ROGUE ONE

A STAR WARS STORY™

ROGUE ONE
A STAR WARS STORY™

JODY HOUSER
Writer

EMILIO LAISO (#1-2, #4-6) & **PAOLO VILLANELLI** (#3)
with **OSCAR BAZALDUA** (#1-2)
Artists

RACHELLE ROSENBERG
Color Artist

VC's CLAYTON COWLES
Letterer

PHIL NOTO
Cover Art

HEATHER ANTOS
Editor

JORDAN D. WHITE
Supervising Editor

C.B. CEBULSKI
Executive Editor

Based on the screenplay by
CHRIS WEITZ and TONY GILROY

Based on a story by
JOHN KNOLL and GARY WHITTA

STAR WARS: ROGUE ONE – CASSIAN & K-2SO SPECIAL #1

DUANE SWIERCZYNSKI
Writer

FERNANDO BLANCO
Artist

MARCELO MAIOLO
Color Artist

VC's CLAYTON COWLES
Letterer

JULIAN TOTINO TEDESCO
Cover Art

HEATHER ANTOS
Assistant Editor

JORDAN D. WHITE
Editor

For Lucasfilm:

MICHAEL SIGLAIN
Creative Director

FRANK PARISI
Senior Editor

JAMES WAUGH, LELAND CHEE, MATT MARTIN, RAYNE ROBERTS
Lucasfilm Story Group

COLLECTION EDITOR: **JENNIFER GRÜNWALD**
ASSISTANT EDITOR: **CAITLIN O'CONNELL**
ASSOCIATE MANAGING EDITOR: **KATERI WOODY**
EDITOR, SPECIAL PROJECTS: **MARK D. BEAZLEY**
VP PRODUCTION & SPECIAL PROJECTS: **JEFF YOUNGQUIST**
SVP PRINT, SALES & MARKETING: **DAVID GABRIEL**
BOOK DESIGNER: **ADAM DEL RE**

EDITOR IN CHIEF: **AXEL ALONSO**
CHIEF CREATIVE OFFICER: **JOE QUESADA**
PRESIDENT: **DAN BUCKLEY**
EXECUTIVE PRODUCER: **ALAN FINE**

STAR WARS: ROGUE ONE ADAPTATION. Contains material originally published in magazine form as STAR WARS: ROGUE ONE ADAPTATION #1-6 and STAR WARS: ROGUE ONE - CASSIAN & K-2SO SPECIAL #1. First printing 2 ISBN# 978-0-7851-9457-6. Published by MARVEL WORLDWIDE, INC., a subsidiary of MARVEL ENTERTAINMENT, LLC. OFFICE OF PUBLICATION: 135 West 50th Street, New York, NY 10020. STAR WARS and related text and illustra are trademarks and/or copyrights, in the United States and other countries, of Lucasfilm Ltd. and/or its affiliates. © & TM Lucasfilm Ltd. No similarity between any of the names, characters, persons, and/or institutions in this maga with those of any living or dead person or institution is intended, and any such similarity which may exist is purely coincidental. Marvel and its logos are TM Marvel Characters, Inc. **Printed in Canada.** DAN BUCKLEY, President, Ma Entertainment; JOE QUESADA, Chief Creative Officer; TOM BREVOORT, SVP of Publishing; DAVID BOGART, SVP of Business Affairs & Operations, Publishing & Partnership; C.B. CEBULSKI, VP of Brand Management & Development, DAVID GABRIEL, SVP of Sales & Marketing, Publishing; JEFF YOUNGQUIST, VP of Production & Special Projects; DAN CARR, Executive Director of Publishing Technology; ALEX MORALES, Director of Publishing Operations; SUSAN CR Production Manager; STAN LEE, Chairman Emeritus. For information regarding advertising in Marvel Comics or on Marvel.com, please contact Vit DeBellis, Integrated Sales Manager, at vdebellis@marvel.com. For Marvel subscri inquiries, please call 888-511-5480. **Manufactured between 9/22/2017 and 10/24/2017 by SOLISCO PRINTERS, SCOTT, QC, CANADA.**

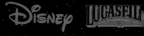

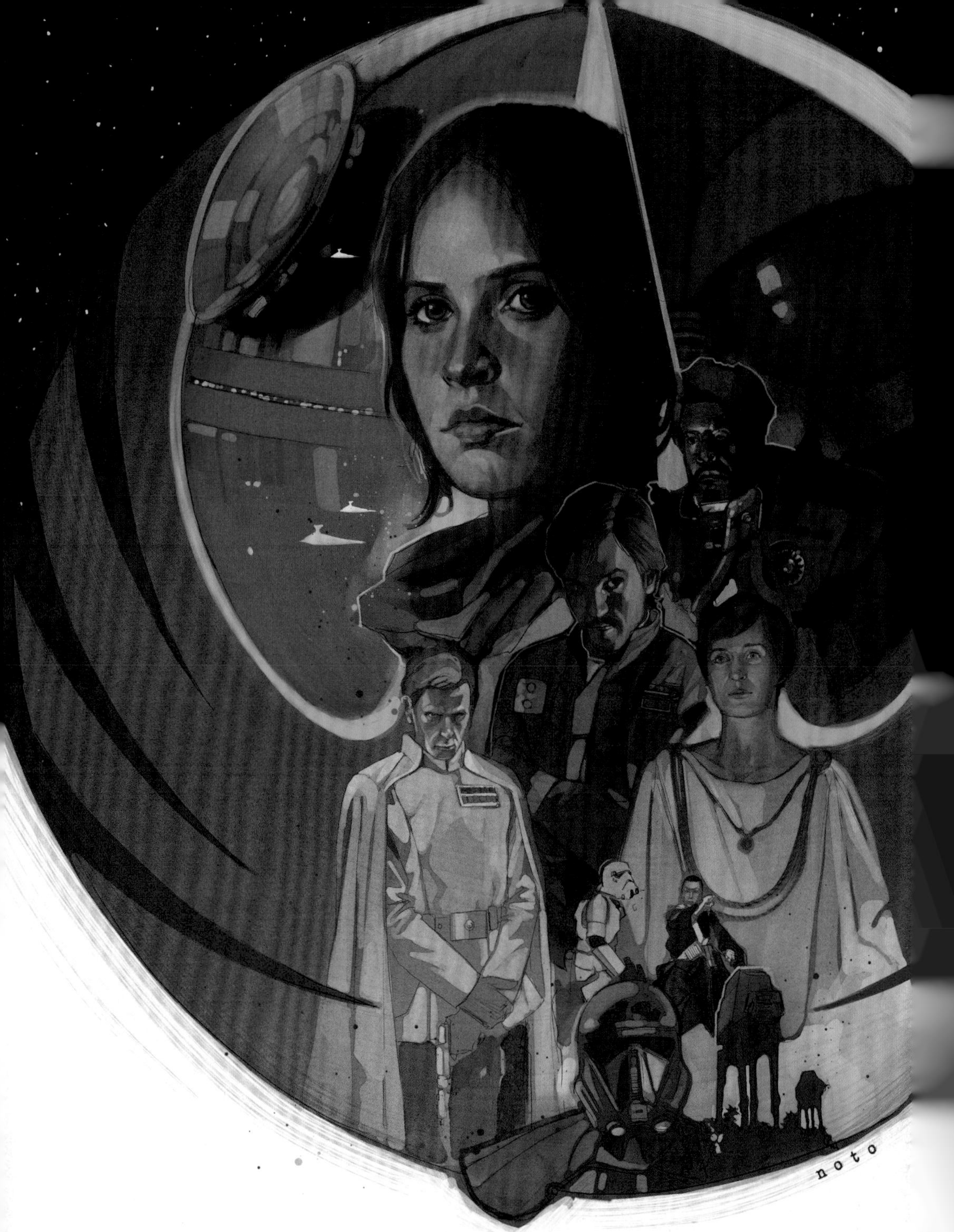
noto

MISSION:
Find and extract Jyn Erso

ALIAS "LIANA HALLIK"

NOTES:
Daughter of Galen Erso (known Imperial research scientist). Goes by the alias "Liana Hallik." Known associate of rebel extremist Saw Gerrera.

SAW GERRERA

GALEN ERSO

STATUS:
Rebel intelligence officers to be dispatched to retrieve target.

CAPTAIN CASSIAN ANDOR

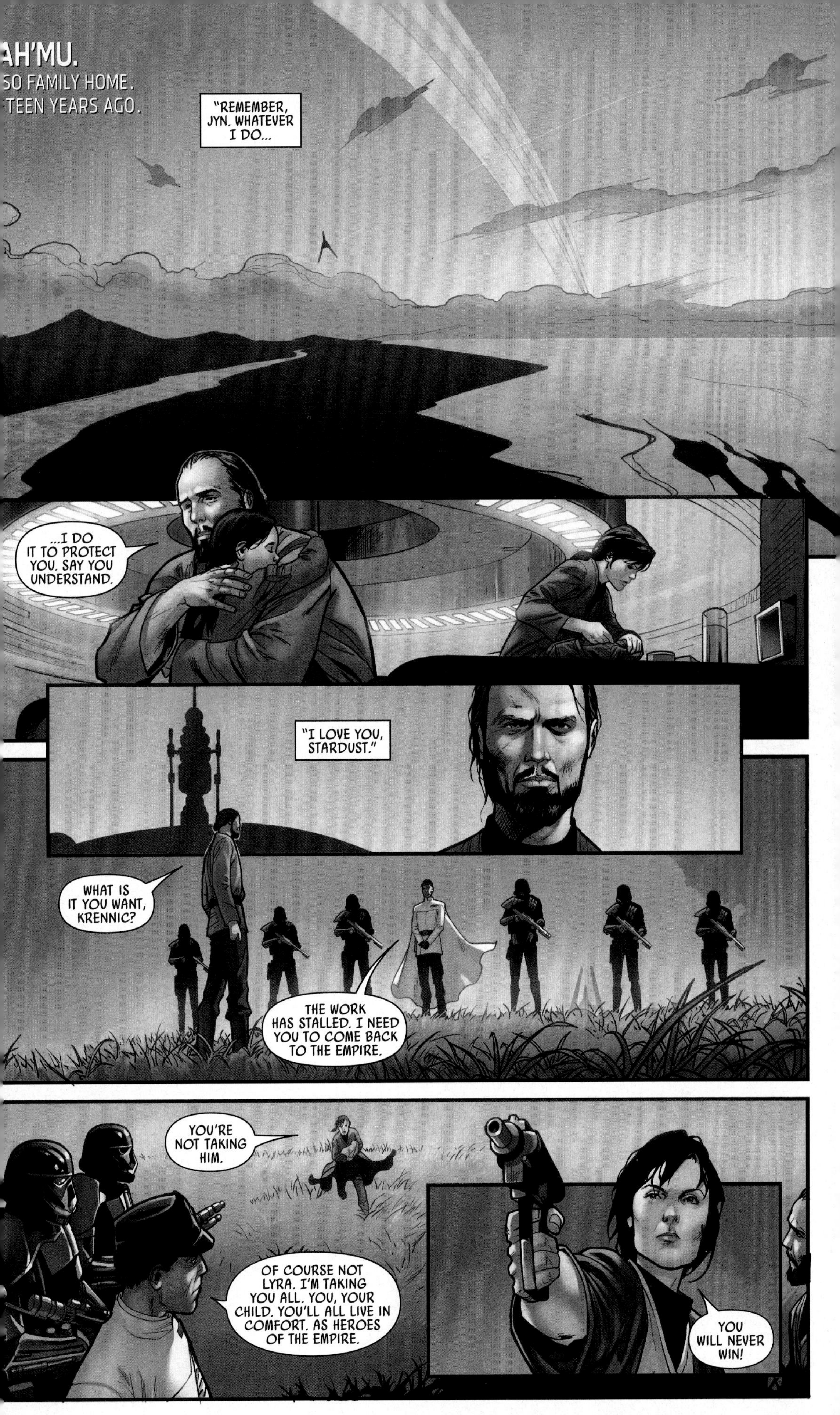
AH'MU.
SO FAMILY HOME.
TEEN YEARS AGO.
"REMEMBER, JYN. WHATEVER I DO...
...I DO IT TO PROTECT YOU. SAY YOU UNDERSTAND.
"I LOVE YOU, STARDUST."
WHAT IS IT YOU WANT, KRENNIC?
THE WORK HAS STALLED. I NEED YOU TO COME BACK TO THE EMPIRE.
YOU'RE NOT TAKING HIM.
OF COURSE NOT LYRA. I'M TAKING YOU ALL. YOU, YOUR CHILD. YOU'LL ALL LIVE IN COMFORT. AS HEROES OF THE EMPIRE.
YOU WILL NEVER WIN!

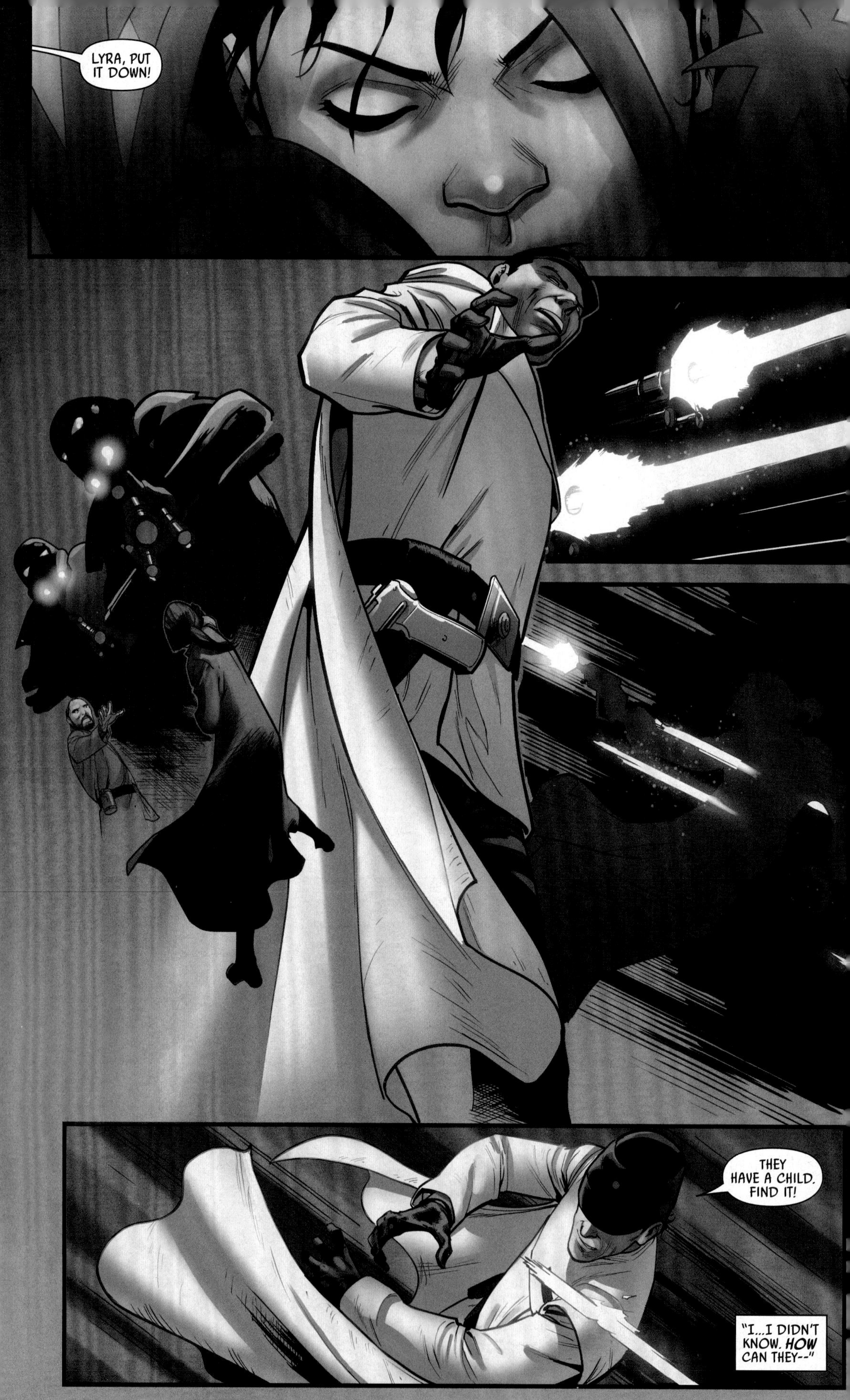
LYRA, PUT IT DOWN!
THEY HAVE A CHILD. FIND IT!
"I...I DIDN'T KNOW. HOW CAN THEY--"

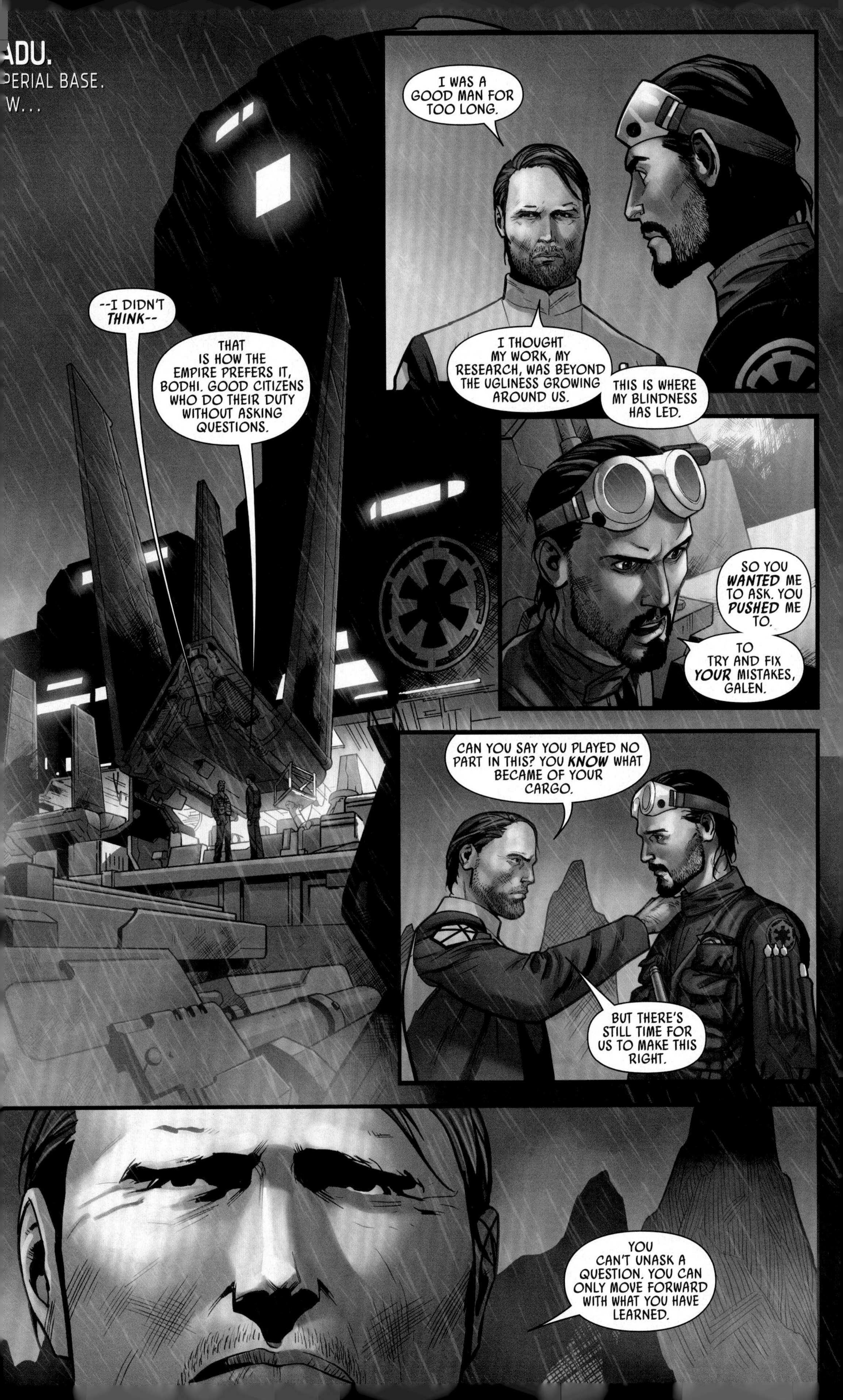

ADU.
PERIAL BASE.
W...
I WAS A GOOD MAN FOR TOO LONG.
I THOUGHT MY WORK, MY RESEARCH, WAS BEYOND THE UGLINESS GROWING AROUND US.
THIS IS WHERE MY BLINDNESS HAS LED.
--I DIDN'T THINK--
THAT IS HOW THE EMPIRE PREFERS IT, BODHI. GOOD CITIZENS WHO DO THEIR DUTY WITHOUT ASKING QUESTIONS.
SO YOU WANTED ME TO ASK. YOU PUSHED ME TO.
TO TRY AND FIX YOUR MISTAKES, GALEN.
CAN YOU SAY YOU PLAYED NO PART IN THIS? YOU KNOW WHAT BECAME OF YOUR CARGO.
BUT THERE'S STILL TIME FOR US TO MAKE THIS RIGHT.
YOU CAN'T UNASK A QUESTION. YOU CAN ONLY MOVE FORWARD WITH WHAT YOU HAVE LEARNED.

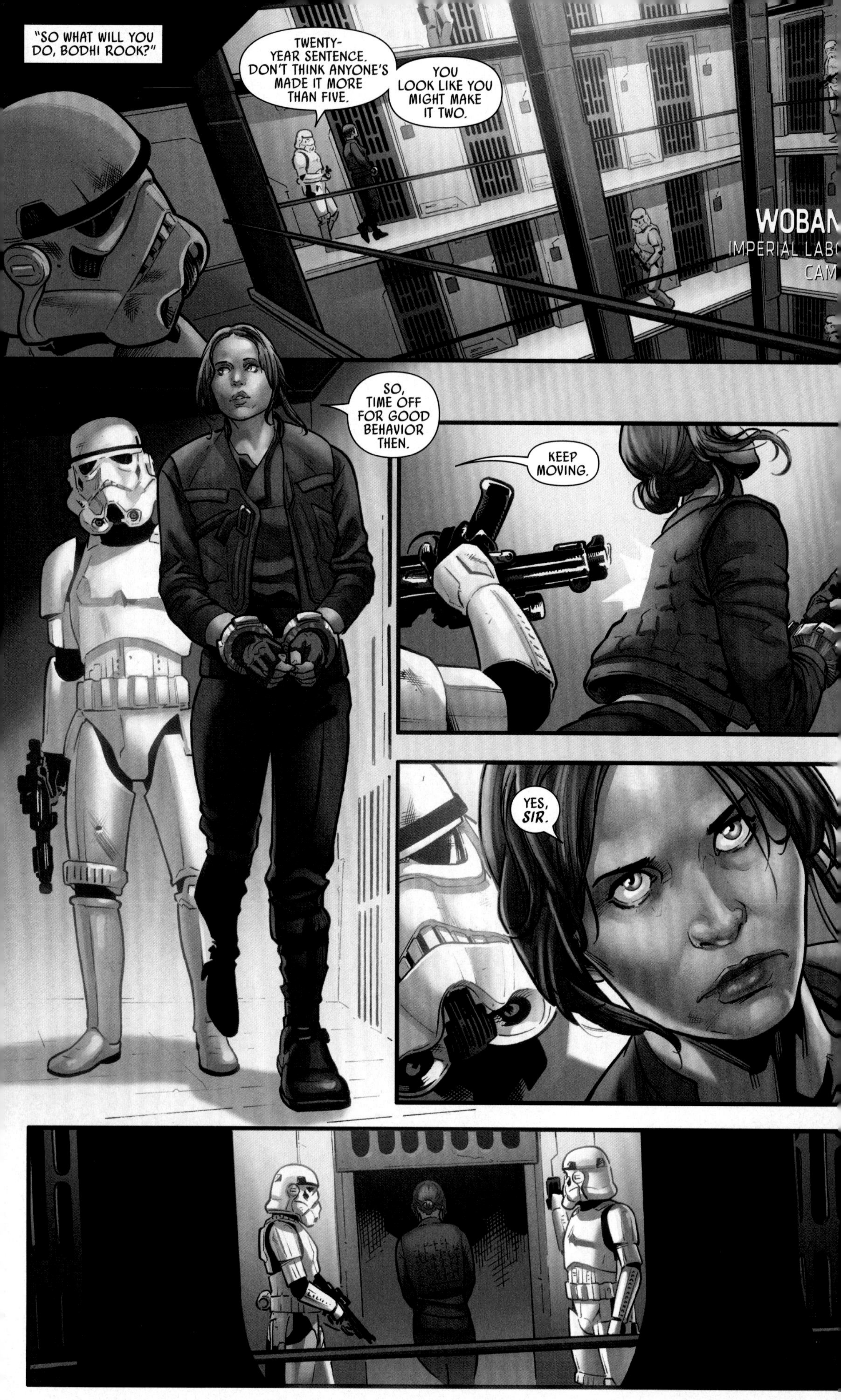
"SO WHAT WILL YOU DO, BODHI ROOK?"
TWENTY-YEAR SENTENCE. DON'T THINK ANYONE'S MADE IT MORE THAN FIVE.
YOU LOOK LIKE YOU MIGHT MAKE IT TWO.
SO, TIME OFF FOR GOOD BEHAVIOR THEN.
KEEP MOVING.
YES, *SIR*.

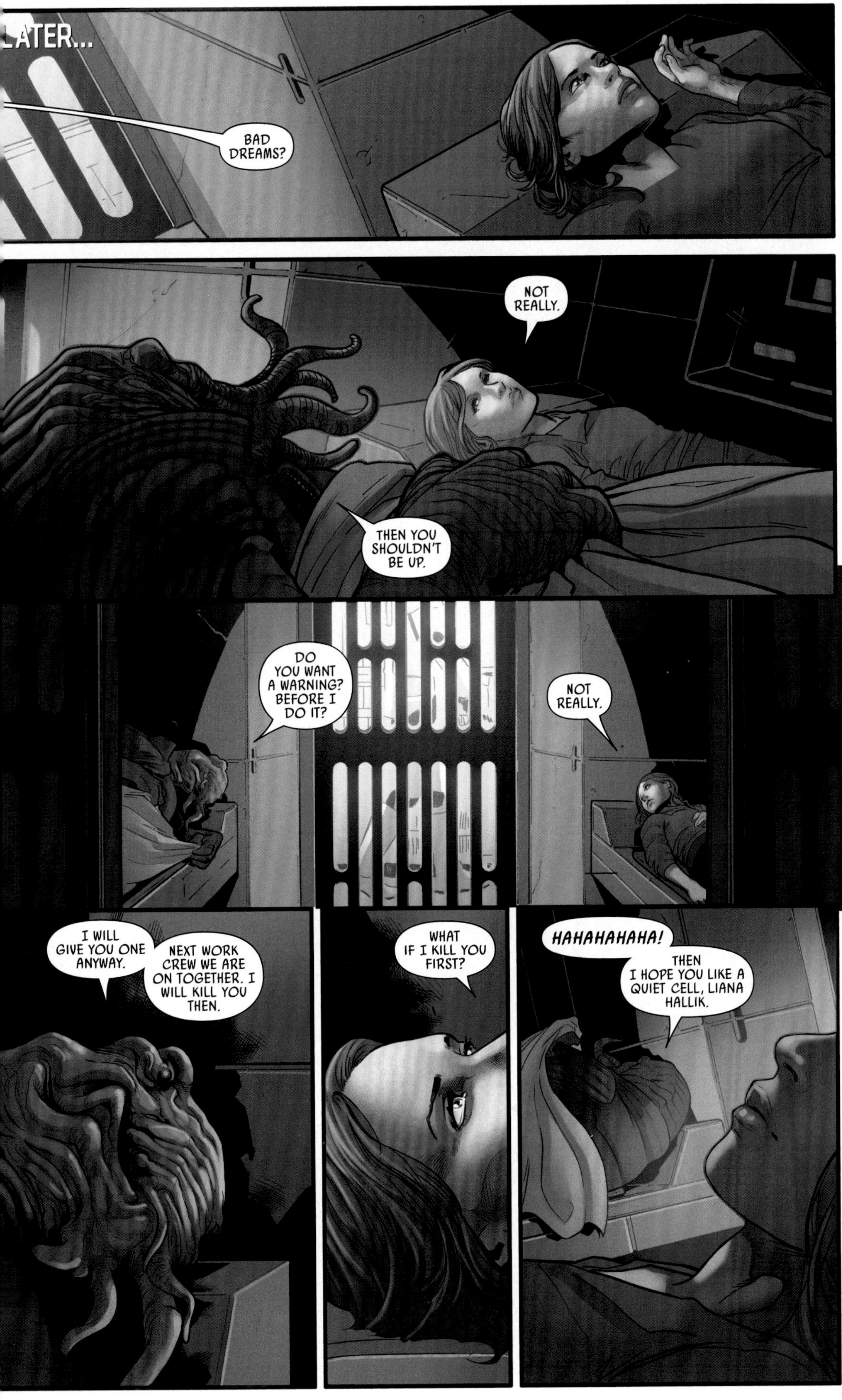
LATER...
BAD DREAMS?
NOT REALLY.
THEN YOU SHOULDN'T BE UP.
DO YOU WANT A WARNING? BEFORE I DO IT?
NOT REALLY.
I WILL GIVE YOU ONE ANYWAY.
NEXT WORK CREW WE ARE ON TOGETHER. I WILL KILL YOU THEN.
WHAT IF I KILL YOU FIRST?
HAHAHAHAHA!
THEN I HOPE YOU LIKE A QUIET CELL, LIANA HALLIK.

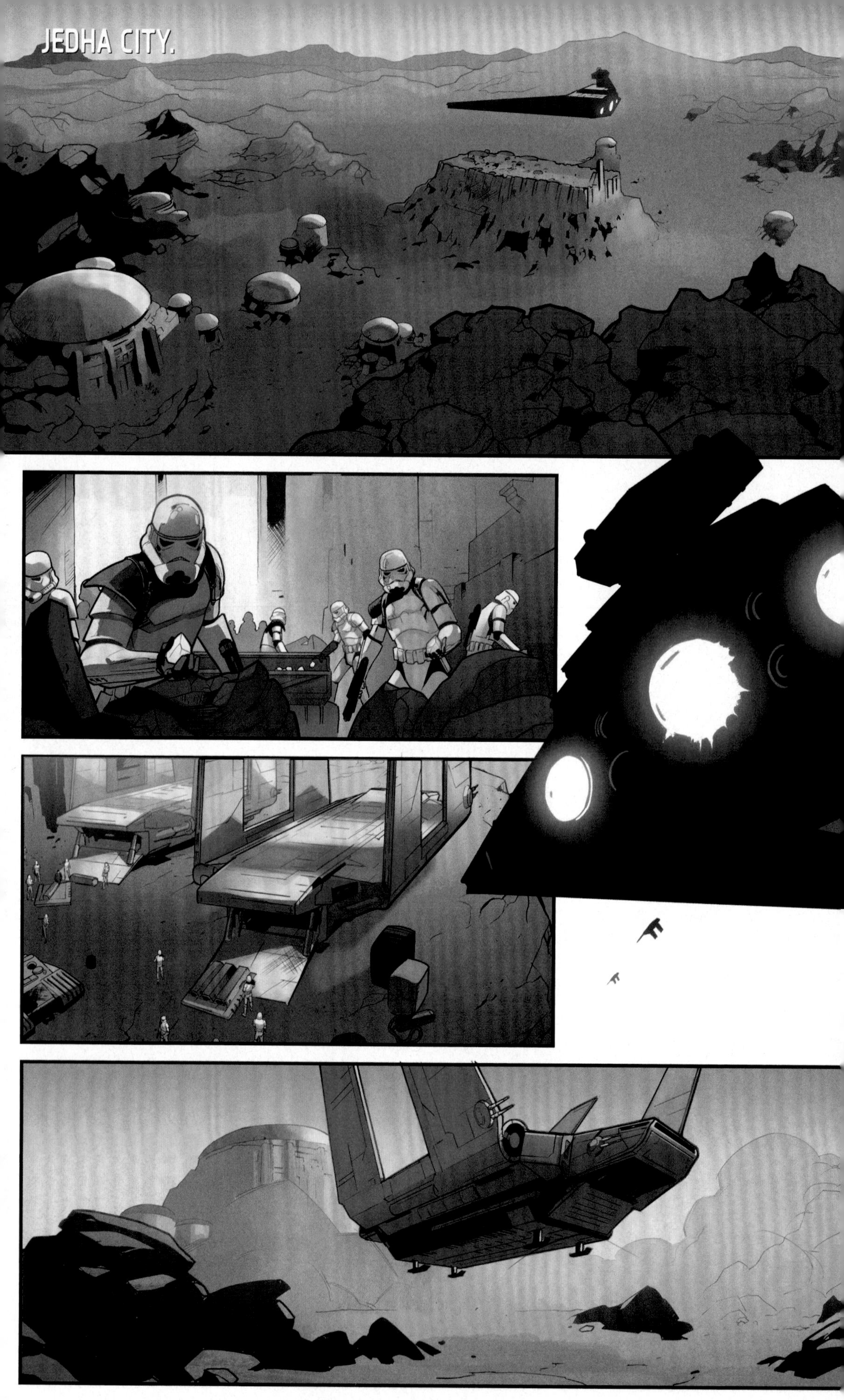
JEDHA CITY.

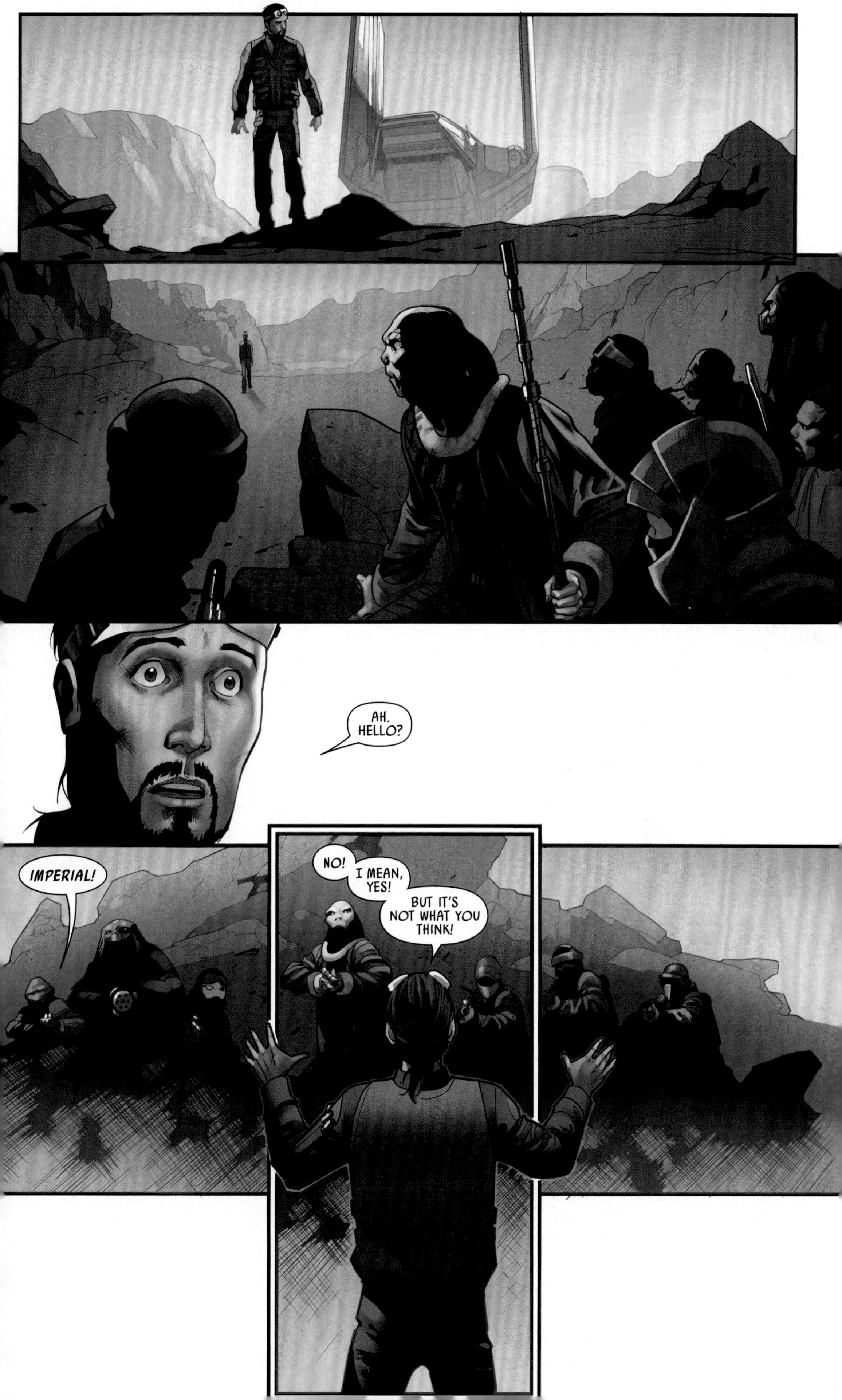
AH. HELLO?
IMPERIAL!
NO!
I MEAN, YES!
BUT IT'S NOT WHAT YOU THINK!

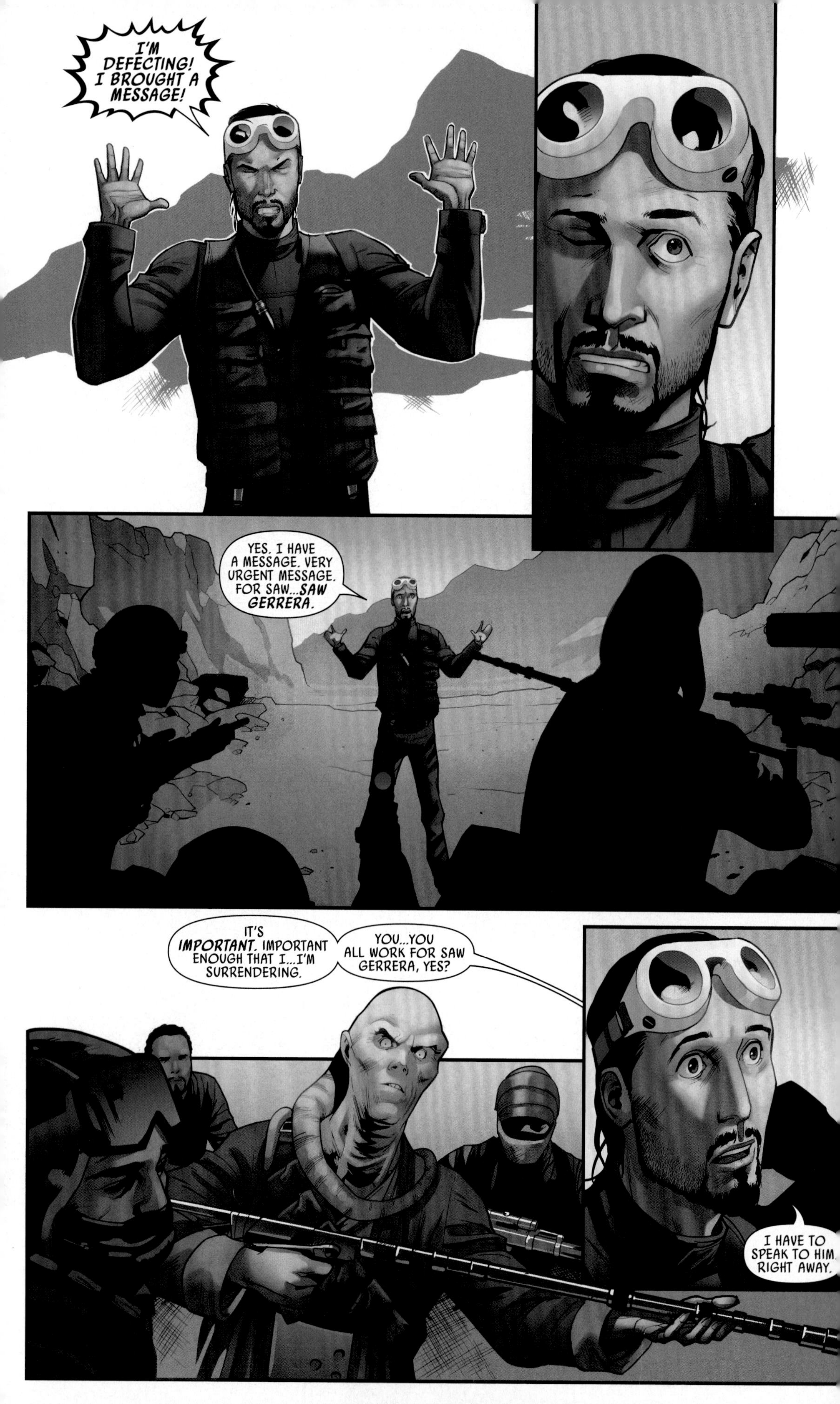
I'M DEFECTING! I BROUGHT A MESSAGE!
YES. I HAVE A MESSAGE. VERY URGENT MESSAGE. FOR SAW...SAW GERRERA.
IT'S IMPORTANT. IMPORTANT ENOUGH THAT I...I'M SURRENDERING.
YOU...YOU ALL WORK FOR SAW GERRERA, YES?
I HAVE TO SPEAK TO HIM RIGHT AWAY.

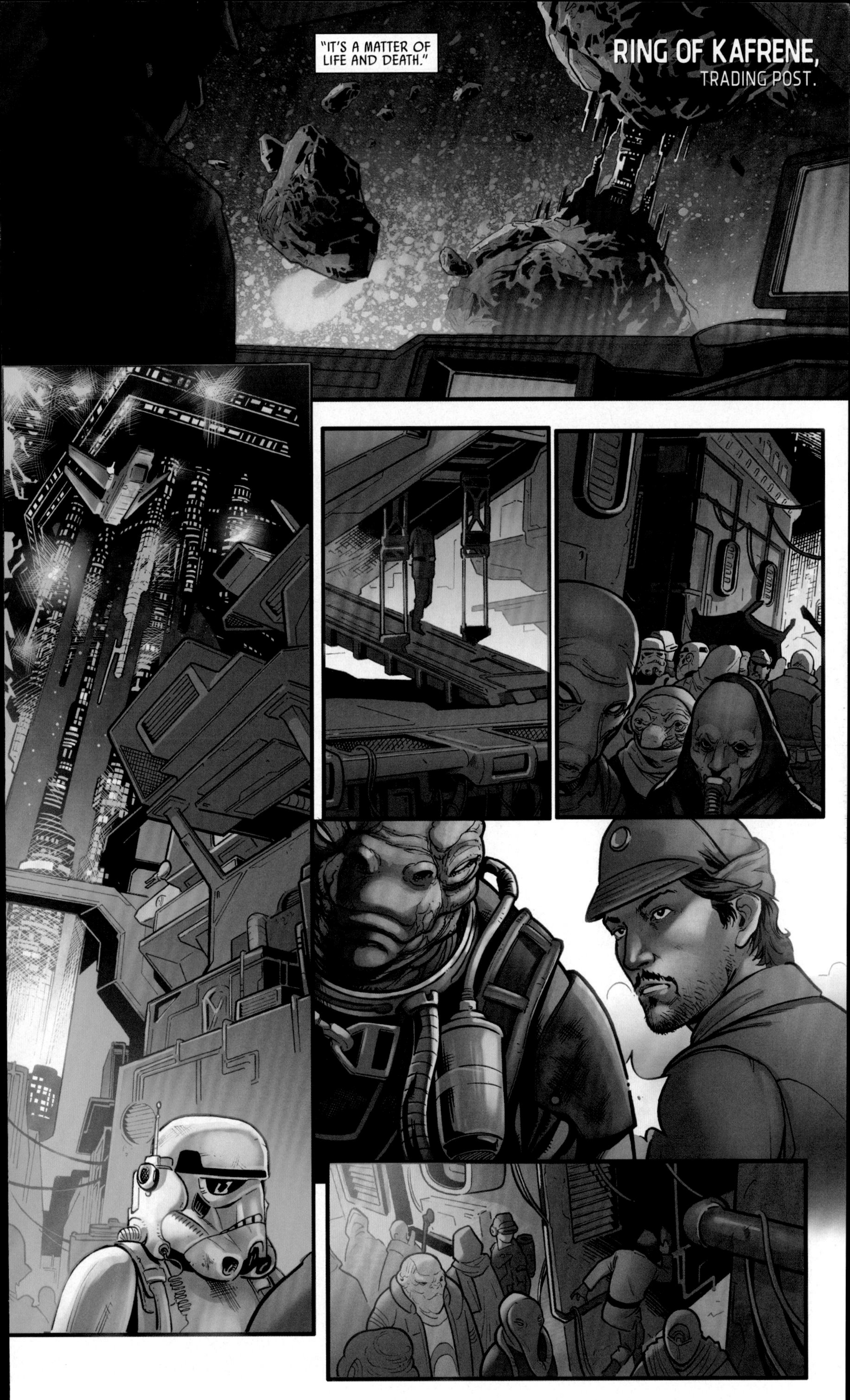
"IT'S A MATTER OF LIFE AND DEATH."
RING OF KAFRENE,
TRADING POST.

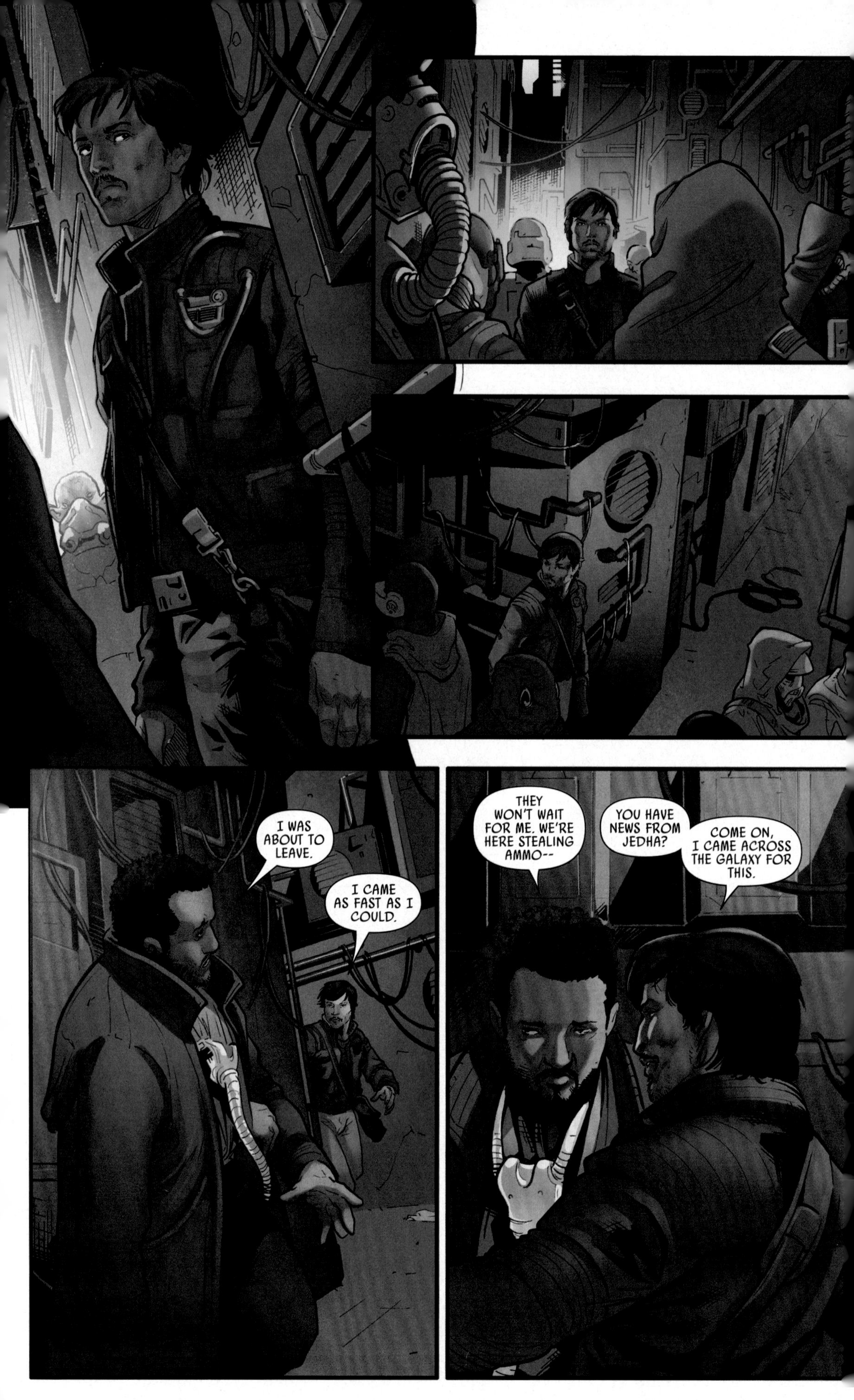
I WAS ABOUT TO LEAVE.
I CAME AS FAST AS I COULD.
THEY WON'T WAIT FOR ME. WE'RE HERE STEALING AMMO--
YOU HAVE NEWS FROM JEDHA?
COME ON, I CAME ACROSS THE GALAXY FOR THIS.

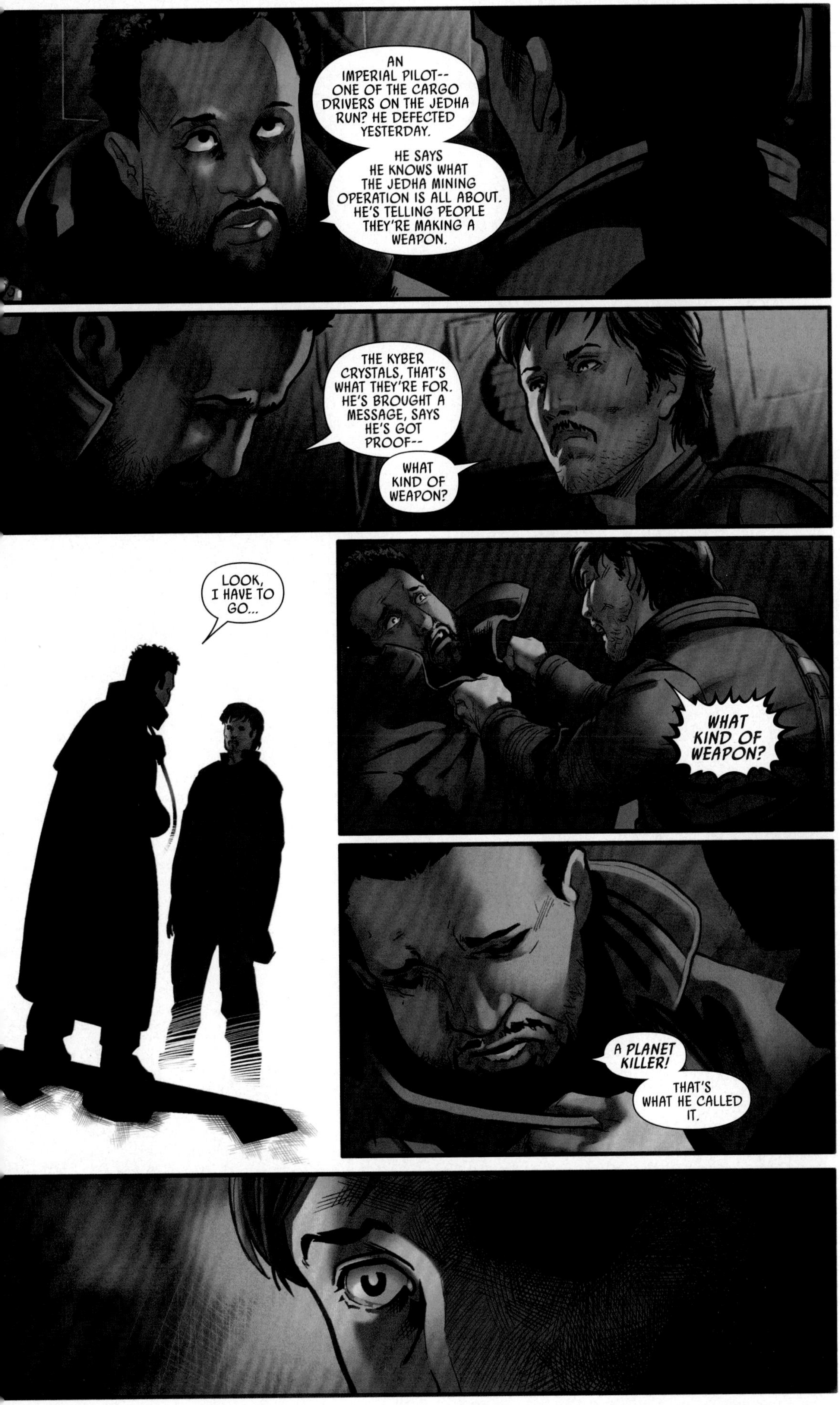
AN IMPERIAL PILOT-- ONE OF THE CARGO DRIVERS ON THE JEDHA RUN? HE DEFECTED YESTERDAY.
HE SAYS HE KNOWS WHAT THE JEDHA MINING OPERATION IS ALL ABOUT. HE'S TELLING PEOPLE THEY'RE MAKING A WEAPON.
THE KYBER CRYSTALS, THAT'S WHAT THEY'RE FOR. HE'S BROUGHT A MESSAGE, SAYS HE'S GOT PROOF--
WHAT KIND OF WEAPON?
LOOK, I HAVE TO GO...
WHAT KIND OF WEAPON?
A *PLANET KILLER!*
THAT'S WHAT HE CALLED IT.

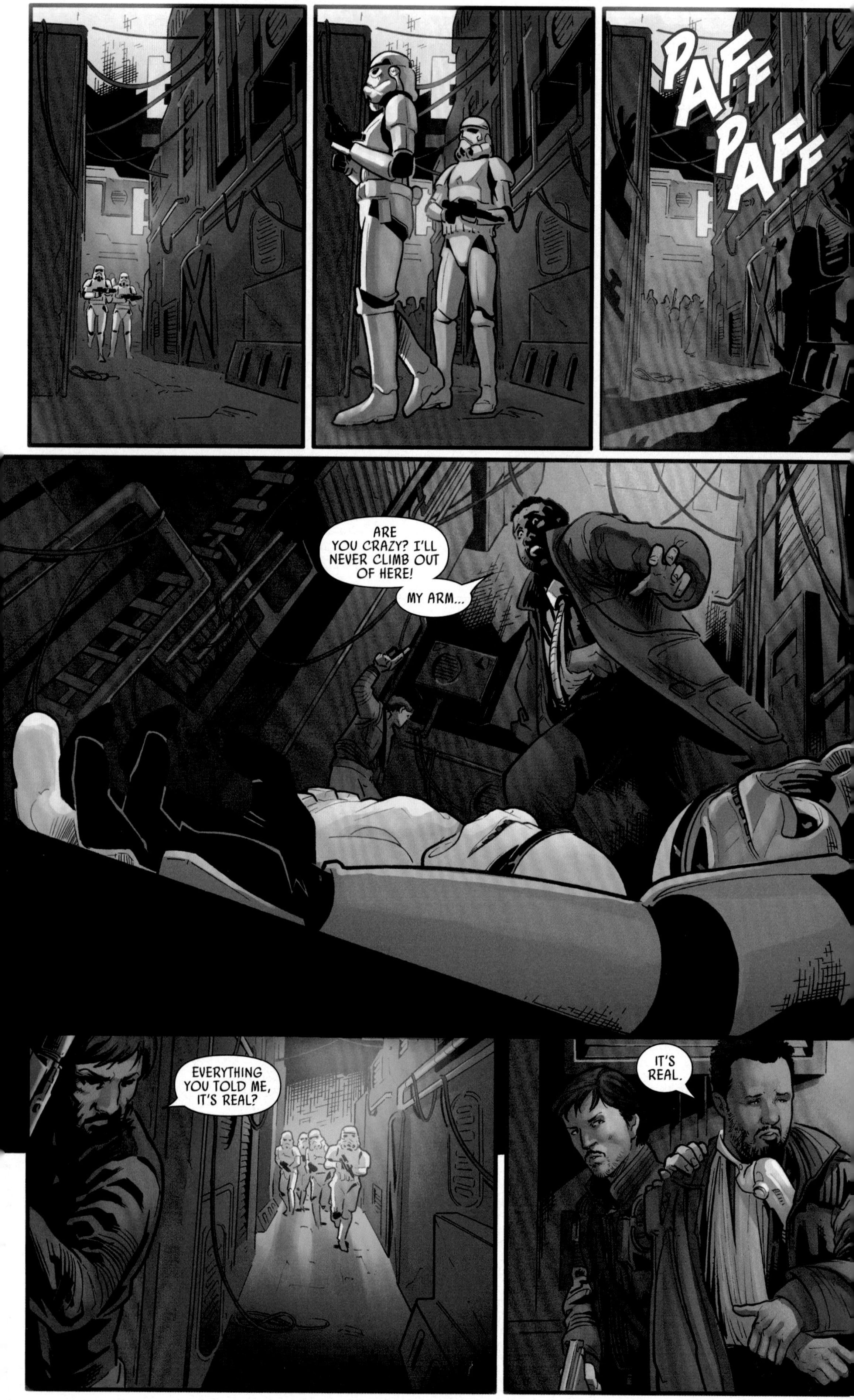
PAFF PAFF
ARE YOU CRAZY? I'LL NEVER CLIMB OUT OF HERE!
MY ARM...
EVERYTHING YOU TOLD ME, IT'S REAL?
IT'S REAL.

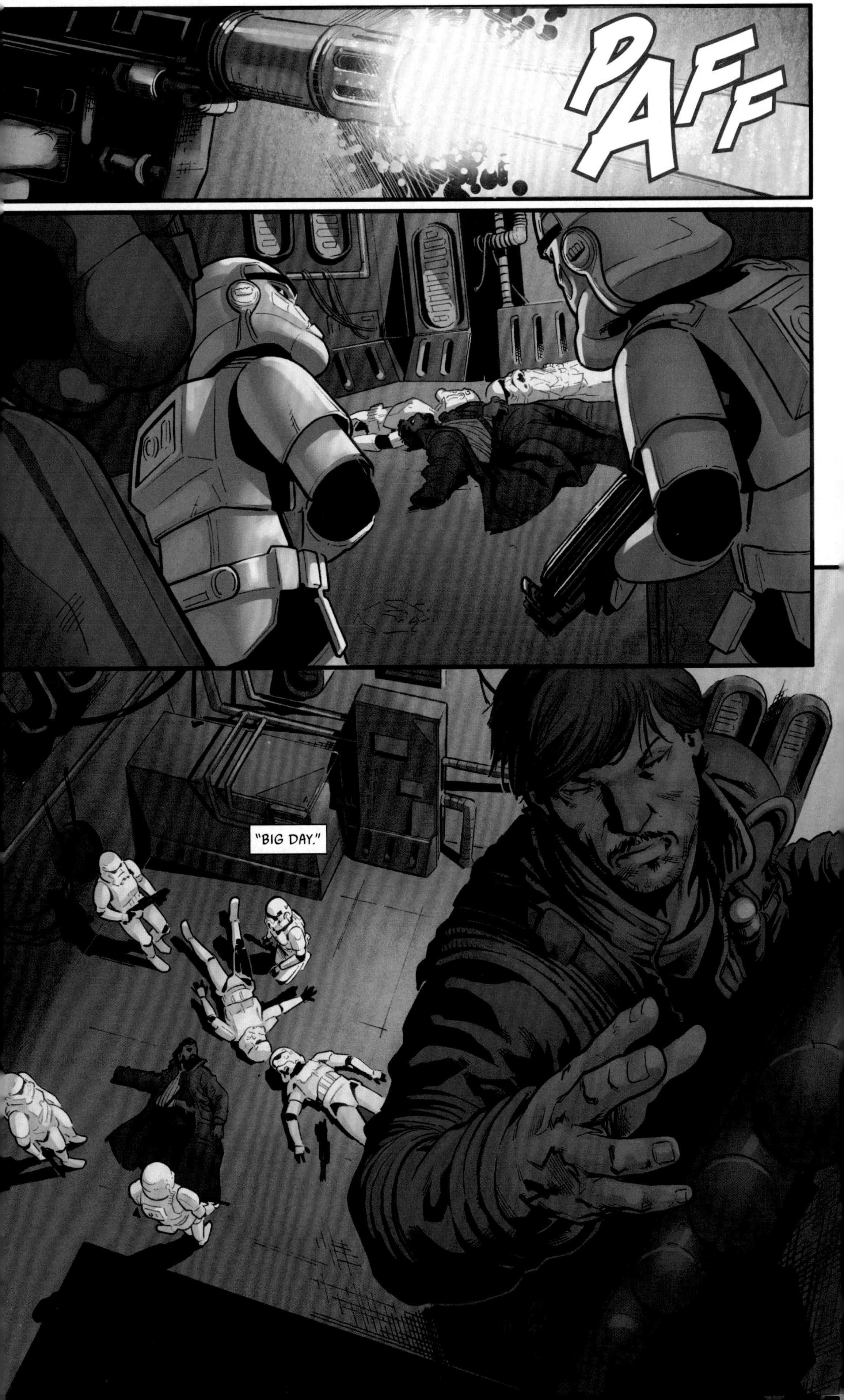
PAFF
"BIG DAY."

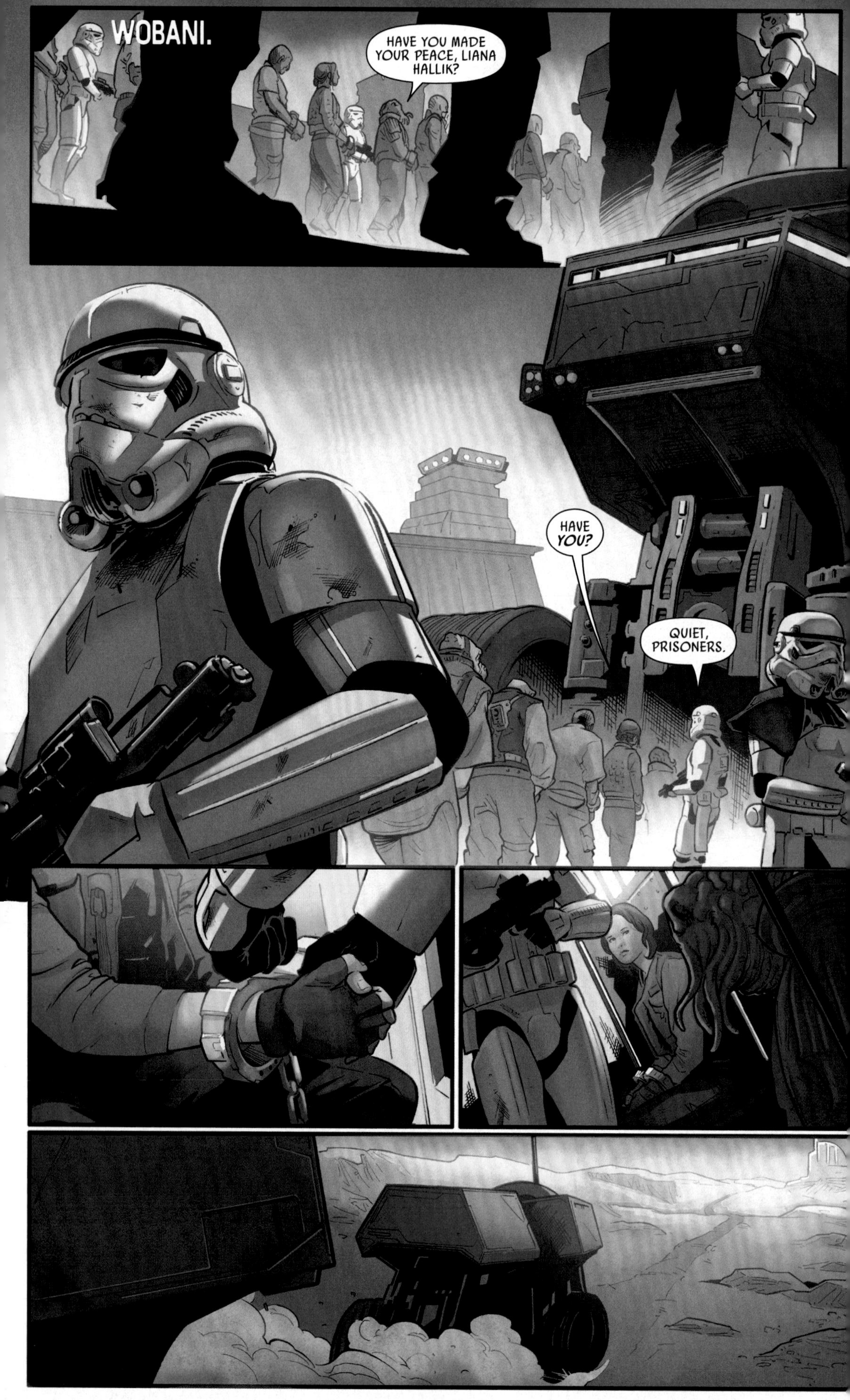
WOBANI.
HAVE YOU MADE YOUR PEACE, LIANA HALLIK?
HAVE *YOU?*
QUIET, PRISONERS.

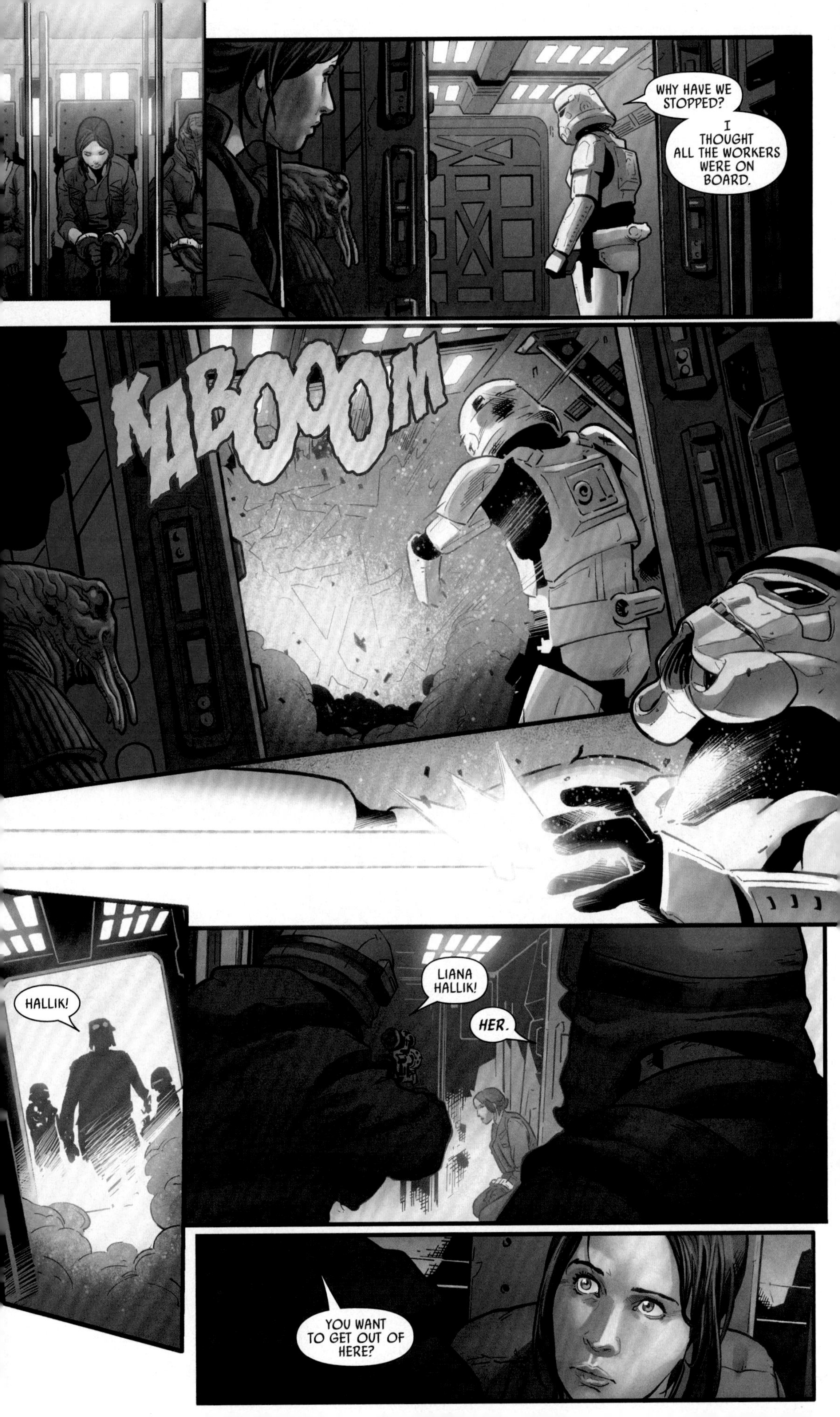

WHY HAVE WE STOPPED?
I THOUGHT ALL THE WORKERS WERE ON BOARD.
KABOOOM
HALLIK!
LIANA HALLIK!
HER.
YOU WANT TO GET OUT OF HERE?

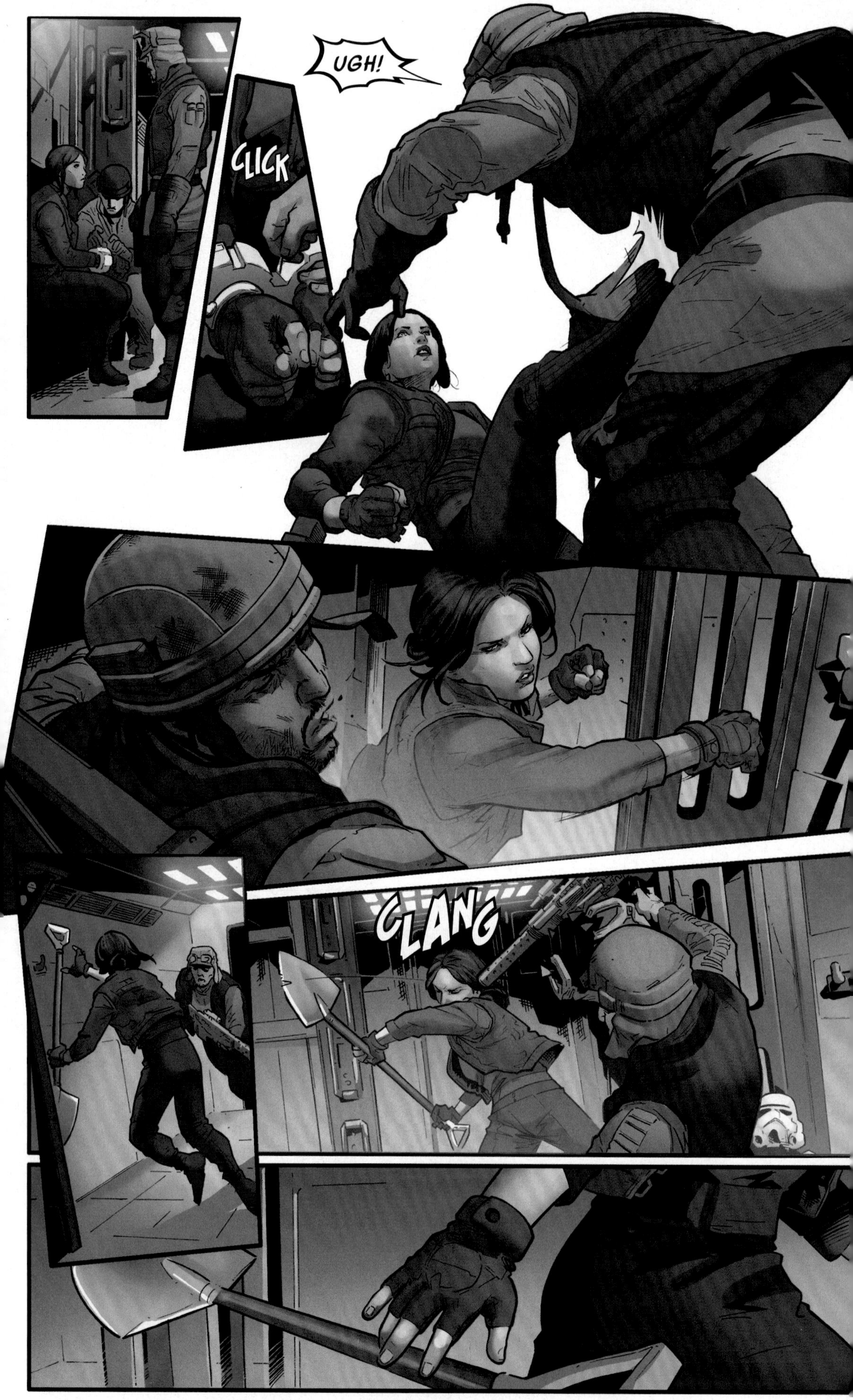
UGH!
CLICK
CLANG

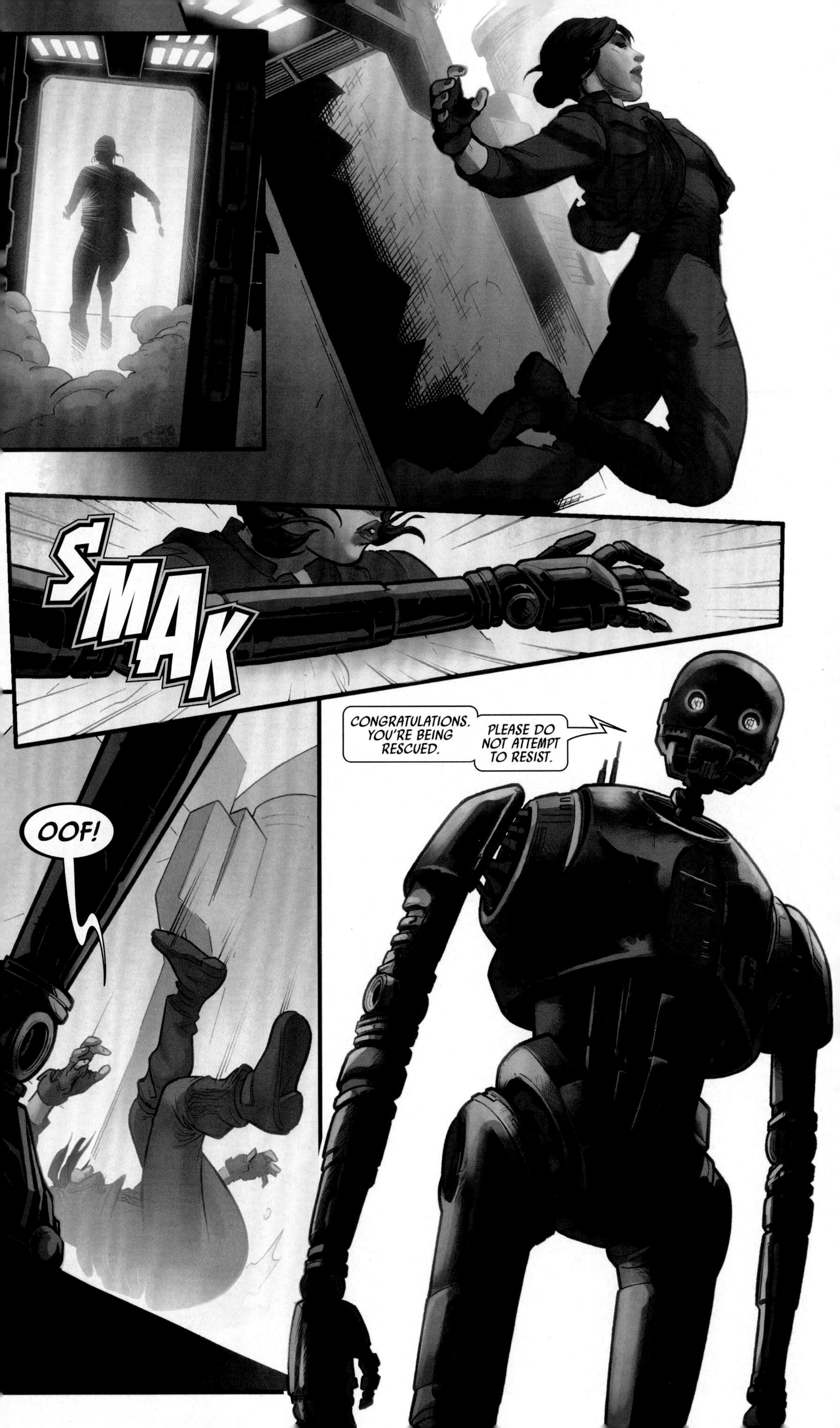
SMAK
OOF!
CONGRATULATIONS. YOU'RE BEING RESCUED.
PLEASE DO NOT ATTEMPT TO RESIST.

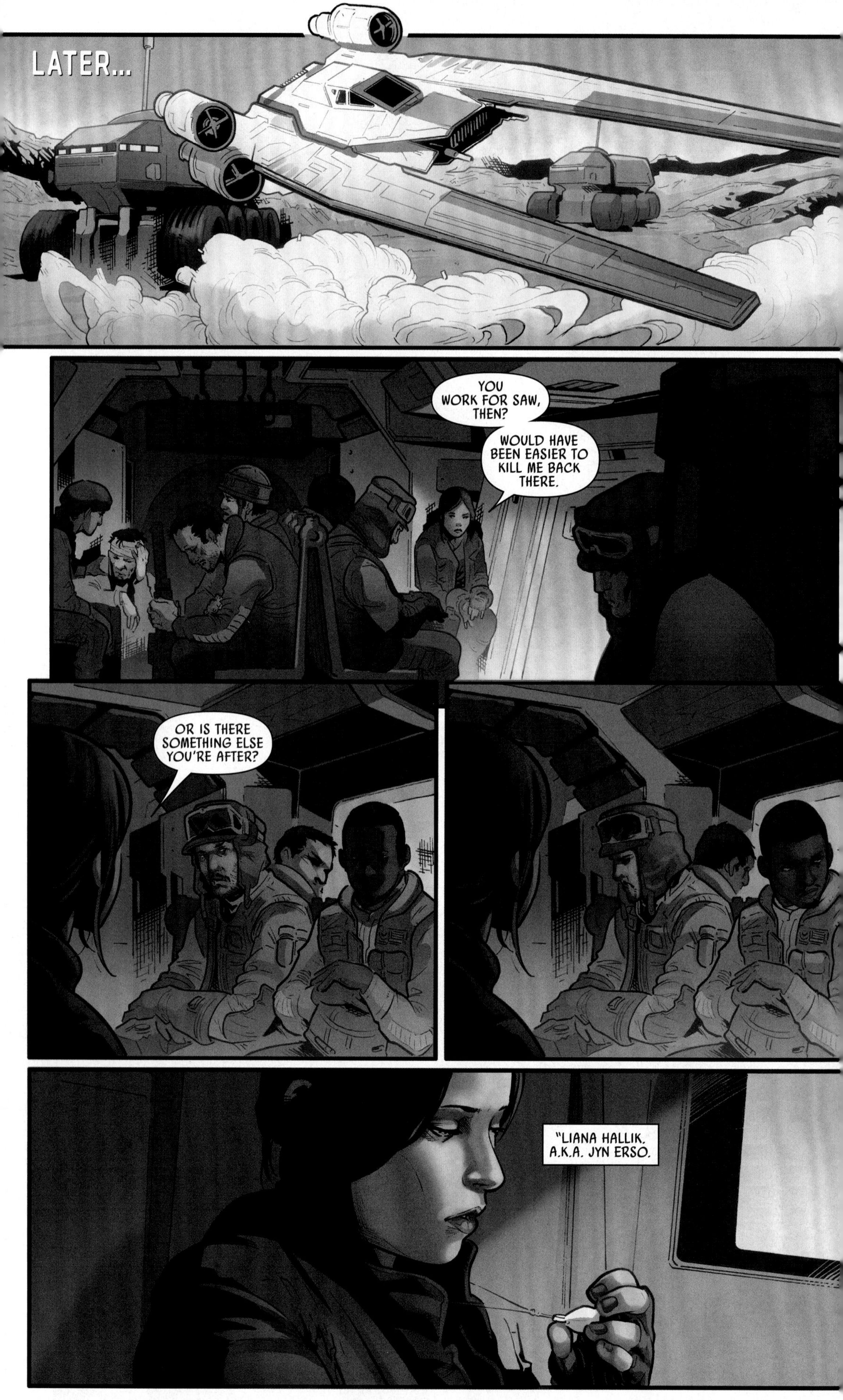
LATER...
YOU WORK FOR SAW, THEN?
WOULD HAVE BEEN EASIER TO KILL ME BACK THERE.
OR IS THERE SOMETHING ELSE YOU'RE AFTER?
"LIANA HALLIK. A.K.A. JYN ERSO.

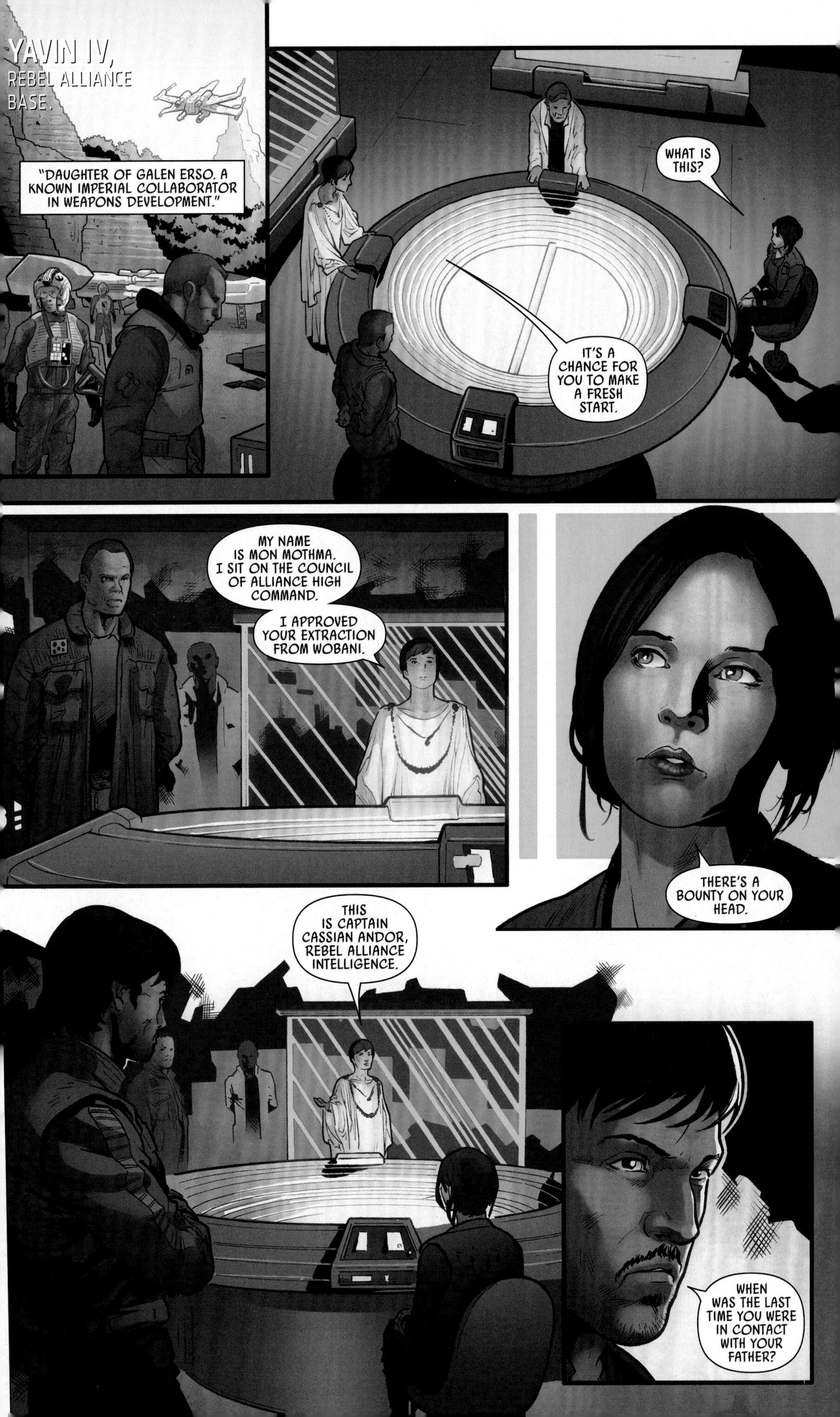

YAVIN IV, REBEL ALLIANCE BASE.
"DAUGHTER OF GALEN ERSO. A KNOWN IMPERIAL COLLABORATOR IN WEAPONS DEVELOPMENT."
WHAT IS THIS?
IT'S A CHANCE FOR YOU TO MAKE A FRESH START.
MY NAME IS MON MOTHMA. I SIT ON THE COUNCIL OF ALLIANCE HIGH COMMAND.
I APPROVED YOUR EXTRACTION FROM WOBANI.
THERE'S A BOUNTY ON YOUR HEAD.
THIS IS CAPTAIN CASSIAN ANDOR, REBEL ALLIANCE INTELLIGENCE.
WHEN WAS THE LAST TIME YOU WERE IN CONTACT WITH YOUR FATHER?

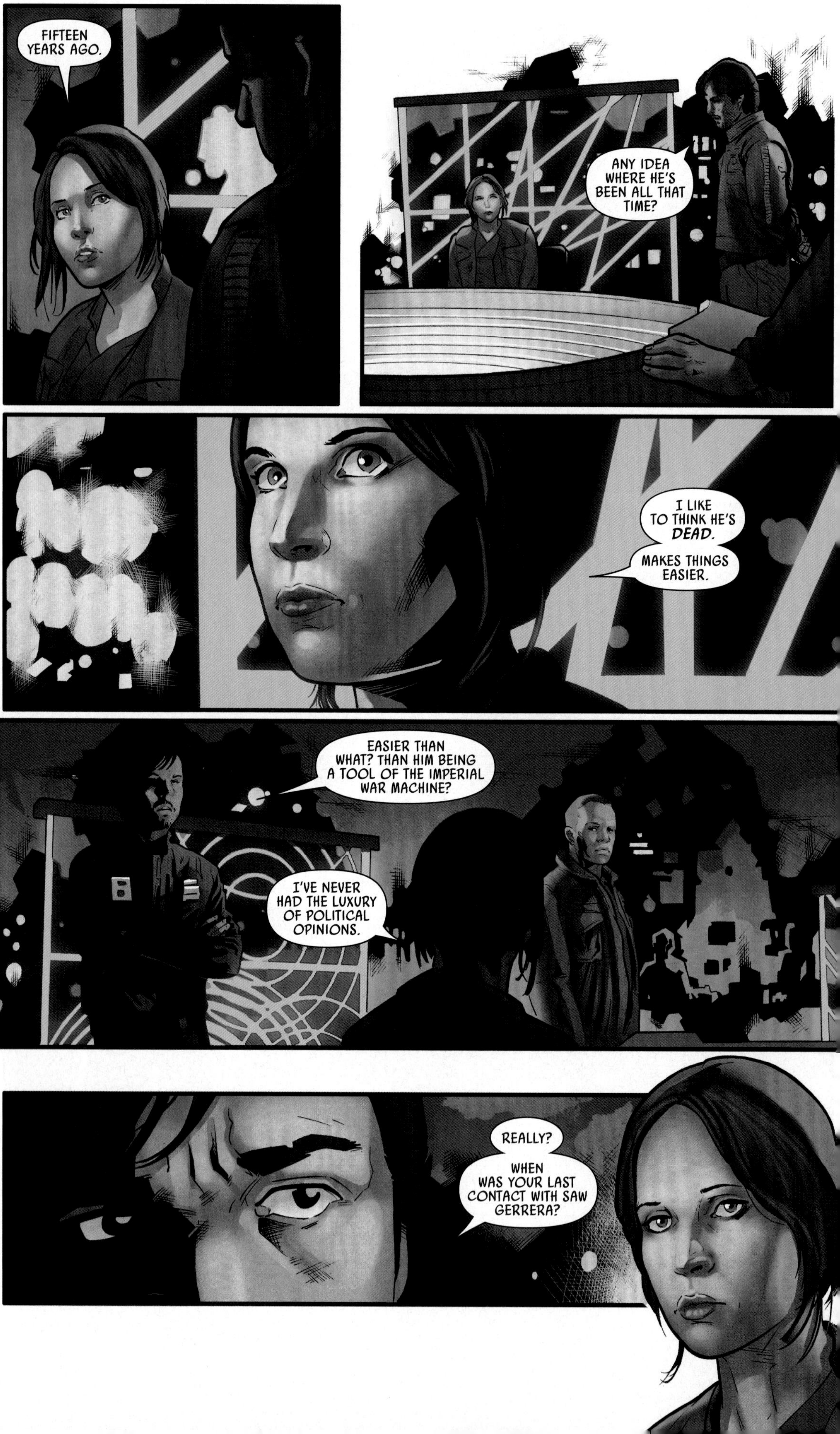
FIFTEEN YEARS AGO.
ANY IDEA WHERE HE'S BEEN ALL THAT TIME?
I LIKE TO THINK HE'S DEAD.
MAKES THINGS EASIER.
EASIER THAN WHAT? THAN HIM BEING A TOOL OF THE IMPERIAL WAR MACHINE?
I'VE NEVER HAD THE LUXURY OF POLITICAL OPINIONS.
REALLY?
WHEN WAS YOUR LAST CONTACT WITH SAW GERRERA?

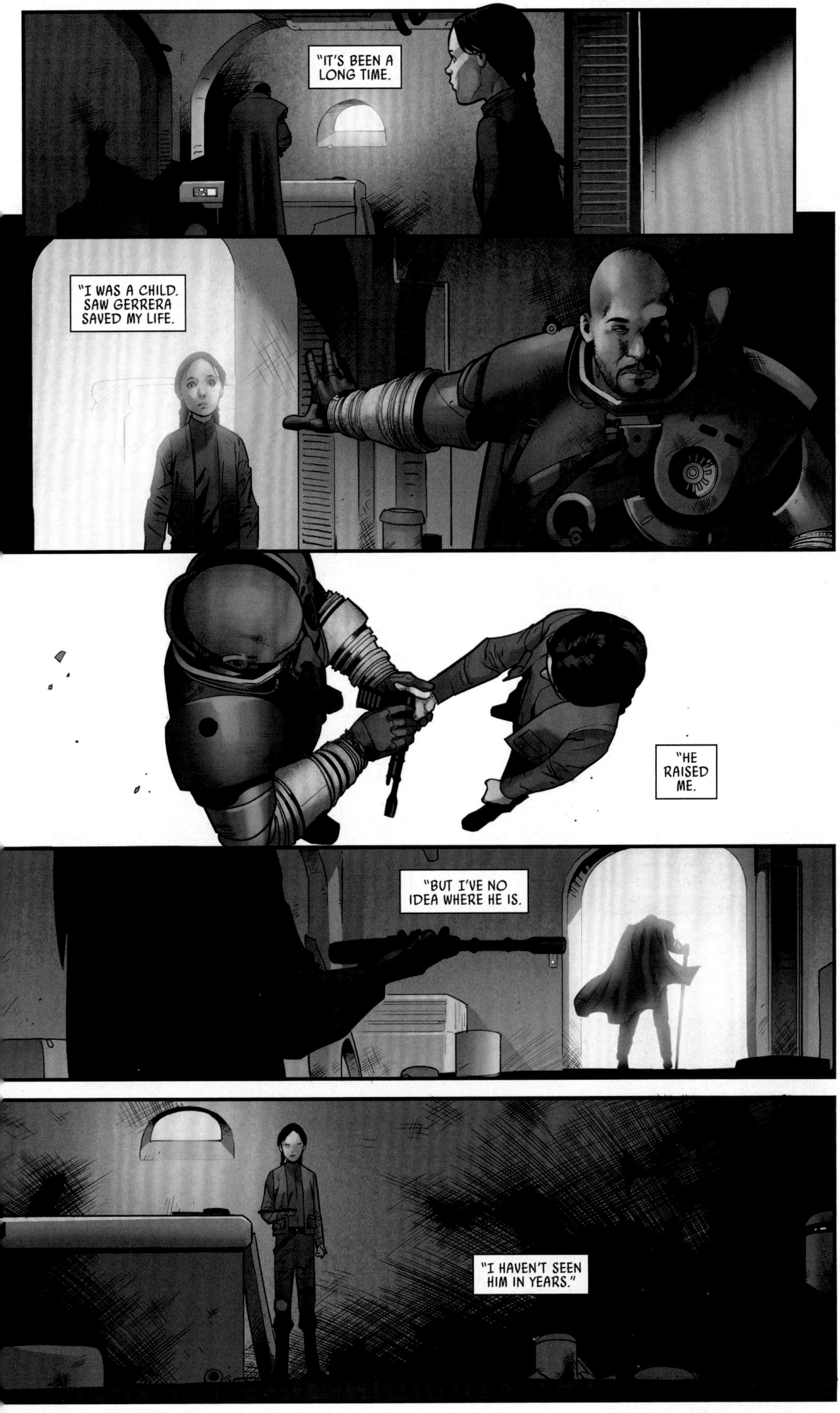
"IT'S BEEN A LONG TIME.
"I WAS A CHILD. SAW GERRERA SAVED MY LIFE.
"HE RAISED ME.
"BUT I'VE NO IDEA WHERE HE IS.
"I HAVEN'T SEEN HIM IN YEARS."

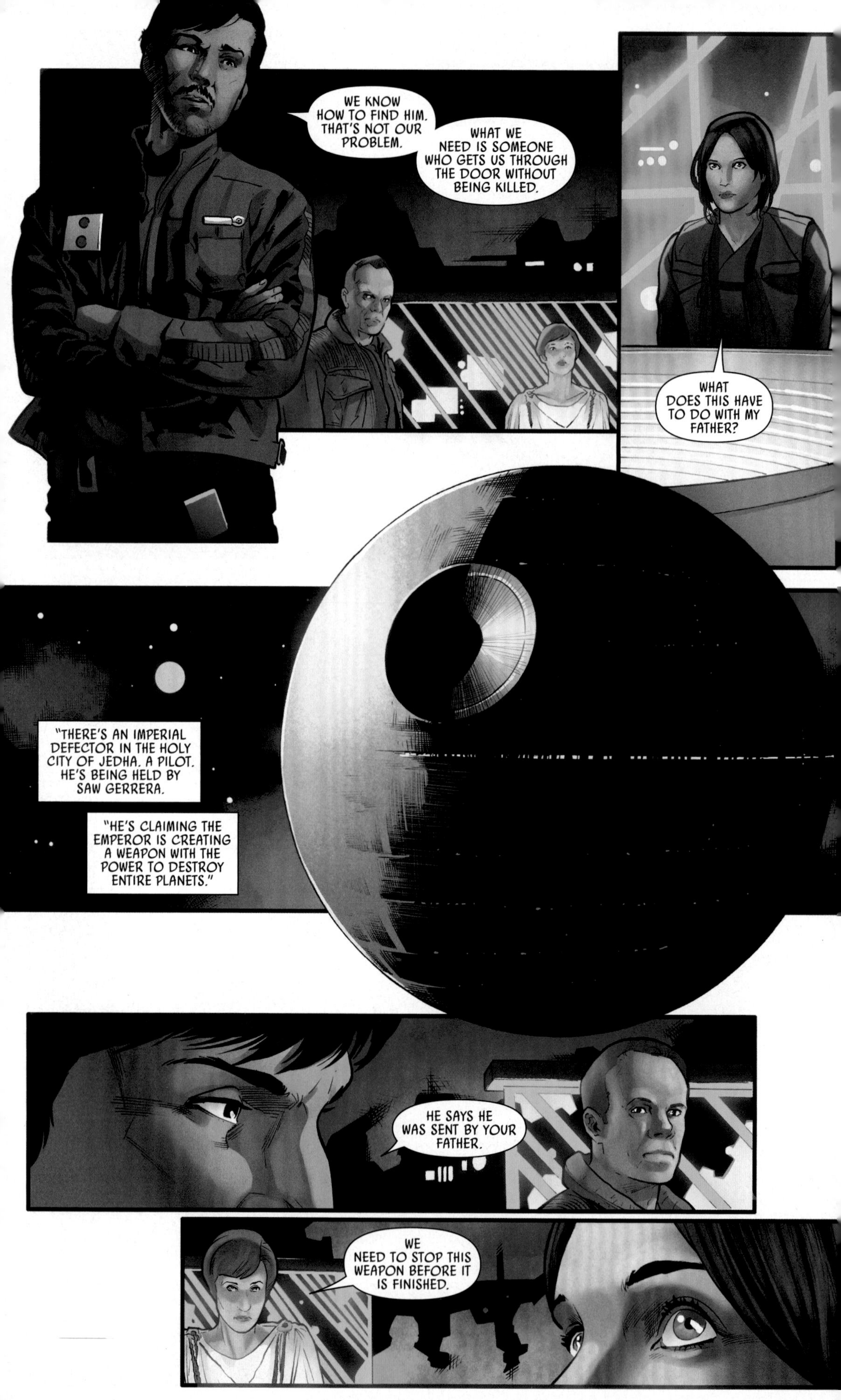
WE KNOW HOW TO FIND HIM. THAT'S NOT OUR PROBLEM.
WHAT WE NEED IS SOMEONE WHO GETS US THROUGH THE DOOR WITHOUT BEING KILLED.
WHAT DOES THIS HAVE TO DO WITH MY FATHER?
"THERE'S AN IMPERIAL DEFECTOR IN THE HOLY CITY OF JEDHA. A PILOT. HE'S BEING HELD BY SAW GERRERA.
"HE'S CLAIMING THE EMPEROR IS CREATING A WEAPON WITH THE POWER TO DESTROY ENTIRE PLANETS."
HE SAYS HE WAS SENT BY YOUR FATHER.
WE NEED TO STOP THIS WEAPON BEFORE IT IS FINISHED.

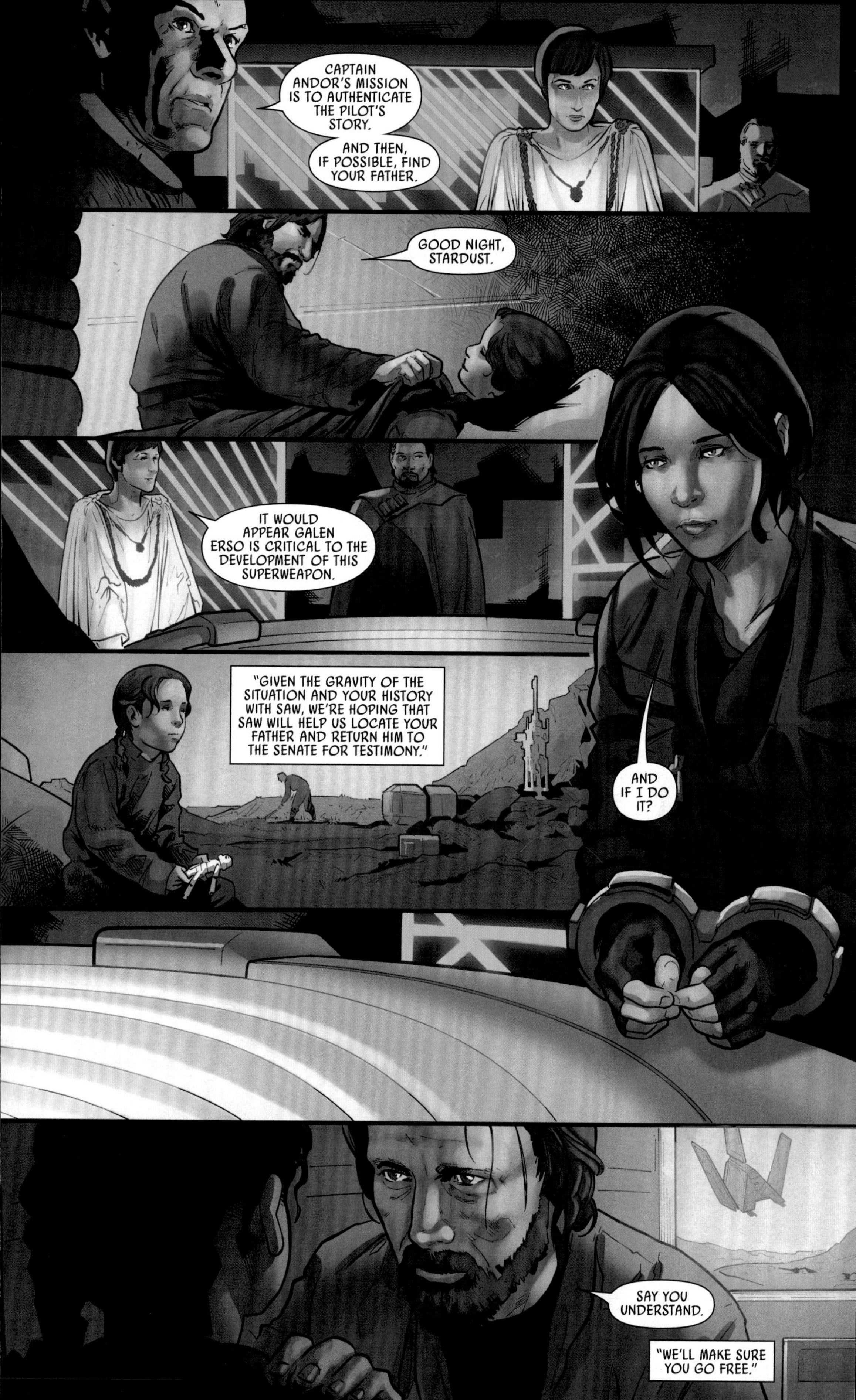

CAPTAIN ANDOR'S MISSION IS TO AUTHENTICATE THE PILOT'S STORY.
AND THEN, IF POSSIBLE, FIND YOUR FATHER.
GOOD NIGHT, STARDUST.
IT WOULD APPEAR GALEN ERSO IS CRITICAL TO THE DEVELOPMENT OF THIS SUPERWEAPON.
"GIVEN THE GRAVITY OF THE SITUATION AND YOUR HISTORY WITH SAW, WE'RE HOPING THAT SAW WILL HELP US LOCATE YOUR FATHER AND RETURN HIM TO THE SENATE FOR TESTIMONY."
AND IF I DO IT?
SAY YOU UNDERSTAND.
"WE'LL MAKE SURE YOU GO FREE."

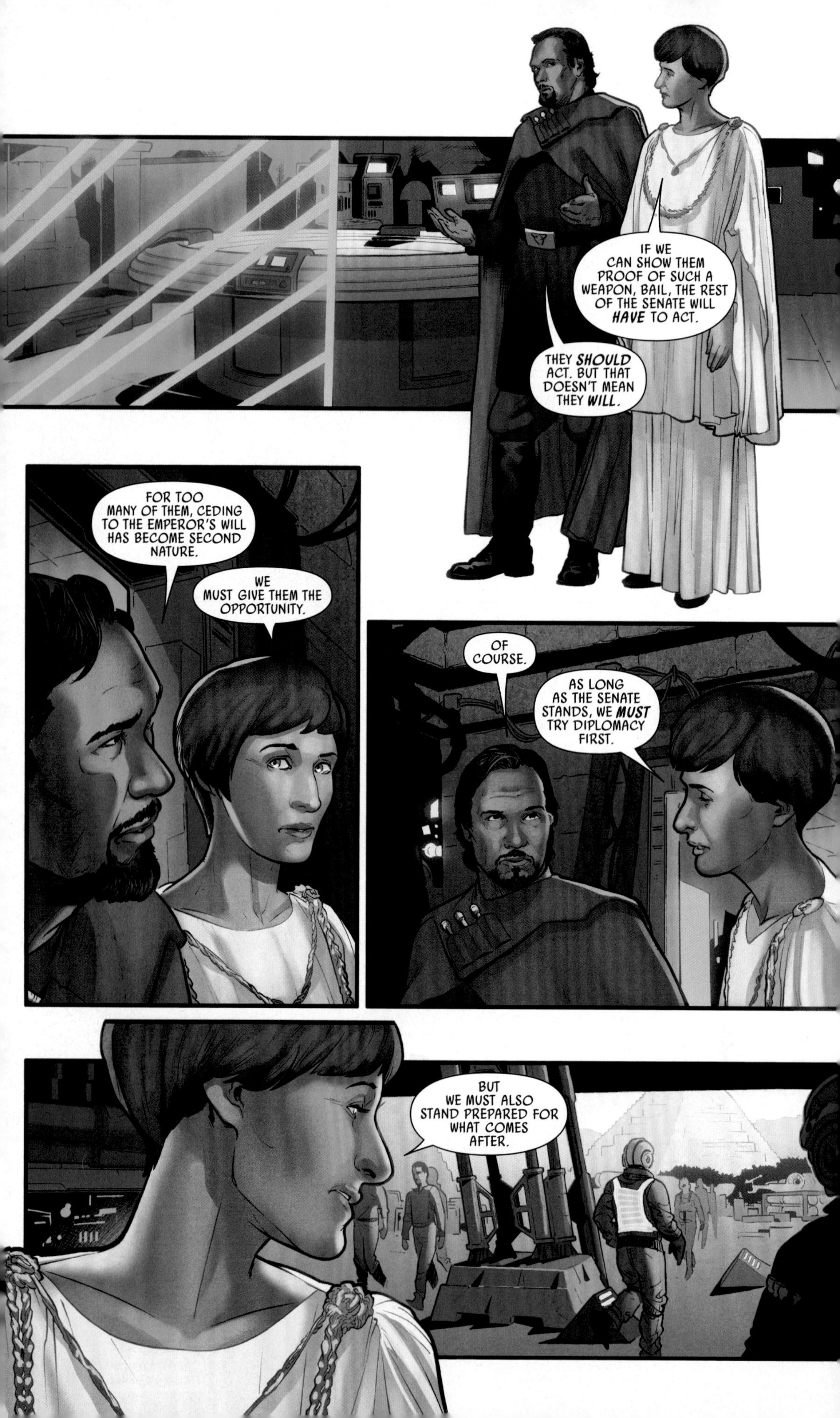
IF WE CAN SHOW THEM PROOF OF SUCH A WEAPON, BAIL, THE REST OF THE SENATE WILL *HAVE* TO ACT.
THEY *SHOULD* ACT. BUT THAT DOESN'T MEAN THEY *WILL*.
FOR TOO MANY OF THEM, CEDING TO THE EMPEROR'S WILL HAS BECOME SECOND NATURE.
WE MUST GIVE THEM THE OPPORTUNITY.
OF COURSE.
AS LONG AS THE SENATE STANDS, WE *MUST* TRY DIPLOMACY FIRST.
BUT WE MUST ALSO STAND PREPARED FOR WHAT COMES AFTER.

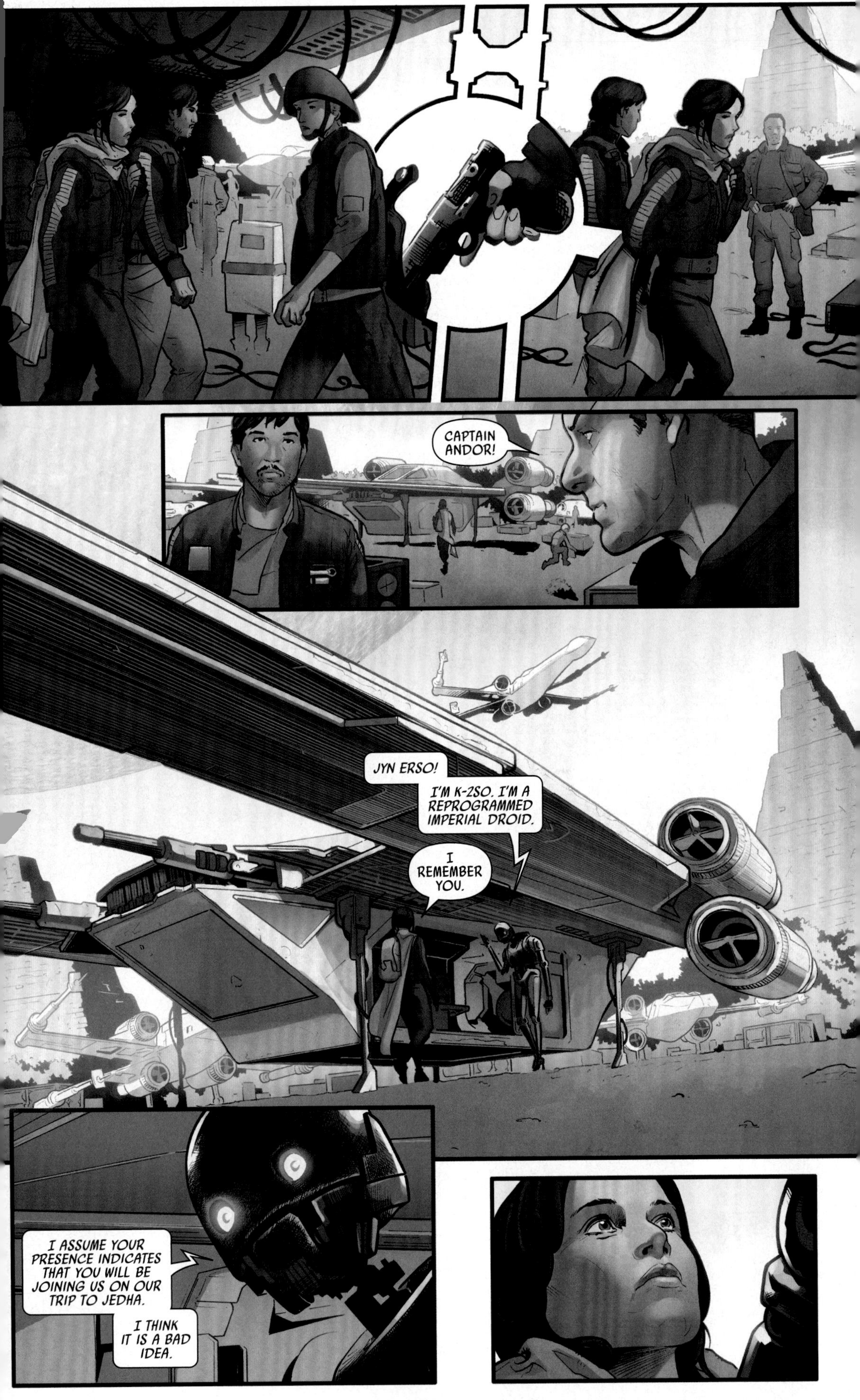
CAPTAIN ANDOR!
JYN ERSO!
I'M K-2SO. I'M A REPROGRAMMED IMPERIAL DROID.
I REMEMBER YOU.
I ASSUME YOUR PRESENCE INDICATES THAT YOU WILL BE JOINING US ON OUR TRIP TO JEDHA.
I THINK IT IS A BAD IDEA.

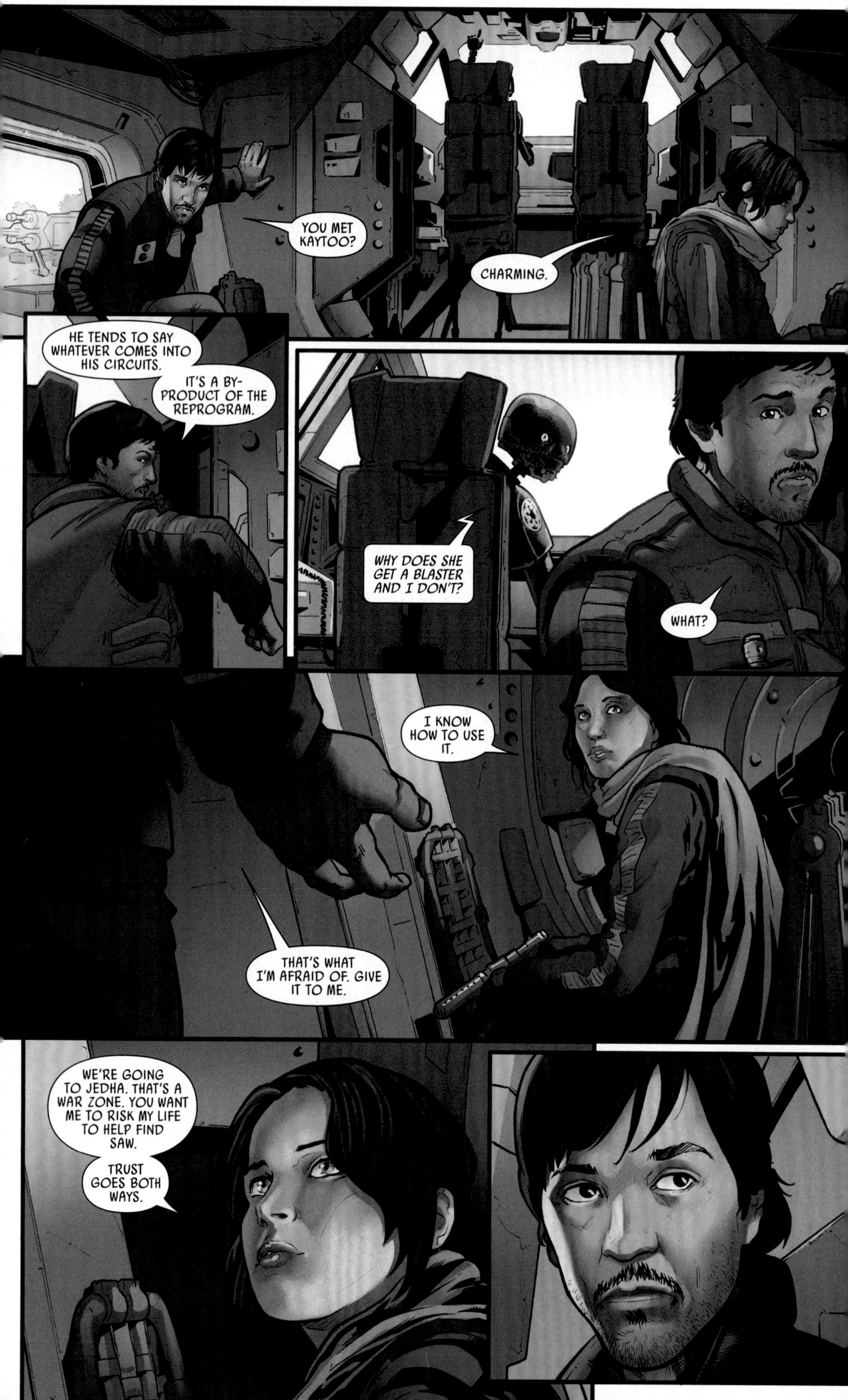
YOU MET KAYTOO?
CHARMING.
HE TENDS TO SAY WHATEVER COMES INTO HIS CIRCUITS.
IT'S A BY-PRODUCT OF THE REPROGRAM.
WHY DOES SHE GET A BLASTER AND I DON'T?
WHAT?
I KNOW HOW TO USE IT.
THAT'S WHAT I'M AFRAID OF. GIVE IT TO ME.
WE'RE GOING TO JEDHA. THAT'S A WAR ZONE. YOU WANT ME TO RISK MY LIFE TO HELP FIND SAW.
TRUST GOES BOTH WAYS.

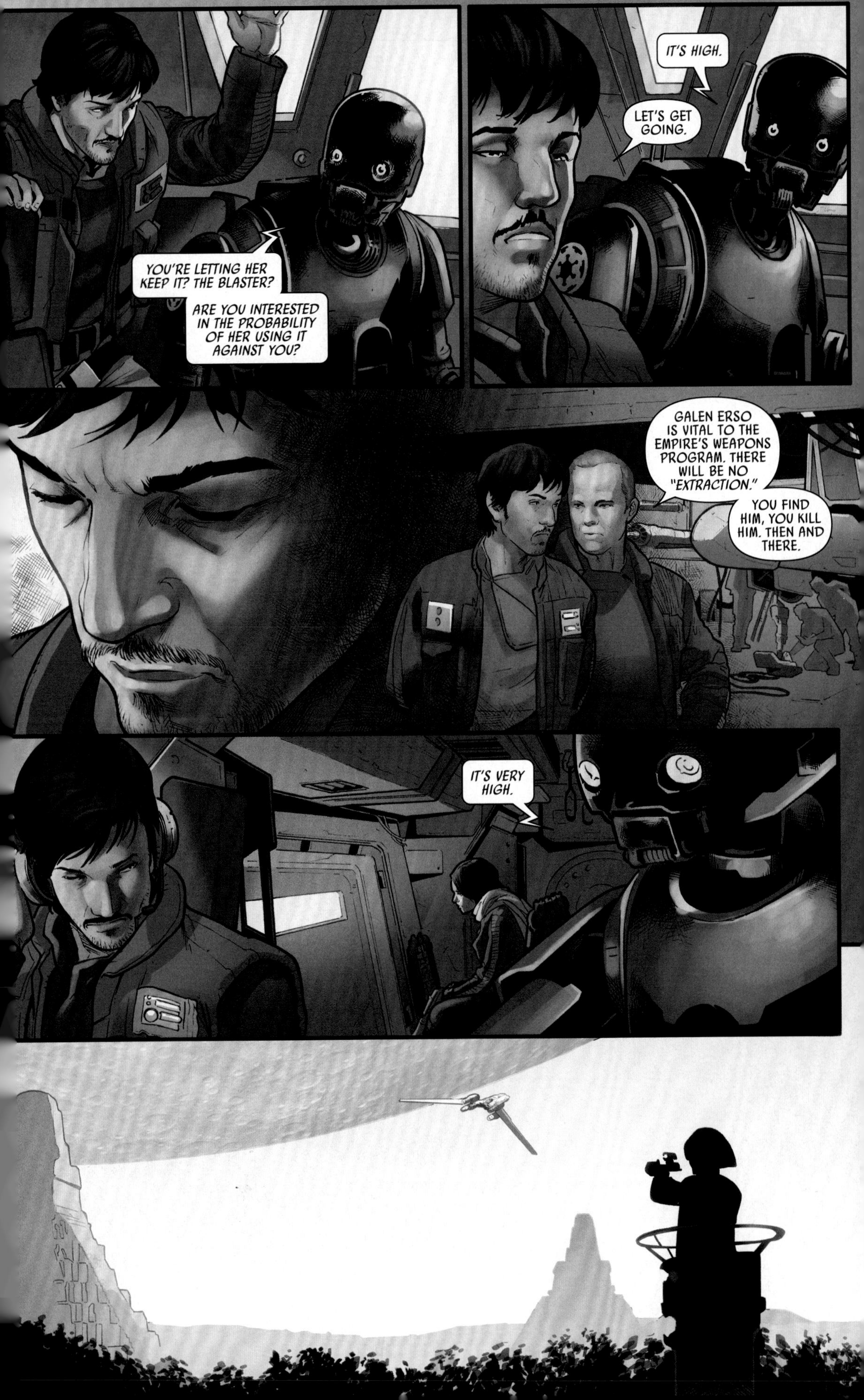
YOU'RE LETTING HER KEEP IT? THE BLASTER?
ARE YOU INTERESTED IN THE PROBABILITY OF HER USING IT AGAINST YOU?
IT'S HIGH.
LET'S GET GOING.
GALEN ERSO IS VITAL TO THE EMPIRE'S WEAPONS PROGRAM. THERE WILL BE NO "EXTRACTION."
YOU FIND HIM, YOU KILL HIM. THEN AND THERE.
IT'S VERY HIGH.

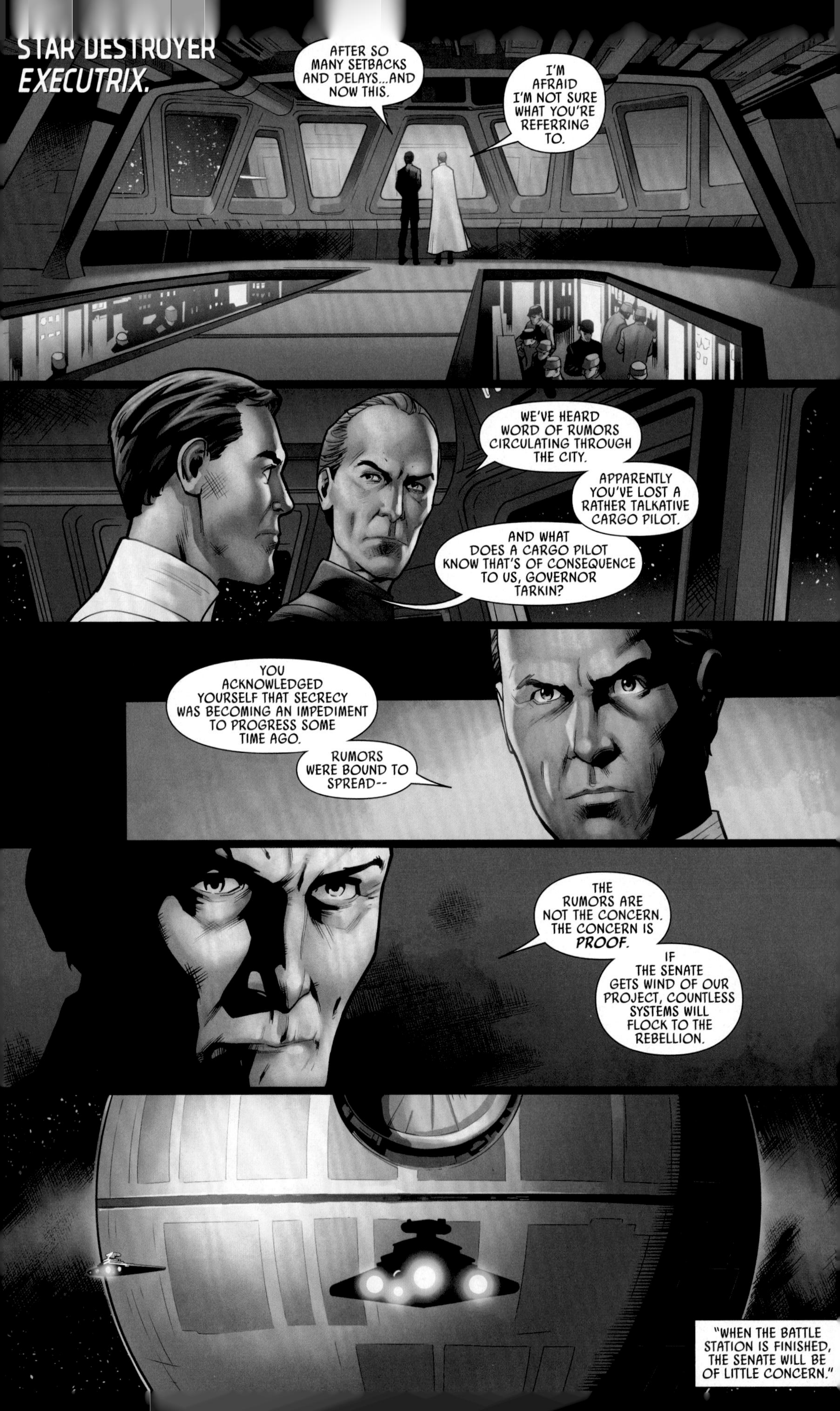
STAR DESTROYER EXECUTRIX.
AFTER SO MANY SETBACKS AND DELAYS...AND NOW THIS.
I'M AFRAID I'M NOT SURE WHAT YOU'RE REFERRING TO.
WE'VE HEARD WORD OF RUMORS CIRCULATING THROUGH THE CITY.
APPARENTLY YOU'VE LOST A RATHER TALKATIVE CARGO PILOT.
AND WHAT DOES A CARGO PILOT KNOW THAT'S OF CONSEQUENCE TO US, GOVERNOR TARKIN?
YOU ACKNOWLEDGED YOURSELF THAT SECRECY WAS BECOMING AN IMPEDIMENT TO PROGRESS SOME TIME AGO.
RUMORS WERE BOUND TO SPREAD--
THE RUMORS ARE NOT THE CONCERN. THE CONCERN IS PROOF.
IF THE SENATE GETS WIND OF OUR PROJECT, COUNTLESS SYSTEMS WILL FLOCK TO THE REBELLION.
"WHEN THE BATTLE STATION IS FINISHED, THE SENATE WILL BE OF LITTLE CONCERN."

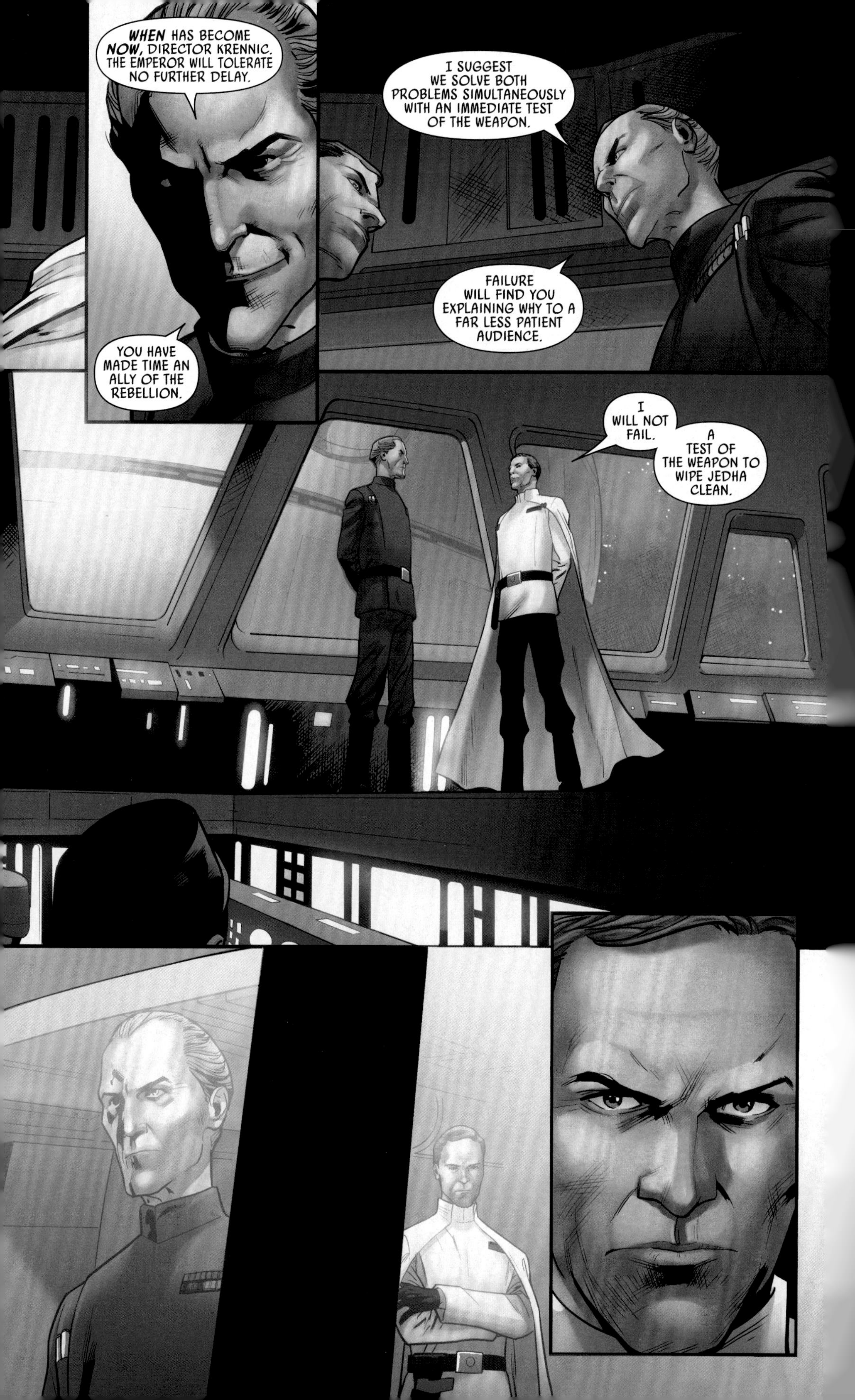
WHEN HAS BECOME NOW, DIRECTOR KRENNIC. THE EMPEROR WILL TOLERATE NO FURTHER DELAY.
YOU HAVE MADE TIME AN ALLY OF THE REBELLION.
I SUGGEST WE SOLVE BOTH PROBLEMS SIMULTANEOUSLY WITH AN IMMEDIATE TEST OF THE WEAPON.
FAILURE WILL FIND YOU EXPLAINING WHY TO A FAR LESS PATIENT AUDIENCE.
I WILL NOT FAIL.
A TEST OF THE WEAPON TO WIPE JEDHA CLEAN.

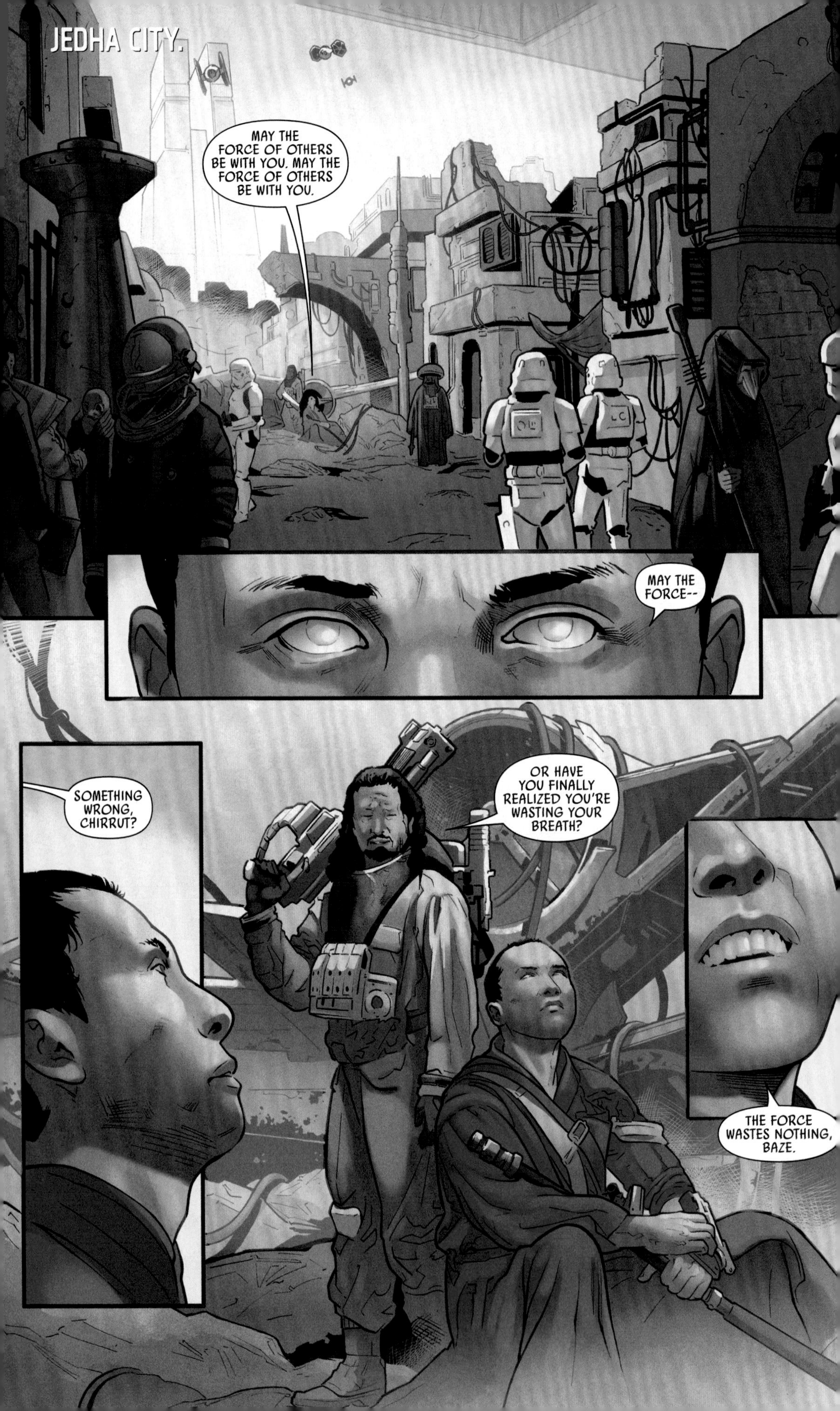
JEDHA CITY.
MAY THE FORCE OF OTHERS BE WITH YOU. MAY THE FORCE OF OTHERS BE WITH YOU.
MAY THE FORCE--
SOMETHING WRONG, CHIRRUT?
OR HAVE YOU FINALLY REALIZED YOU'RE WASTING YOUR BREATH?
THE FORCE WASTES NOTHING, BAZE.

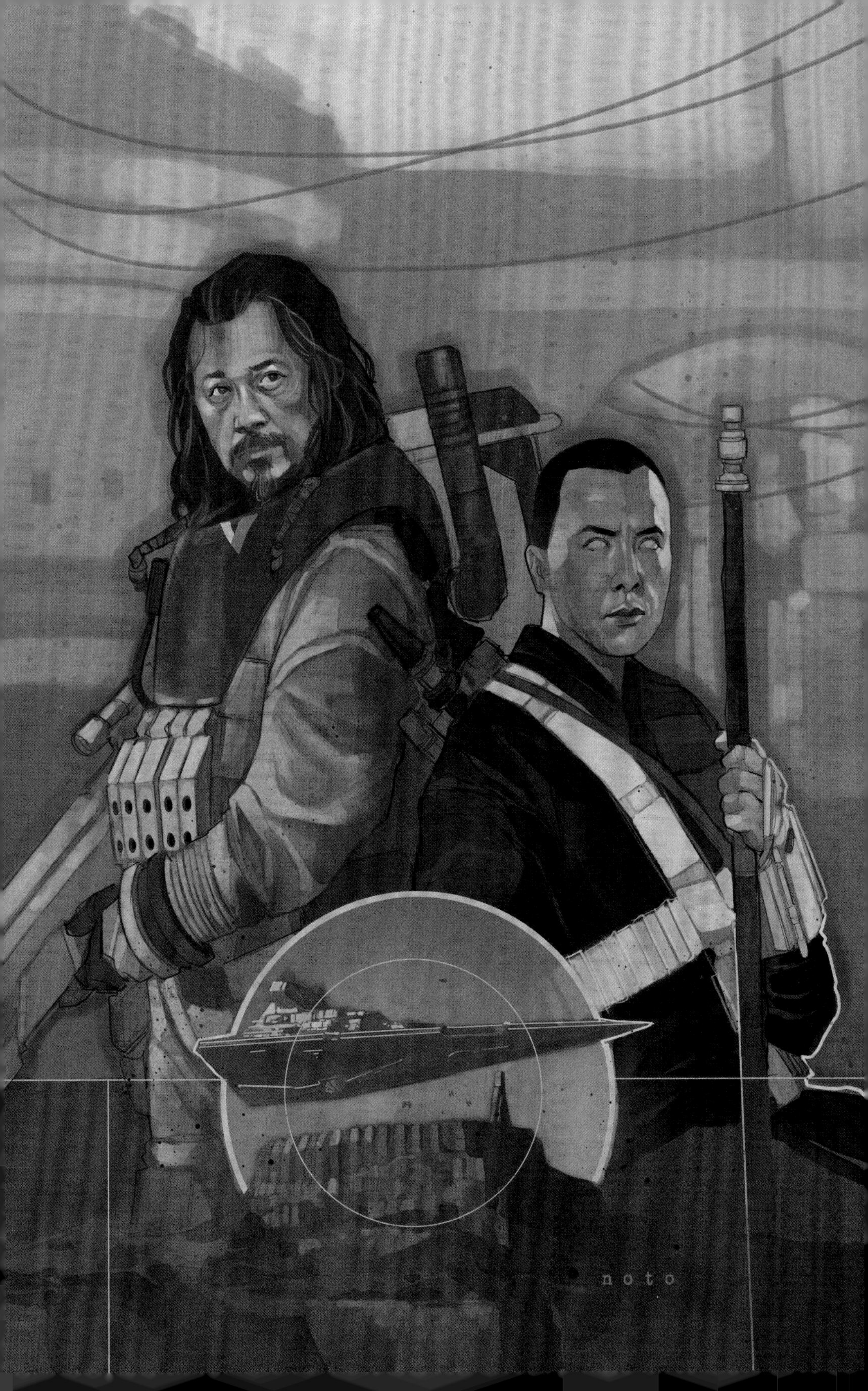
noto

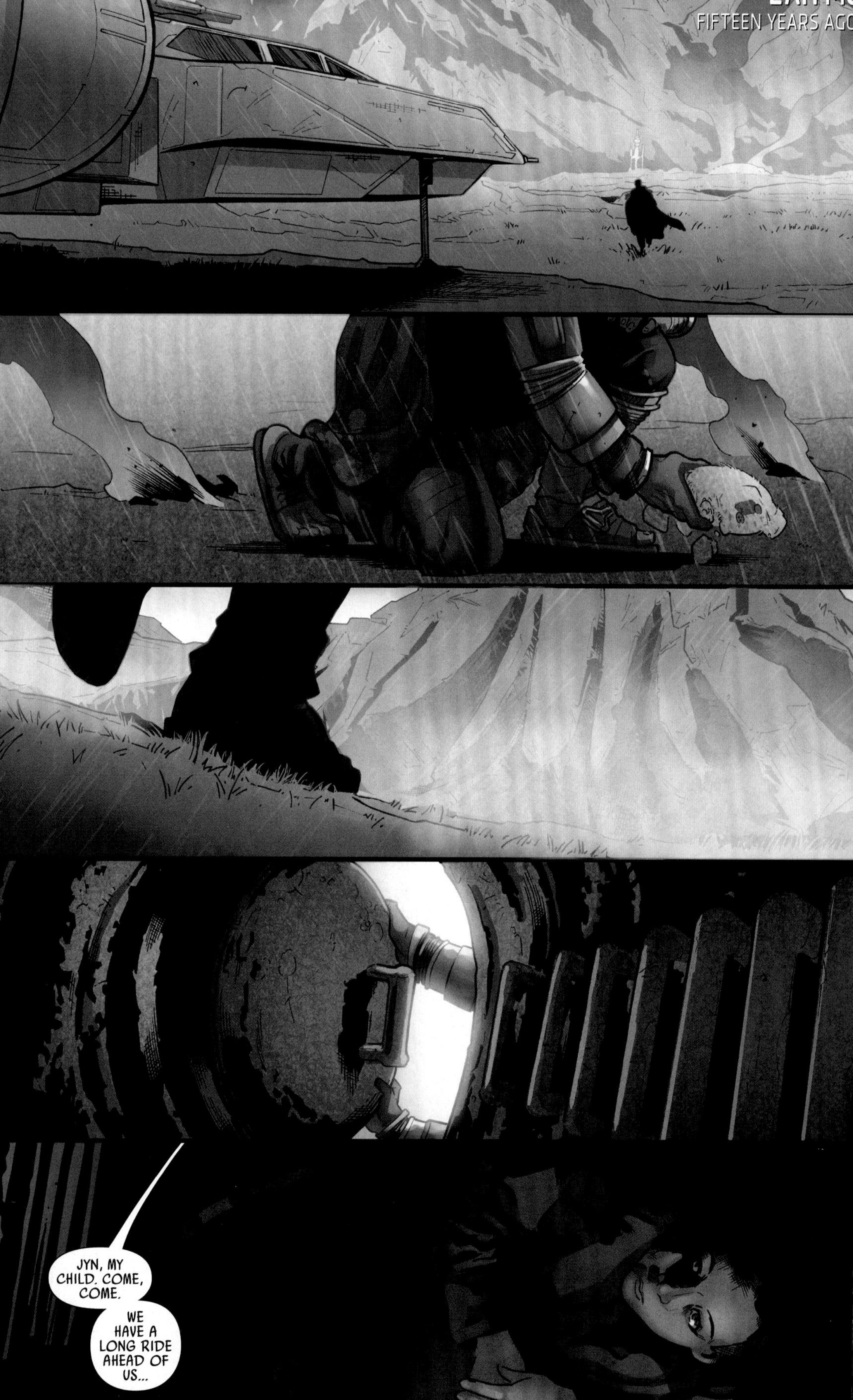
FIFTEEN YEARS AG
JYN, MY CHILD. COME, COME.
WE HAVE A LONG RIDE AHEAD OF US...

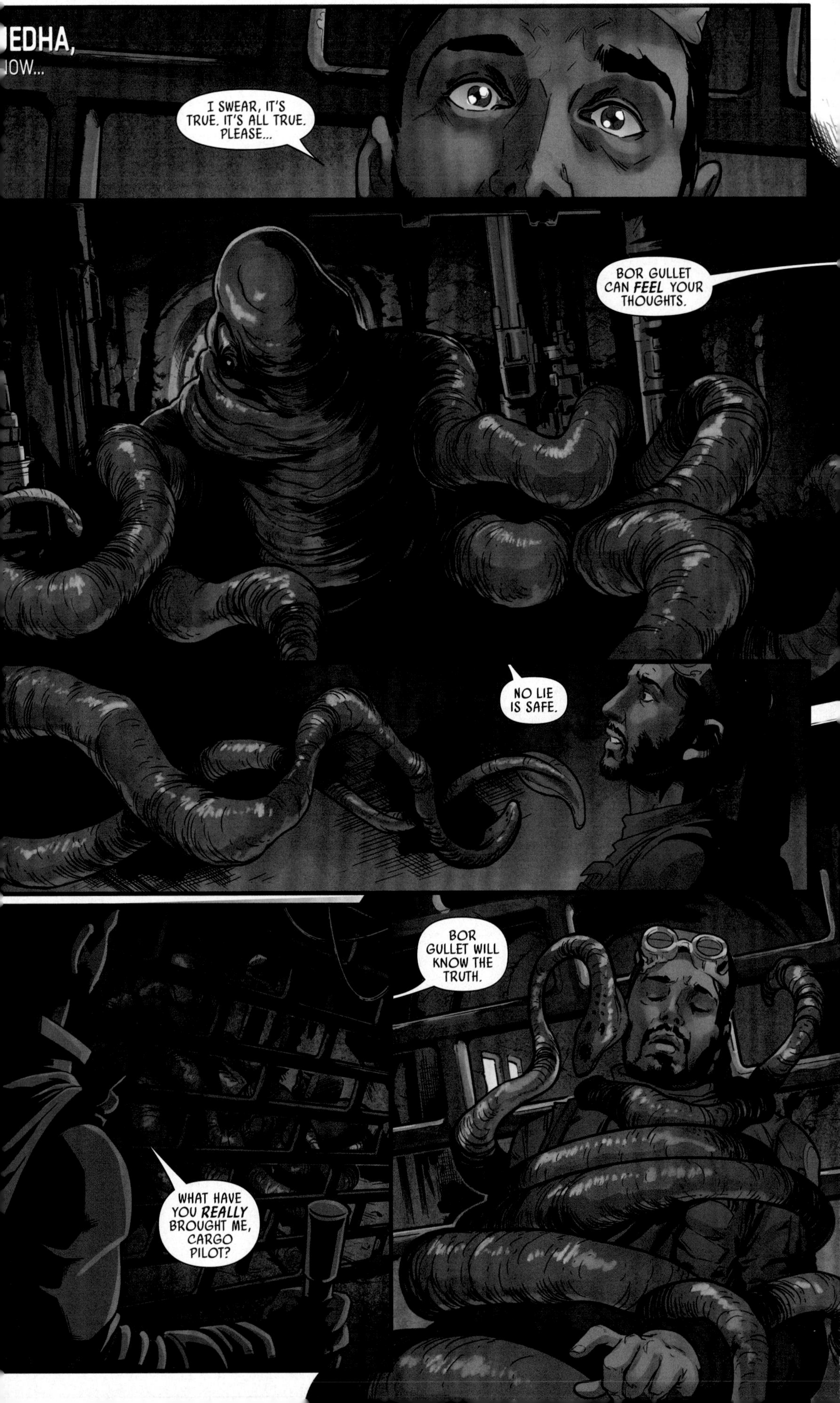

EDHA,
IOW...
I SWEAR, IT'S TRUE. IT'S ALL TRUE. PLEASE...
BOR GULLET CAN FEEL YOUR THOUGHTS.
NO LIE IS SAFE.
BOR GULLET WILL KNOW THE TRUTH.
WHAT HAVE YOU REALLY BROUGHT ME, CARGO PILOT?

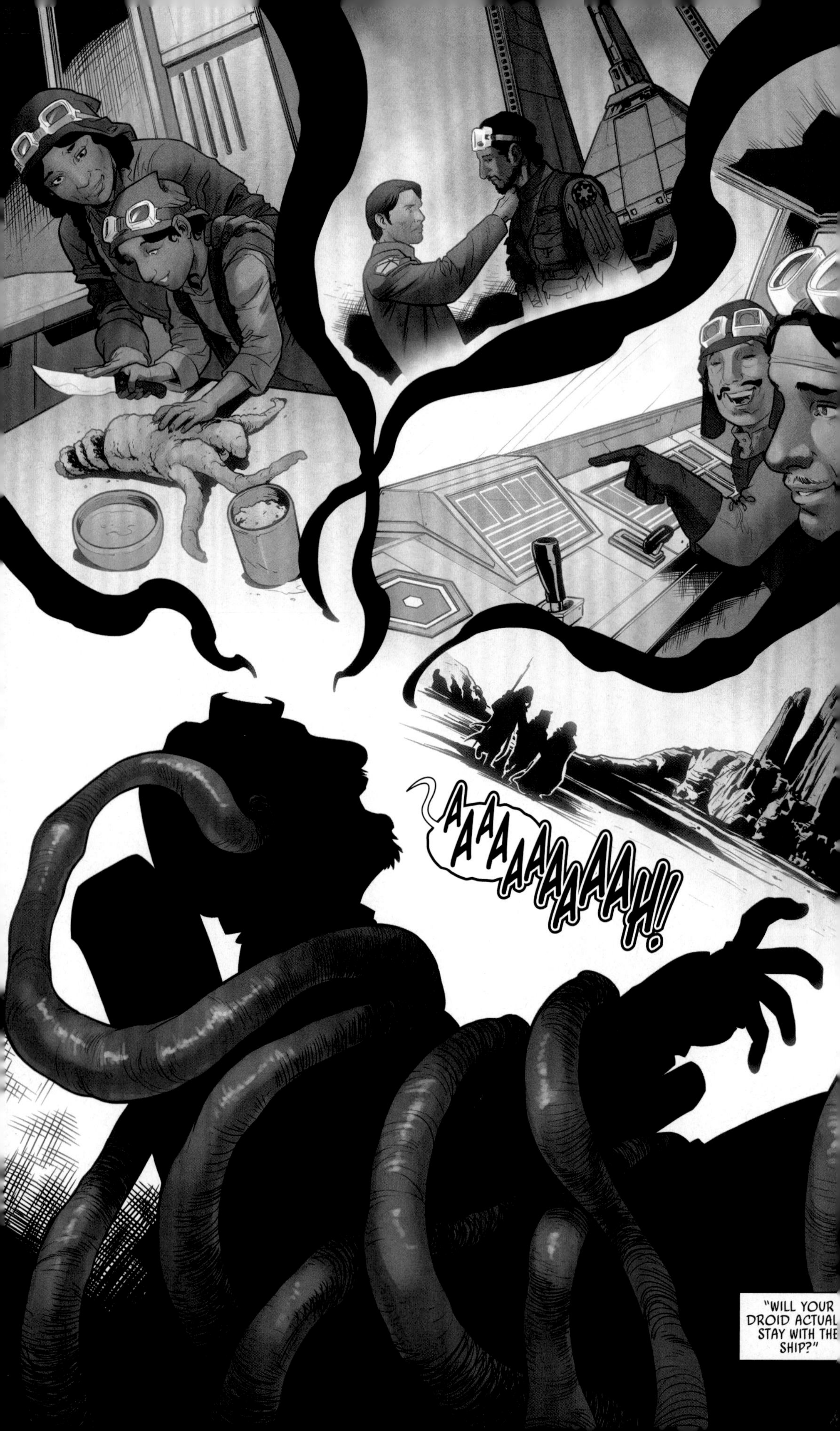
AAAAAAAAAAAH!!
"WILL YOUR DROID ACTUAL STAY WITH THE SHIP?"

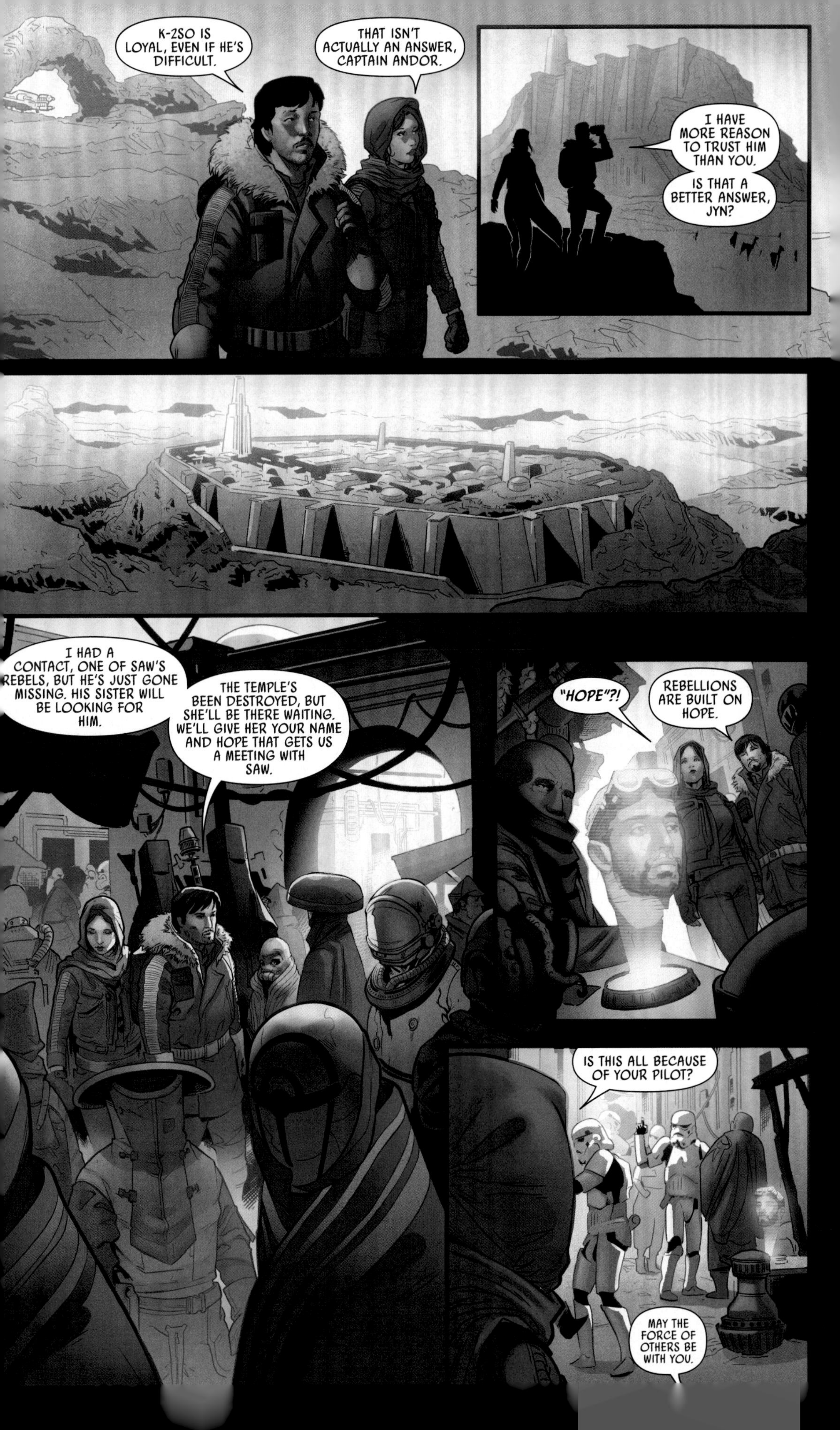
K-2SO IS LOYAL, EVEN IF HE'S DIFFICULT.
THAT ISN'T ACTUALLY AN ANSWER, CAPTAIN ANDOR.
I HAVE MORE REASON TO TRUST HIM THAN YOU.
IS THAT A BETTER ANSWER, JYN?
I HAD A CONTACT, ONE OF SAW'S REBELS, BUT HE'S JUST GONE MISSING. HIS SISTER WILL BE LOOKING FOR HIM.
THE TEMPLE'S BEEN DESTROYED, BUT SHE'LL BE THERE WAITING. WE'LL GIVE HER YOUR NAME AND HOPE THAT GETS US A MEETING WITH SAW.
"HOPE"?!
REBELLIONS ARE BUILT ON HOPE.
IS THIS ALL BECAUSE OF YOUR PILOT?
MAY THE FORCE OF OTHERS BE WITH YOU.

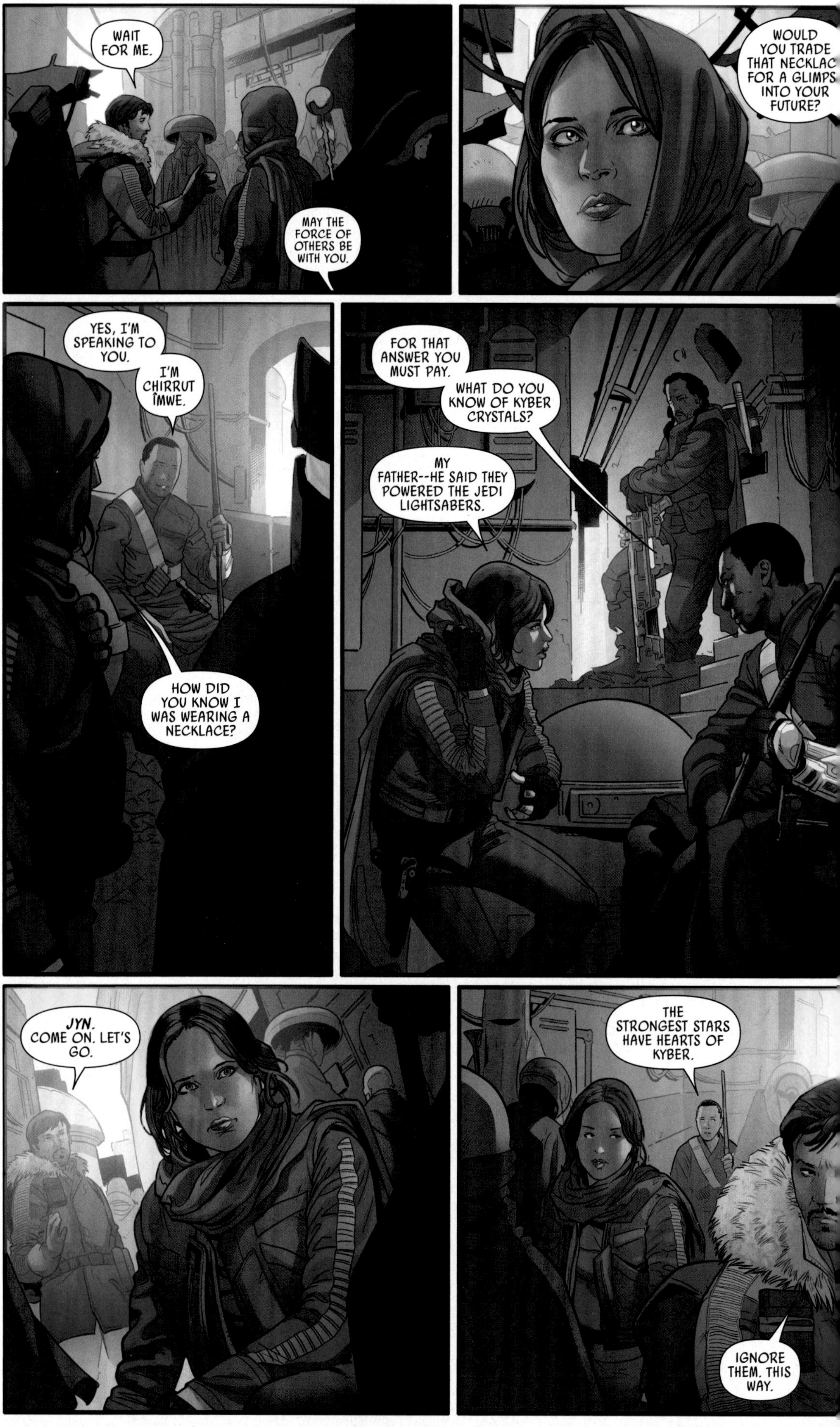
WAIT FOR ME.
MAY THE FORCE OF OTHERS BE WITH YOU.
WOULD YOU TRADE THAT NECKLAC FOR A GLIMPS INTO YOUR FUTURE?
YES, I'M SPEAKING TO YOU.
I'M CHIRRUT ÎMWE.
HOW DID YOU KNOW I WAS WEARING A NECKLACE?
FOR THAT ANSWER YOU MUST PAY.
WHAT DO YOU KNOW OF KYBER CRYSTALS?
MY FATHER--HE SAID THEY POWERED THE JEDI LIGHTSABERS.
JYN. COME ON. LET'S GO.
THE STRONGEST STARS HAVE HEARTS OF KYBER.
IGNORE THEM. THIS WAY.

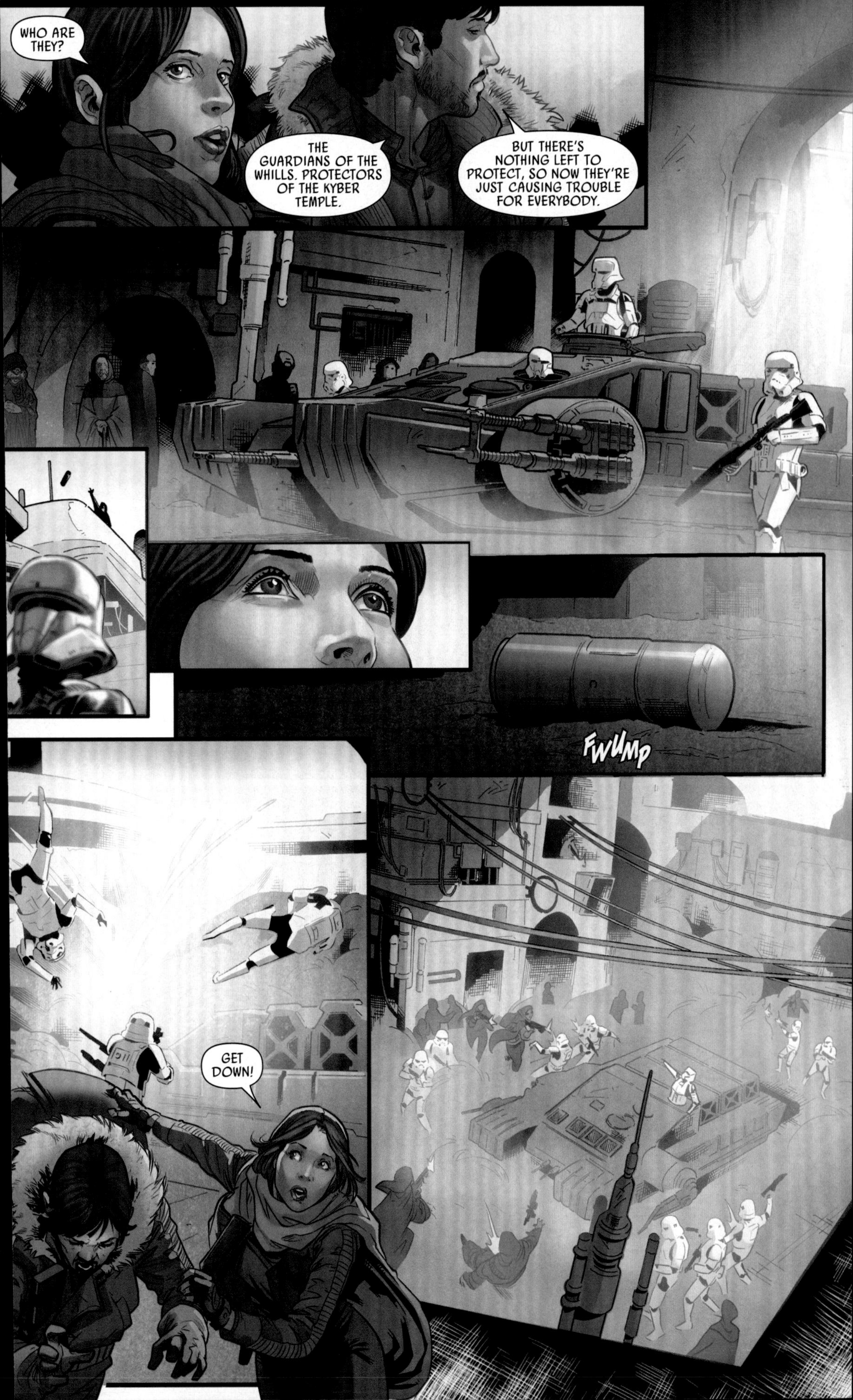
WHO ARE THEY?
THE GUARDIANS OF THE WHILLS. PROTECTORS OF THE KYBER TEMPLE.
BUT THERE'S NOTHING LEFT TO PROTECT, SO NOW THEY'RE JUST CAUSING TROUBLE FOR EVERYBODY.
FWUMP
GET DOWN!

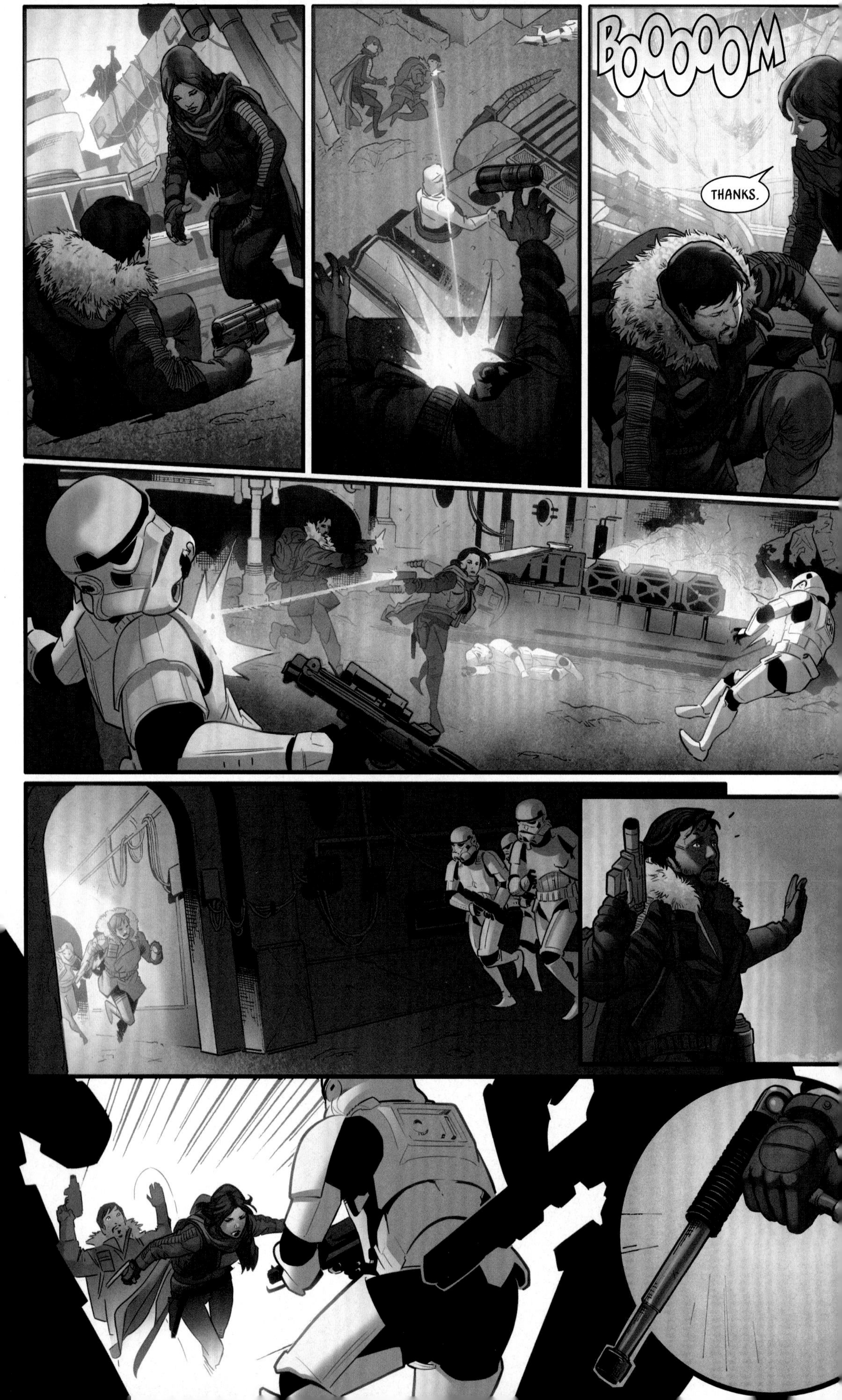
BOOOOOM
THANKS.

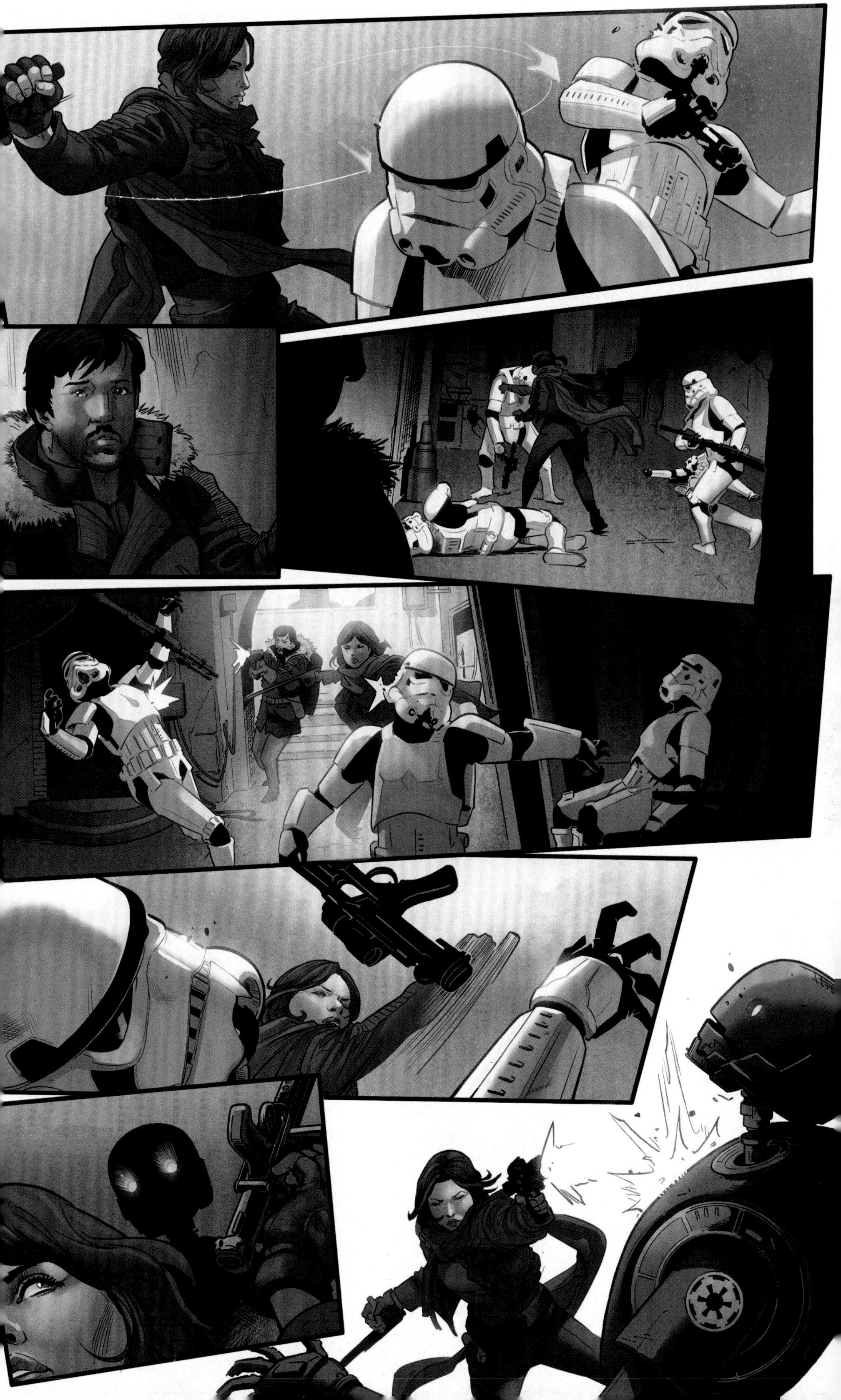

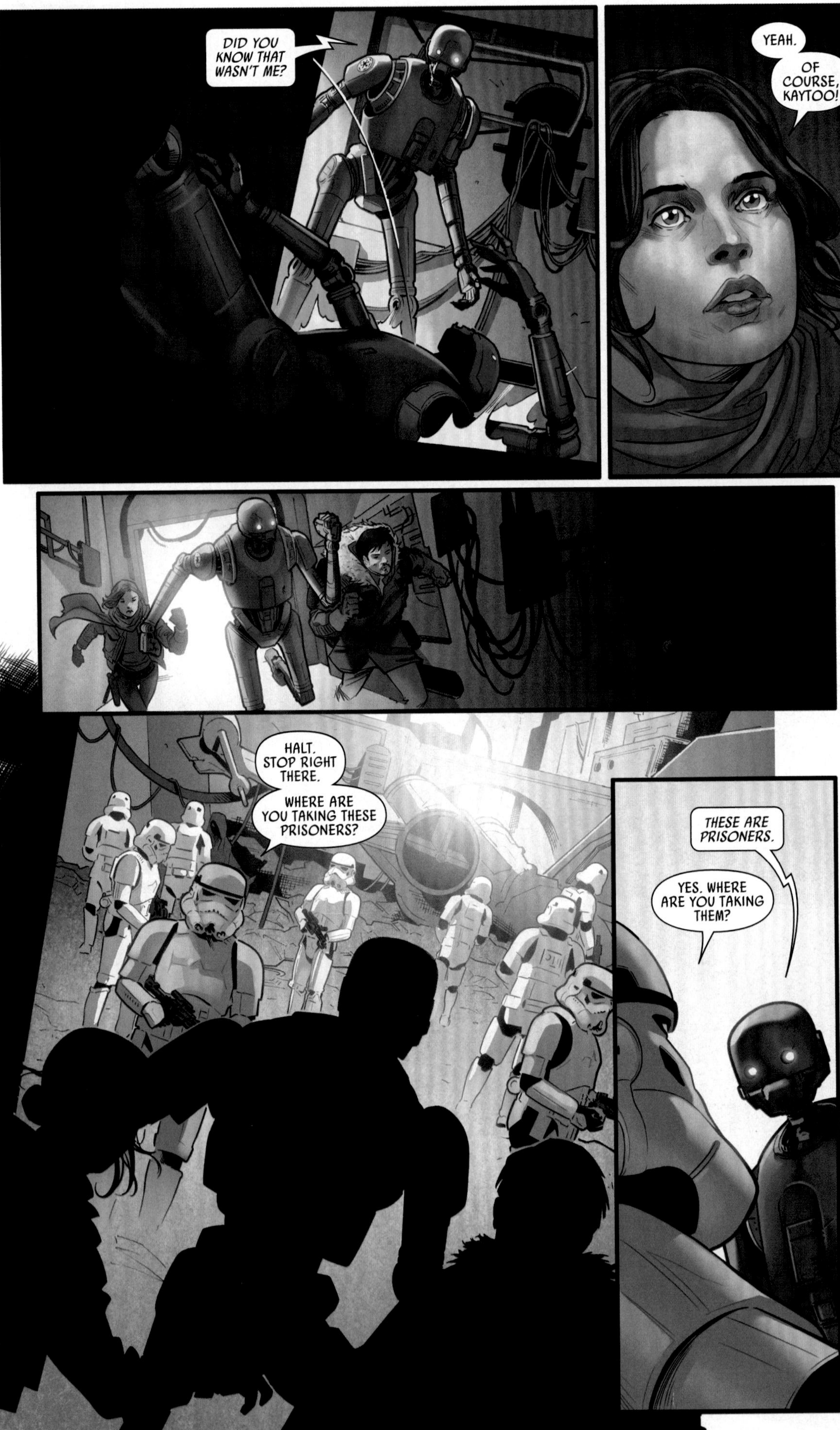
DID YOU KNOW THAT WASN'T ME?
YEAH.
OF COURSE, KAYTOO!
HALT. STOP RIGHT THERE.
WHERE ARE YOU TAKING THESE PRISONERS?
THESE ARE PRISONERS.
YES. WHERE ARE YOU TAKING THEM?

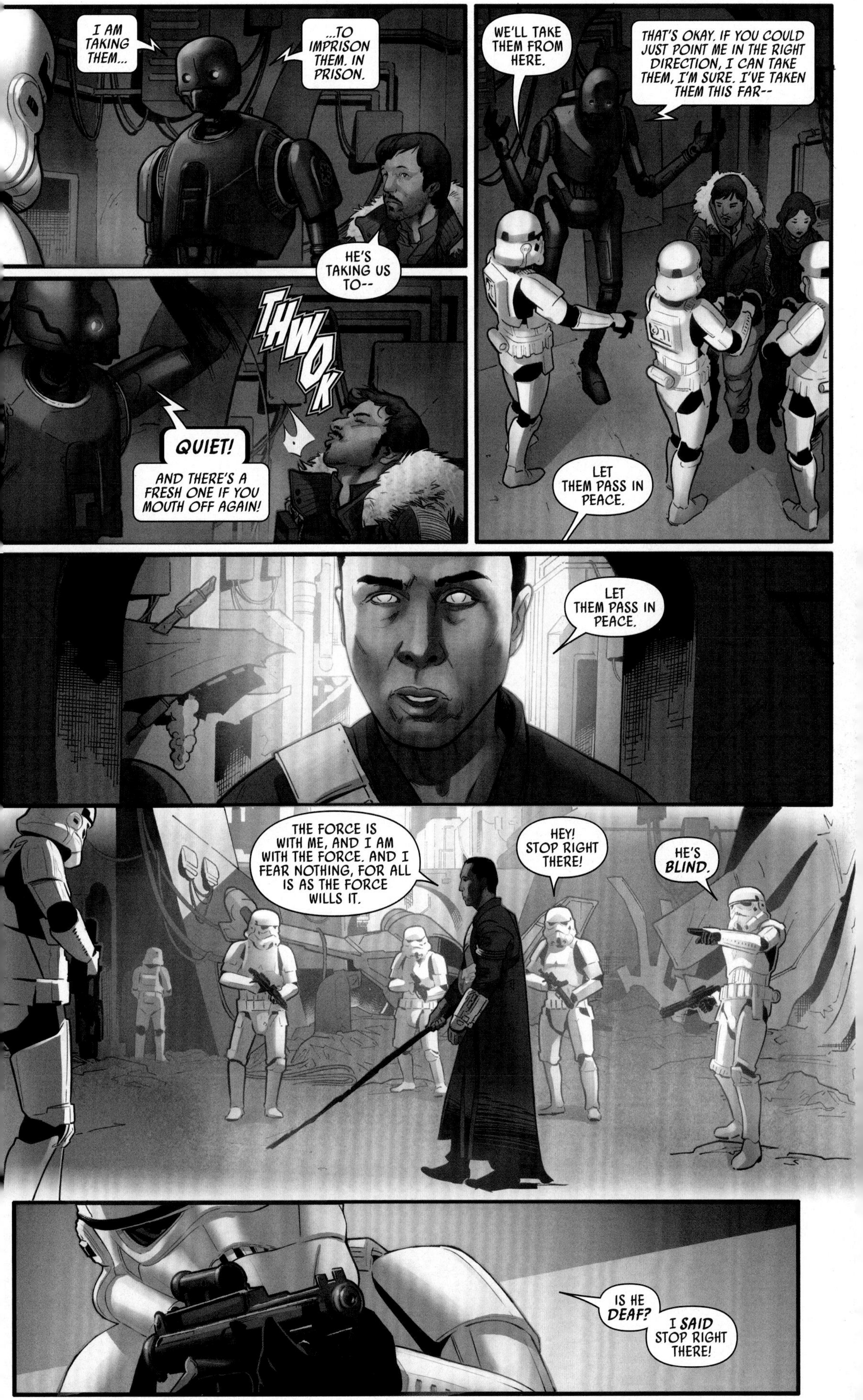
I AM TAKING THEM...
...TO IMPRISON THEM. IN PRISON.
HE'S TAKING US TO--
THWOK
QUIET!
AND THERE'S A FRESH ONE IF YOU MOUTH OFF AGAIN!
WE'LL TAKE THEM FROM HERE.
THAT'S OKAY. IF YOU COULD JUST POINT ME IN THE RIGHT DIRECTION, I CAN TAKE THEM, I'M SURE. I'VE TAKEN THEM THIS FAR--
LET THEM PASS IN PEACE.
LET THEM PASS IN PEACE.
THE FORCE IS WITH ME, AND I AM WITH THE FORCE. AND I FEAR NOTHING, FOR ALL IS AS THE FORCE WILLS IT.
HEY! STOP RIGHT THERE!
HE'S BLIND.
IS HE DEAF?
I SAID STOP RIGHT THERE!

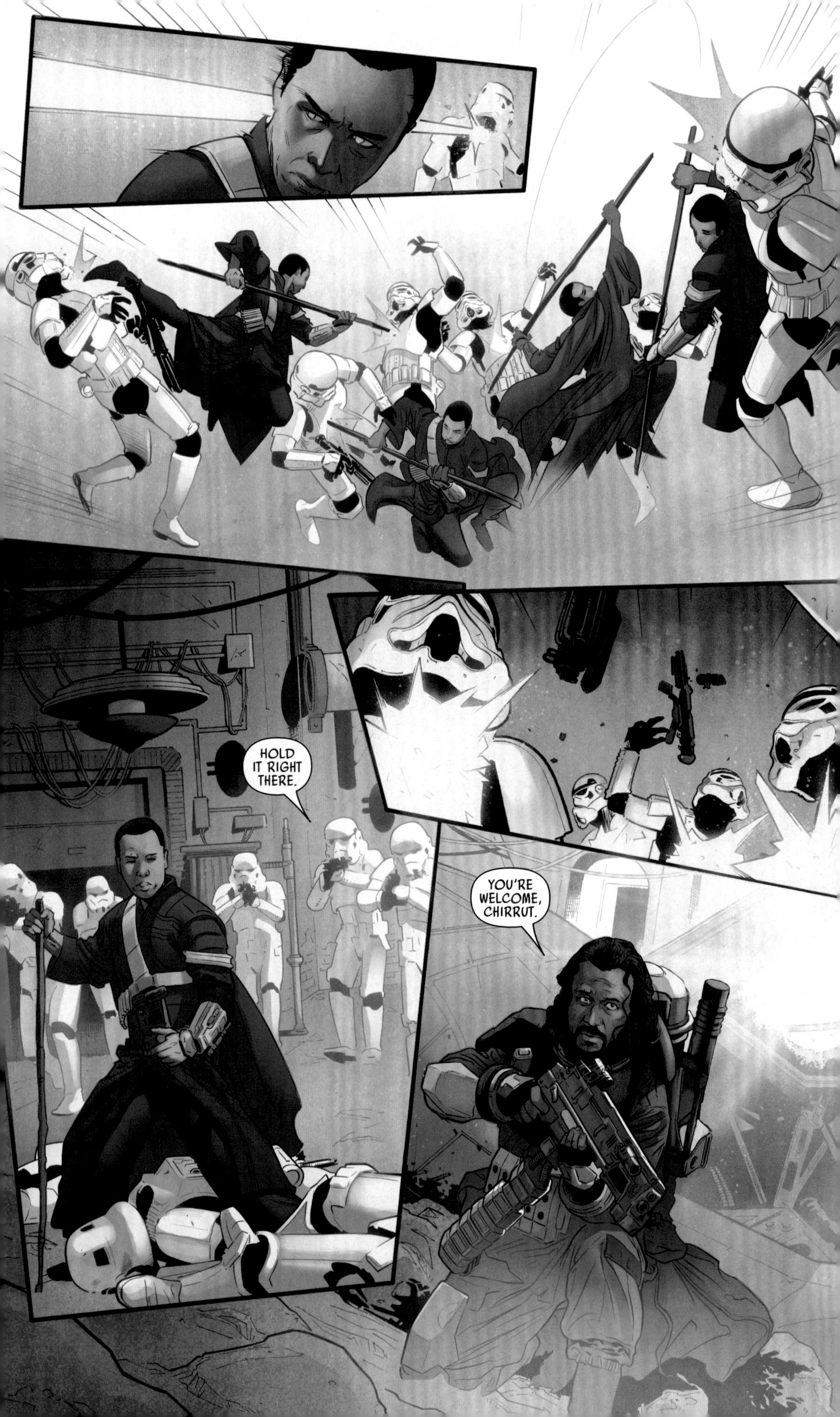
HOLD IT RIGHT THERE.
YOU'RE WELCOME, CHIRRUT.

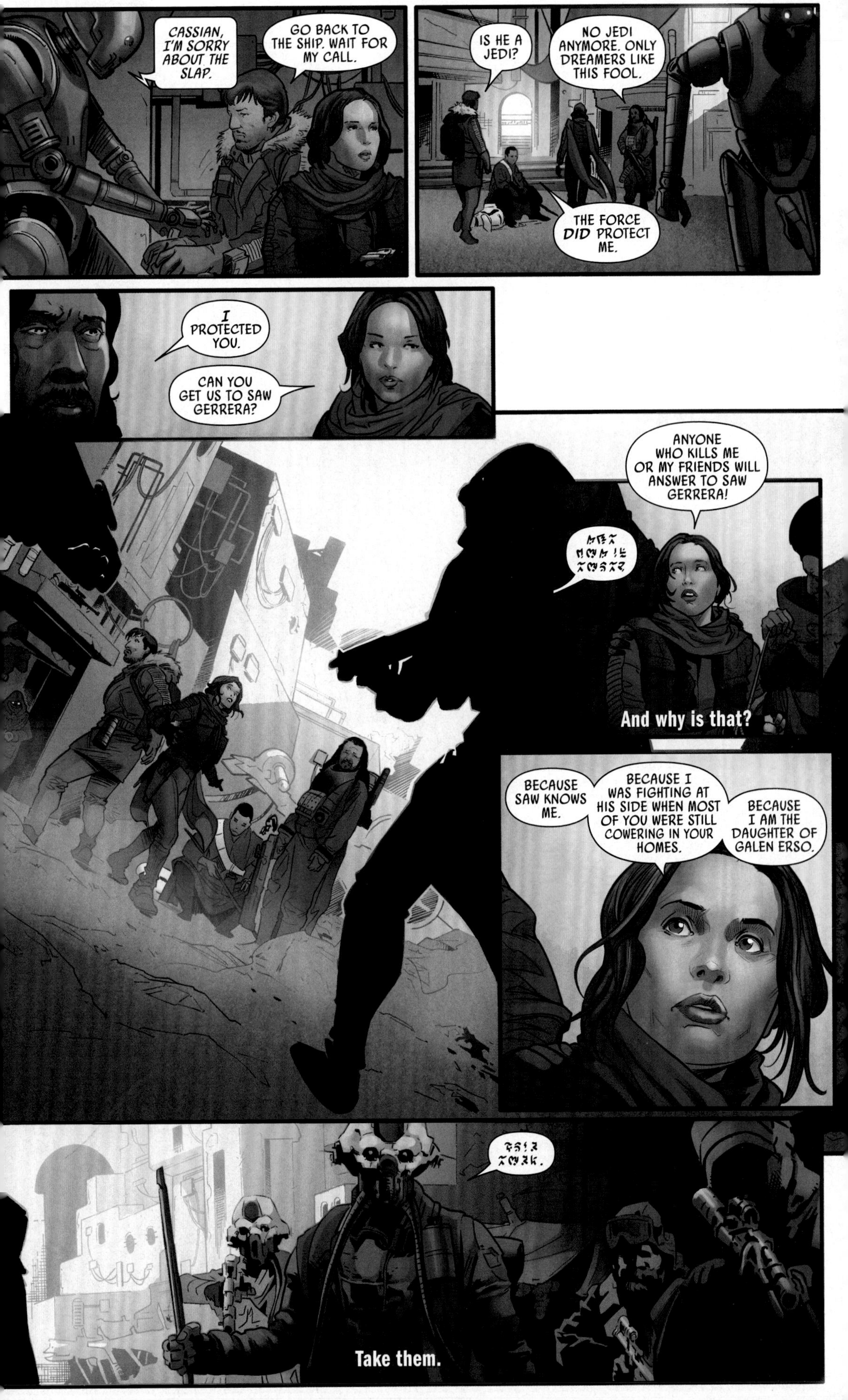
CASSIAN, I'M SORRY ABOUT THE SLAP.
GO BACK TO THE SHIP. WAIT FOR MY CALL.
IS HE A JEDI?
NO JEDI ANYMORE. ONLY DREAMERS LIKE THIS FOOL.
THE FORCE DID PROTECT ME.
I PROTECTED YOU.
CAN YOU GET US TO SAW GERRERA?
ANYONE WHO KILLS ME OR MY FRIENDS WILL ANSWER TO SAW GERRERA!
And why is that?
BECAUSE SAW KNOWS ME.
BECAUSE I WAS FIGHTING AT HIS SIDE WHEN MOST OF YOU WERE STILL COWERING IN YOUR HOMES.
BECAUSE I AM THE DAUGHTER OF GALEN ERSO.
Take them.

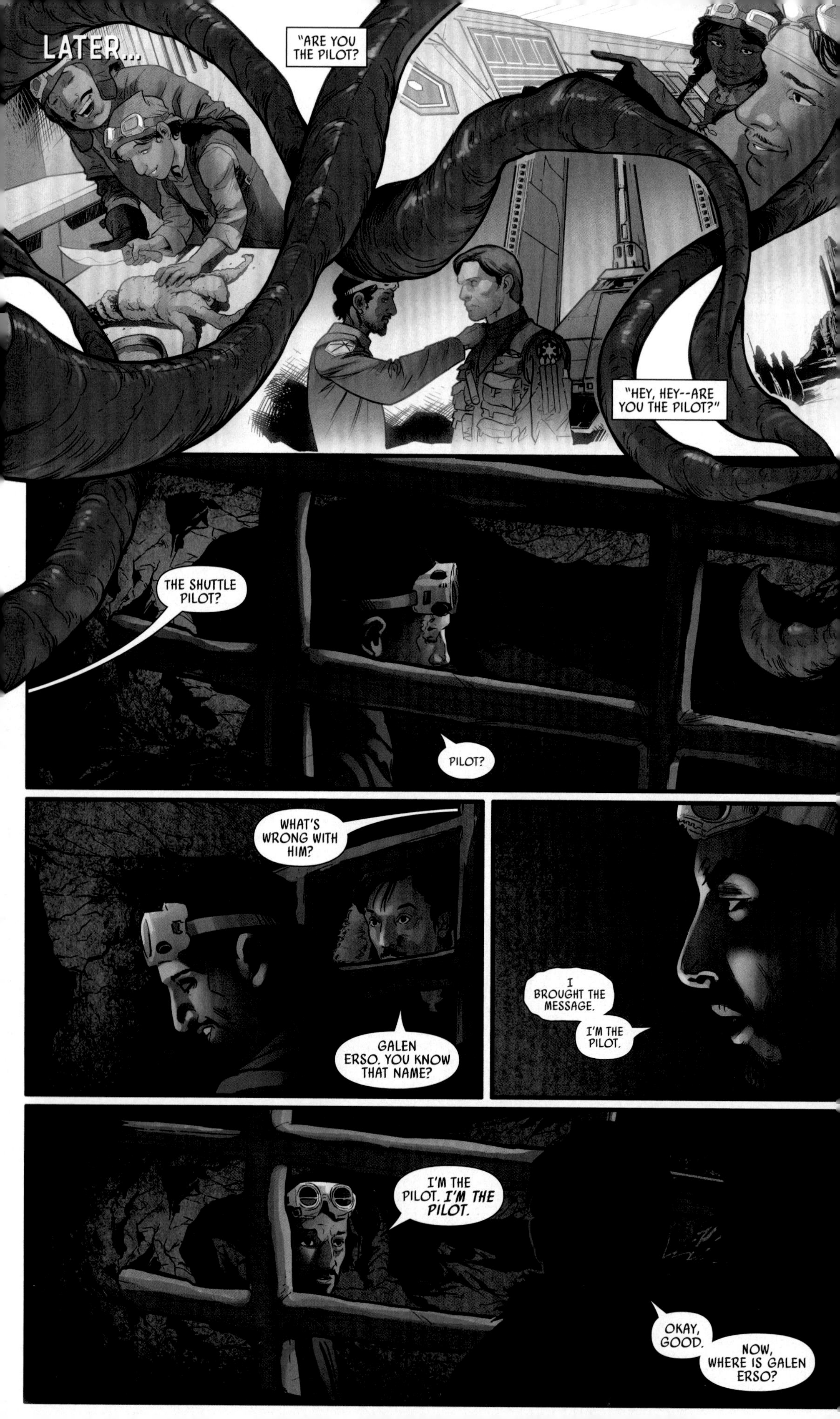
LATER...
"ARE YOU THE PILOT?
"HEY, HEY--ARE YOU THE PILOT?"
THE SHUTTLE PILOT?
PILOT?
WHAT'S WRONG WITH HIM?
GALEN ERSO. YOU KNOW THAT NAME?
I BROUGHT THE MESSAGE.
I'M THE PILOT.
I'M THE PILOT. *I'M THE PILOT.*
OKAY, GOOD.
NOW, WHERE IS GALEN ERSO?

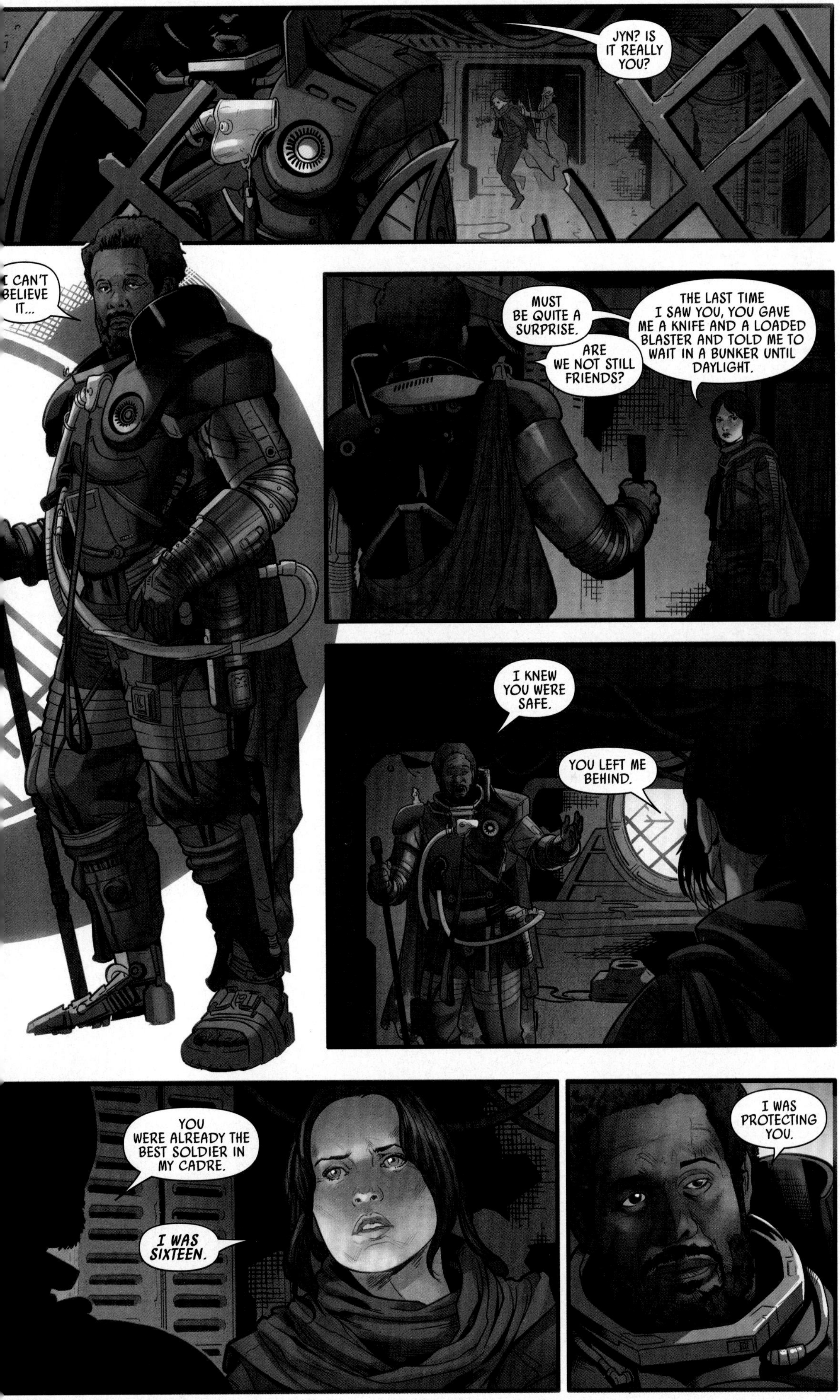
JYN? IS IT REALLY YOU?
I CAN'T BELIEVE IT...
MUST BE QUITE A SURPRISE.
ARE WE NOT STILL FRIENDS?
THE LAST TIME I SAW YOU, YOU GAVE ME A KNIFE AND A LOADED BLASTER AND TOLD ME TO WAIT IN A BUNKER UNTIL DAYLIGHT.
I KNEW YOU WERE SAFE.
YOU LEFT ME BEHIND.
YOU WERE ALREADY THE BEST SOLDIER IN MY CADRE.
I WAS SIXTEEN.
I WAS PROTECTING YOU.

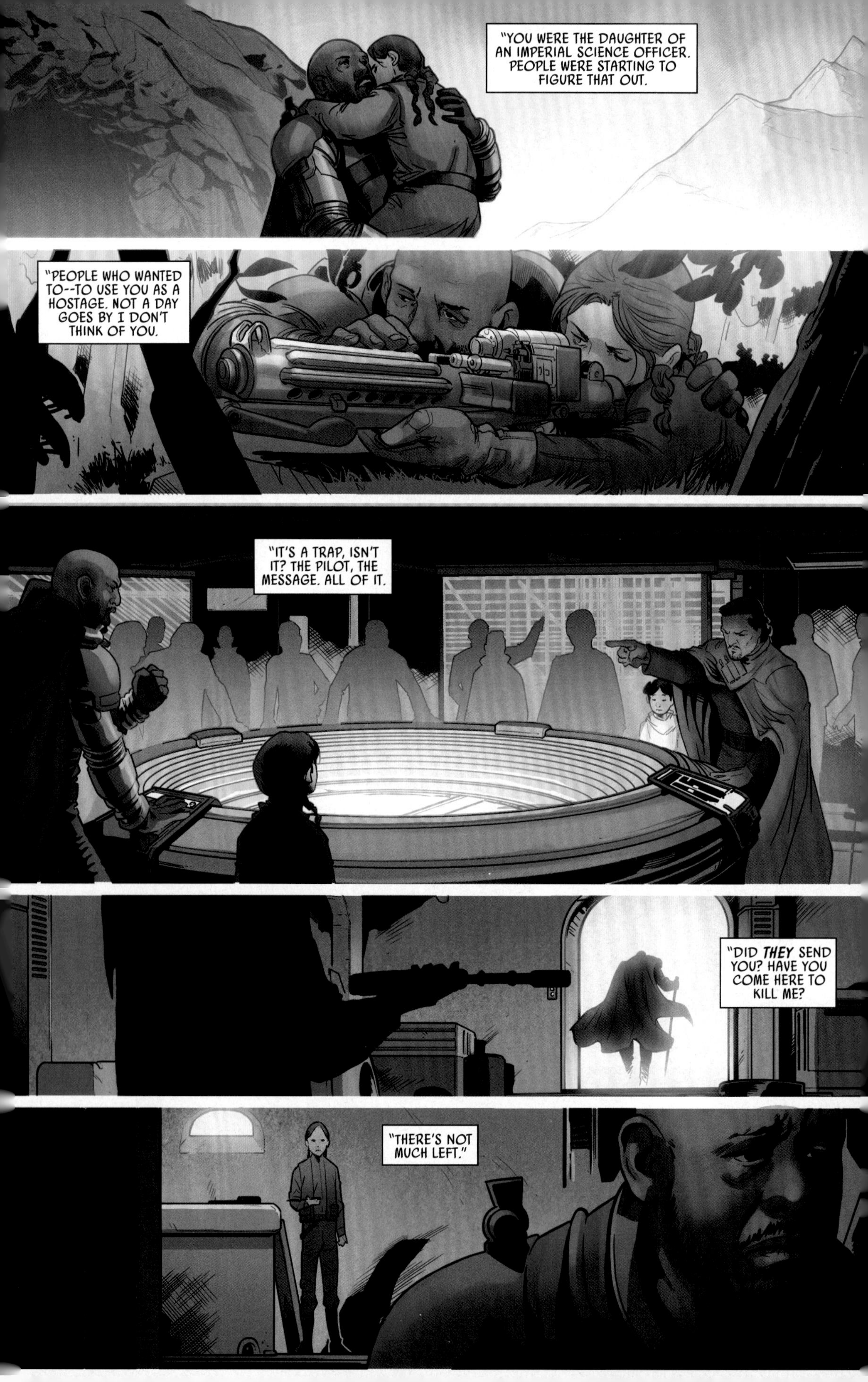
"YOU WERE THE DAUGHTER OF AN IMPERIAL SCIENCE OFFICER. PEOPLE WERE STARTING TO FIGURE THAT OUT.
"PEOPLE WHO WANTED TO--TO USE YOU AS A HOSTAGE. NOT A DAY GOES BY I DON'T THINK OF YOU.
"IT'S A TRAP, ISN'T IT? THE PILOT, THE MESSAGE. ALL OF IT.
"DID *THEY* SEND YOU? HAVE YOU COME HERE TO KILL ME?
"THERE'S NOT MUCH LEFT."

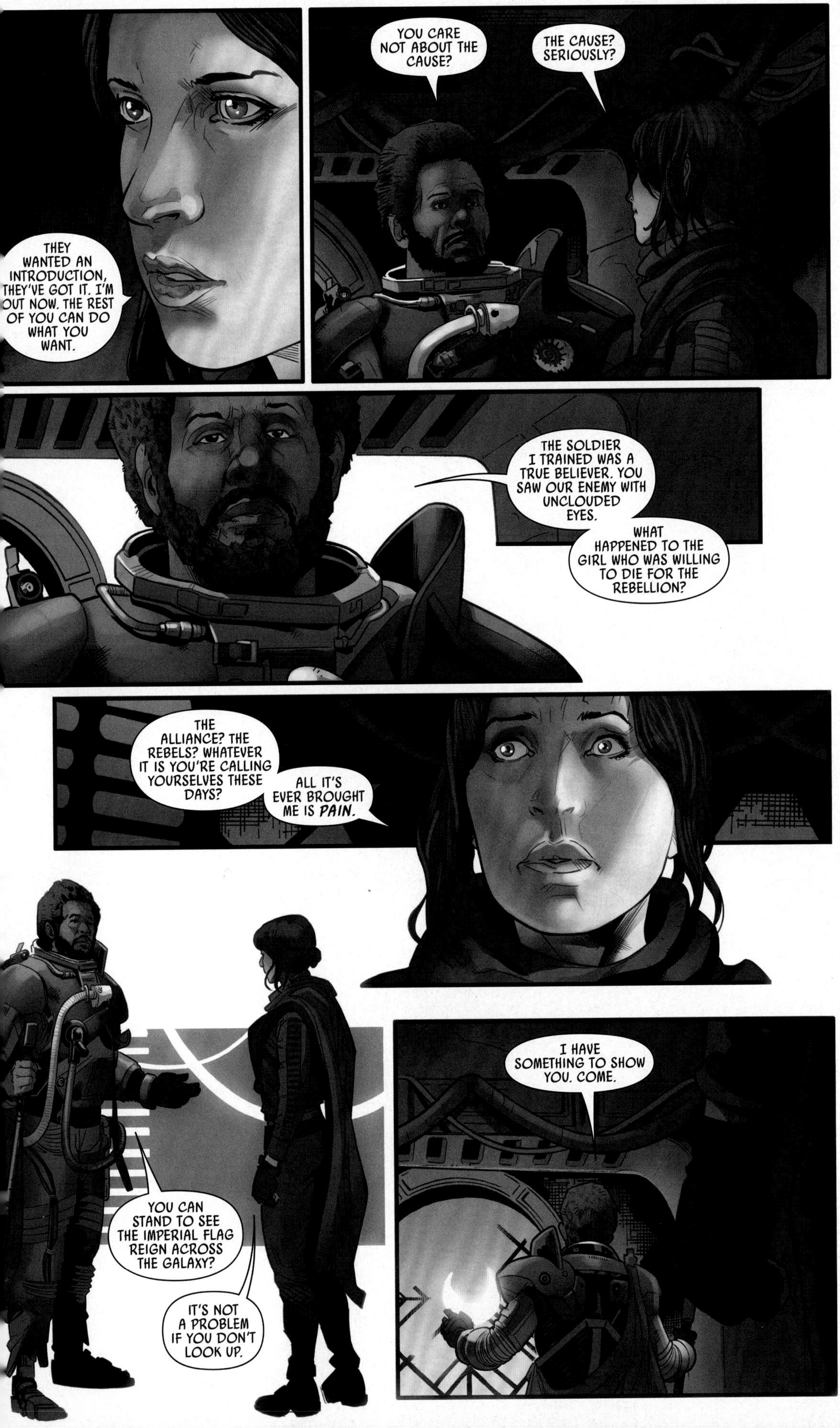
THEY WANTED AN INTRODUCTION, THEY'VE GOT IT. I'M OUT NOW. THE REST OF YOU CAN DO WHAT YOU WANT.
YOU CARE NOT ABOUT THE CAUSE?
THE CAUSE? SERIOUSLY?
THE SOLDIER I TRAINED WAS A TRUE BELIEVER. YOU SAW OUR ENEMY WITH UNCLOUDED EYES.
WHAT HAPPENED TO THE GIRL WHO WAS WILLING TO DIE FOR THE REBELLION?
THE ALLIANCE? THE REBELS? WHATEVER IT IS YOU'RE CALLING YOURSELVES THESE DAYS?
ALL IT'S EVER BROUGHT ME IS *PAIN*.
YOU CAN STAND TO SEE THE IMPERIAL FLAG REIGN ACROSS THE GALAXY?
IT'S NOT A PROBLEM IF YOU DON'T LOOK UP.
I HAVE SOMETHING TO SHOW YOU. COME.

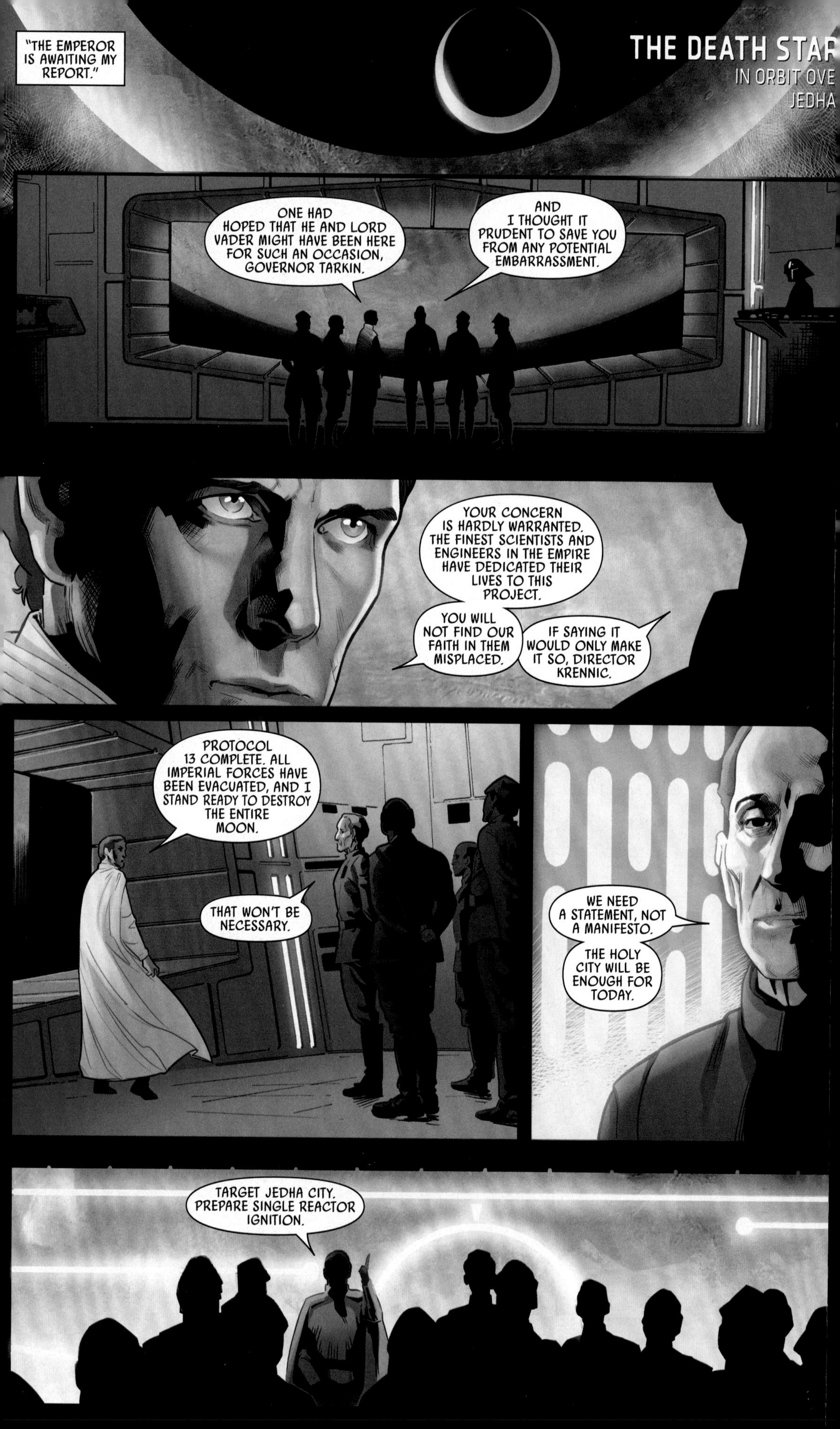
"THE EMPEROR IS AWAITING MY REPORT."
THE DEATH STAR
IN ORBIT OVE
JEDHA
ONE HAD HOPED THAT HE AND LORD VADER MIGHT HAVE BEEN HERE FOR SUCH AN OCCASION, GOVERNOR TARKIN.
AND I THOUGHT IT PRUDENT TO SAVE YOU FROM ANY POTENTIAL EMBARRASSMENT.
YOUR CONCERN IS HARDLY WARRANTED. THE FINEST SCIENTISTS AND ENGINEERS IN THE EMPIRE HAVE DEDICATED THEIR LIVES TO THIS PROJECT.
YOU WILL NOT FIND OUR FAITH IN THEM MISPLACED.
IF SAYING IT WOULD ONLY MAKE IT SO, DIRECTOR KRENNIC.
PROTOCOL 13 COMPLETE. ALL IMPERIAL FORCES HAVE BEEN EVACUATED, AND I STAND READY TO DESTROY THE ENTIRE MOON.
THAT WON'T BE NECESSARY.
WE NEED A STATEMENT, NOT A MANIFESTO.
THE HOLY CITY WILL BE ENOUGH FOR TODAY.
TARGET JEDHA CITY. PREPARE SINGLE REACTOR IGNITION.

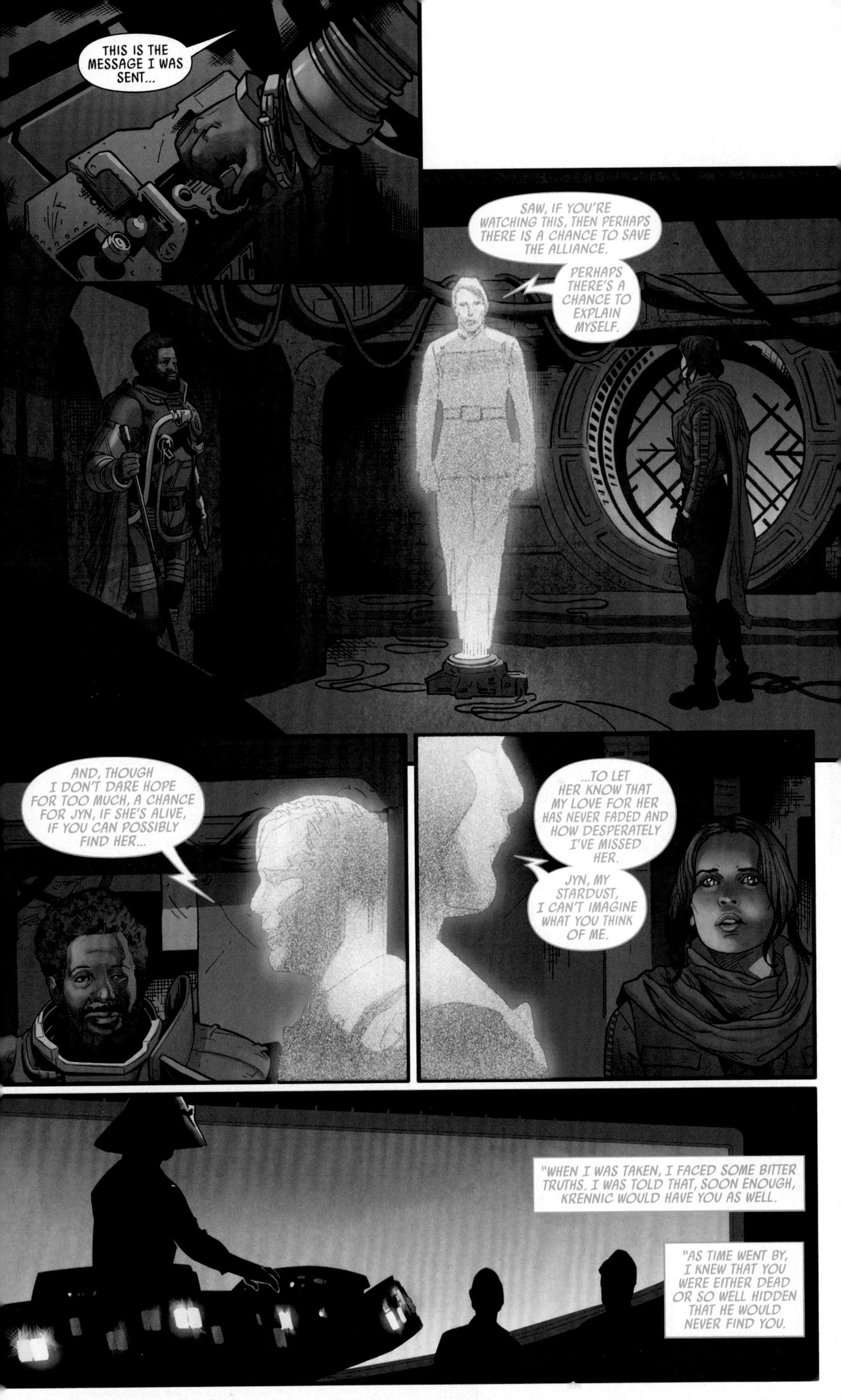
THIS IS THE MESSAGE I WAS SENT...
SAW, IF YOU'RE WATCHING THIS, THEN PERHAPS THERE IS A CHANCE TO SAVE THE ALLIANCE.
PERHAPS THERE'S A CHANCE TO EXPLAIN MYSELF.
AND, THOUGH I DON'T DARE HOPE FOR TOO MUCH, A CHANCE FOR JYN, IF SHE'S ALIVE, IF YOU CAN POSSIBLY FIND HER...
...TO LET HER KNOW THAT MY LOVE FOR HER HAS NEVER FADED AND HOW DESPERATELY I'VE MISSED HER.
JYN, MY STARDUST, I CAN'T IMAGINE WHAT YOU THINK OF ME.
"WHEN I WAS TAKEN, I FACED SOME BITTER TRUTHS. I WAS TOLD THAT, SOON ENOUGH, KRENNIC WOULD HAVE YOU AS WELL.
"AS TIME WENT BY, I KNEW THAT YOU WERE EITHER DEAD OR SO WELL HIDDEN THAT HE WOULD NEVER FIND YOU.

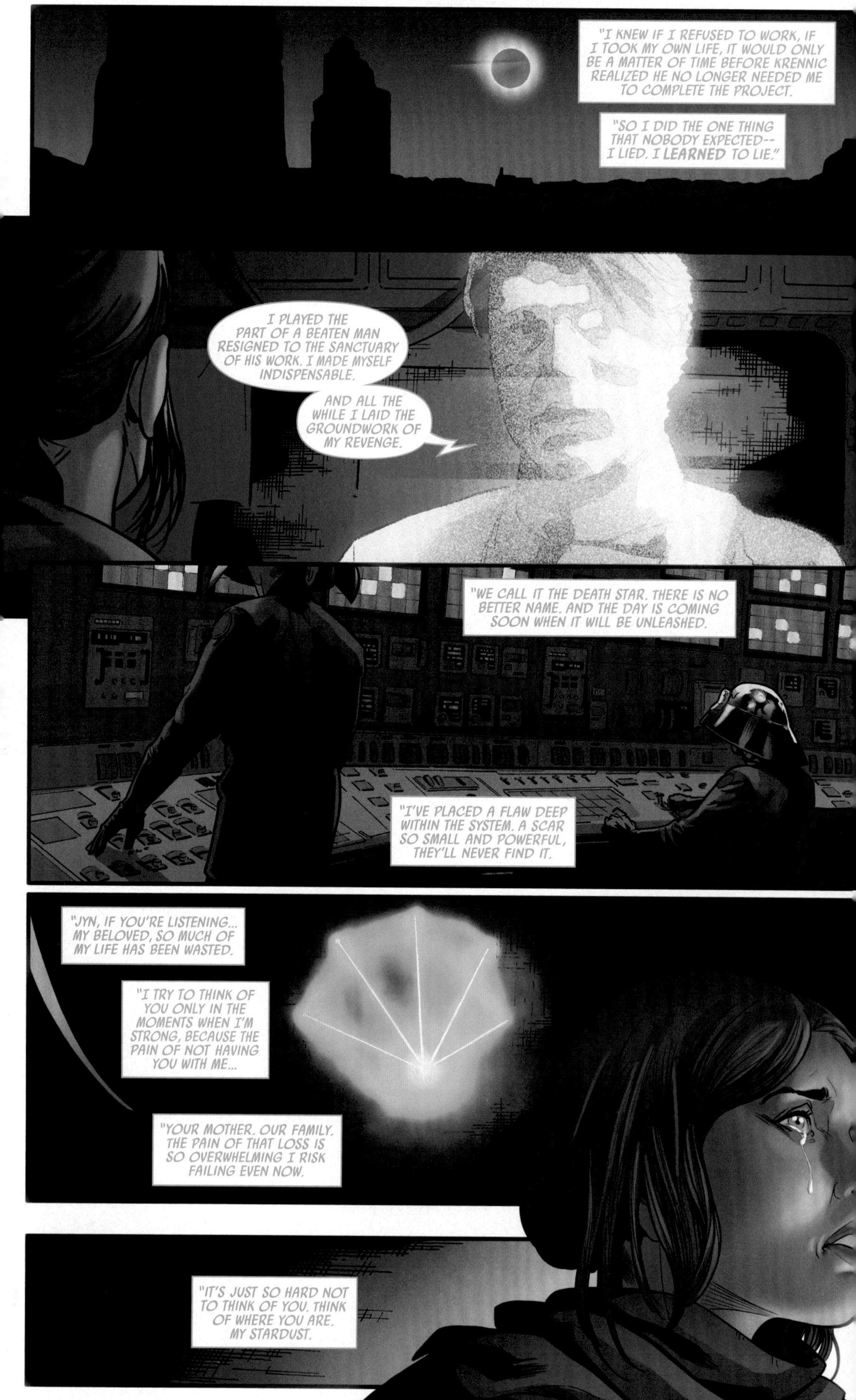
"I KNEW IF I REFUSED TO WORK, IF I TOOK MY OWN LIFE, IT WOULD ONLY BE A MATTER OF TIME BEFORE KRENNIC REALIZED HE NO LONGER NEEDED ME TO COMPLETE THE PROJECT.
"SO I DID THE ONE THING THAT NOBODY EXPECTED-- I LIED. I LEARNED TO LIE."
I PLAYED THE PART OF A BEATEN MAN RESIGNED TO THE SANCTUARY OF HIS WORK. I MADE MYSELF INDISPENSABLE.
AND ALL THE WHILE I LAID THE GROUNDWORK OF MY REVENGE.
"WE CALL IT THE DEATH STAR. THERE IS NO BETTER NAME. AND THE DAY IS COMING SOON WHEN IT WILL BE UNLEASHED.
"I'VE PLACED A FLAW DEEP WITHIN THE SYSTEM. A SCAR SO SMALL AND POWERFUL, THEY'LL NEVER FIND IT.
"JYN, IF YOU'RE LISTENING... MY BELOVED, SO MUCH OF MY LIFE HAS BEEN WASTED.
"I TRY TO THINK OF YOU ONLY IN THE MOMENTS WHEN I'M STRONG, BECAUSE THE PAIN OF NOT HAVING YOU WITH ME...
"YOUR MOTHER. OUR FAMILY. THE PAIN OF THAT LOSS IS SO OVERWHELMING I RISK FAILING EVEN NOW.
"IT'S JUST SO HARD NOT TO THINK OF YOU. THINK OF WHERE YOU ARE. MY STARDUST.

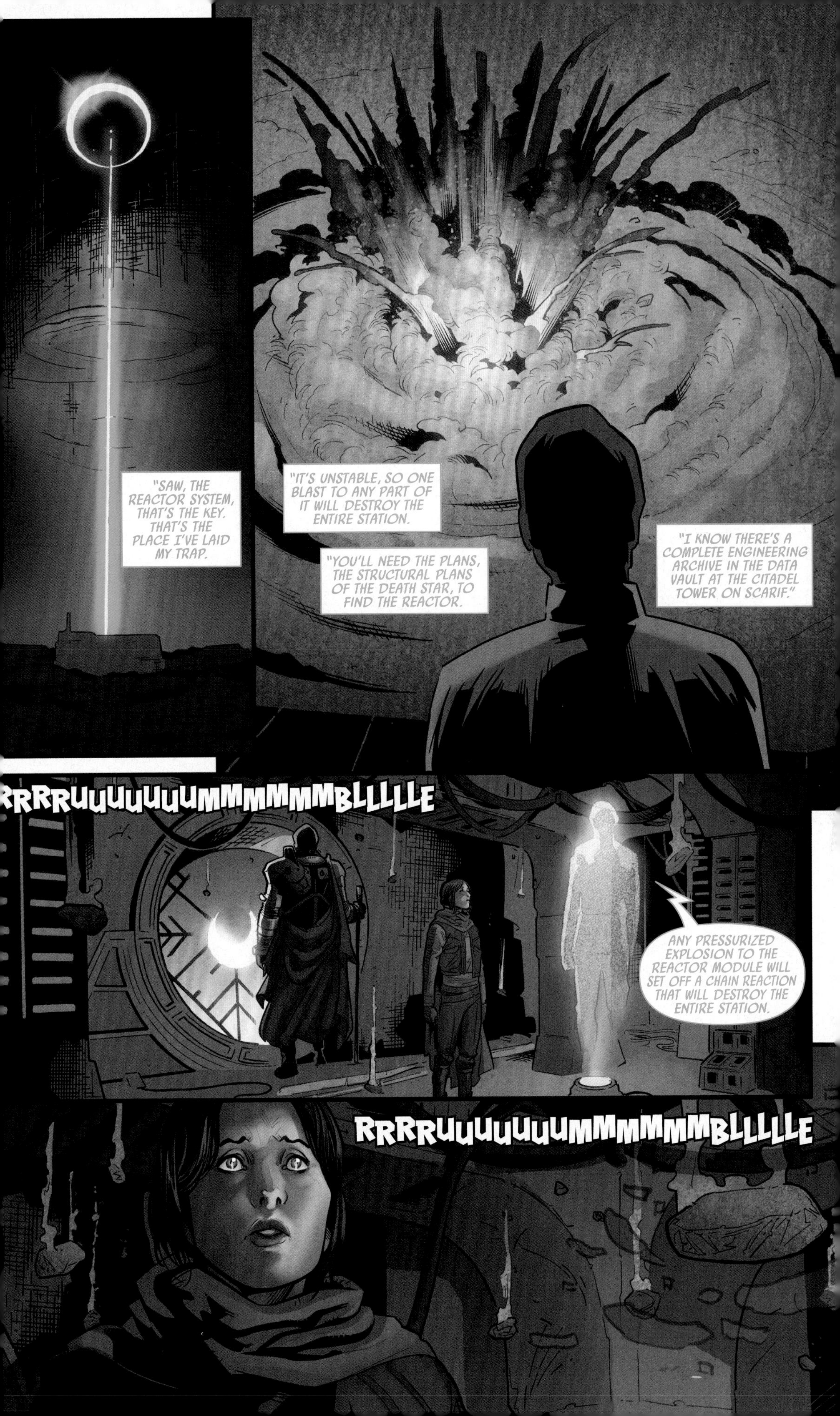
"SAW, THE REACTOR SYSTEM, THAT'S THE KEY. THAT'S THE PLACE I'VE LAID MY TRAP.
"IT'S UNSTABLE, SO ONE BLAST TO ANY PART OF IT WILL DESTROY THE ENTIRE STATION.
"YOU'LL NEED THE PLANS, THE STRUCTURAL PLANS OF THE DEATH STAR, TO FIND THE REACTOR.
"I KNOW THERE'S A COMPLETE ENGINEERING ARCHIVE IN THE DATA VAULT AT THE CITADEL TOWER ON SCARIF."
RRRRUUUUUUUUMMMMMMMBLLLLLE
ANY PRESSURIZED EXPLOSION TO THE REACTOR MODULE WILL SET OFF A CHAIN REACTION THAT WILL DESTROY THE ENTIRE STATION.
RRRRUUUUUUUUMMMMMMMBLLLLLE

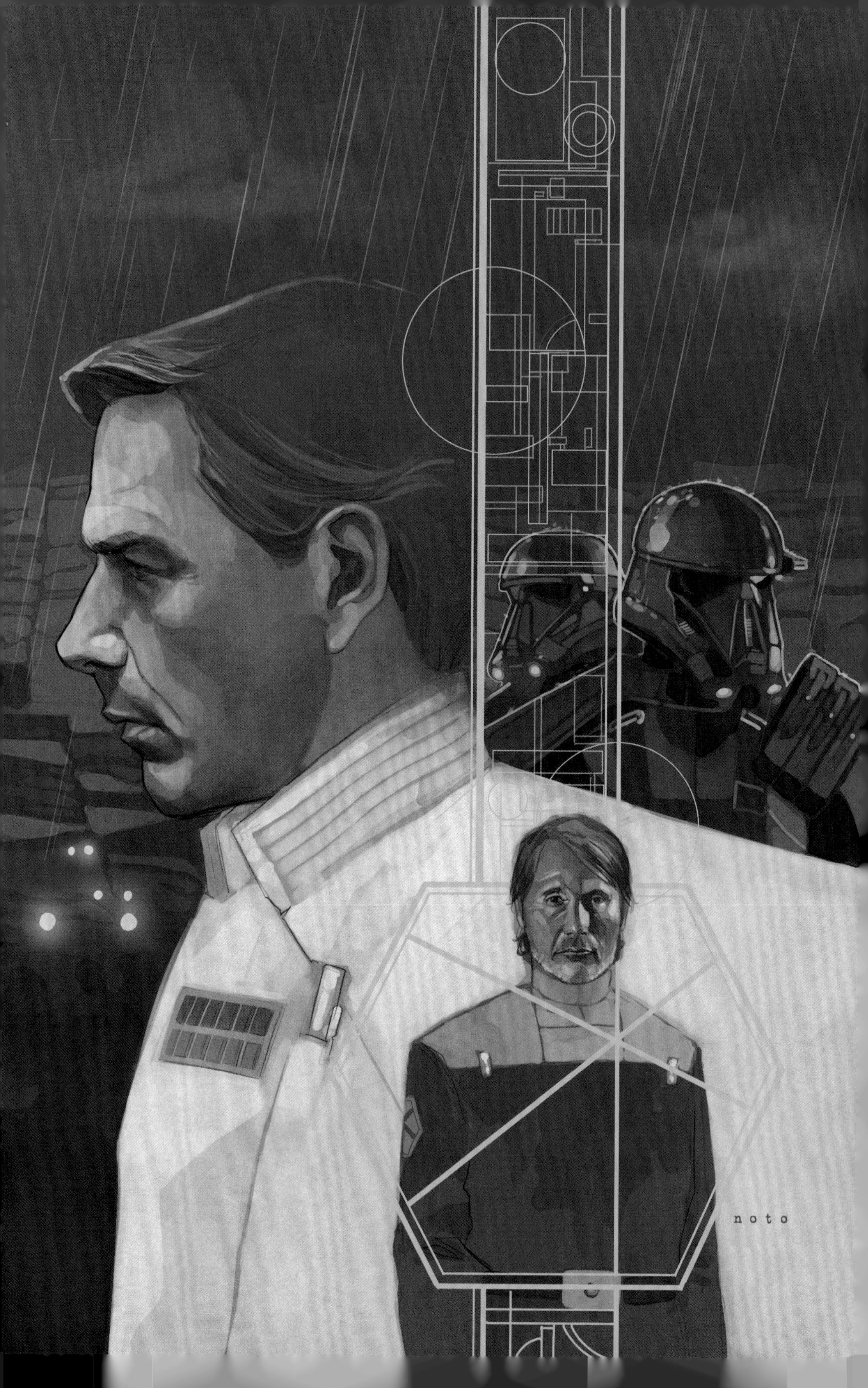
noto

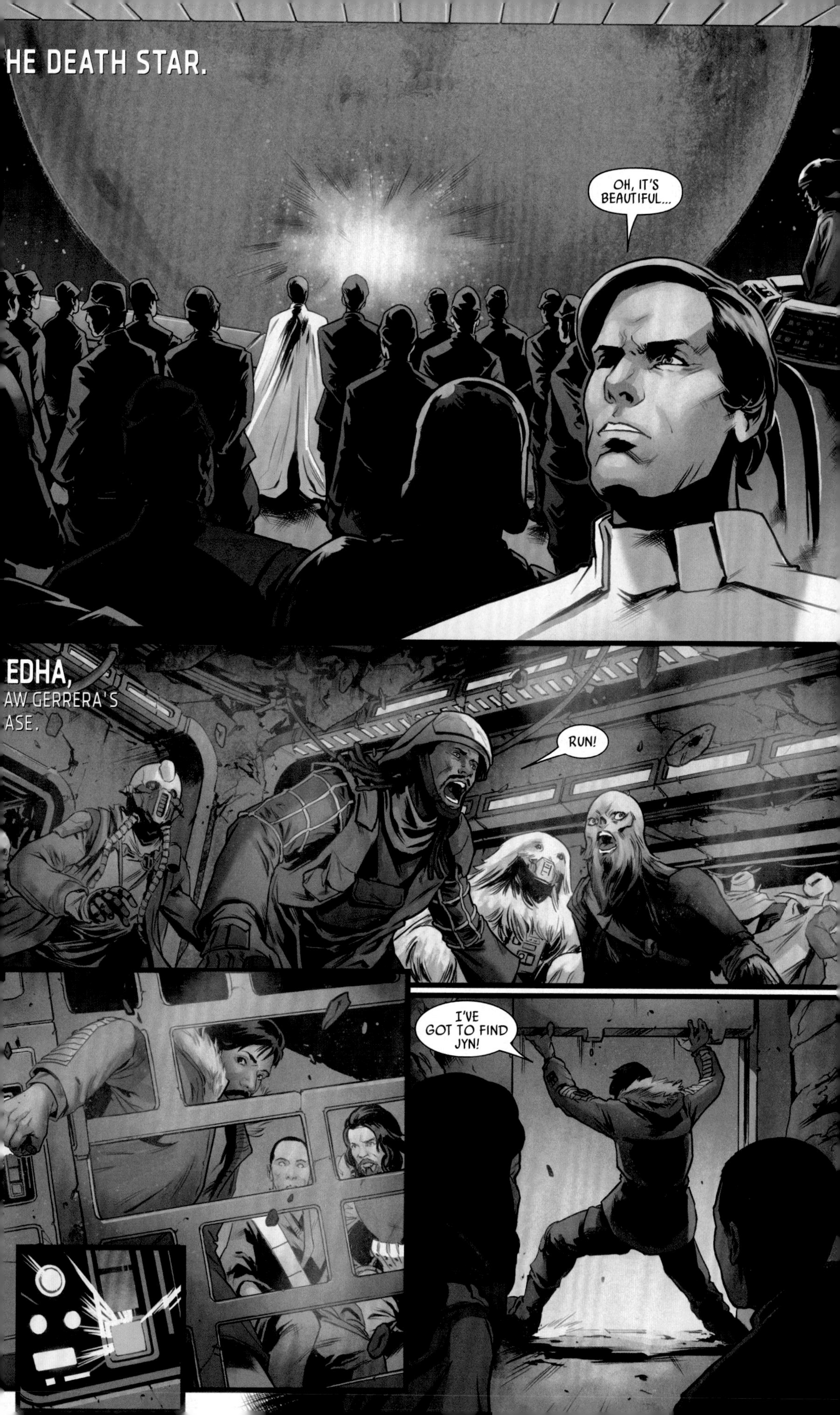
HE DEATH STAR.
OH, IT'S BEAUTIFUL...
EDHA,
AW GERRERA'S
ASE.
RUN!
I'VE GOT TO FIND JYN!

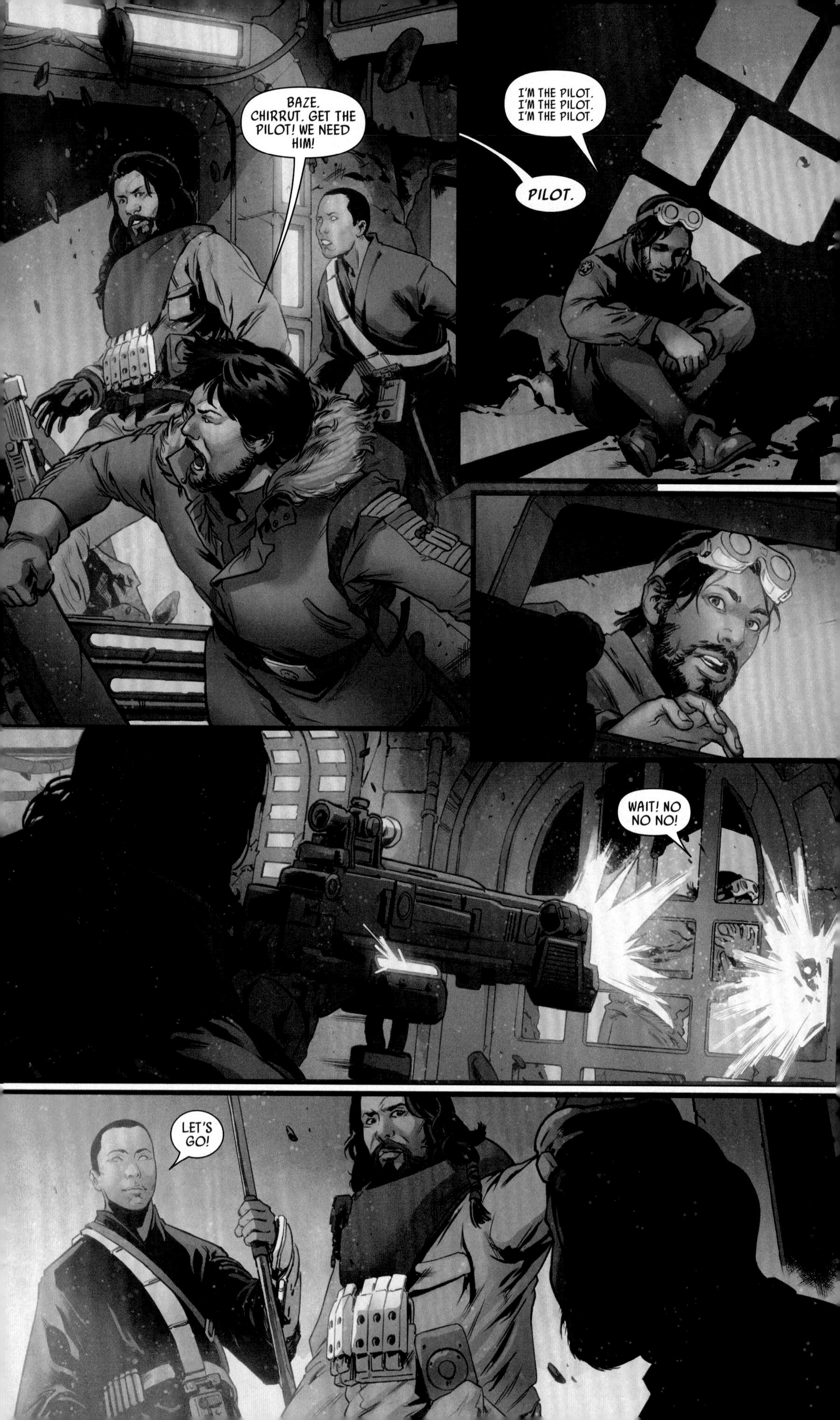
BAZE. CHIRRUT. GET THE PILOT! WE NEED HIM!
I'M THE PILOT. I'M THE PILOT. I'M THE PILOT.
PILOT.
WAIT! NO NO NO!
LET'S GO!

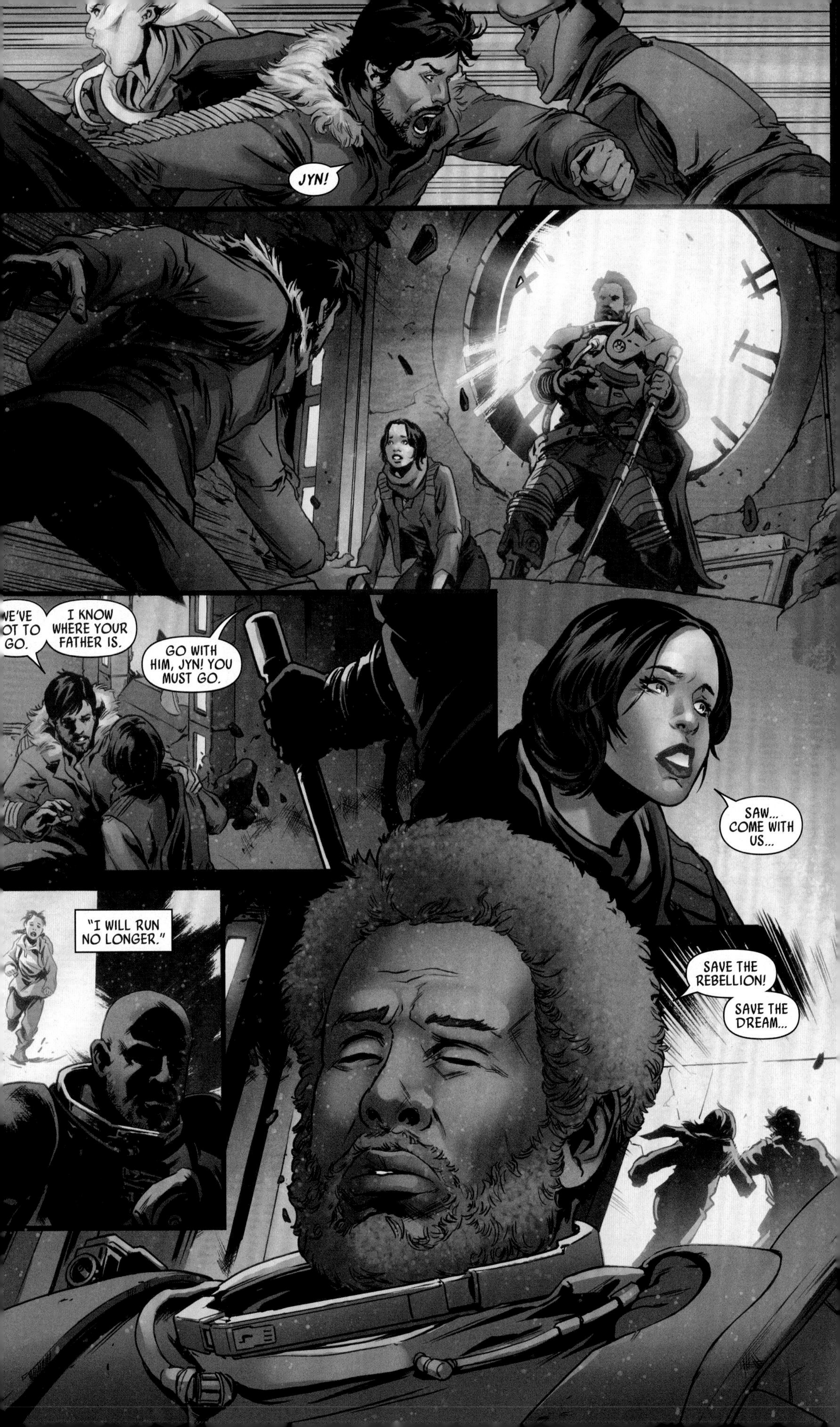
JYN!
WE'VE OT TO GO.
I KNOW WHERE YOUR FATHER IS.
GO WITH HIM, JYN! YOU MUST GO.
SAW... COME WITH US...
"I WILL RUN NO LONGER."
SAVE THE REBELLION!
SAVE THE DREAM...

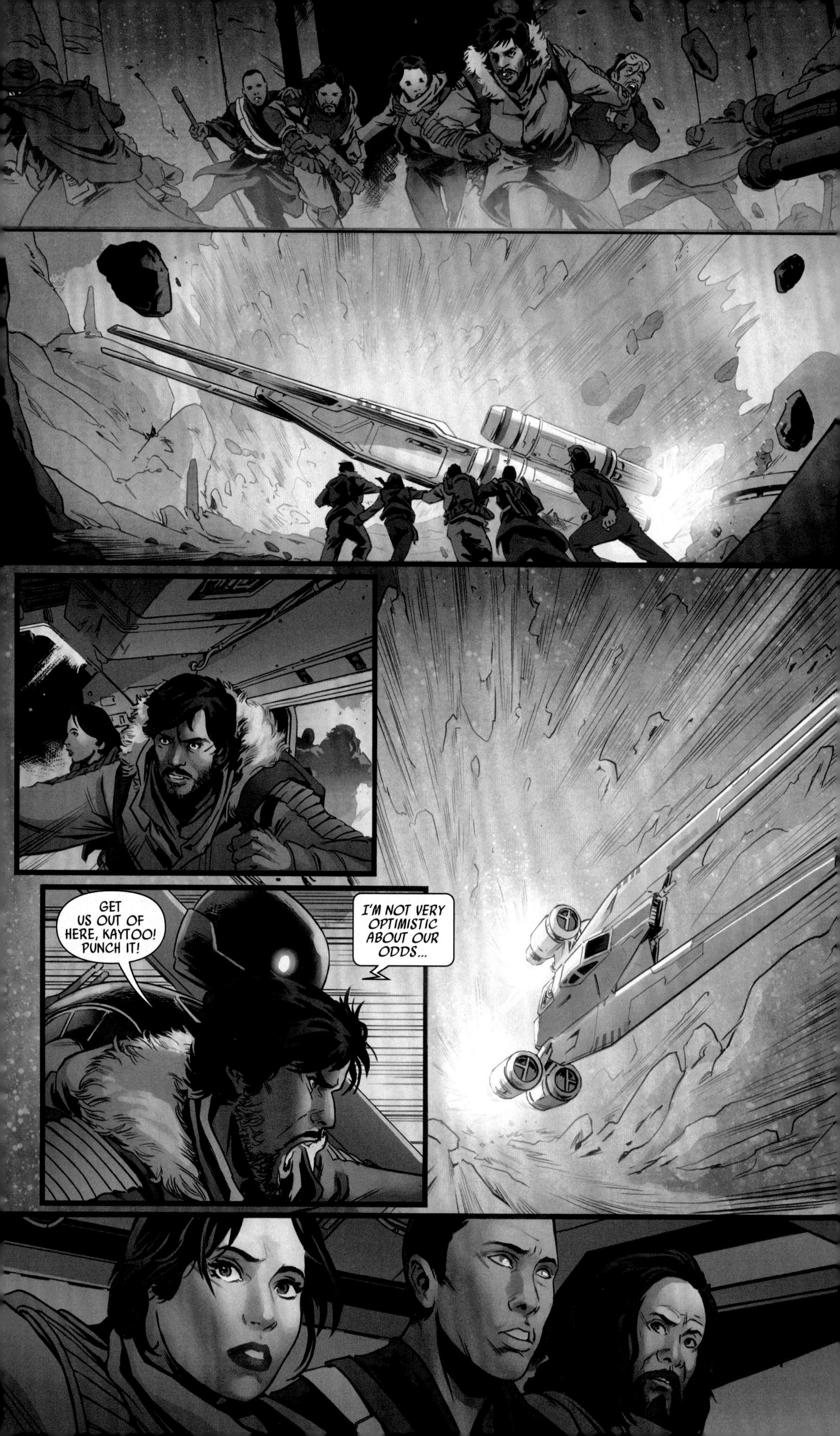
GET US OUT OF HERE, KAYTOO! PUNCH IT!
I'M NOT VERY OPTIMISTIC ABOUT OUR ODDS...

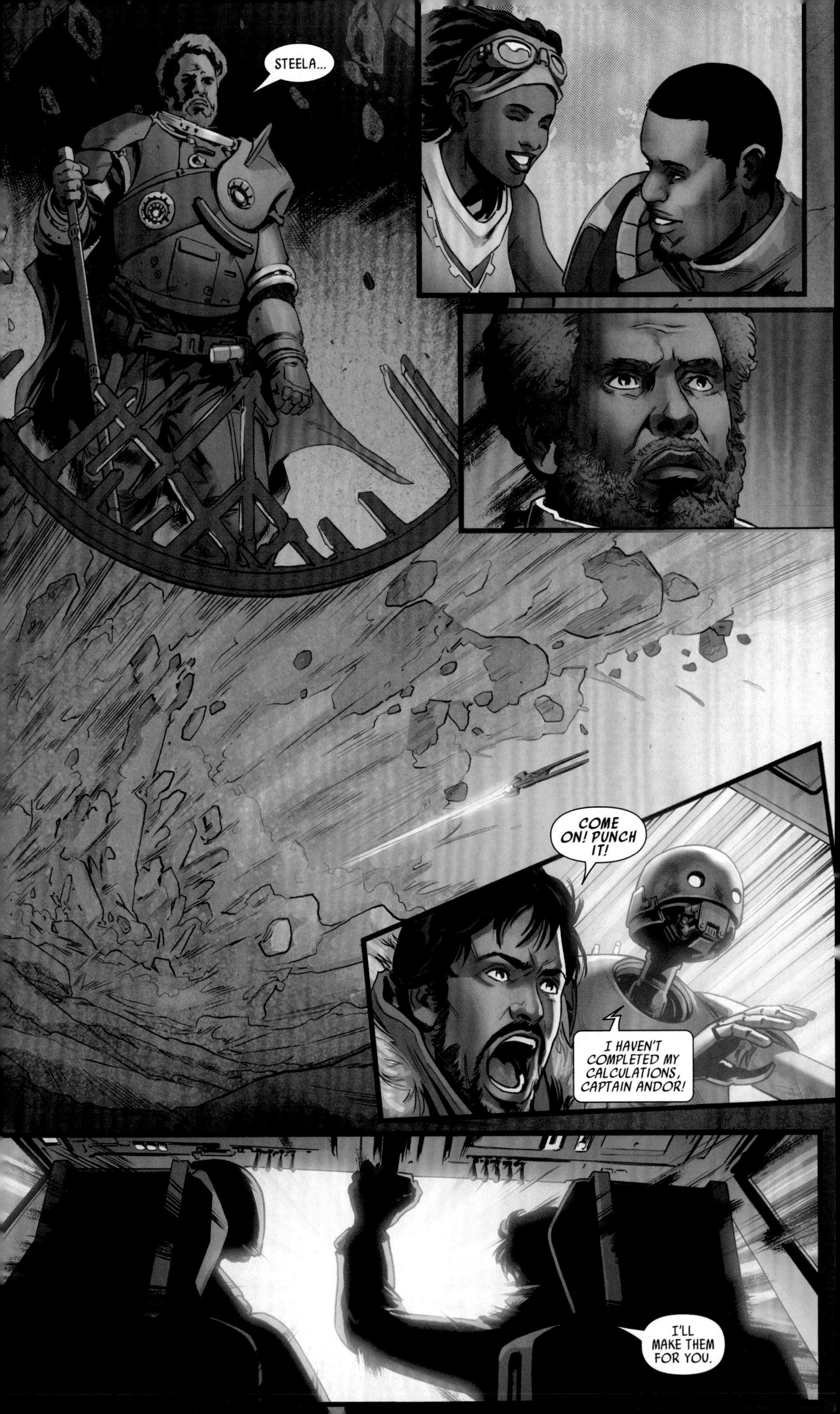
STEELA...
COME ON! PUNCH IT!
I HAVEN'T COMPLETED MY CALCULATIONS, CAPTAIN ANDOR!
I'LL MAKE THEM FOR YOU.

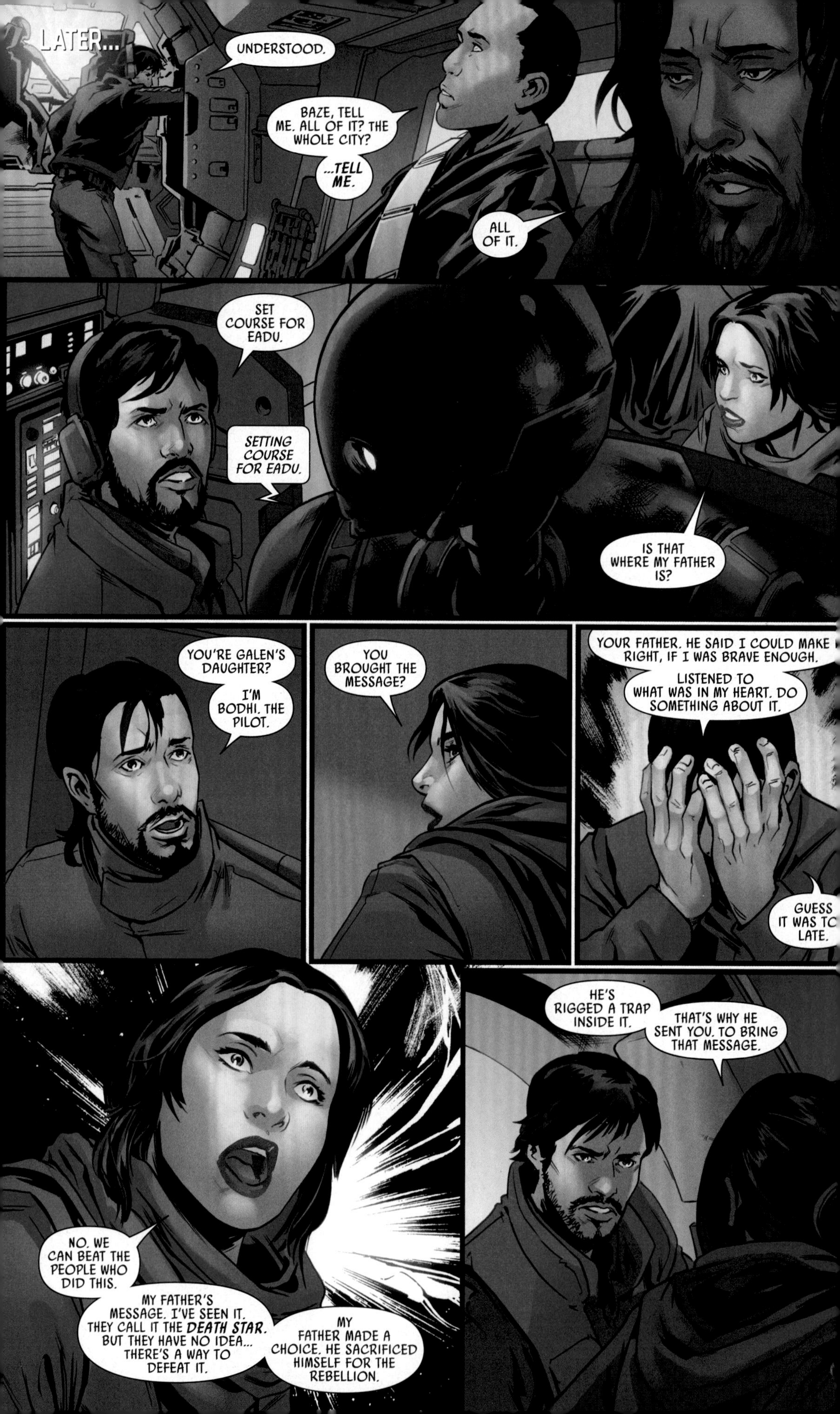
LATER...
UNDERSTOOD.
BAZE, TELL ME. ALL OF IT? THE WHOLE CITY?
...TELL ME.
ALL OF IT.
SET COURSE FOR EADU.
SETTING COURSE FOR EADU.
IS THAT WHERE MY FATHER IS?
YOU'RE GALEN'S DAUGHTER?
I'M BODHI. THE PILOT.
YOU BROUGHT THE MESSAGE?
YOUR FATHER. HE SAID I COULD MAKE RIGHT, IF I WAS BRAVE ENOUGH.
LISTENED TO WHAT WAS IN MY HEART. DO SOMETHING ABOUT IT.
GUESS IT WAS TO LATE.
NO. WE CAN BEAT THE PEOPLE WHO DID THIS.
MY FATHER'S MESSAGE. I'VE SEEN IT. THEY CALL IT THE DEATH STAR. BUT THEY HAVE NO IDEA... THERE'S A WAY TO DEFEAT IT.
MY FATHER MADE A CHOICE. HE SACRIFICED HIMSELF FOR THE REBELLION.
HE'S RIGGED A TRAP INSIDE IT.
THAT'S WHY HE SENT YOU. TO BRING THAT MESSAGE.

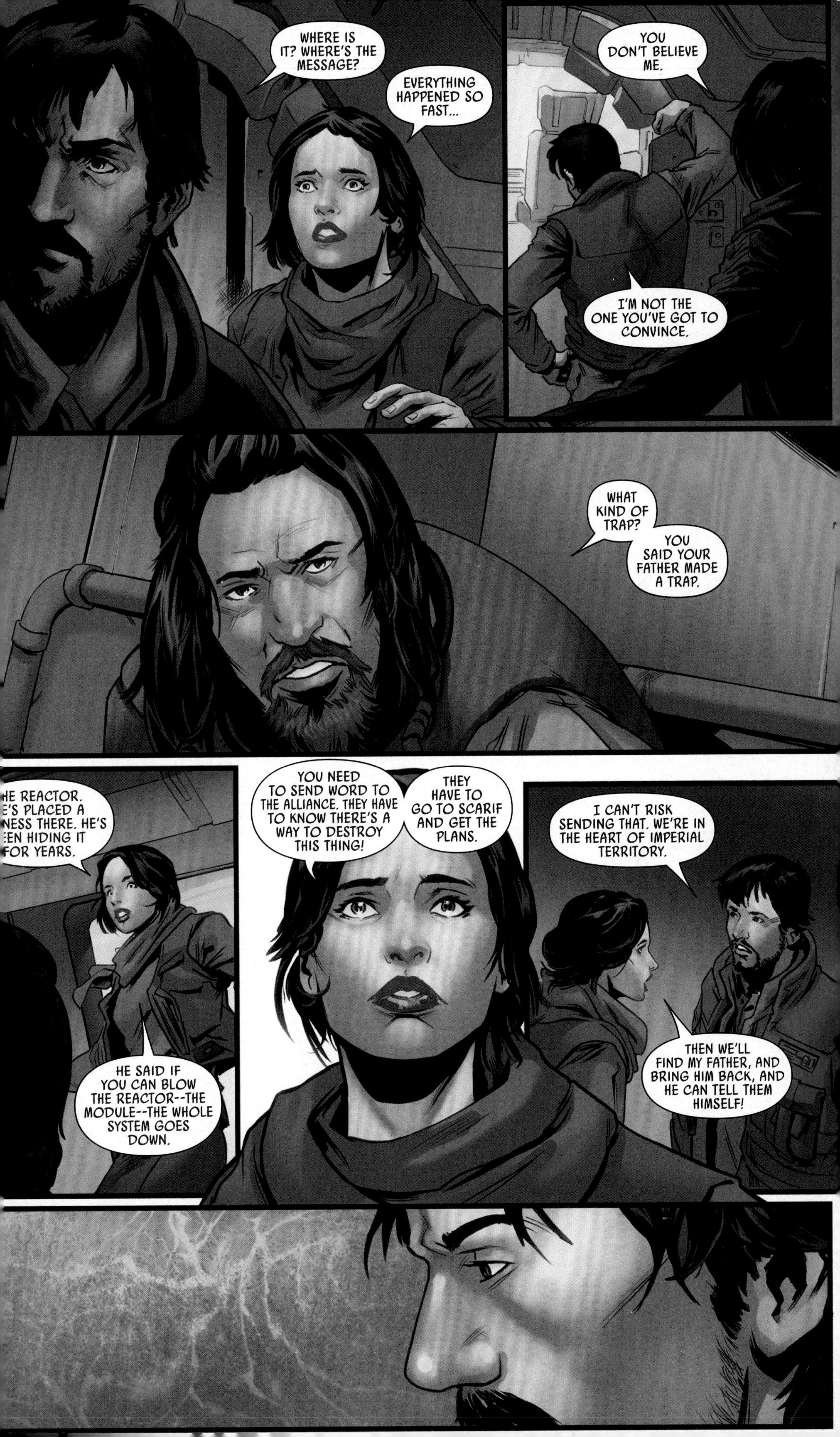
WHERE IS IT? WHERE'S THE MESSAGE?
EVERYTHING HAPPENED SO FAST...
YOU DON'T BELIEVE ME.
I'M NOT THE ONE YOU'VE GOT TO CONVINCE.
WHAT KIND OF TRAP?
YOU SAID YOUR FATHER MADE A TRAP.
HE REACTOR. E'S PLACED A NESS THERE. HE'S EEN HIDING IT FOR YEARS.
HE SAID IF YOU CAN BLOW THE REACTOR--THE MODULE--THE WHOLE SYSTEM GOES DOWN.
YOU NEED TO SEND WORD TO THE ALLIANCE. THEY HAVE TO KNOW THERE'S A WAY TO DESTROY THIS THING!
THEY HAVE TO GO TO SCARIF AND GET THE PLANS.
I CAN'T RISK SENDING THAT. WE'RE IN THE HEART OF IMPERIAL TERRITORY.
THEN WE'LL FIND MY FATHER, AND BRING HIM BACK, AND HE CAN TELL THEM HIMSELF!

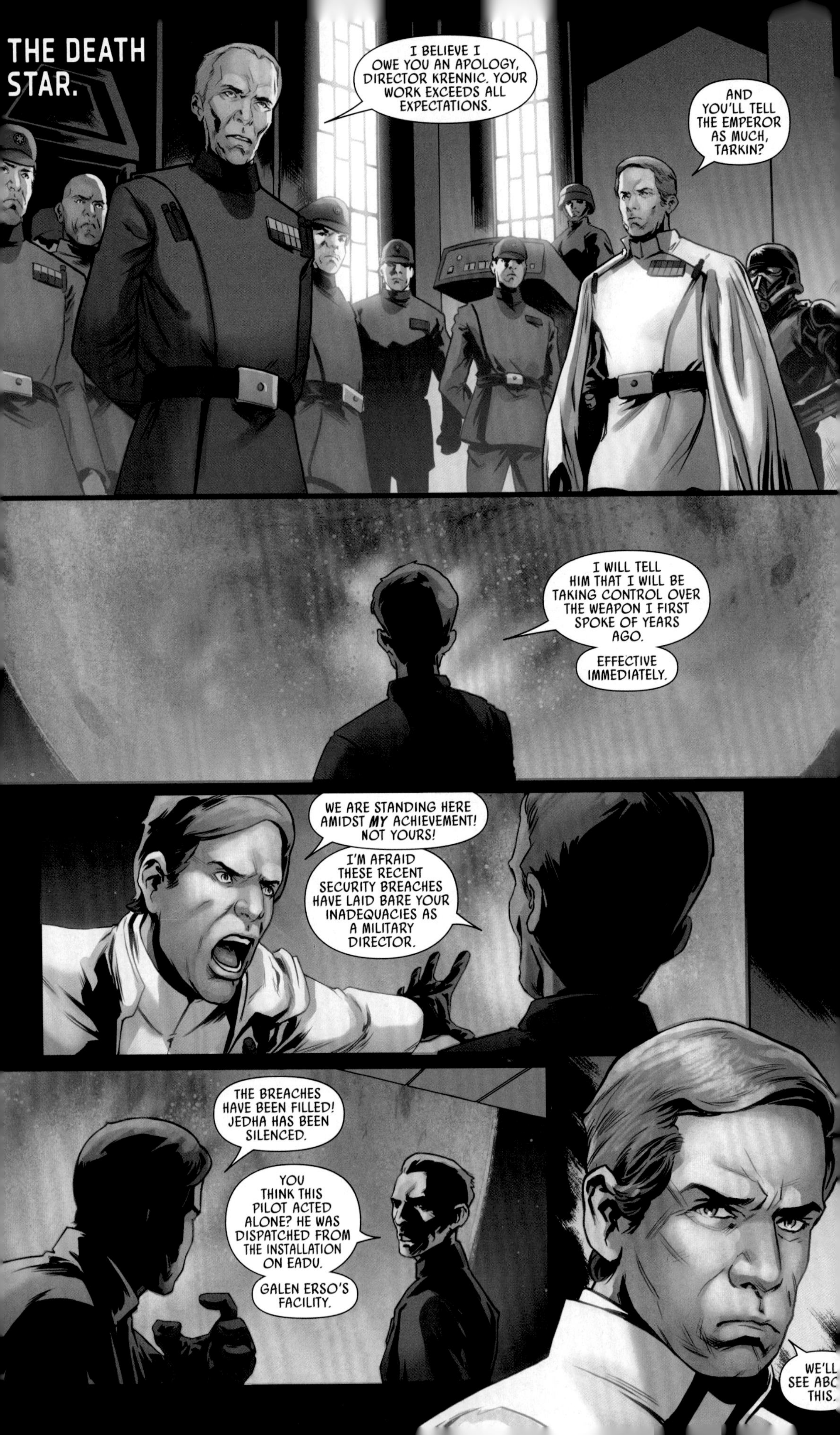
THE DEATH STAR.
I BELIEVE I OWE YOU AN APOLOGY, DIRECTOR KRENNIC. YOUR WORK EXCEEDS ALL EXPECTATIONS.
AND YOU'LL TELL THE EMPEROR AS MUCH, TARKIN?
I WILL TELL HIM THAT I WILL BE TAKING CONTROL OVER THE WEAPON I FIRST SPOKE OF YEARS AGO.
EFFECTIVE IMMEDIATELY.
WE ARE STANDING HERE AMIDST MY ACHIEVEMENT! NOT YOURS!
I'M AFRAID THESE RECENT SECURITY BREACHES HAVE LAID BARE YOUR INADEQUACIES AS A MILITARY DIRECTOR.
THE BREACHES HAVE BEEN FILLED! JEDHA HAS BEEN SILENCED.
YOU THINK THIS PILOT ACTED ALONE? HE WAS DISPATCHED FROM THE INSTALLATION ON EADU.
GALEN ERSO'S FACILITY.
WE'LL SEE ABO THIS.

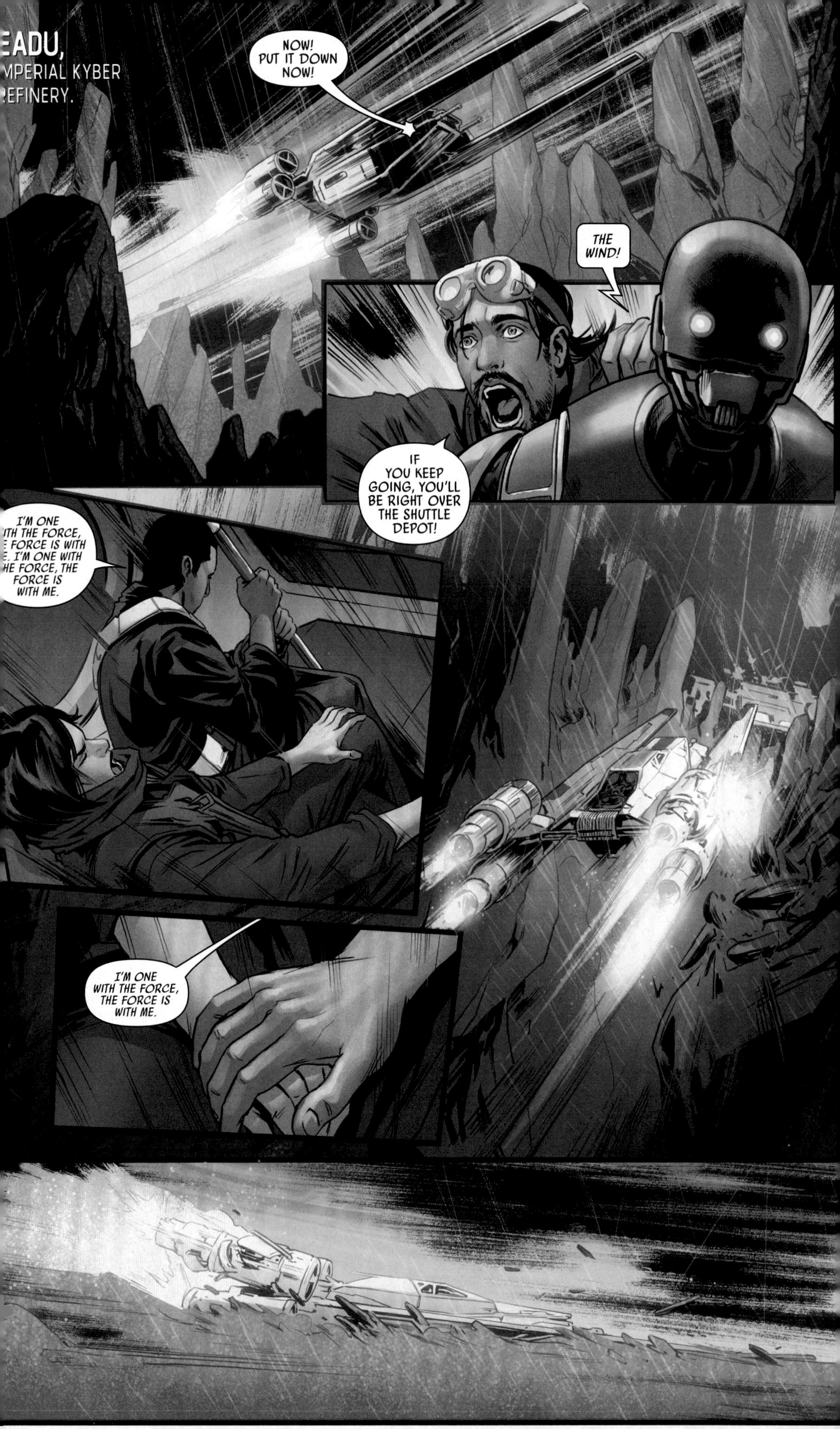
EADU,
MPERIAL KYBER
REFINERY.
NOW! PUT IT DOWN NOW!
THE WIND!
IF YOU KEEP GOING, YOU'LL BE RIGHT OVER THE SHUTTLE DEPOT!
I'M ONE ITH THE FORCE, E FORCE IS WITH E. I'M ONE WITH HE FORCE, THE FORCE IS WITH ME.
I'M ONE WITH THE FORCE, THE FORCE IS WITH ME.

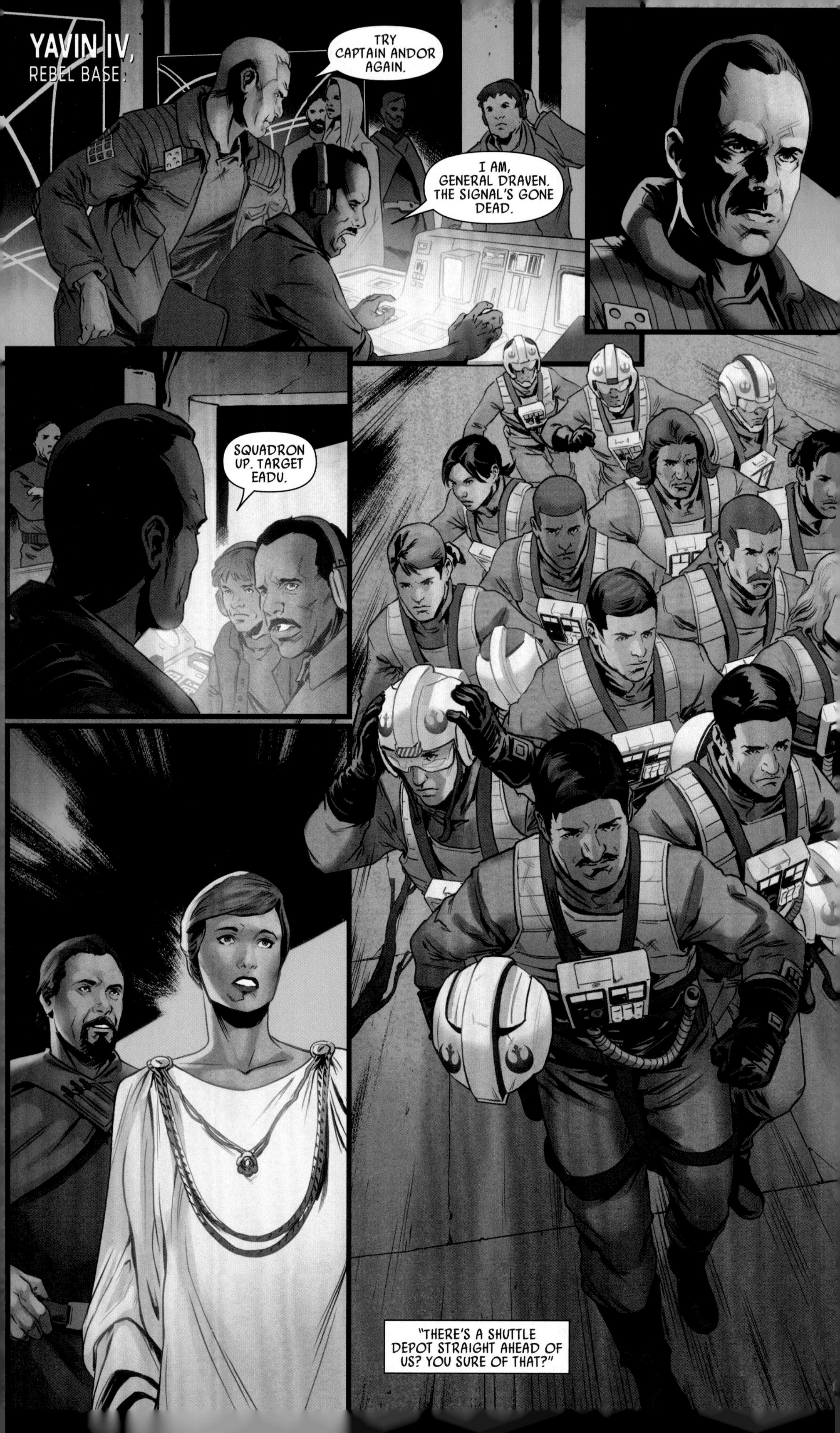
YAVIN IV,
REBEL BASE.
TRY CAPTAIN ANDOR AGAIN.
I AM, GENERAL DRAVEN. THE SIGNAL'S GONE DEAD.
SQUADRON UP. TARGET EADU.
"THERE'S A SHUTTLE DEPOT STRAIGHT AHEAD OF US? YOU SURE OF THAT?"

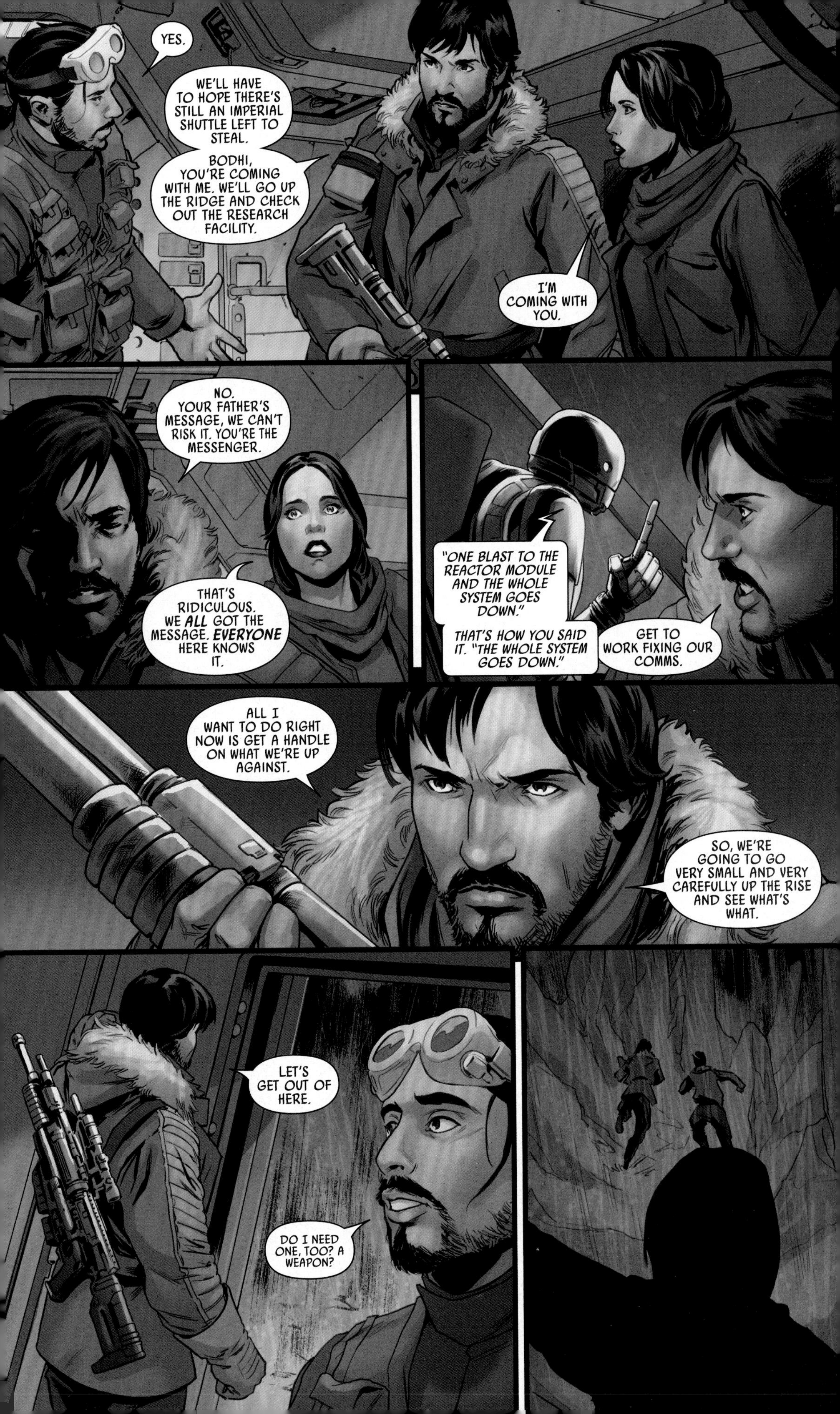
YES.
WE'LL HAVE TO HOPE THERE'S STILL AN IMPERIAL SHUTTLE LEFT TO STEAL.
BODHI, YOU'RE COMING WITH ME. WE'LL GO UP THE RIDGE AND CHECK OUT THE RESEARCH FACILITY.
I'M COMING WITH YOU.
NO. YOUR FATHER'S MESSAGE, WE CAN'T RISK IT. YOU'RE THE MESSENGER.
THAT'S RIDICULOUS. WE ALL GOT THE MESSAGE. EVERYONE HERE KNOWS IT.
"ONE BLAST TO THE REACTOR MODULE AND THE WHOLE SYSTEM GOES DOWN."
THAT'S HOW YOU SAID IT. "THE WHOLE SYSTEM GOES DOWN."
GET TO WORK FIXING OUR COMMS.
ALL I WANT TO DO RIGHT NOW IS GET A HANDLE ON WHAT WE'RE UP AGAINST.
SO, WE'RE GOING TO GO VERY SMALL AND VERY CAREFULLY UP THE RISE AND SEE WHAT'S WHAT.
LET'S GET OUT OF HERE.
DO I NEED ONE, TOO? A WEAPON?

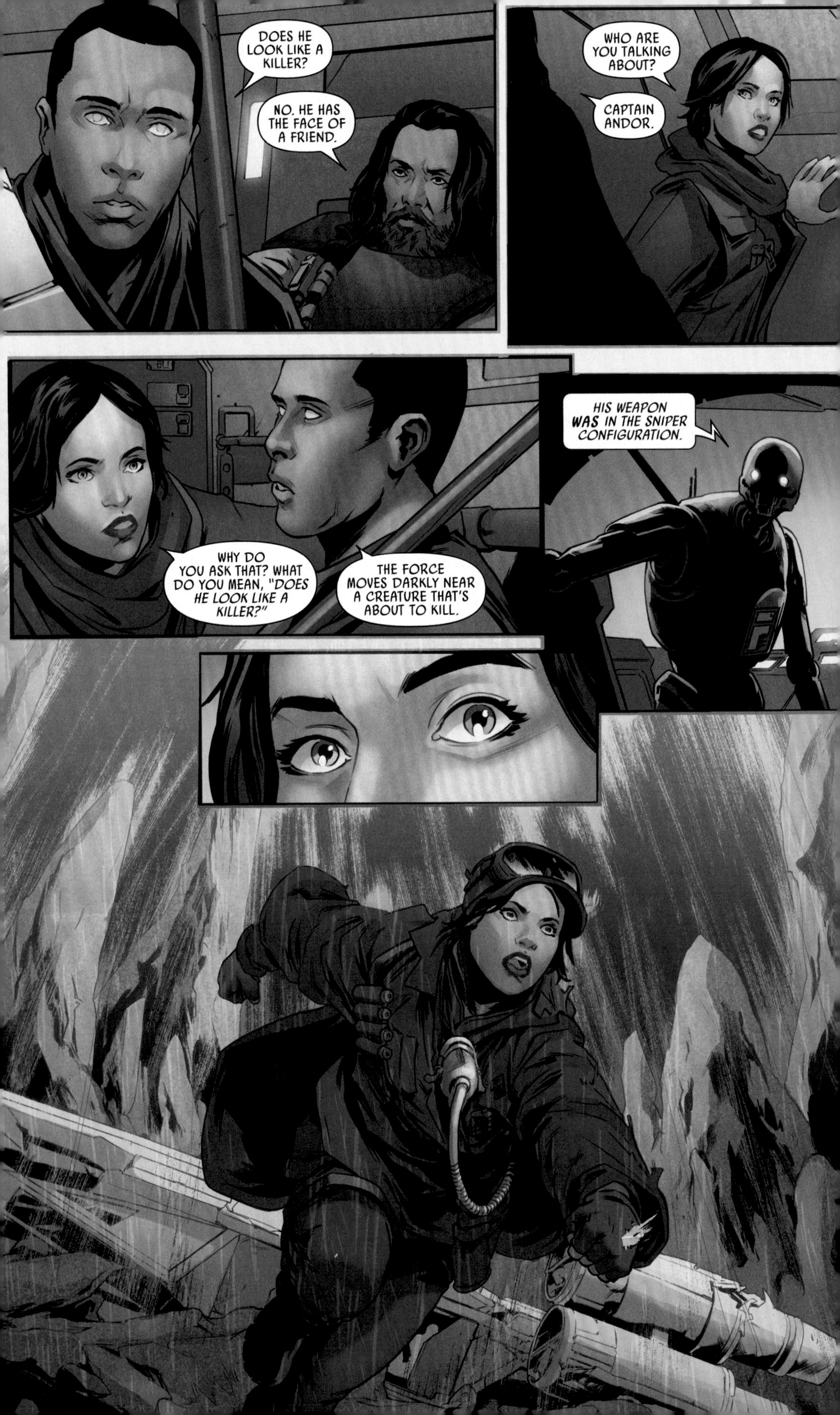
DOES HE LOOK LIKE A KILLER?
NO. HE HAS THE FACE OF A FRIEND.
WHO ARE YOU TALKING ABOUT?
CAPTAIN ANDOR.
WHY DO YOU ASK THAT? WHAT DO YOU MEAN, "DOES HE LOOK LIKE A KILLER?"
THE FORCE MOVES DARKLY NEAR A CREATURE THAT'S ABOUT TO KILL.
HIS WEAPON WAS IN THE SNIPER CONFIGURATION.

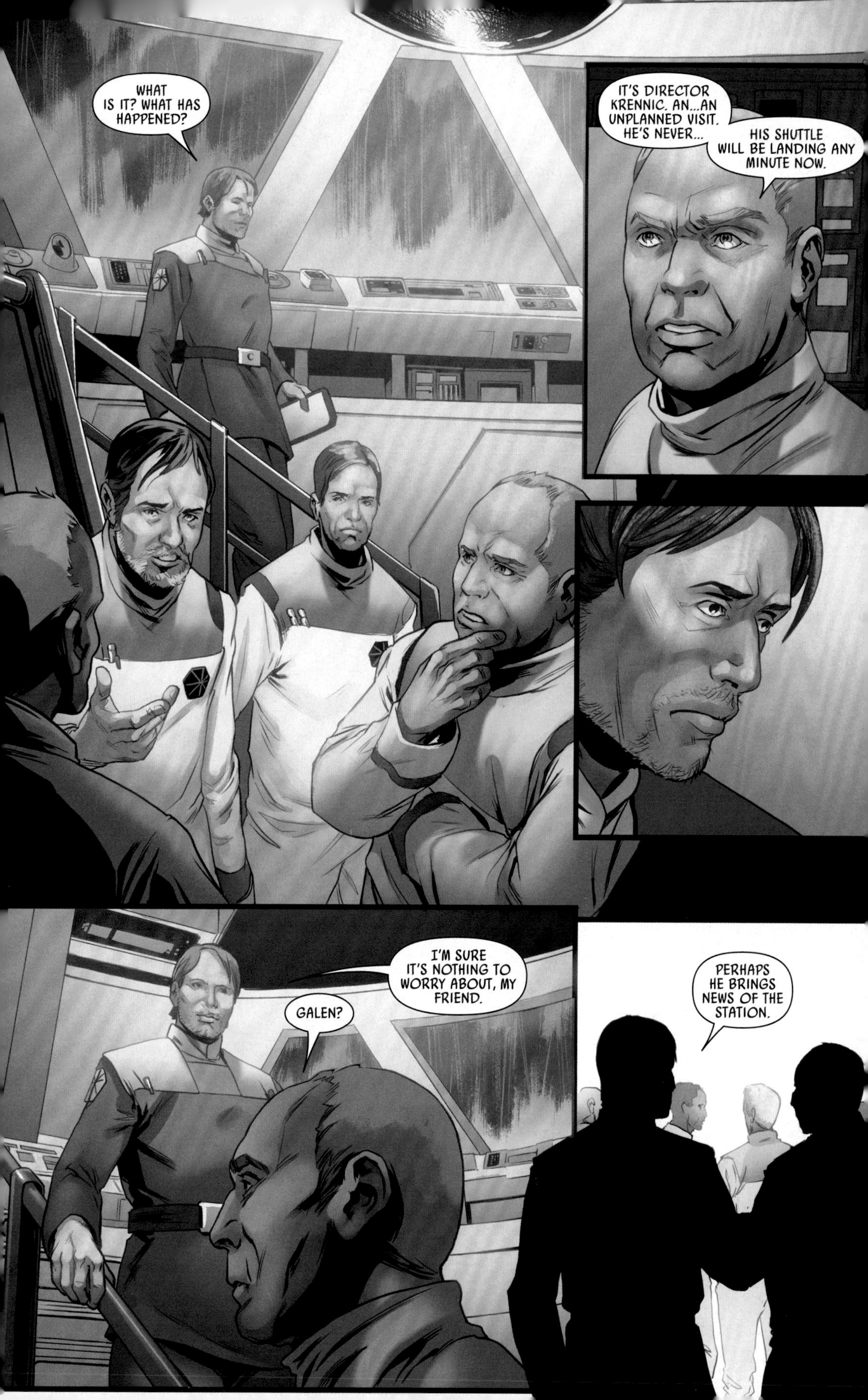
WHAT IS IT? WHAT HAS HAPPENED?
IT'S DIRECTOR KRENNIC. AN...AN UNPLANNED VISIT. HE'S NEVER...
HIS SHUTTLE WILL BE LANDING ANY MINUTE NOW.
GALEN?
I'M SURE IT'S NOTHING TO WORRY ABOUT, MY FRIEND.
PERHAPS HE BRINGS NEWS OF THE STATION.

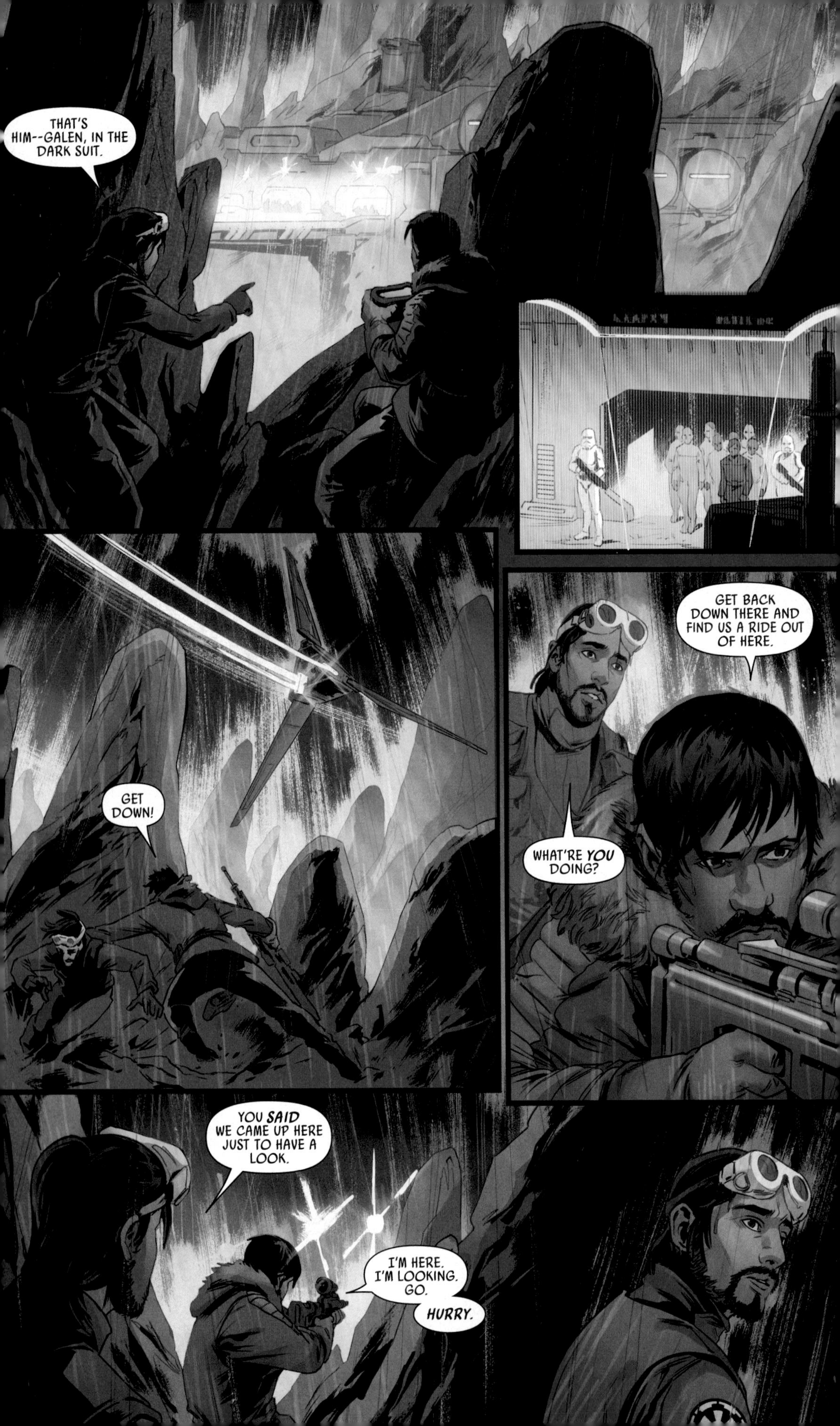
THAT'S HIM--GALEN, IN THE DARK SUIT.
GET DOWN!
GET BACK DOWN THERE AND FIND US A RIDE OUT OF HERE.
WHAT'RE *YOU* DOING?
YOU *SAID* WE CAME UP HERE JUST TO HAVE A LOOK.
I'M HERE. I'M LOOKING. GO.
HURRY.

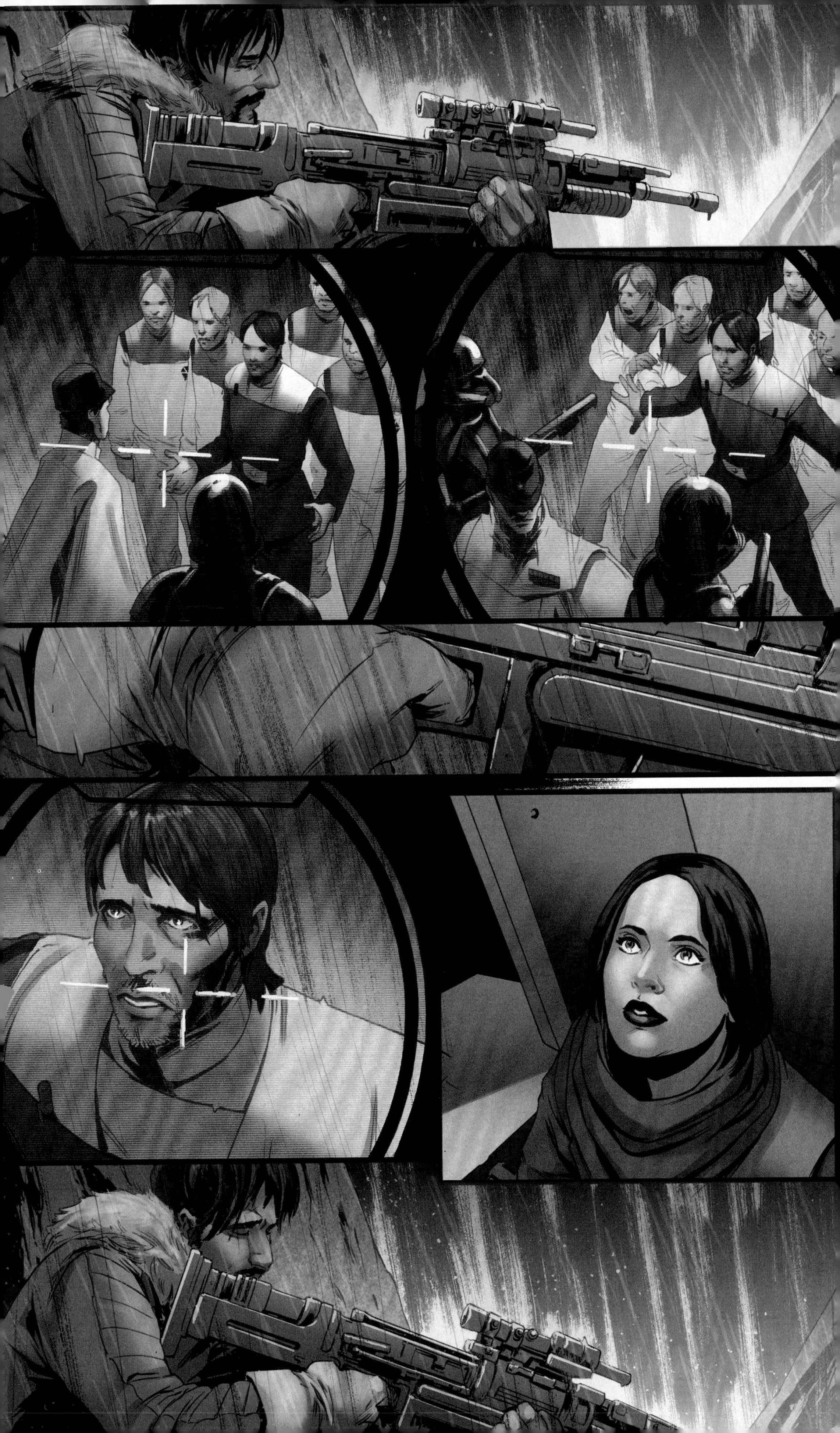

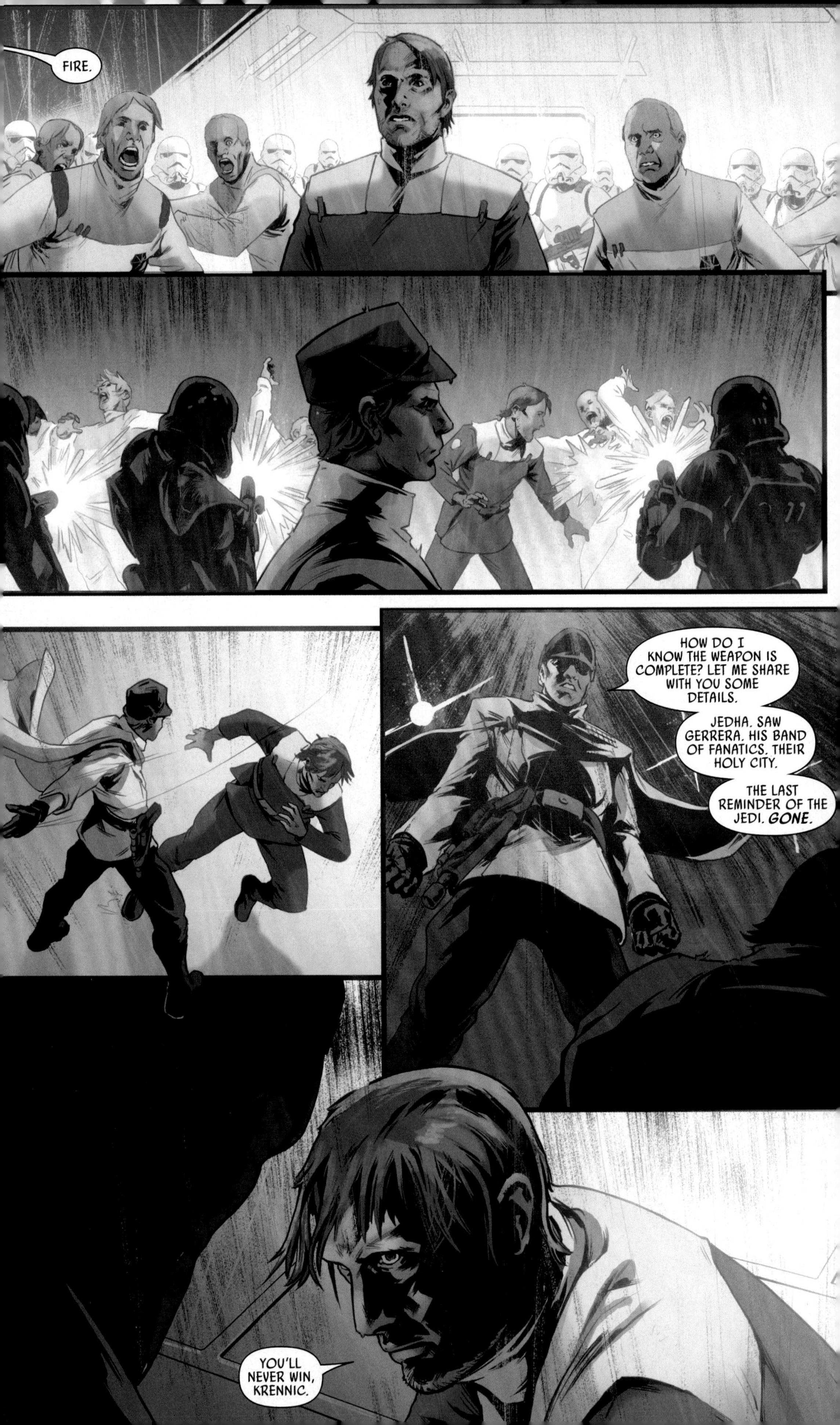
FIRE.
HOW DO I KNOW THE WEAPON IS COMPLETE? LET ME SHARE WITH YOU SOME DETAILS.
JEDHA. SAW GERRERA. HIS BAND OF FANATICS. THEIR HOLY CITY.
THE LAST REMINDER OF THE JEDI. *GONE.*
YOU'LL NEVER WIN, KRENNIC.

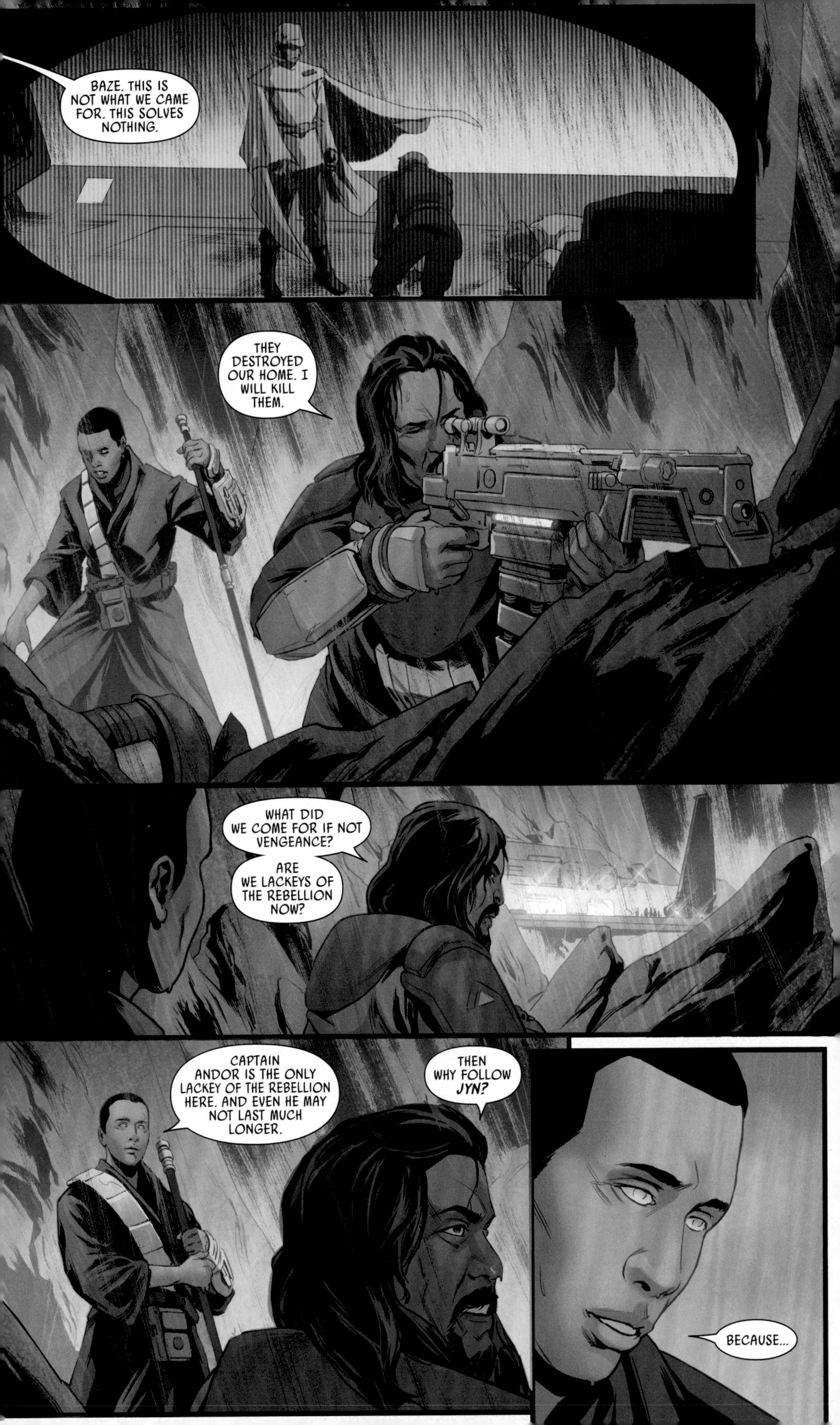
BAZE. THIS IS NOT WHAT WE CAME FOR. THIS SOLVES NOTHING.
THEY DESTROYED OUR HOME. I WILL KILL THEM.
WHAT DID WE COME FOR IF NOT VENGEANCE?
ARE WE LACKEYS OF THE REBELLION NOW?
CAPTAIN ANDOR IS THE ONLY LACKEY OF THE REBELLION HERE. AND EVEN HE MAY NOT LAST MUCH LONGER.
THEN WHY FOLLOW *JYN?*
BECAUSE...

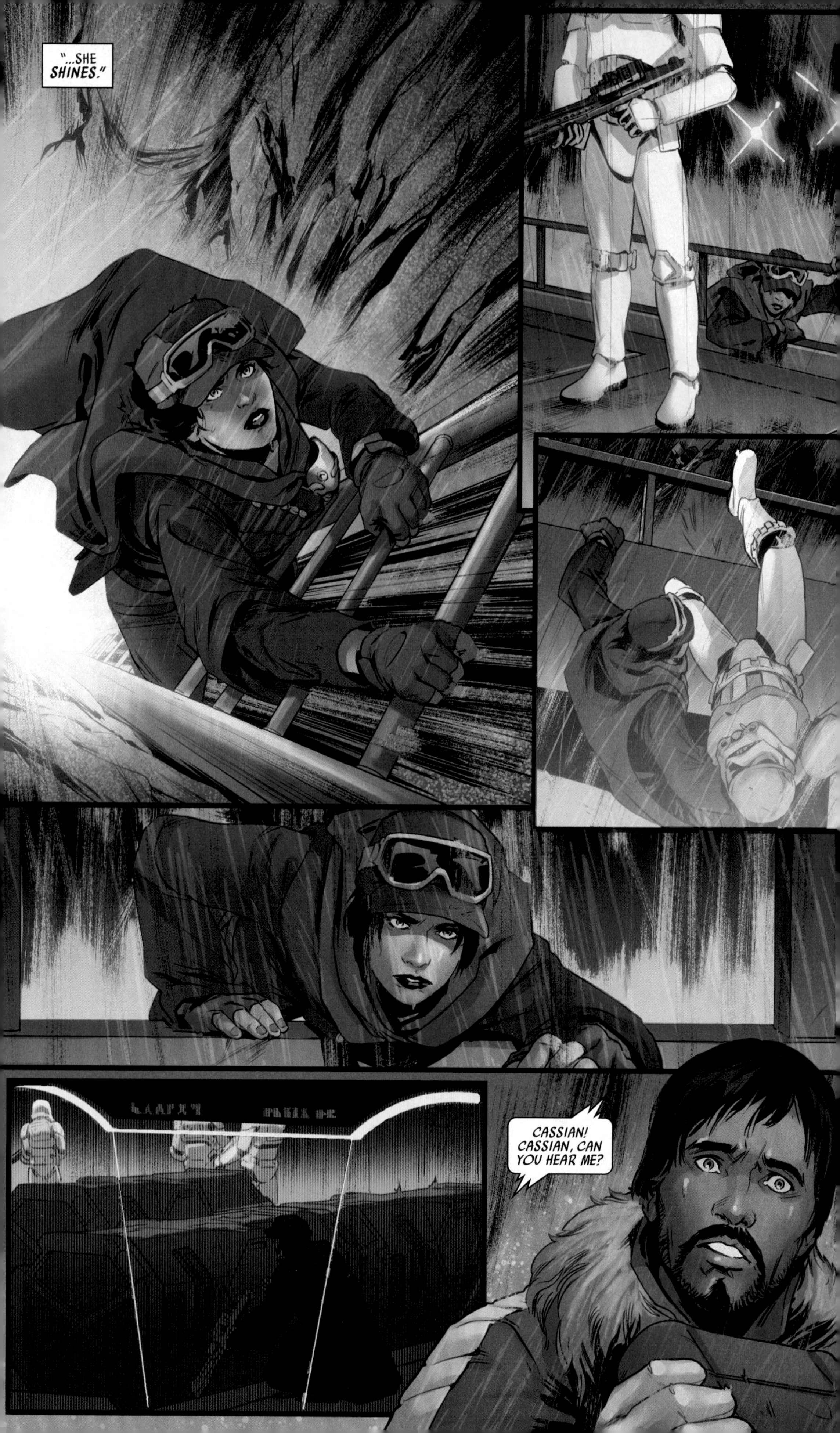
"...SHE SHINES."
CASSIAN! CASSIAN, CAN YOU HEAR ME?

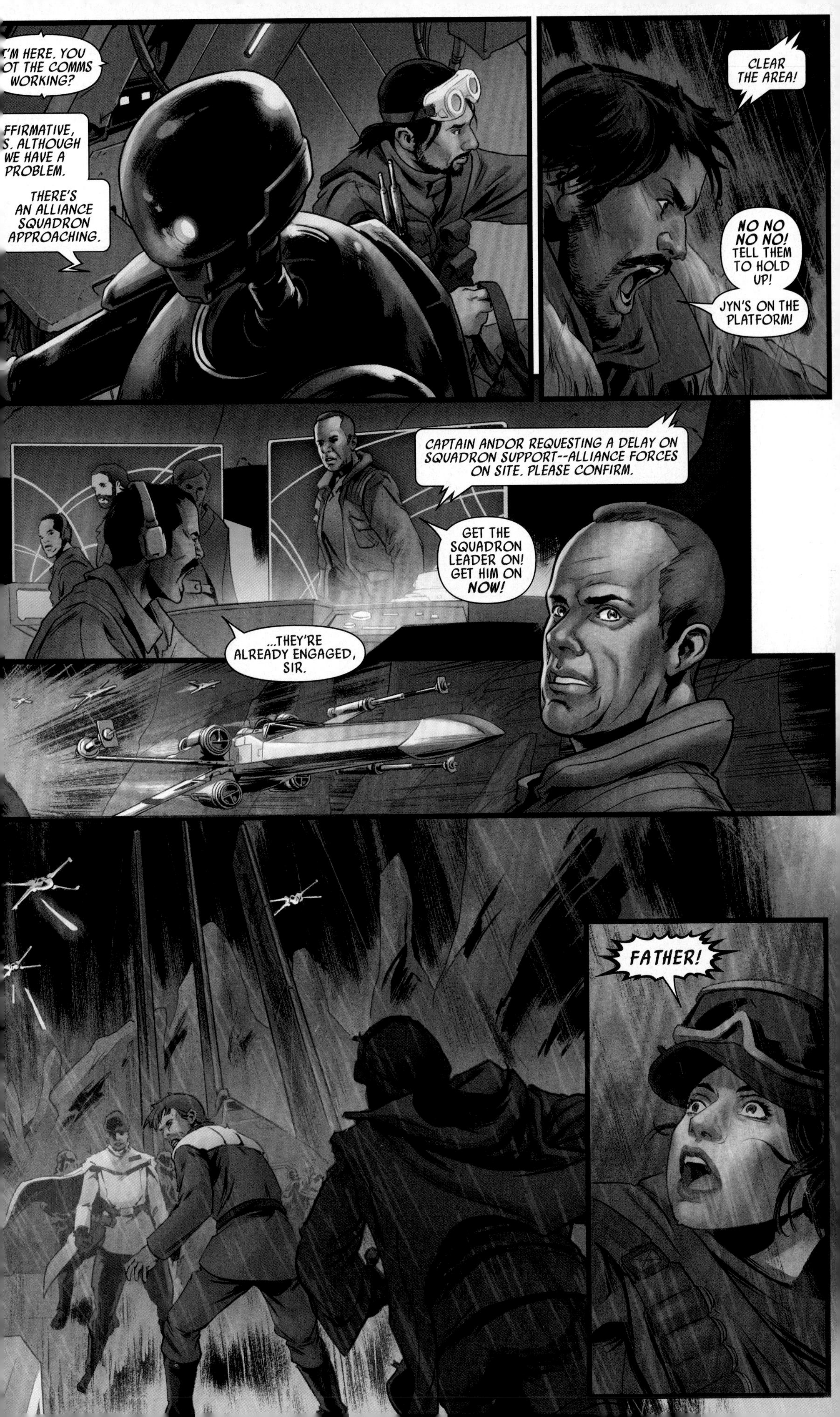
'M HERE. YOU OT THE COMMS WORKING?
FFIRMATIVE, S. ALTHOUGH WE HAVE A PROBLEM.
THERE'S AN ALLIANCE SQUADRON APPROACHING.
CLEAR THE AREA!
NO NO NO NO! TELL THEM TO HOLD UP!
JYN'S ON THE PLATFORM!
CAPTAIN ANDOR REQUESTING A DELAY ON SQUADRON SUPPORT--ALLIANCE FORCES ON SITE. PLEASE CONFIRM.
GET THE SQUADRON LEADER ON! GET HIM ON NOW!
...THEY'RE ALREADY ENGAGED, SIR.
FATHER!

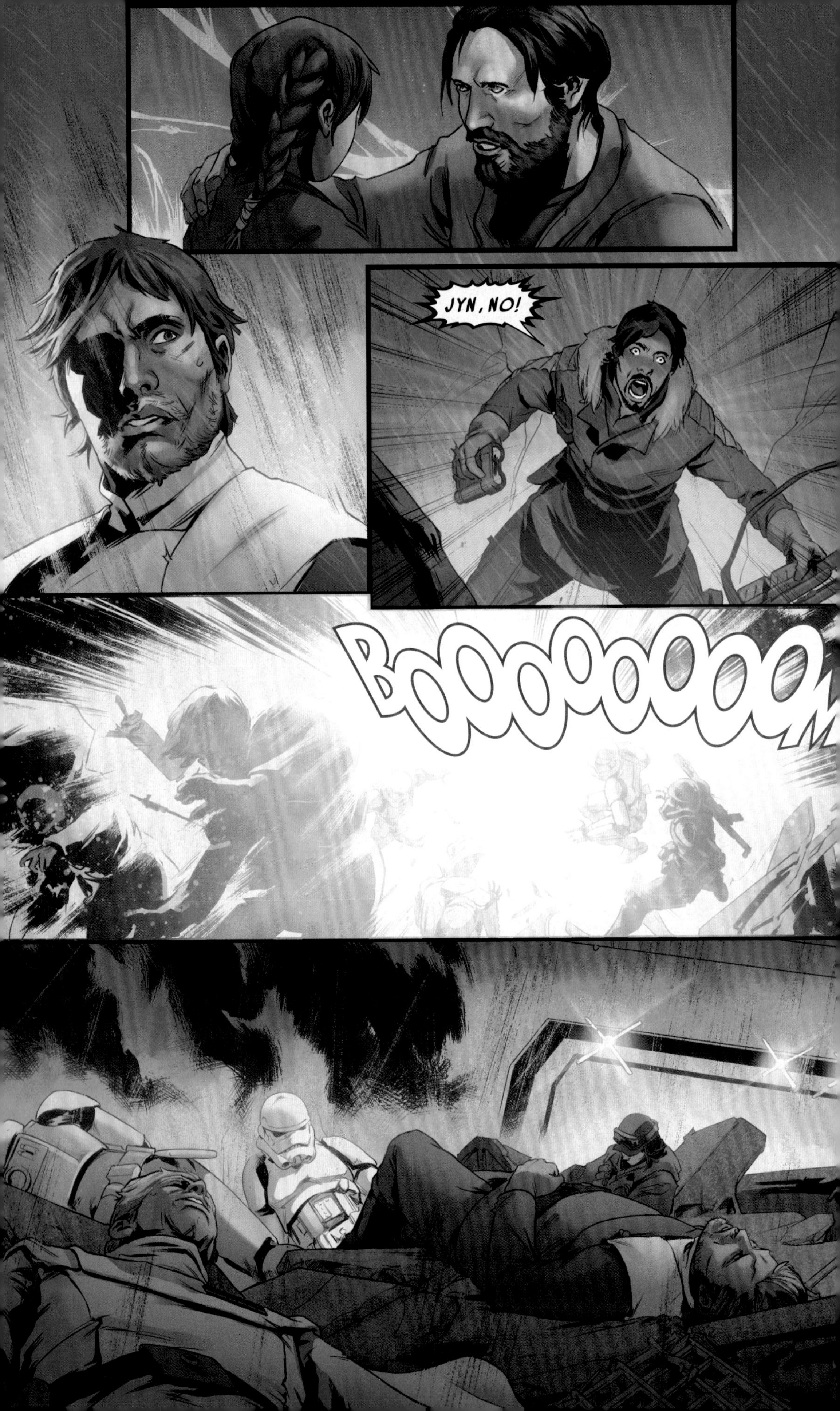
JYN, NO!
BOOOOOOOOM

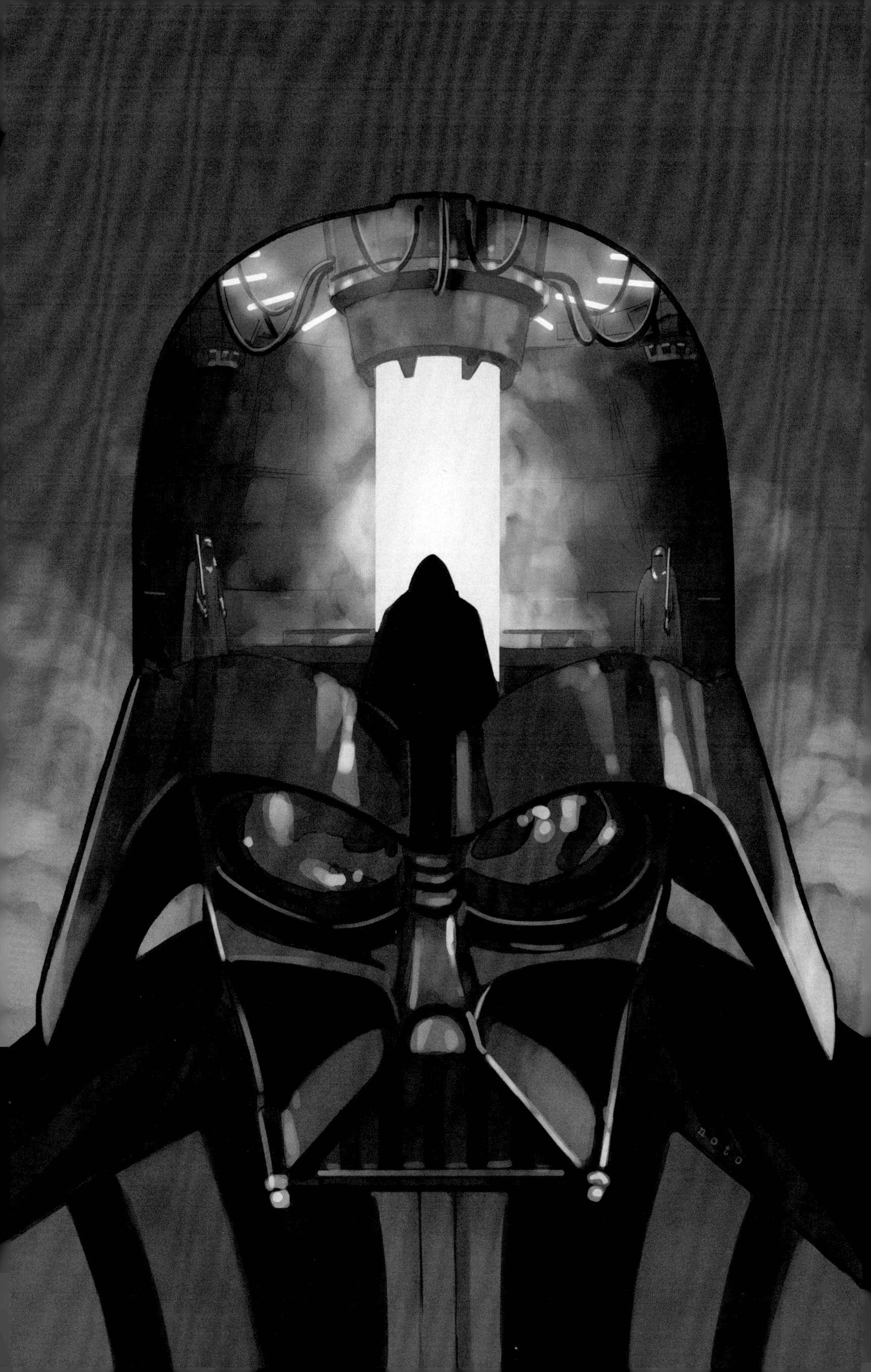
noto

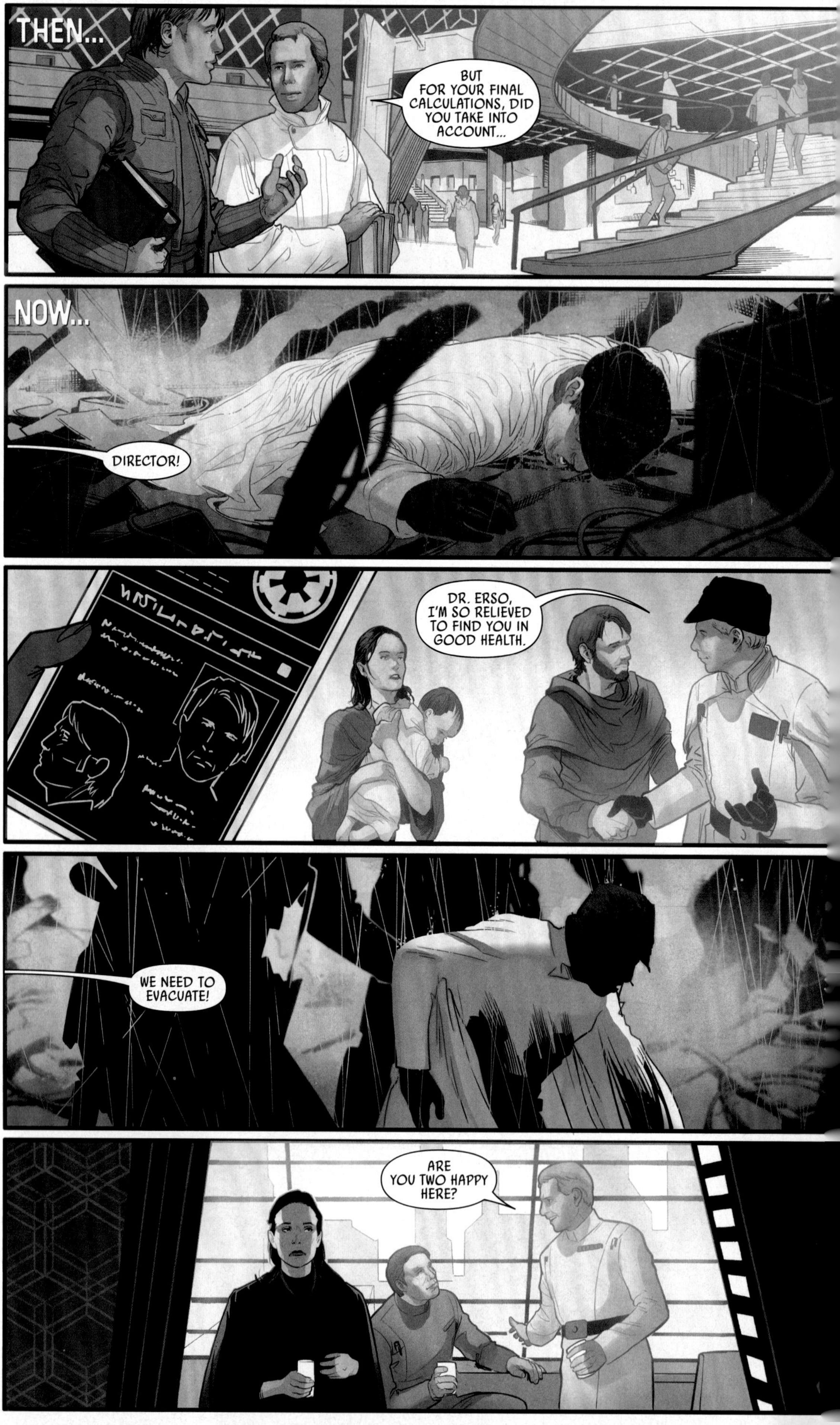
THEN...
BUT FOR YOUR FINAL CALCULATIONS, DID YOU TAKE INTO ACCOUNT...
NOW...
DIRECTOR!
DR. ERSO, I'M SO RELIEVED TO FIND YOU IN GOOD HEALTH.
WE NEED TO EVACUATE!
ARE YOU TWO HAPPY HERE?

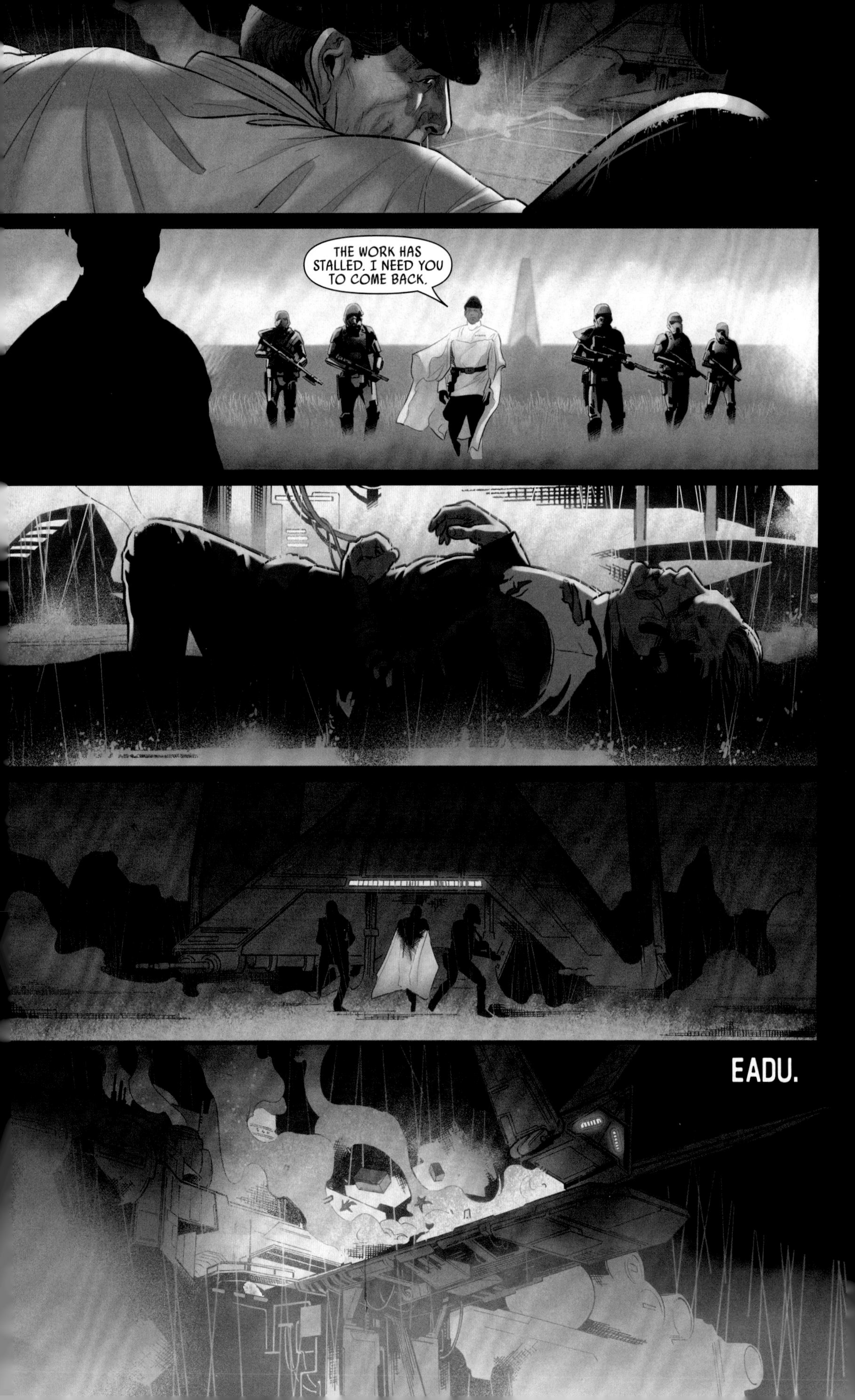
THE WORK HAS STALLED. I NEED YOU TO COME BACK.
EADU.

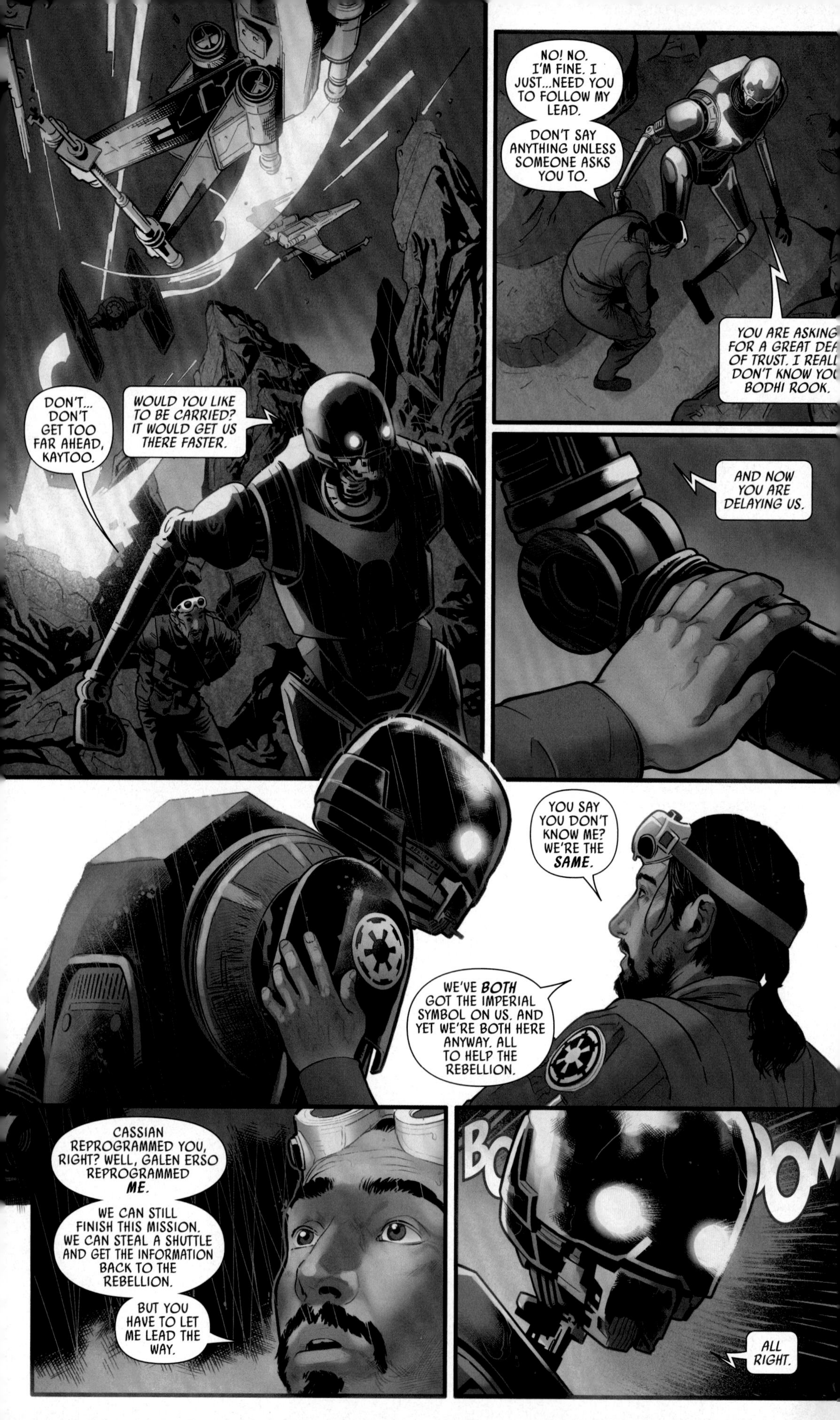
DON'T... DON'T GET TOO FAR AHEAD, KAYTOO.
WOULD YOU LIKE TO BE CARRIED? IT WOULD GET US THERE FASTER.
NO! NO. I'M FINE. I JUST...NEED YOU TO FOLLOW MY LEAD.
DON'T SAY ANYTHING UNLESS SOMEONE ASKS YOU TO.
YOU ARE ASKING FOR A GREAT DEA OF TRUST. I REALL DON'T KNOW YOU BODHI ROOK.
AND NOW YOU ARE DELAYING US.
YOU SAY YOU DON'T KNOW ME? WE'RE THE SAME.
WE'VE BOTH GOT THE IMPERIAL SYMBOL ON US. AND YET WE'RE BOTH HERE ANYWAY. ALL TO HELP THE REBELLION.
CASSIAN REPROGRAMMED YOU, RIGHT? WELL, GALEN ERSO REPROGRAMMED ME.
WE CAN STILL FINISH THIS MISSION. WE CAN STEAL A SHUTTLE AND GET THE INFORMATION BACK TO THE REBELLION.
BUT YOU HAVE TO LET ME LEAD THE WAY.
ALL RIGHT.

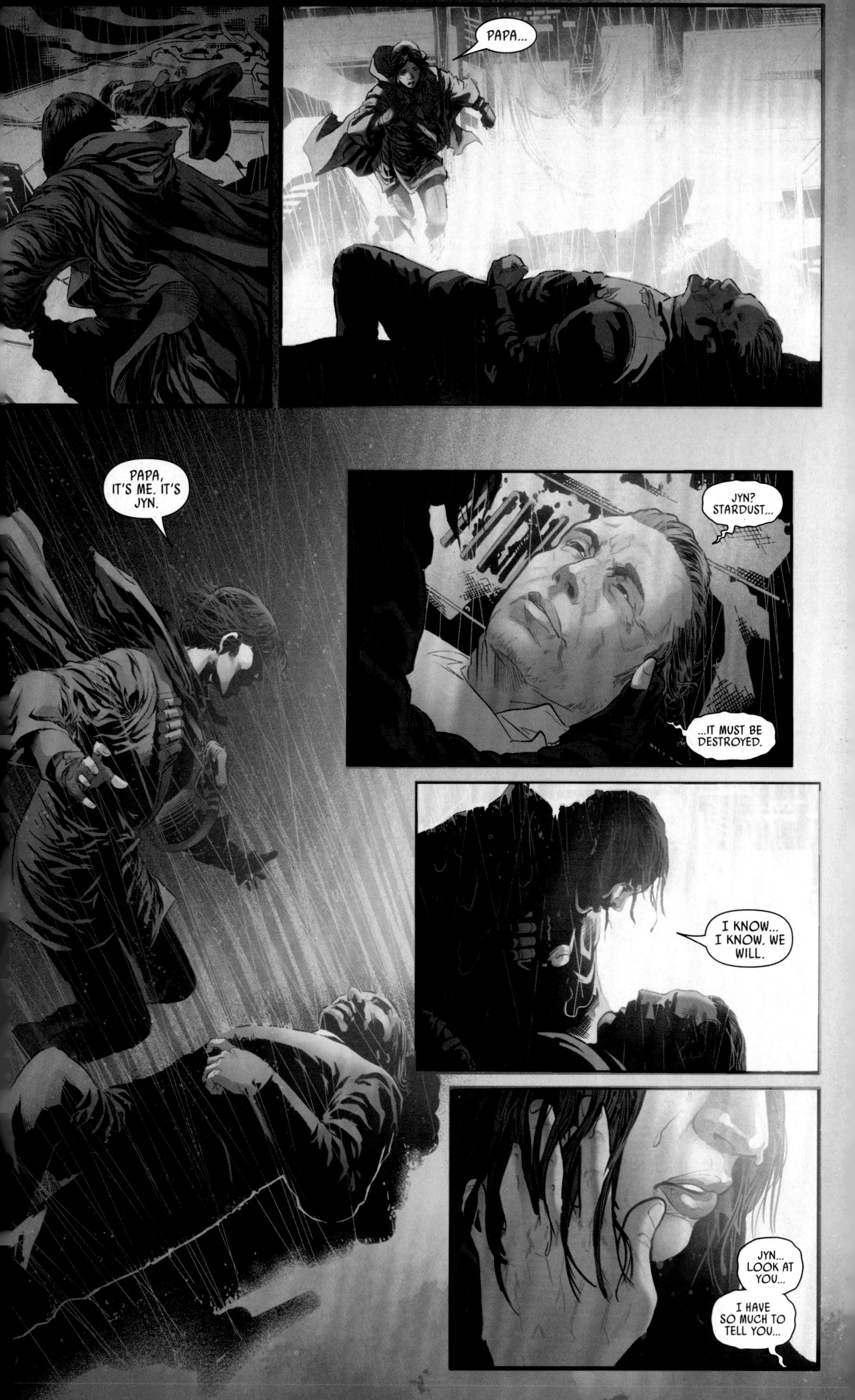
PAPA...
PAPA, IT'S ME. IT'S JYN.
JYN? STARDUST...
...IT MUST BE DESTROYED.
I KNOW... I KNOW. WE WILL.
JYN... LOOK AT YOU...
I HAVE SO MUCH TO TELL YOU...

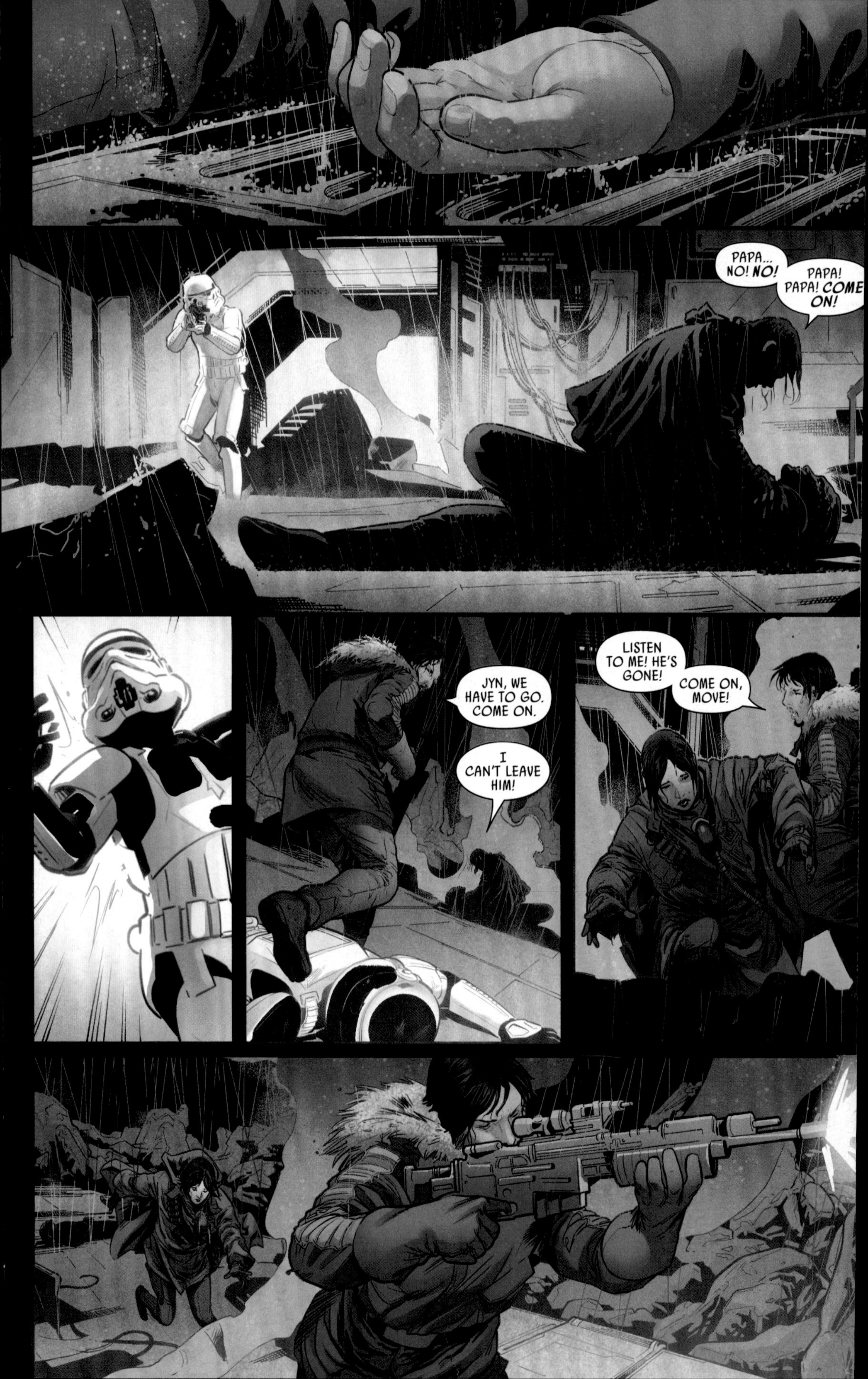
PAPA... NO! NO!
PAPA! PAPA! COME ON!
JYN, WE HAVE TO GO. COME ON.
I CAN'T LEAVE HIM!
LISTEN TO ME! HE'S GONE!
COME ON, MOVE!

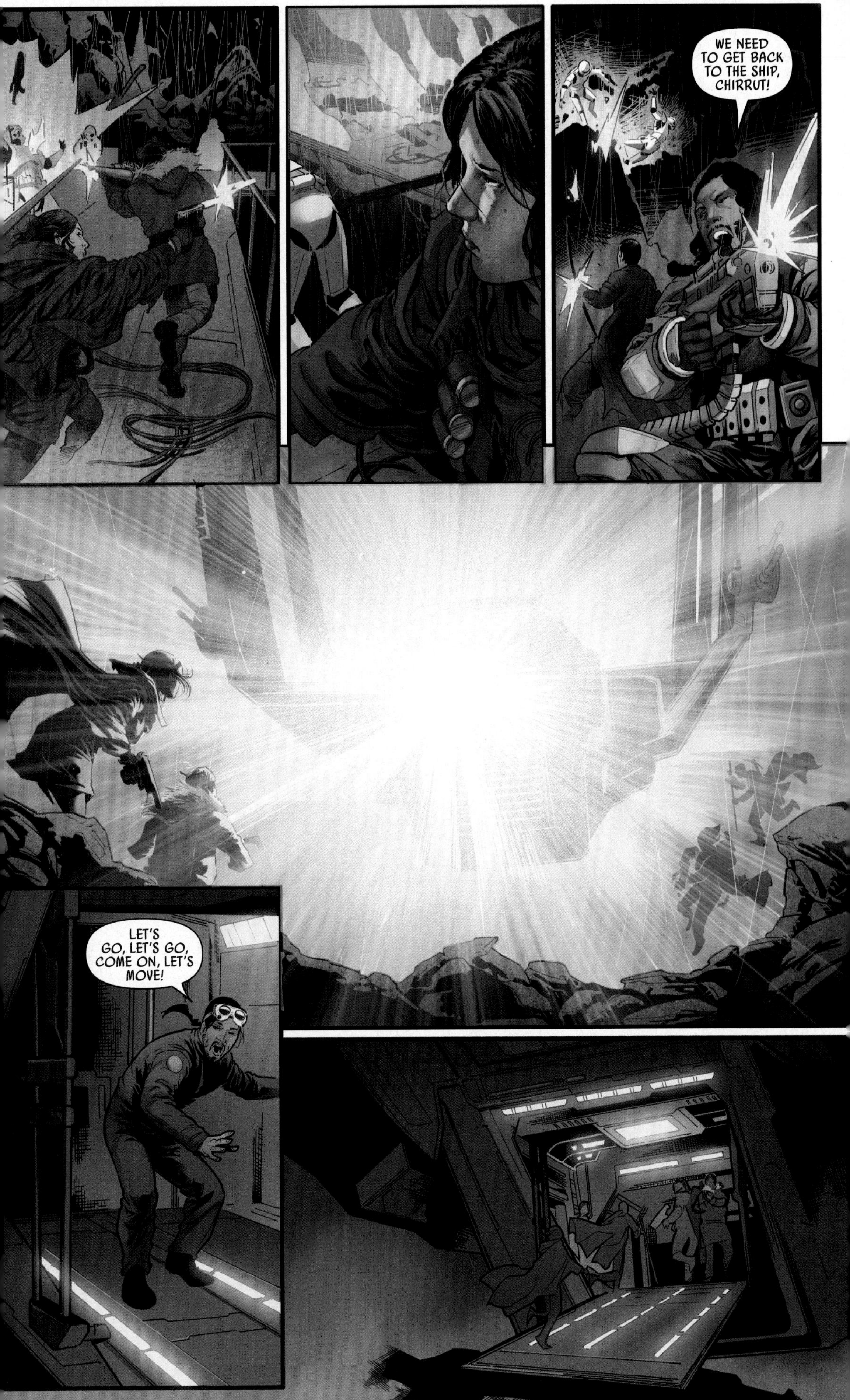
WE NEED TO GET BACK TO THE SHIP, CHIRRUT!
LET'S GO, LET'S GO, COME ON, LET'S MOVE!

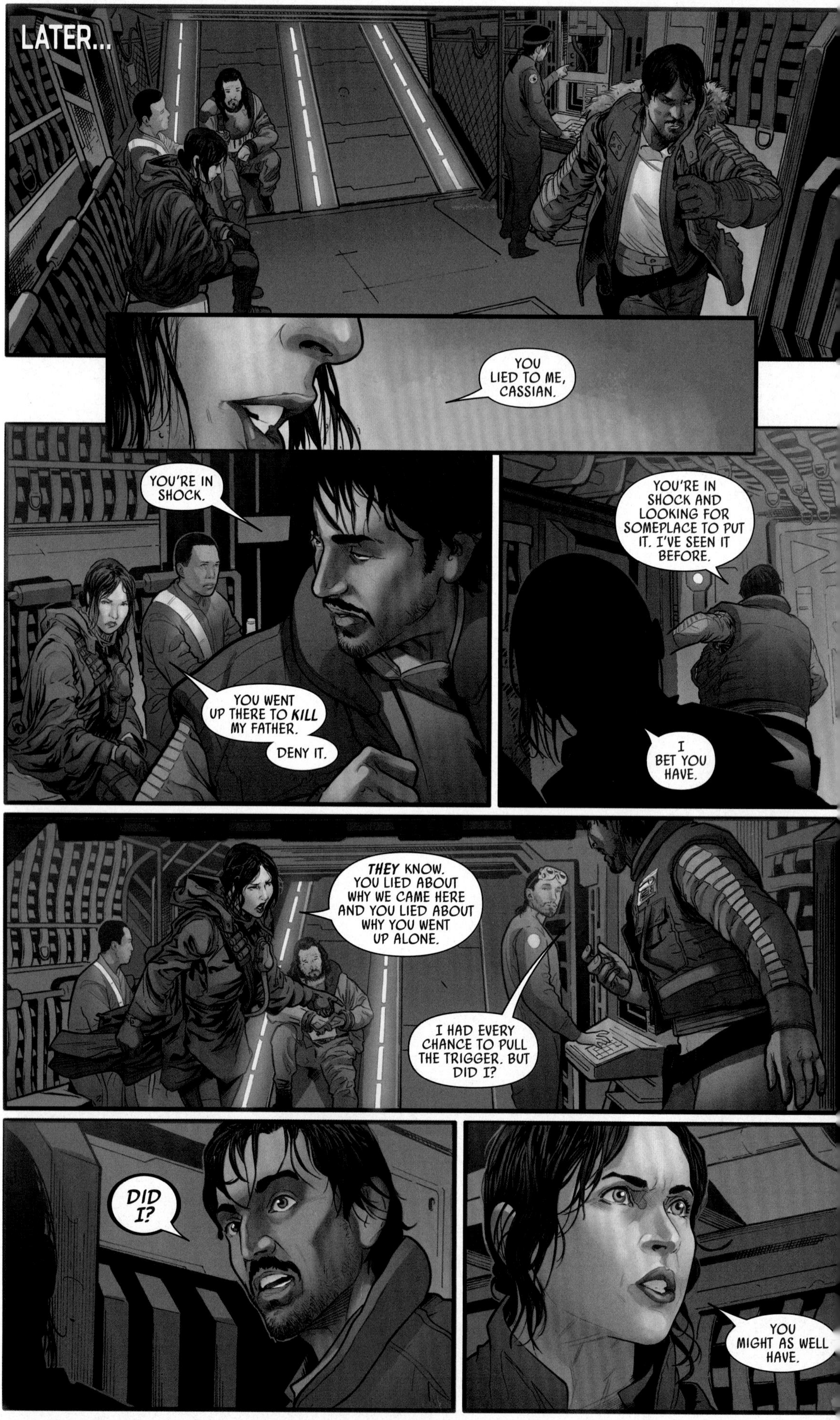
LATER...
YOU LIED TO ME, CASSIAN.
YOU'RE IN SHOCK.
YOU WENT UP THERE TO KILL MY FATHER.
DENY IT.
YOU'RE IN SHOCK AND LOOKING FOR SOMEPLACE TO PUT IT. I'VE SEEN IT BEFORE.
I BET YOU HAVE.
THEY KNOW. YOU LIED ABOUT WHY WE CAME HERE AND YOU LIED ABOUT WHY YOU WENT UP ALONE.
I HAD EVERY CHANCE TO PULL THE TRIGGER. BUT DID I?
DID I?
YOU MIGHT AS WELL HAVE.

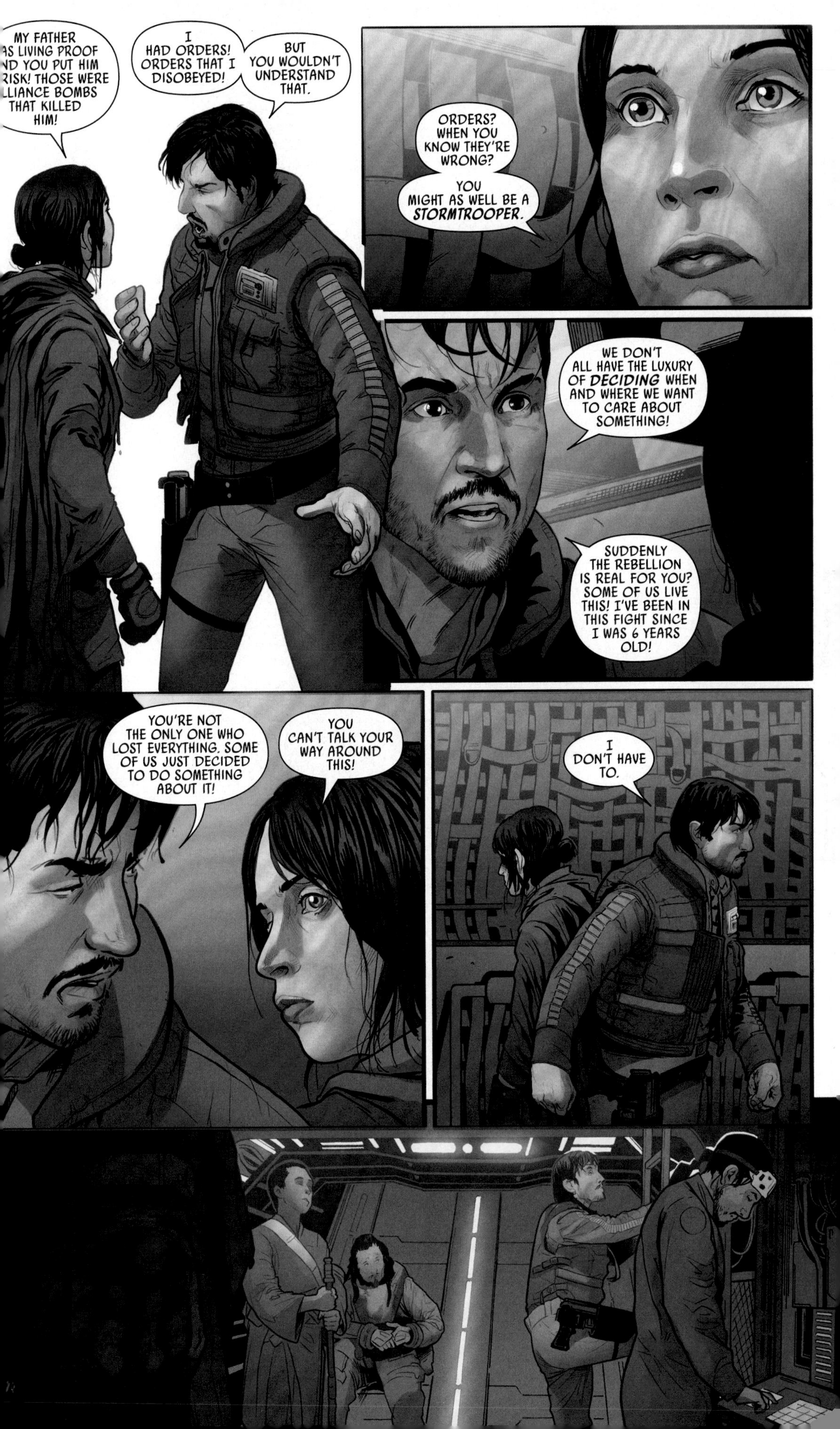
MY FATHER AS LIVING PROOF ND YOU PUT HIM RISK! THOSE WERE LLIANCE BOMBS THAT KILLED HIM!
I HAD ORDERS! ORDERS THAT I DISOBEYED!
BUT YOU WOULDN'T UNDERSTAND THAT.
ORDERS? WHEN YOU KNOW THEY'RE WRONG?
YOU MIGHT AS WELL BE A STORMTROOPER.
WE DON'T ALL HAVE THE LUXURY OF DECIDING WHEN AND WHERE WE WANT TO CARE ABOUT SOMETHING!
SUDDENLY THE REBELLION IS REAL FOR YOU? SOME OF US LIVE THIS! I'VE BEEN IN THIS FIGHT SINCE I WAS 6 YEARS OLD!
YOU'RE NOT THE ONLY ONE WHO LOST EVERYTHING. SOME OF US JUST DECIDED TO DO SOMETHING ABOUT IT!
YOU CAN'T TALK YOUR WAY AROUND THIS!
I DON'T HAVE TO.

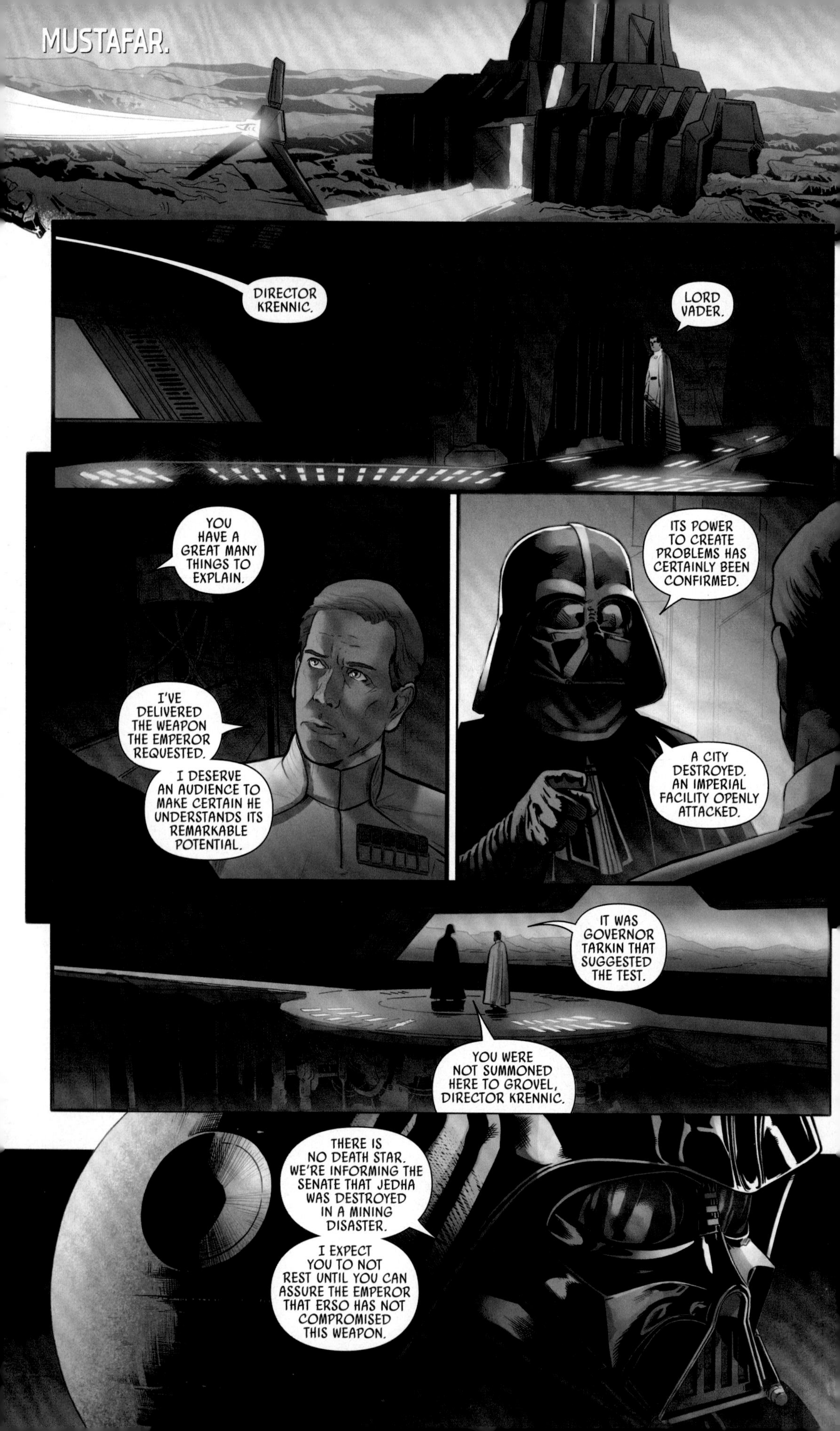
MUSTAFAR.
DIRECTOR KRENNIC.
LORD VADER.
YOU HAVE A GREAT MANY THINGS TO EXPLAIN.
I'VE DELIVERED THE WEAPON THE EMPEROR REQUESTED.
I DESERVE AN AUDIENCE TO MAKE CERTAIN HE UNDERSTANDS ITS REMARKABLE POTENTIAL.
ITS POWER TO CREATE PROBLEMS HAS CERTAINLY BEEN CONFIRMED.
A CITY DESTROYED. AN IMPERIAL FACILITY OPENLY ATTACKED.
IT WAS GOVERNOR TARKIN THAT SUGGESTED THE TEST.
YOU WERE NOT SUMMONED HERE TO GROVEL, DIRECTOR KRENNIC.
THERE IS NO DEATH STAR. WE'RE INFORMING THE SENATE THAT JEDHA WAS DESTROYED IN A MINING DISASTER.
I EXPECT YOU TO NOT REST UNTIL YOU CAN ASSURE THE EMPEROR THAT ERSO HAS NOT COMPROMISED THIS WEAPON.

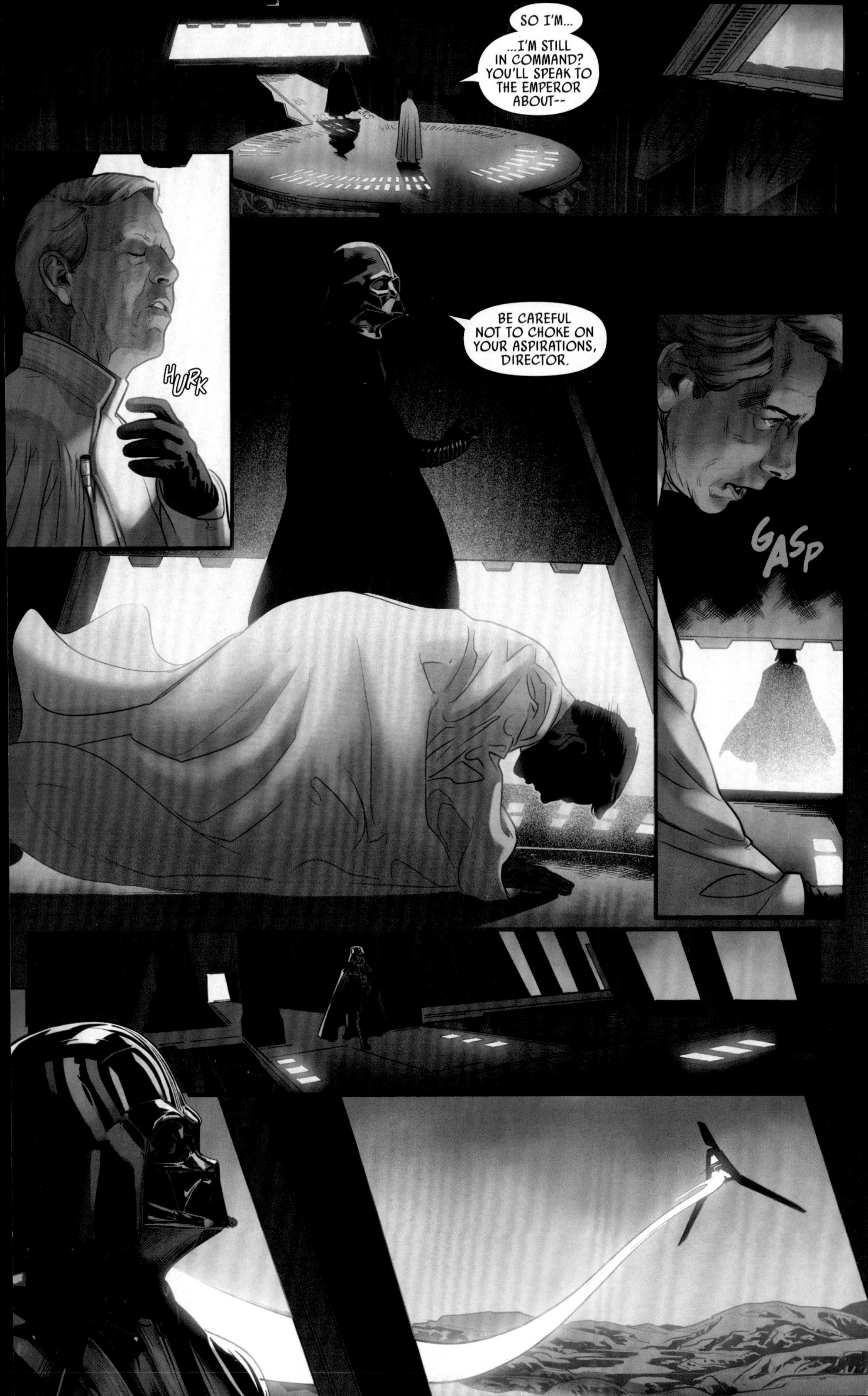
SO I'M...
...I'M STILL IN COMMAND? YOU'LL SPEAK TO THE EMPEROR ABOUT--
HURK
BE CAREFUL NOT TO CHOKE ON YOUR ASPIRATIONS, DIRECTOR.
GASP

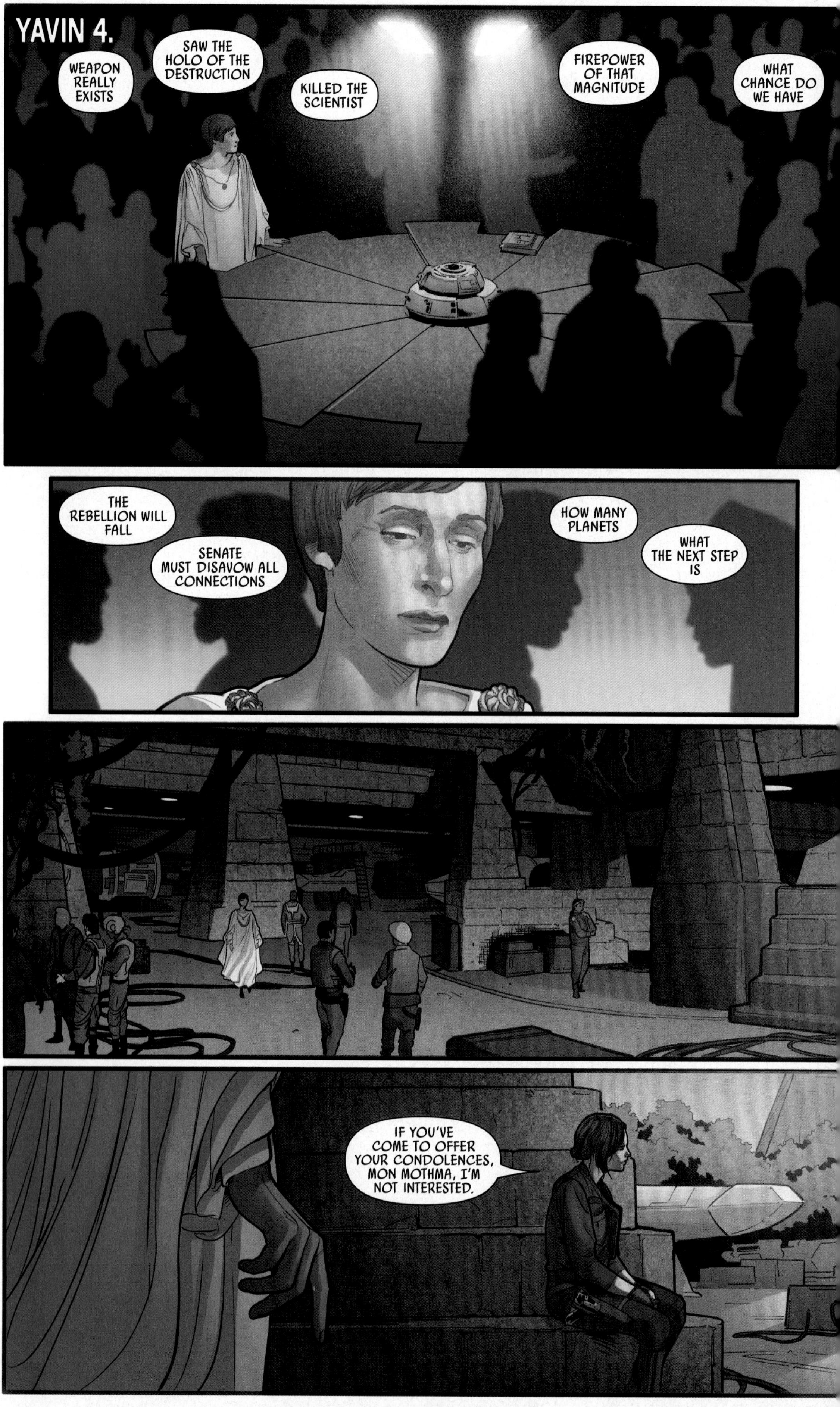
YAVIN 4.
WEAPON REALLY EXISTS
SAW THE HOLO OF THE DESTRUCTION
KILLED THE SCIENTIST
FIREPOWER OF THAT MAGNITUDE
WHAT CHANCE DO WE HAVE
THE REBELLION WILL FALL
SENATE MUST DISAVOW ALL CONNECTIONS
HOW MANY PLANETS
WHAT THE NEXT STEP IS
IF YOU'VE COME TO OFFER YOUR CONDOLENCES, MON MOTHMA, I'M NOT INTERESTED.

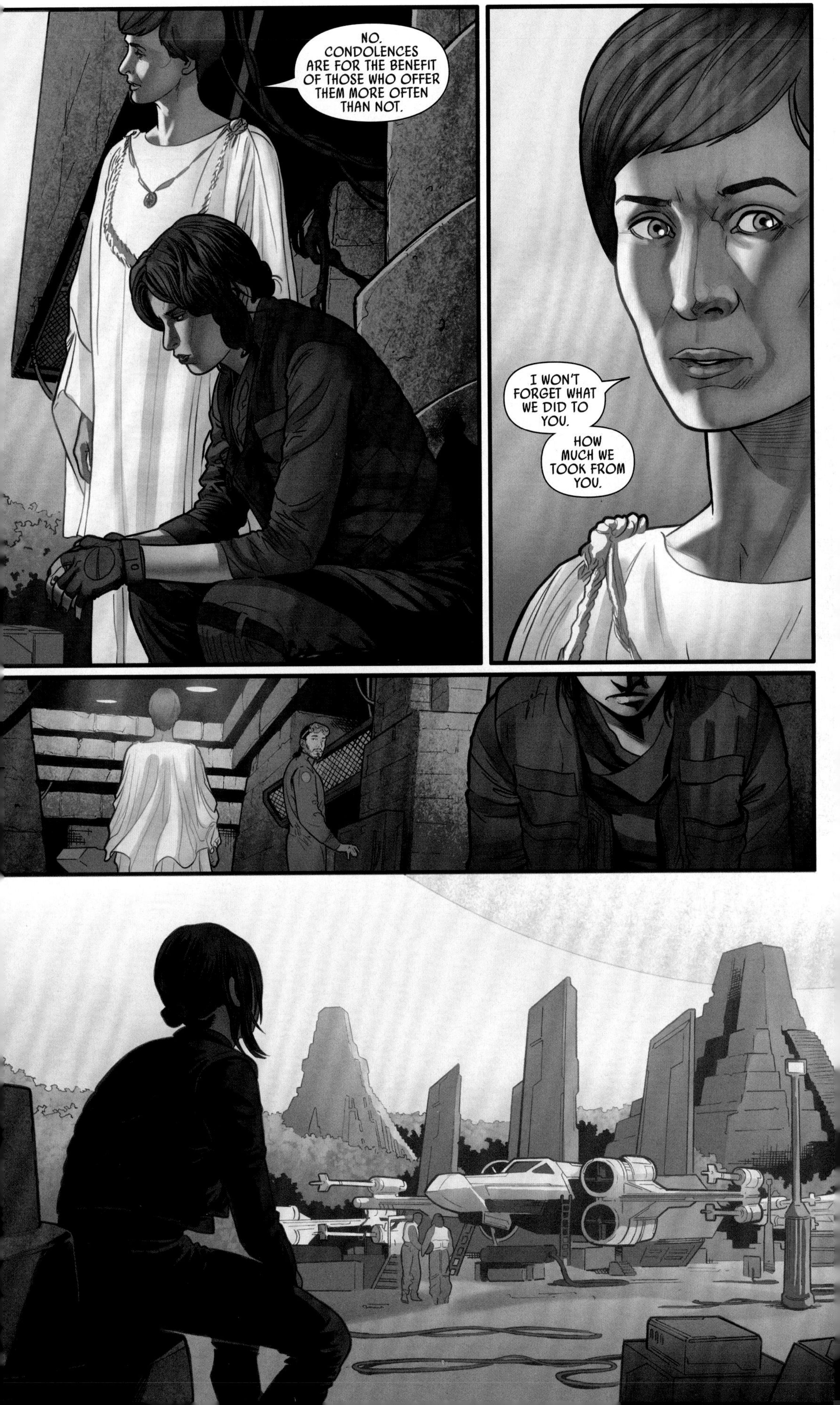
NO. CONDOLENCES ARE FOR THE BENEFIT OF THOSE WHO OFFER THEM MORE OFTEN THAN NOT.
I WON'T FORGET WHAT WE DID TO YOU.
HOW MUCH WE TOOK FROM YOU.

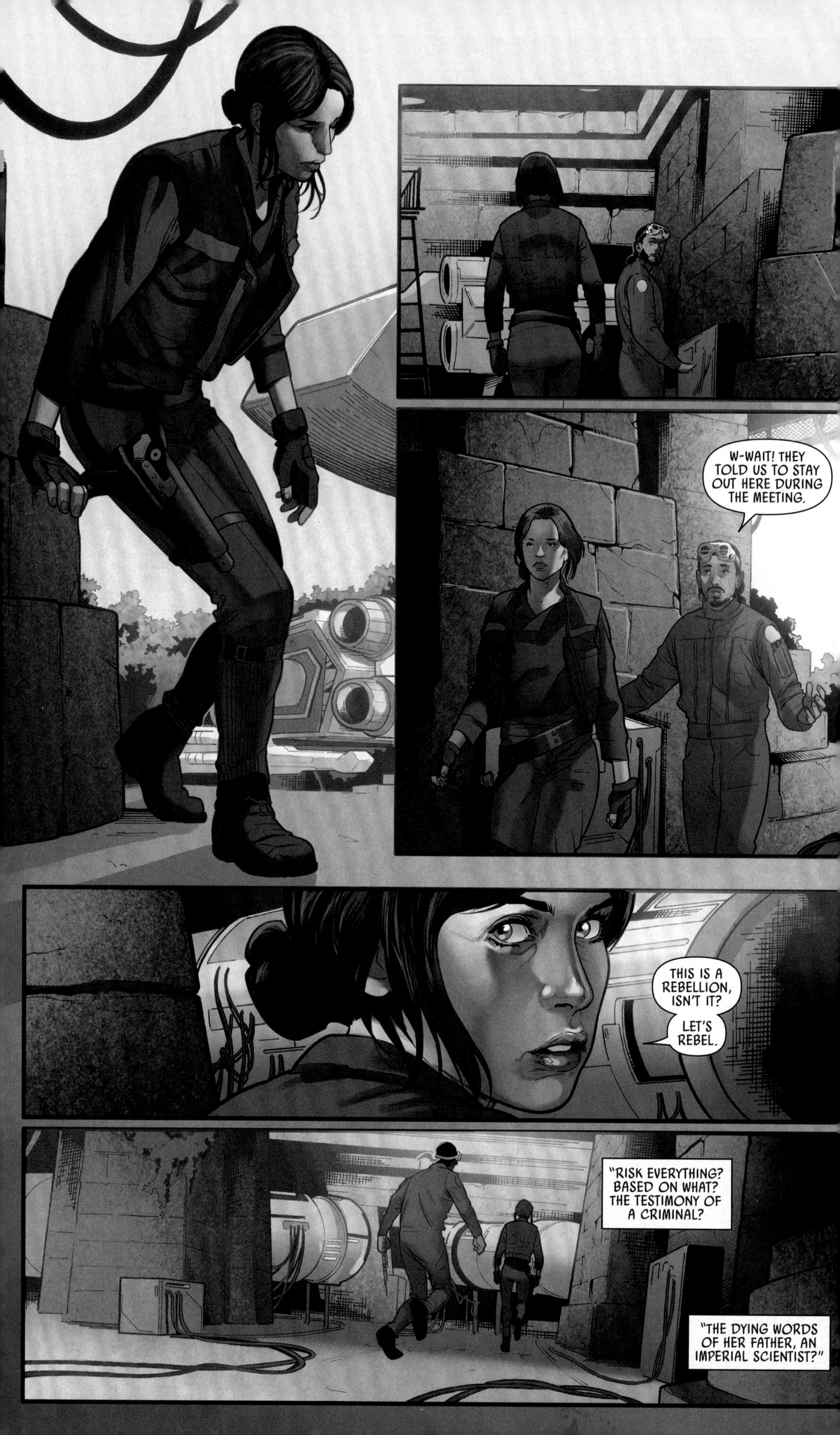
W-WAIT! THEY TOLD US TO STAY OUT HERE DURING THE MEETING.
THIS IS A REBELLION, ISN'T IT?
LET'S REBEL.
"RISK EVERYTHING? BASED ON WHAT? THE TESTIMONY OF A CRIMINAL?
"THE DYING WORDS OF HER FATHER, AN IMPERIAL SCIENTIST?"

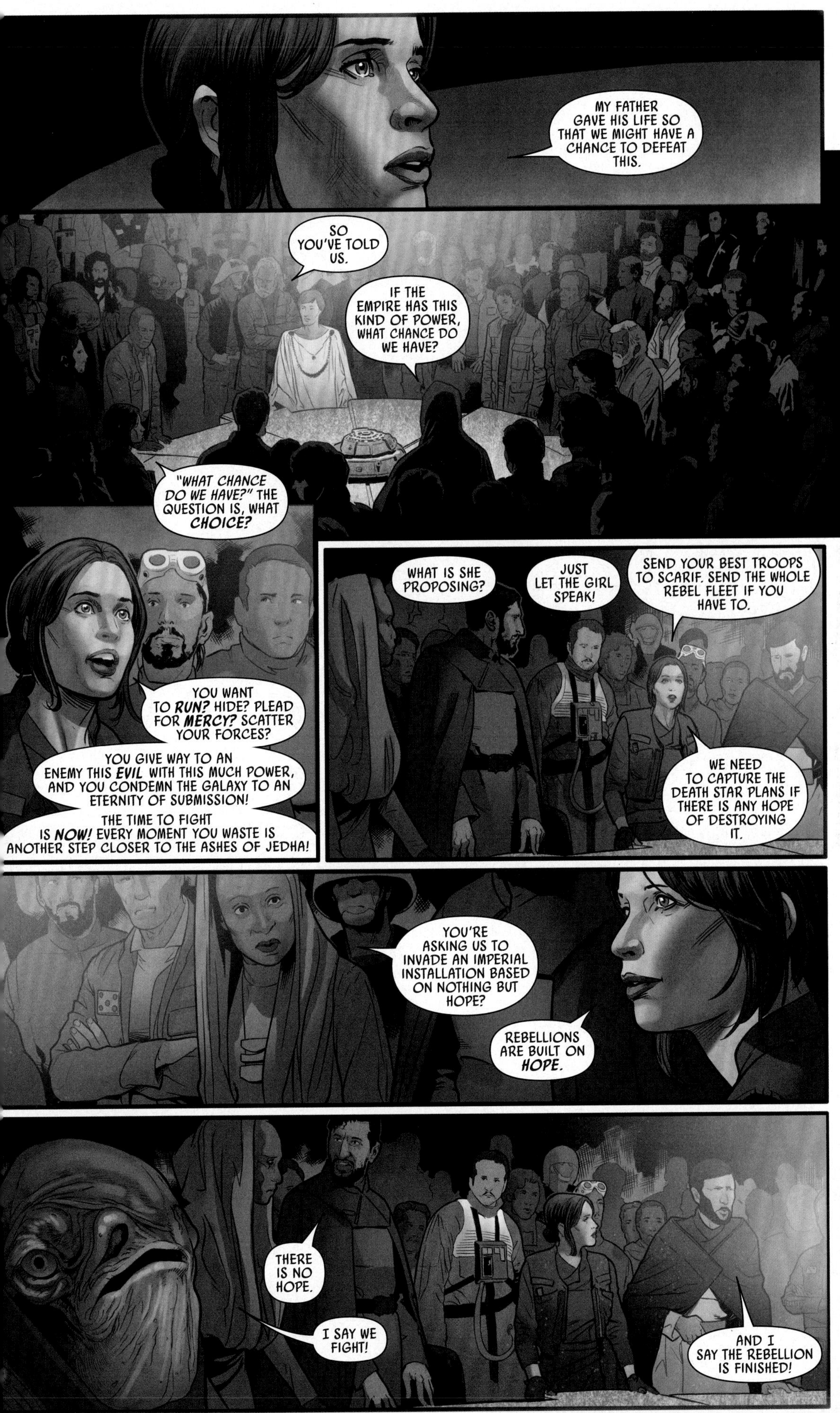

MY FATHER GAVE HIS LIFE SO THAT WE MIGHT HAVE A CHANCE TO DEFEAT THIS.
SO YOU'VE TOLD US.
IF THE EMPIRE HAS THIS KIND OF POWER, WHAT CHANCE DO WE HAVE?
"WHAT CHANCE DO WE HAVE?" THE QUESTION IS, WHAT CHOICE?
YOU WANT TO RUN? HIDE? PLEAD FOR MERCY? SCATTER YOUR FORCES?
YOU GIVE WAY TO AN ENEMY THIS EVIL WITH THIS MUCH POWER, AND YOU CONDEMN THE GALAXY TO AN ETERNITY OF SUBMISSION!
THE TIME TO FIGHT IS NOW! EVERY MOMENT YOU WASTE IS ANOTHER STEP CLOSER TO THE ASHES OF JEDHA!
WHAT IS SHE PROPOSING?
JUST LET THE GIRL SPEAK!
SEND YOUR BEST TROOPS TO SCARIF. SEND THE WHOLE REBEL FLEET IF YOU HAVE TO.
WE NEED TO CAPTURE THE DEATH STAR PLANS IF THERE IS ANY HOPE OF DESTROYING IT.
YOU'RE ASKING US TO INVADE AN IMPERIAL INSTALLATION BASED ON NOTHING BUT HOPE?
REBELLIONS ARE BUILT ON HOPE.
THERE IS NO HOPE.
I SAY WE FIGHT!
AND I SAY THE REBELLION IS FINISHED!

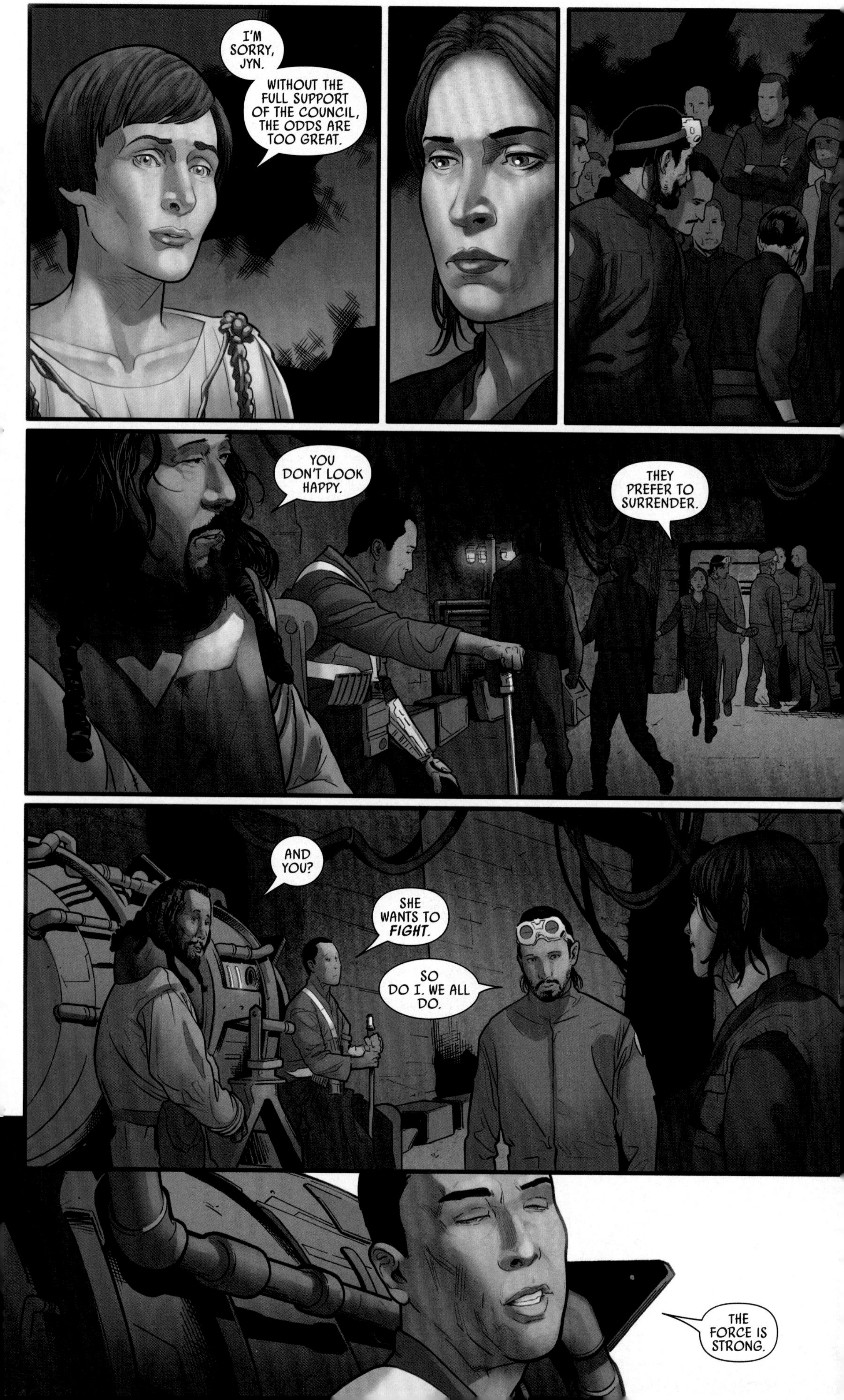
I'M SORRY, JYN.
WITHOUT THE FULL SUPPORT OF THE COUNCIL, THE ODDS ARE TOO GREAT.
YOU DON'T LOOK HAPPY.
THEY PREFER TO SURRENDER.
AND YOU?
SHE WANTS TO *FIGHT*.
SO DO I. WE ALL DO.
THE FORCE IS STRONG.

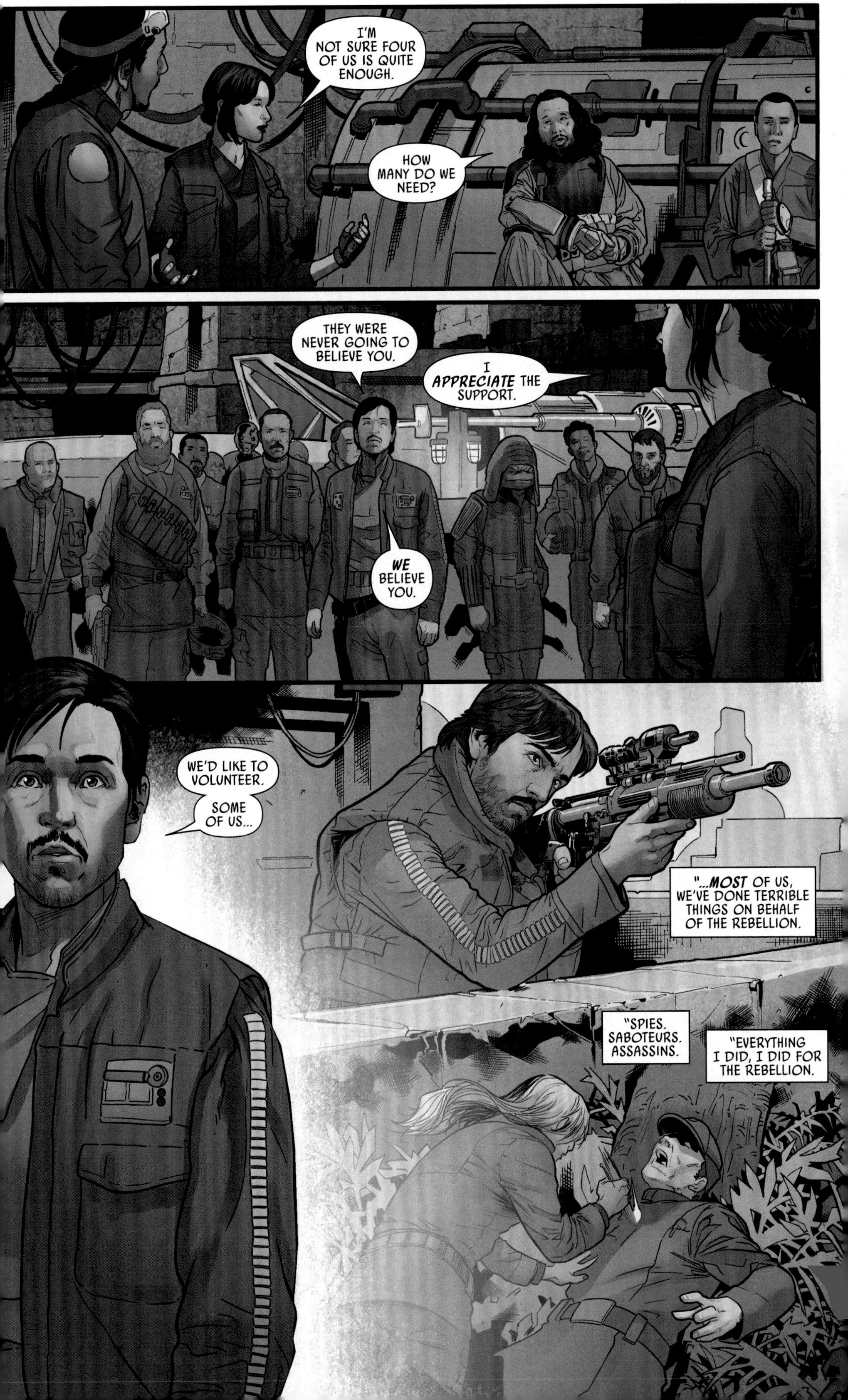
I'M NOT SURE FOUR OF US IS QUITE ENOUGH.
HOW MANY DO WE NEED?
THEY WERE NEVER GOING TO BELIEVE YOU.
I APPRECIATE THE SUPPORT.
WE BELIEVE YOU.
WE'D LIKE TO VOLUNTEER.
SOME OF US...
"...MOST OF US, WE'VE DONE TERRIBLE THINGS ON BEHALF OF THE REBELLION.
"SPIES. SABOTEURS. ASSASSINS.
"EVERYTHING I DID, I DID FOR THE REBELLION.

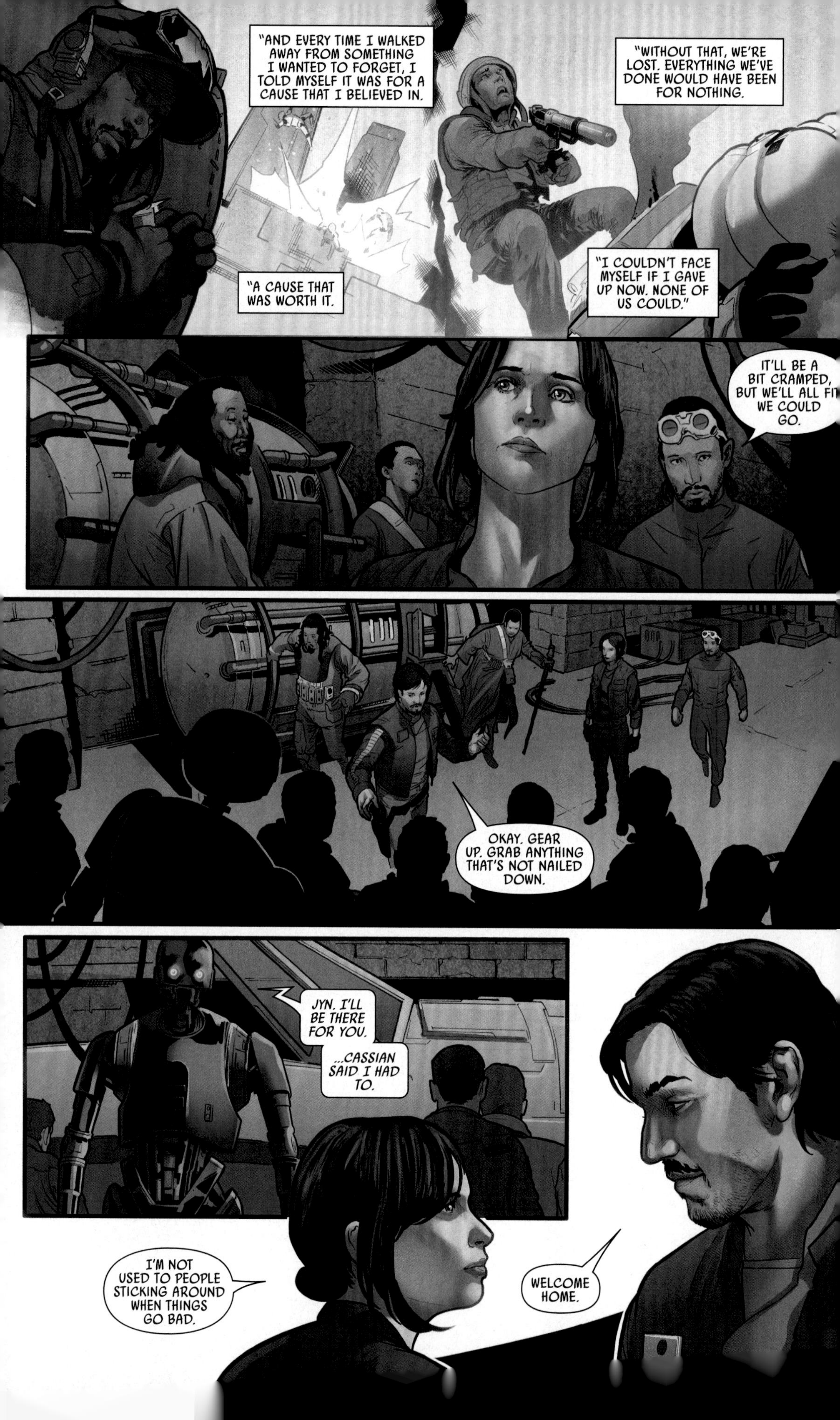
"AND EVERY TIME I WALKED AWAY FROM SOMETHING I WANTED TO FORGET, I TOLD MYSELF IT WAS FOR A CAUSE THAT I BELIEVED IN.
"A CAUSE THAT WAS WORTH IT.
"WITHOUT THAT, WE'RE LOST. EVERYTHING WE'VE DONE WOULD HAVE BEEN FOR NOTHING.
"I COULDN'T FACE MYSELF IF I GAVE UP NOW. NONE OF US COULD."
IT'LL BE A BIT CRAMPED, BUT WE'LL ALL FI WE COULD GO.
OKAY. GEAR UP. GRAB ANYTHING THAT'S NOT NAILED DOWN.
JYN. I'LL BE THERE FOR YOU.
...CASSIAN SAID I HAD TO.
I'M NOT USED TO PEOPLE STICKING AROUND WHEN THINGS GO BAD.
WELCOME HOME.

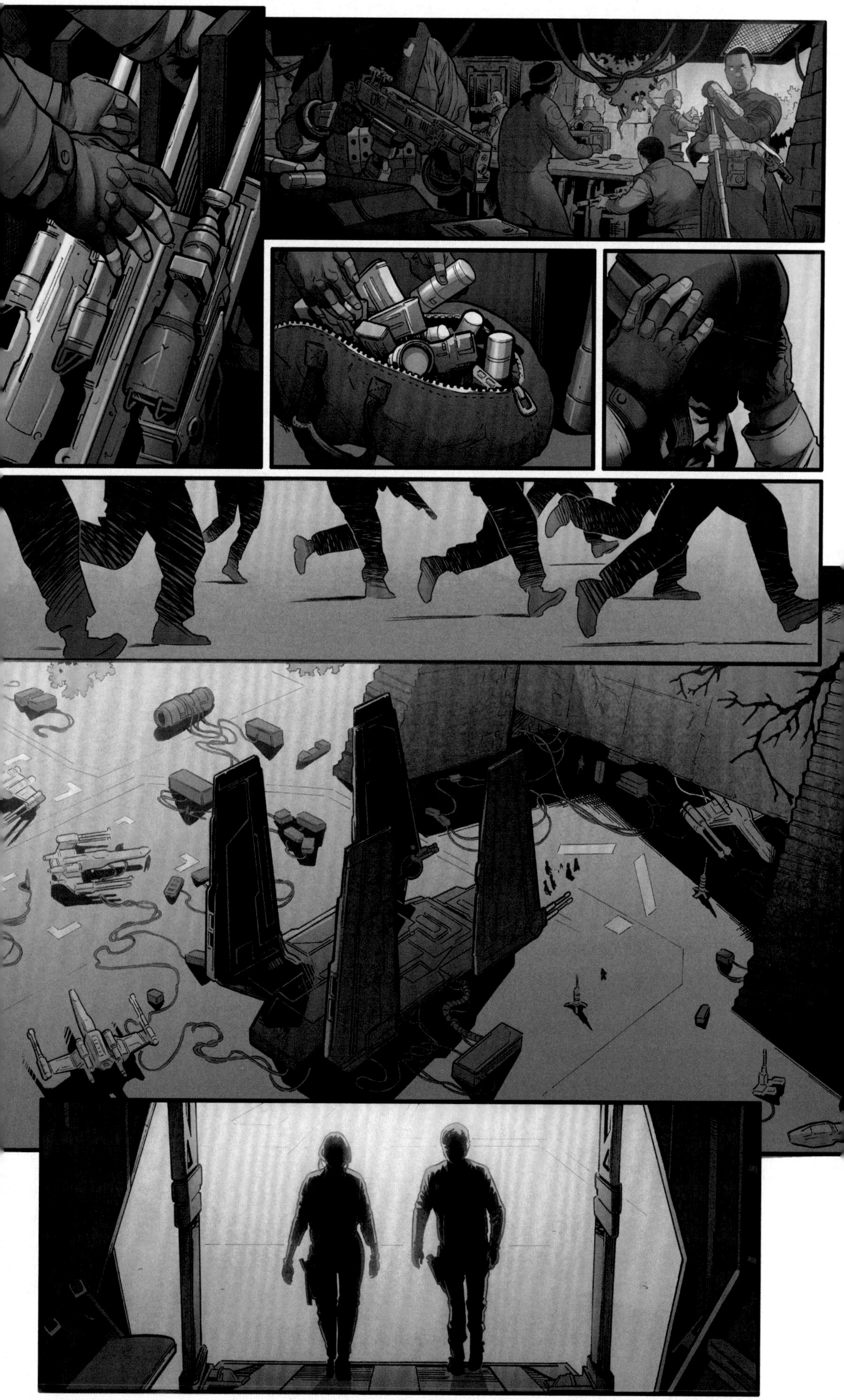

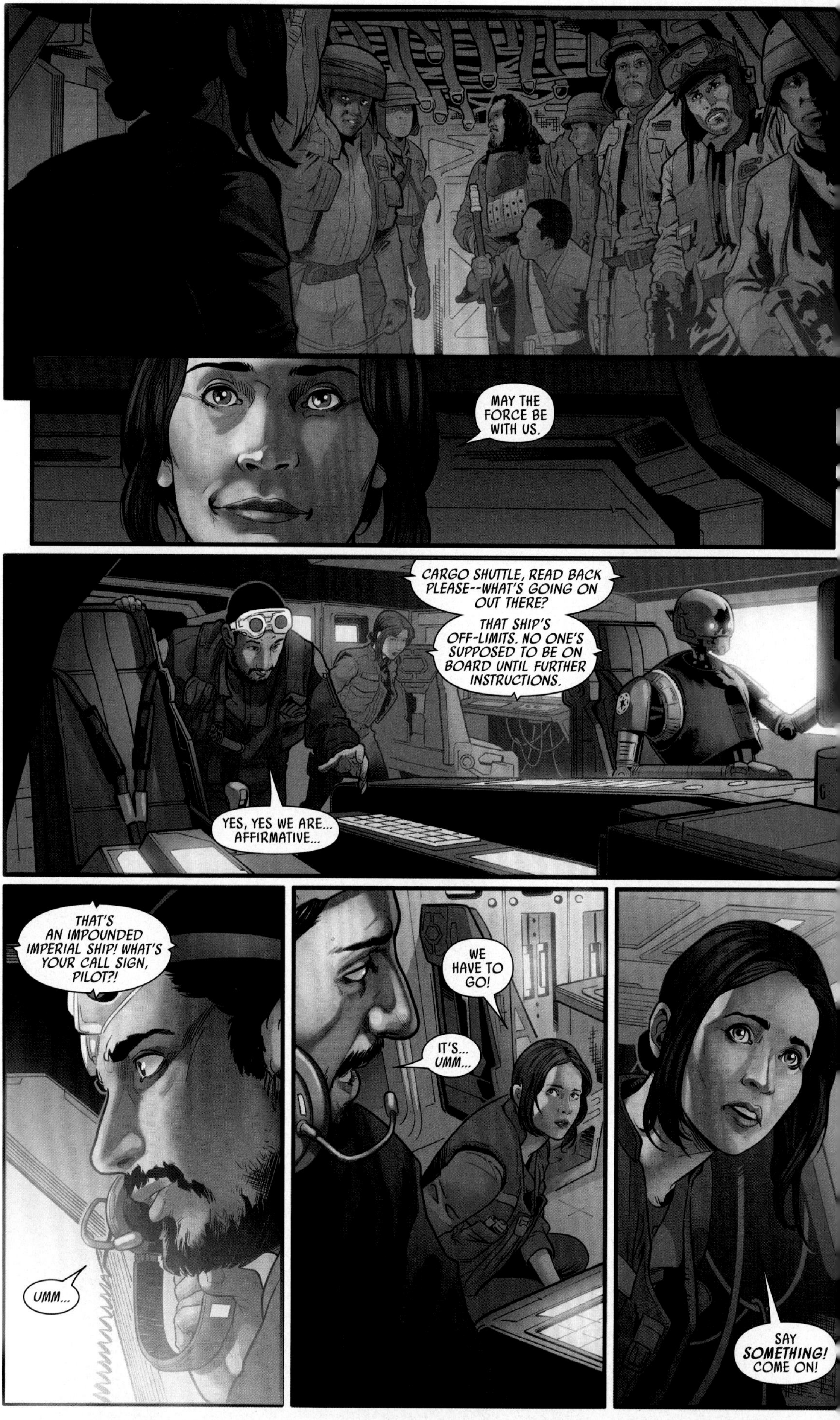
MAY THE FORCE BE WITH US.
CARGO SHUTTLE, READ BACK PLEASE--WHAT'S GOING ON OUT THERE?
THAT SHIP'S OFF-LIMITS. NO ONE'S SUPPOSED TO BE ON BOARD UNTIL FURTHER INSTRUCTIONS.
YES, YES WE ARE... AFFIRMATIVE...
THAT'S AN IMPOUNDED IMPERIAL SHIP! WHAT'S YOUR CALL SIGN, PILOT?!
UMM...
WE HAVE TO GO!
IT'S... UMM...
SAY *SOMETHING!* COME ON!

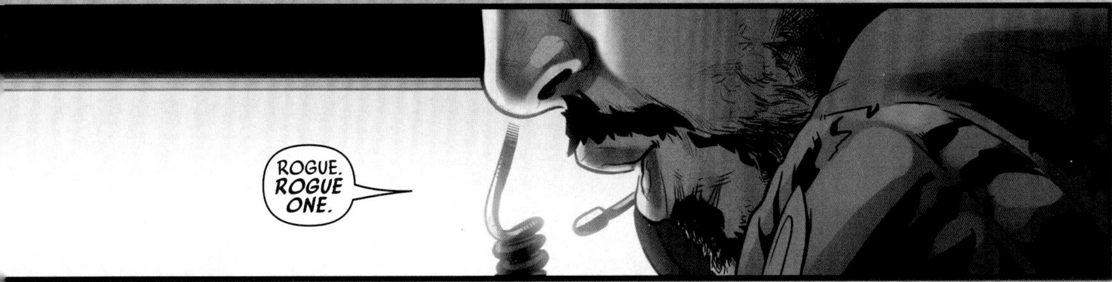
ROGUE. ROGUE ONE.
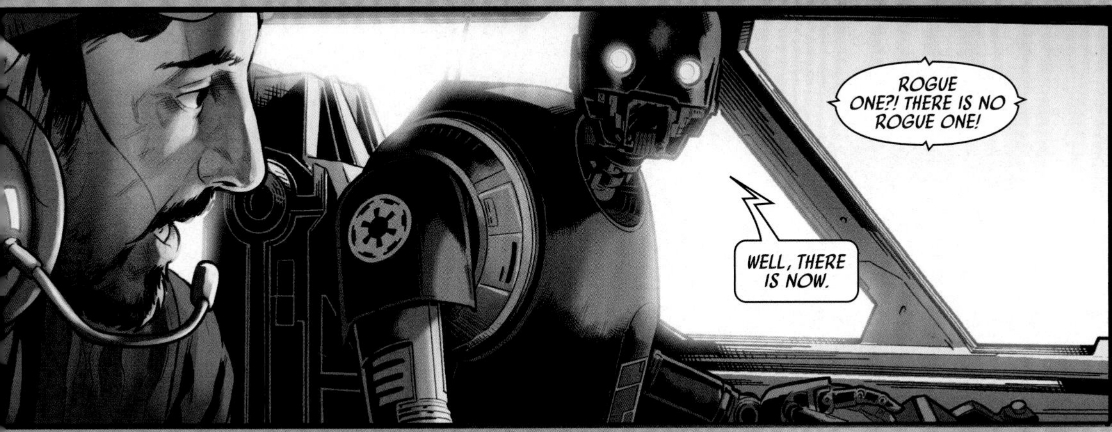
ROGUE ONE?! THERE IS NO ROGUE ONE!
WELL, THERE IS NOW.
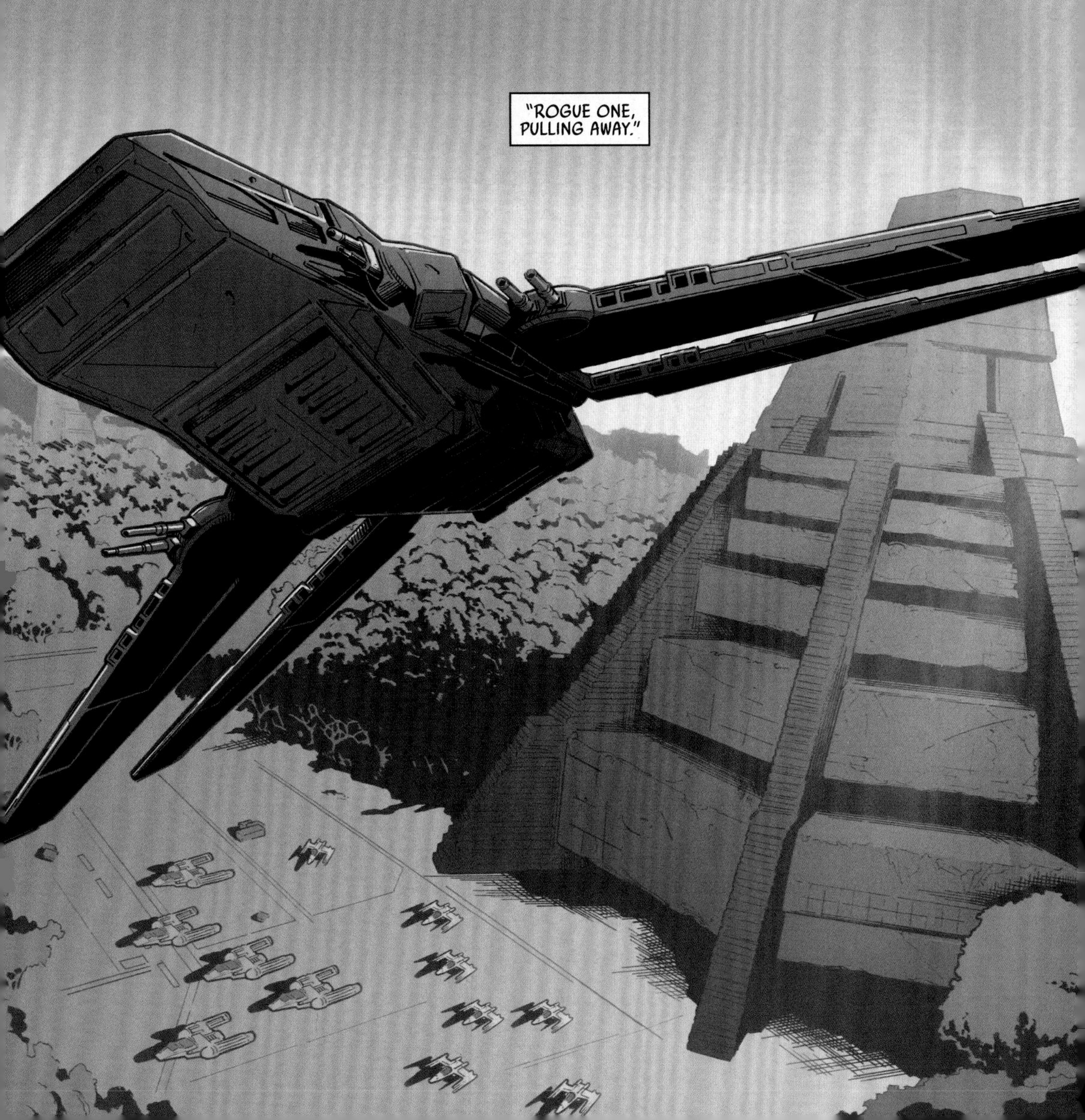
"ROGUE ONE, PULLING AWAY."

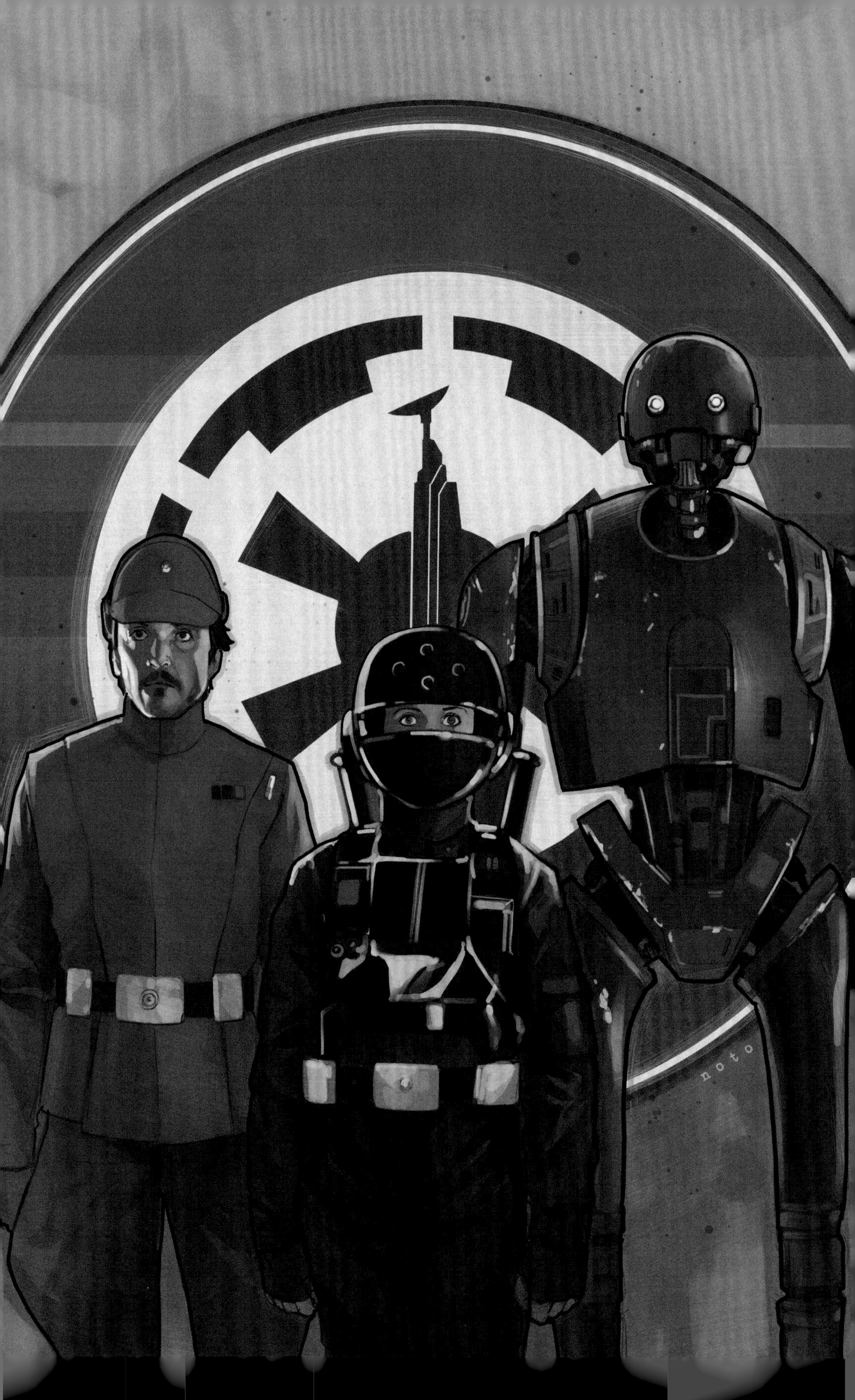
noto

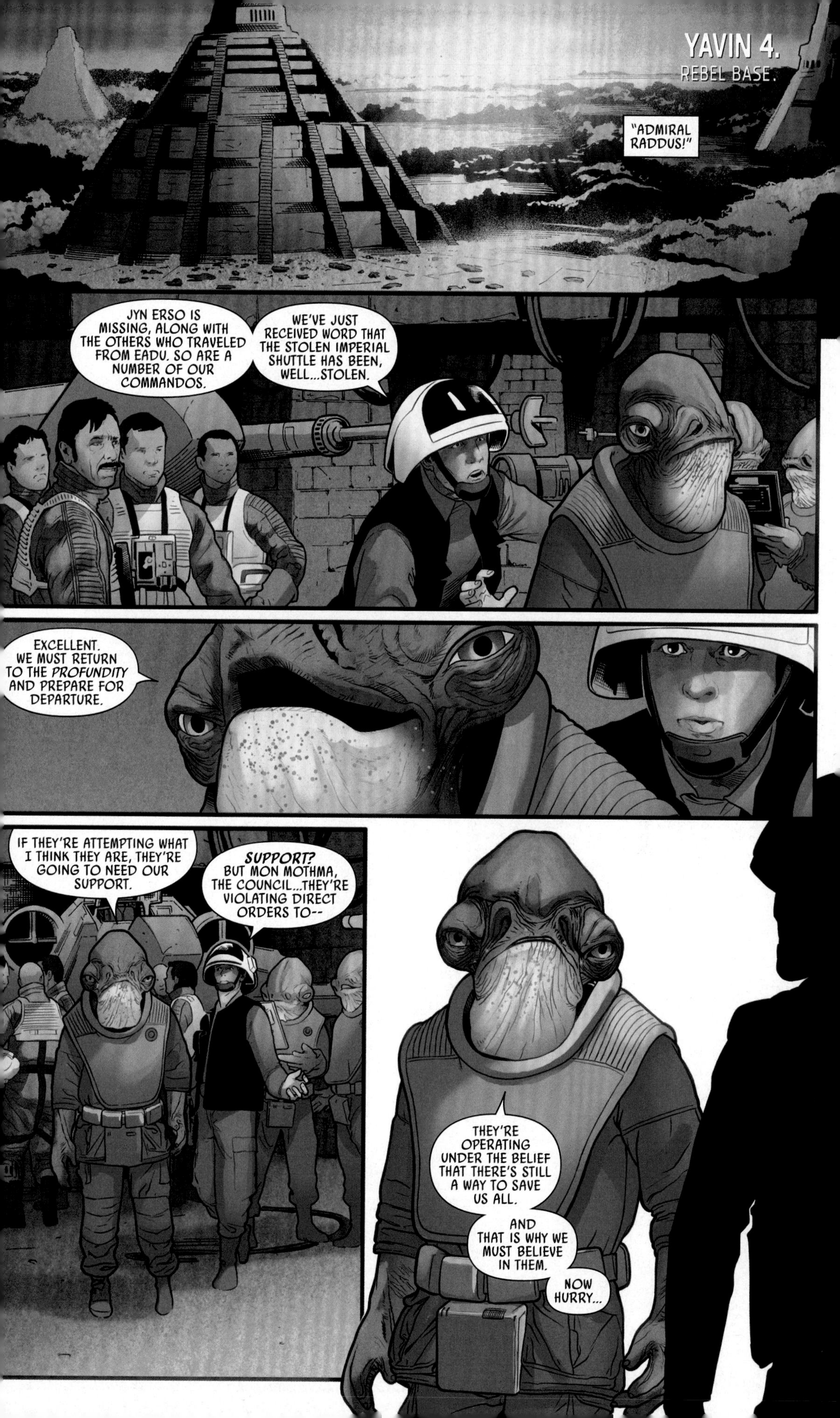
YAVIN 4.
REBEL BASE.
"ADMIRAL RADDUS!"
JYN ERSO IS MISSING, ALONG WITH THE OTHERS WHO TRAVELED FROM EADU. SO ARE A NUMBER OF OUR COMMANDOS.
WE'VE JUST RECEIVED WORD THAT THE STOLEN IMPERIAL SHUTTLE HAS BEEN, WELL...STOLEN.
EXCELLENT. WE MUST RETURN TO THE *PROFUNDITY* AND PREPARE FOR DEPARTURE.
IF THEY'RE ATTEMPTING WHAT I THINK THEY ARE, THEY'RE GOING TO NEED OUR SUPPORT.
SUPPORT? BUT MON MOTHMA, THE COUNCIL...THEY'RE VIOLATING DIRECT ORDERS TO--
THEY'RE OPERATING UNDER THE BELIEF THAT THERE'S STILL A WAY TO SAVE US ALL.
AND THAT IS WHY WE MUST BELIEVE IN THEM.
NOW HURRY...

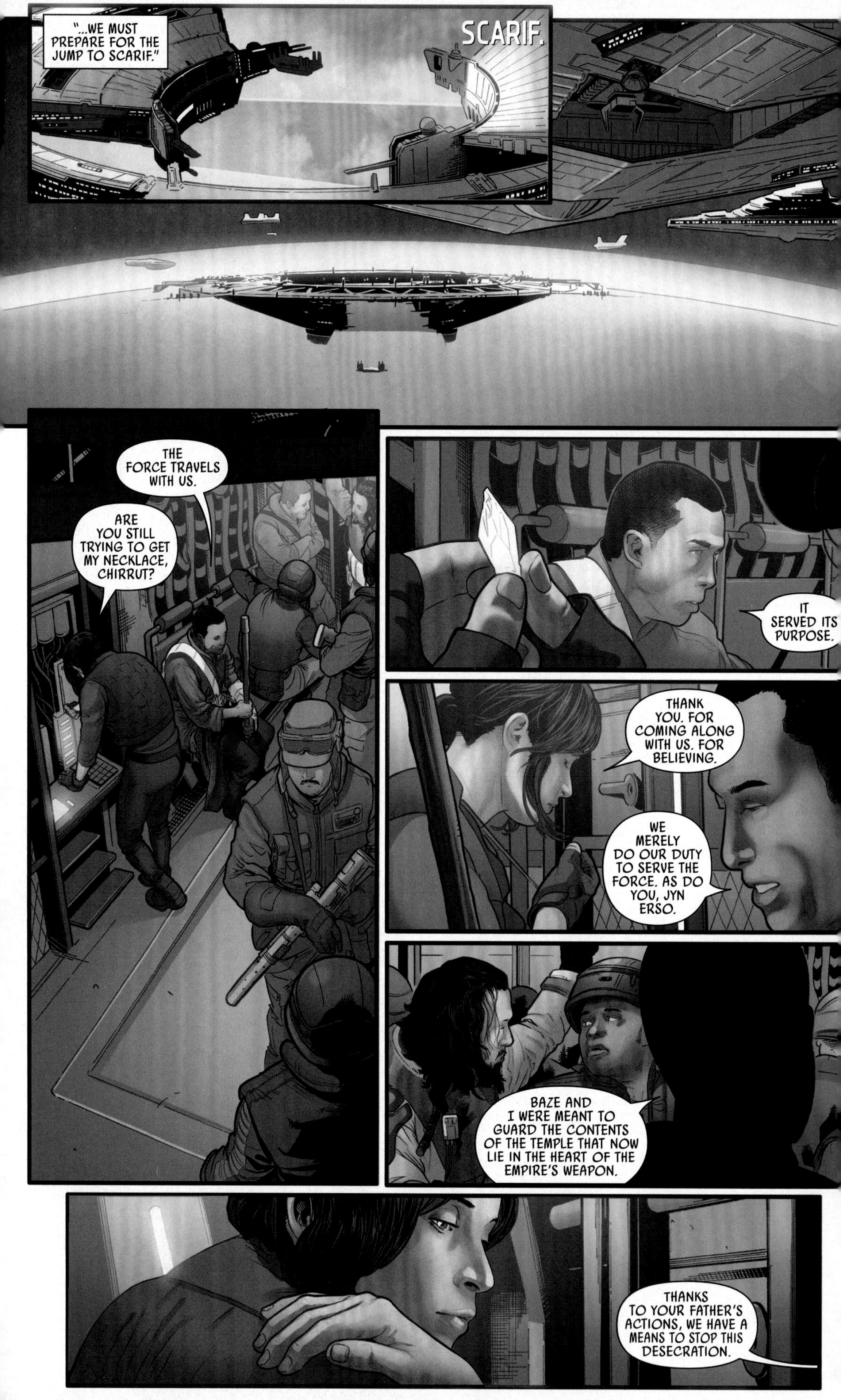
"...WE MUST PREPARE FOR THE JUMP TO SCARIF."
SCARIF.
THE FORCE TRAVELS WITH US.
ARE YOU STILL TRYING TO GET MY NECKLACE, CHIRRUT?
IT SERVED ITS PURPOSE.
THANK YOU. FOR COMING ALONG WITH US. FOR BELIEVING.
WE MERELY DO OUR DUTY TO SERVE THE FORCE. AS DO YOU, JYN ERSO.
BAZE AND I WERE MEANT TO GUARD THE CONTENTS OF THE TEMPLE THAT NOW LIE IN THE HEART OF THE EMPIRE'S WEAPON.
THANKS TO YOUR FATHER'S ACTIONS, WE HAVE A MEANS TO STOP THIS DESECRATION.

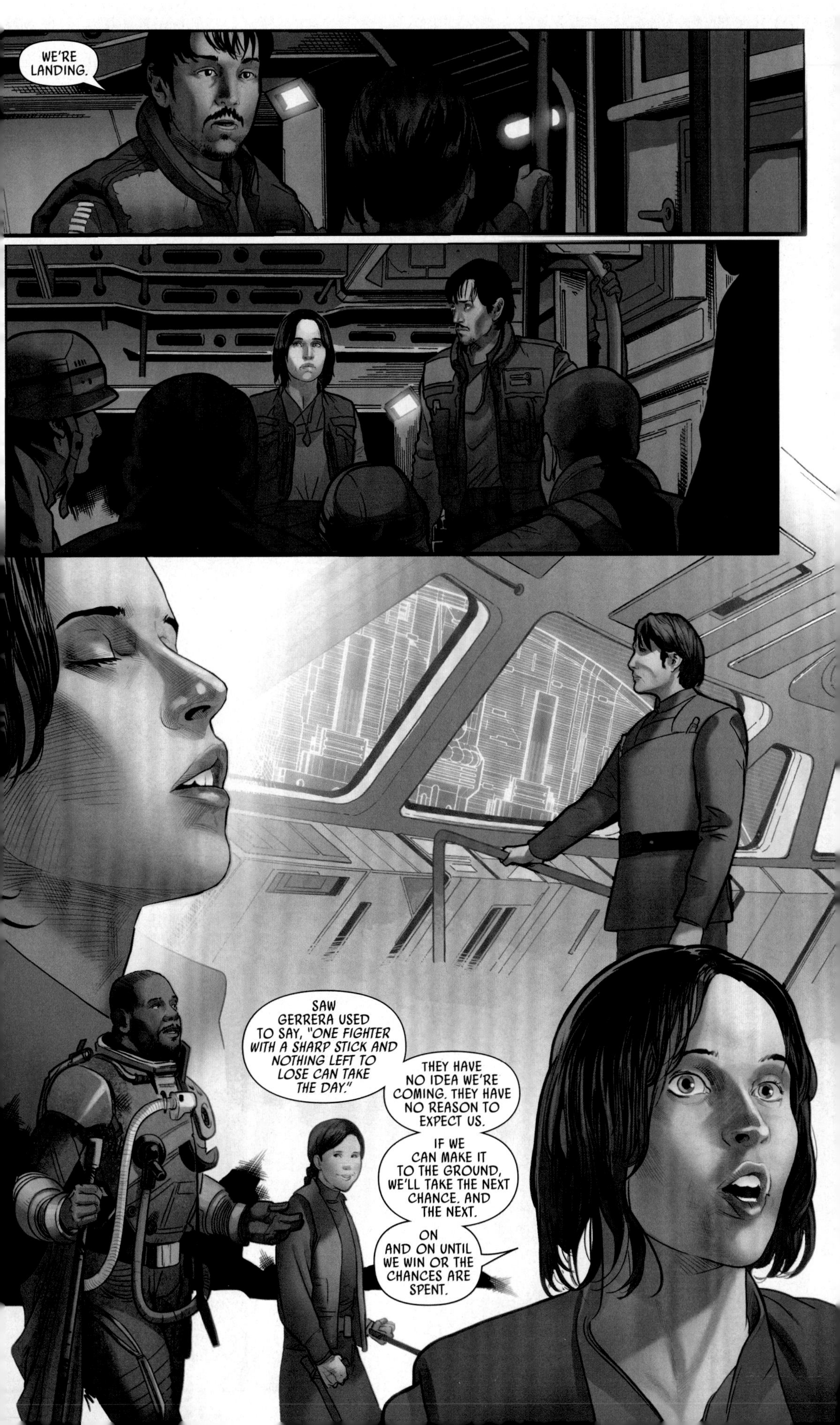
WE'RE LANDING.
SAW GERRERA USED TO SAY, "ONE FIGHTER WITH A SHARP STICK AND NOTHING LEFT TO LOSE CAN TAKE THE DAY."
THEY HAVE NO IDEA WE'RE COMING. THEY HAVE NO REASON TO EXPECT US.
IF WE CAN MAKE IT TO THE GROUND, WE'LL TAKE THE NEXT CHANCE. AND THE NEXT.
ON AND ON UNTIL WE WIN OR THE CHANCES ARE SPENT.

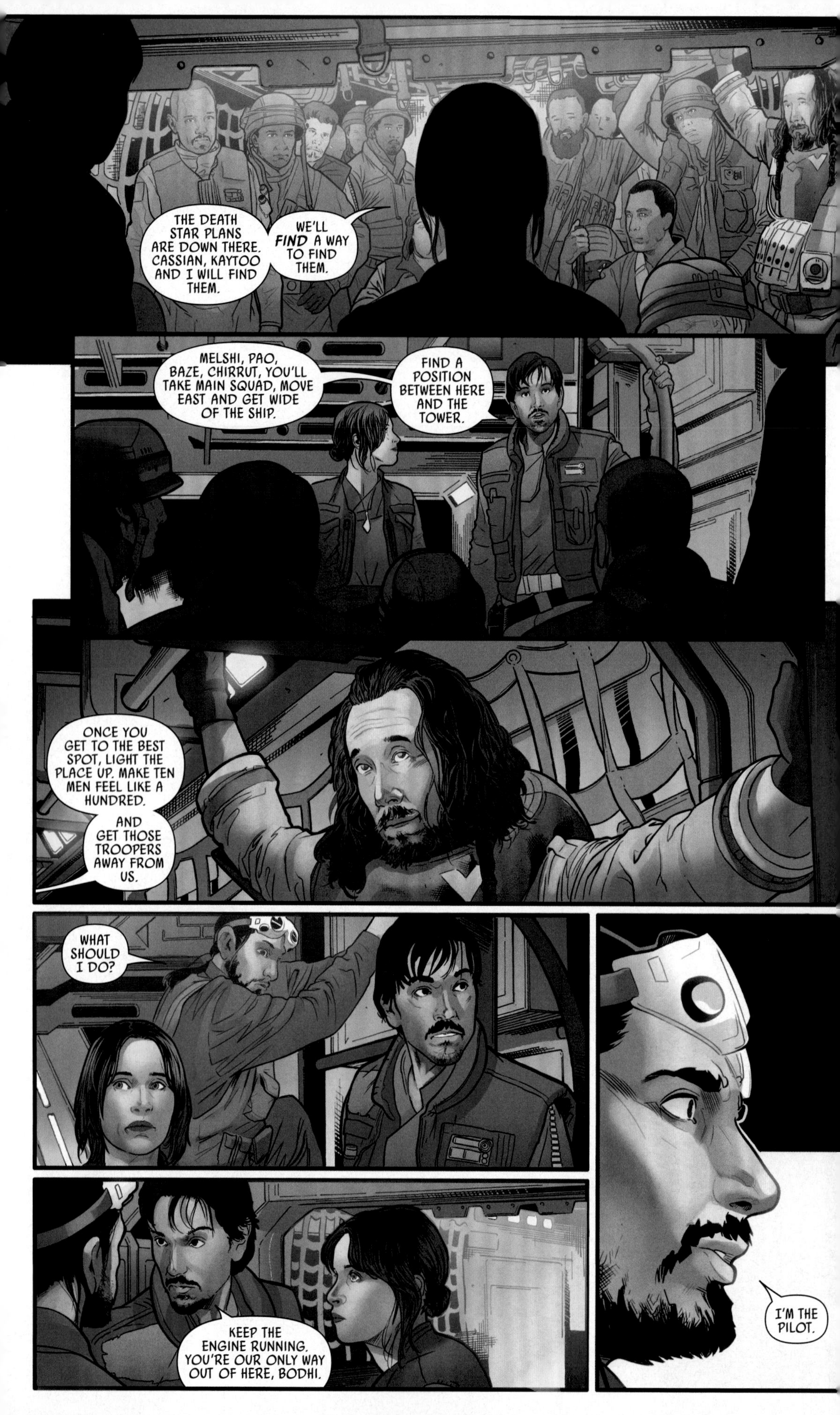
THE DEATH STAR PLANS ARE DOWN THERE. CASSIAN, KAYTOO AND I WILL FIND THEM.
WE'LL FIND A WAY TO FIND THEM.
MELSHI, PAO, BAZE, CHIRRUT, YOU'LL TAKE MAIN SQUAD, MOVE EAST AND GET WIDE OF THE SHIP.
FIND A POSITION BETWEEN HERE AND THE TOWER.
ONCE YOU GET TO THE BEST SPOT, LIGHT THE PLACE UP. MAKE TEN MEN FEEL LIKE A HUNDRED.
AND GET THOSE TROOPERS AWAY FROM US.
WHAT SHOULD I DO?
KEEP THE ENGINE RUNNING. YOU'RE OUR ONLY WAY OUT OF HERE, BODHI.
I'M THE PILOT.

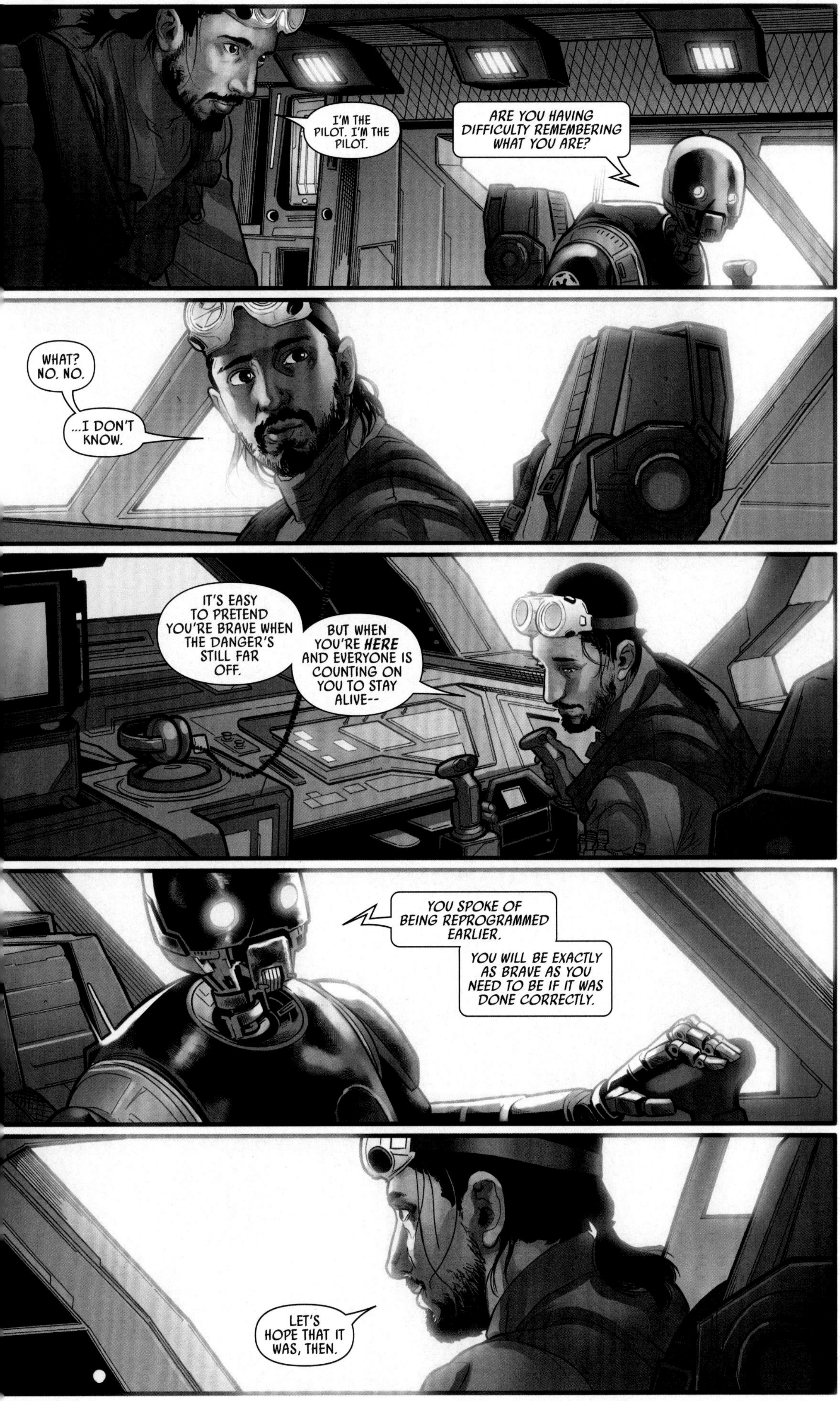

I'M THE PILOT. I'M THE PILOT.
ARE YOU HAVING DIFFICULTY REMEMBERING WHAT YOU ARE?
WHAT? NO. NO.
...I DON'T KNOW.
IT'S EASY TO PRETEND YOU'RE BRAVE WHEN THE DANGER'S STILL FAR OFF.
BUT WHEN YOU'RE *HERE* AND EVERYONE IS COUNTING ON YOU TO STAY ALIVE--
YOU SPOKE OF BEING REPROGRAMMED EARLIER.
YOU WILL BE EXACTLY AS BRAVE AS YOU NEED TO BE IF IT WAS DONE CORRECTLY.
LET'S HOPE THAT IT WAS, THEN.

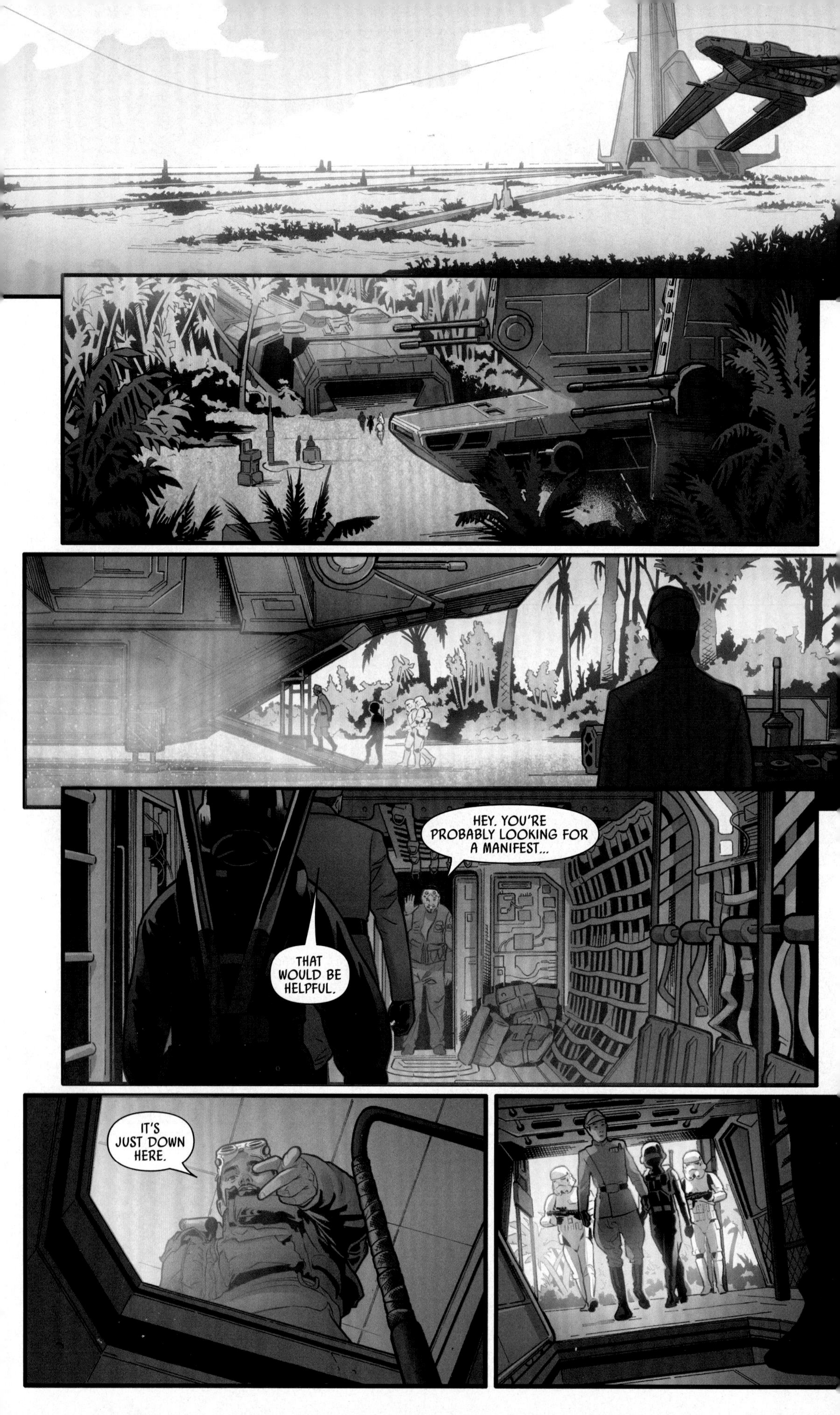
HEY. YOU'RE PROBABLY LOOKING FOR A MANIFEST...
THAT WOULD BE HELPFUL.
IT'S JUST DOWN HERE.

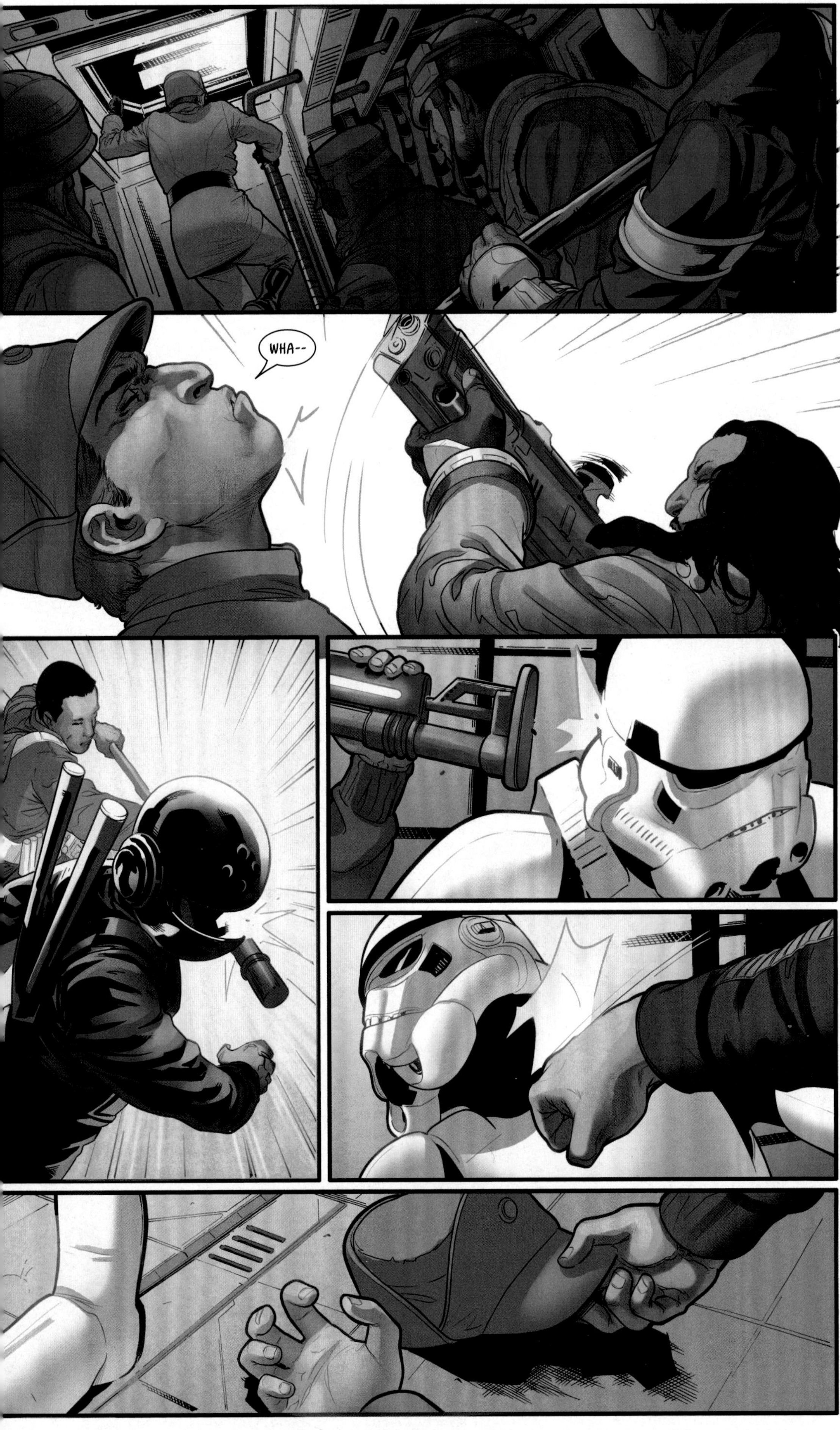
WHA--

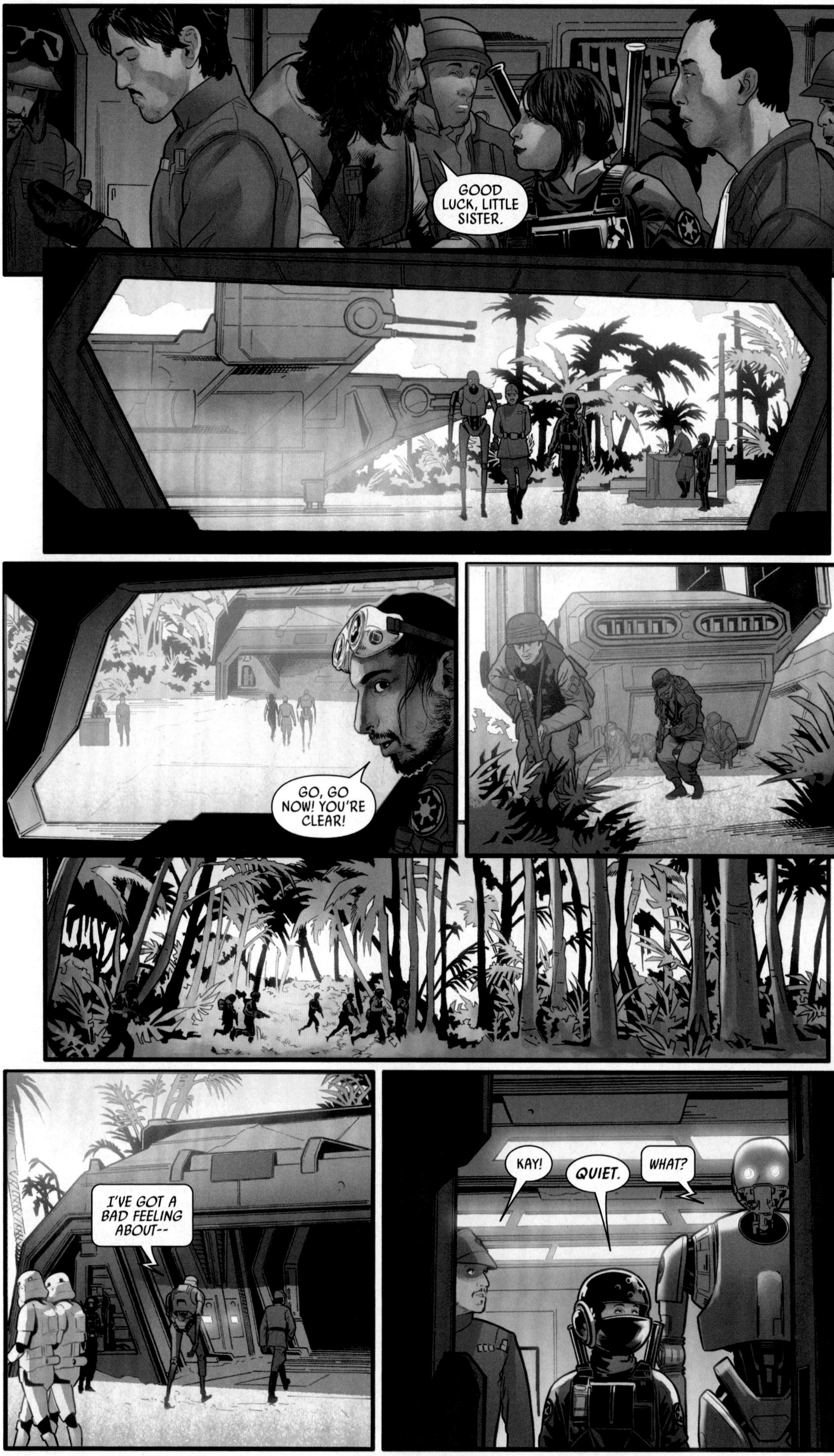

GOOD LUCK, LITTLE SISTER.
GO, GO NOW! YOU'RE CLEAR!
I'VE GOT A BAD FEELING ABOUT--
KAY!
QUIET.
WHAT?

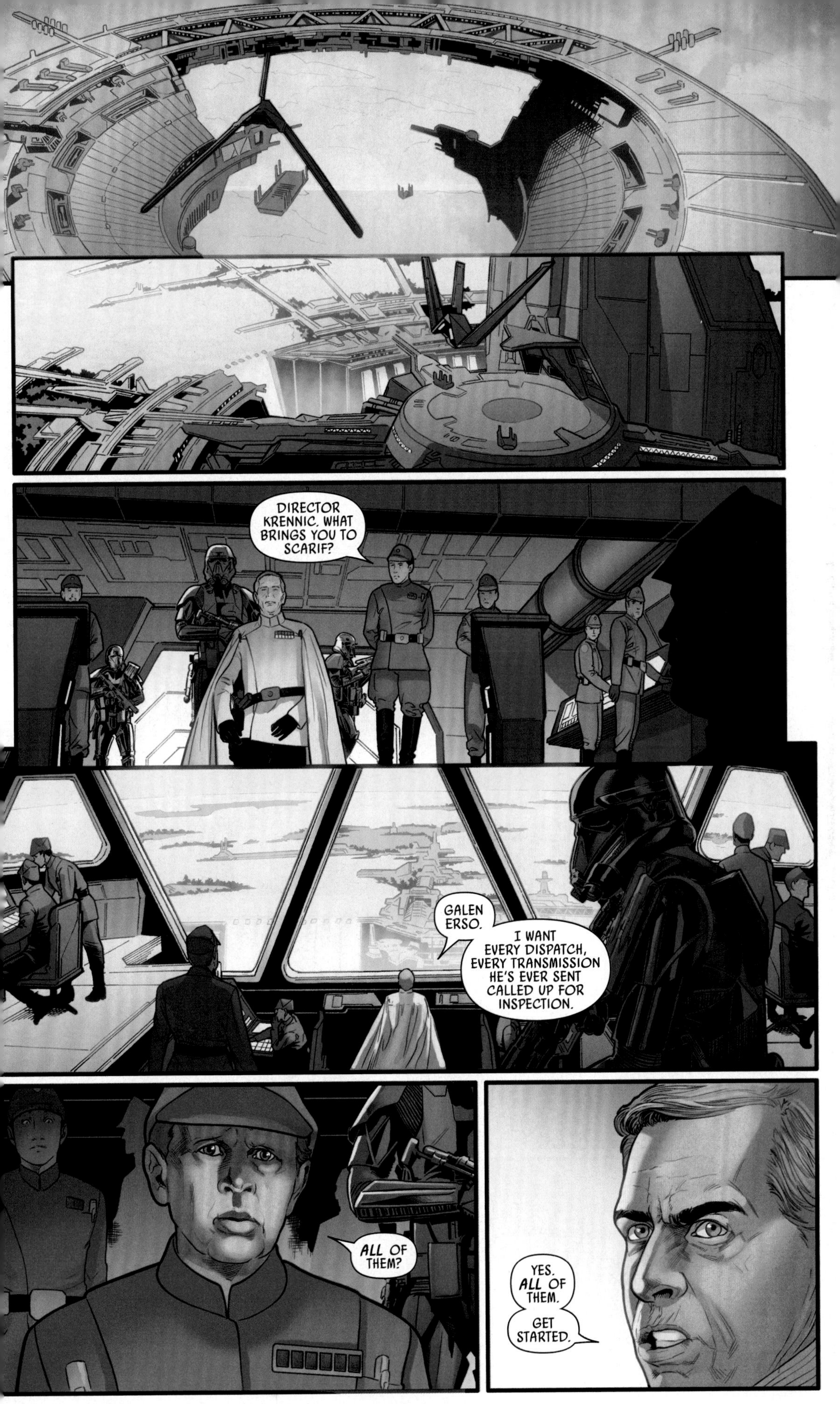
DIRECTOR KRENNIC. WHAT BRINGS YOU TO SCARIF?
GALEN ERSO.
I WANT EVERY DISPATCH, EVERY TRANSMISSION HE'S EVER SENT CALLED UP FOR INSPECTION.
ALL OF THEM?
YES. ALL OF THEM.
GET STARTED.

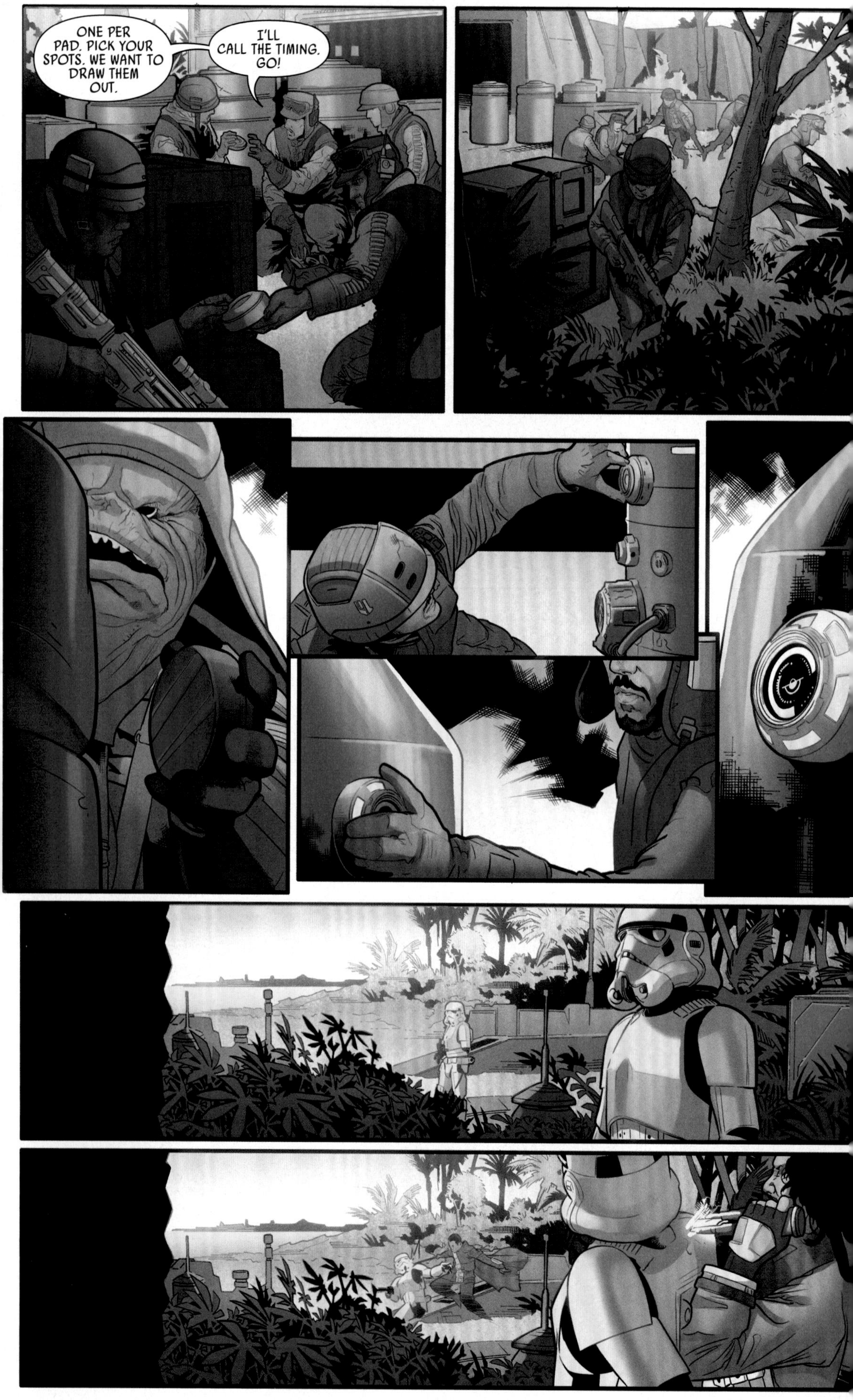
ONE PER PAD. PICK YOUR SPOTS. WE WANT TO DRAW THEM OUT.
I'LL CALL THE TIMING. GO!

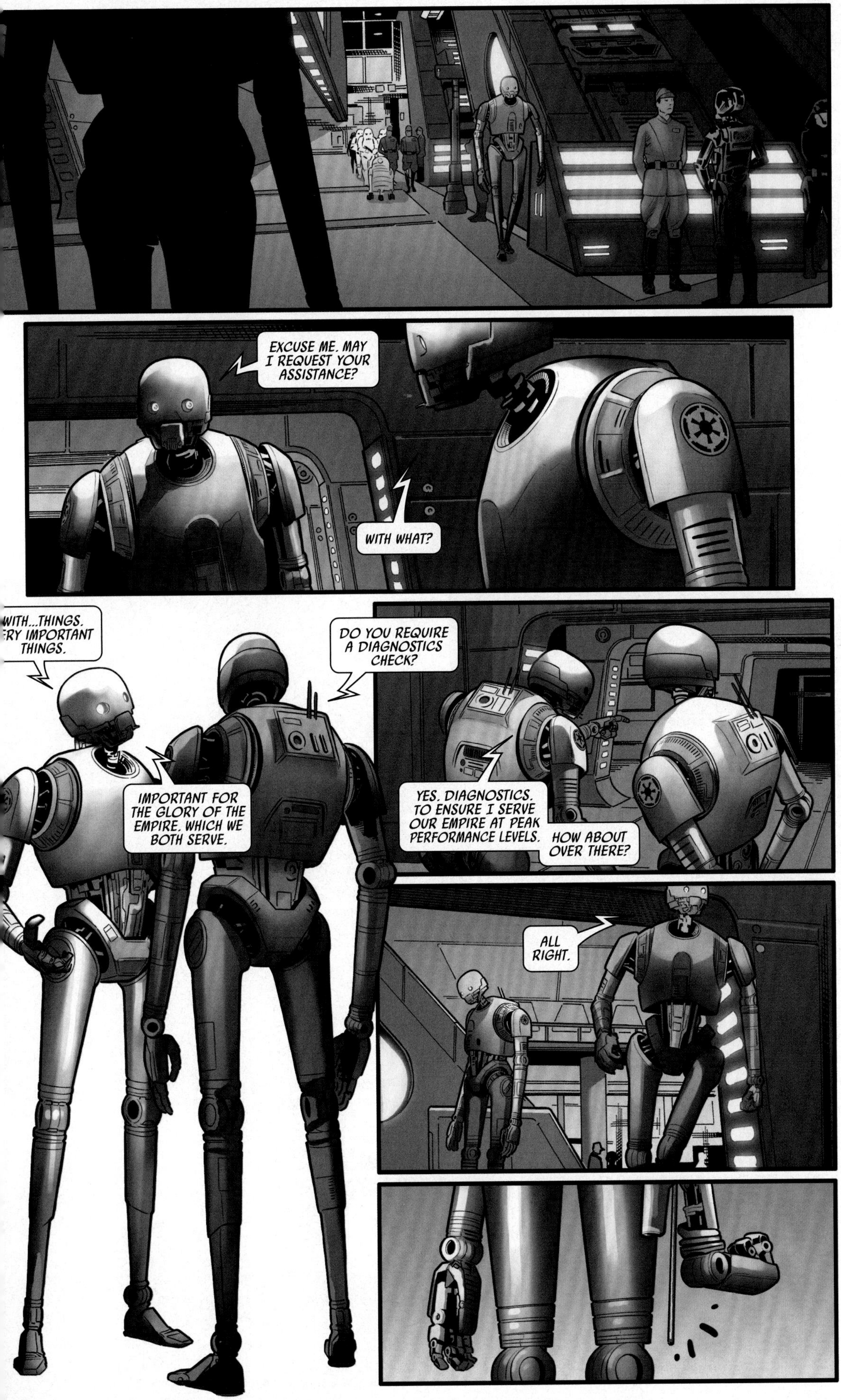
EXCUSE ME. MAY I REQUEST YOUR ASSISTANCE?
WITH WHAT?
WITH...THINGS. ERY IMPORTANT THINGS.
DO YOU REQUIRE A DIAGNOSTICS CHECK?
IMPORTANT FOR THE GLORY OF THE EMPIRE. WHICH WE BOTH SERVE.
YES. DIAGNOSTICS. TO ENSURE I SERVE OUR EMPIRE AT PEAK PERFORMANCE LEVELS.
HOW ABOUT OVER THERE?
ALL RIGHT.

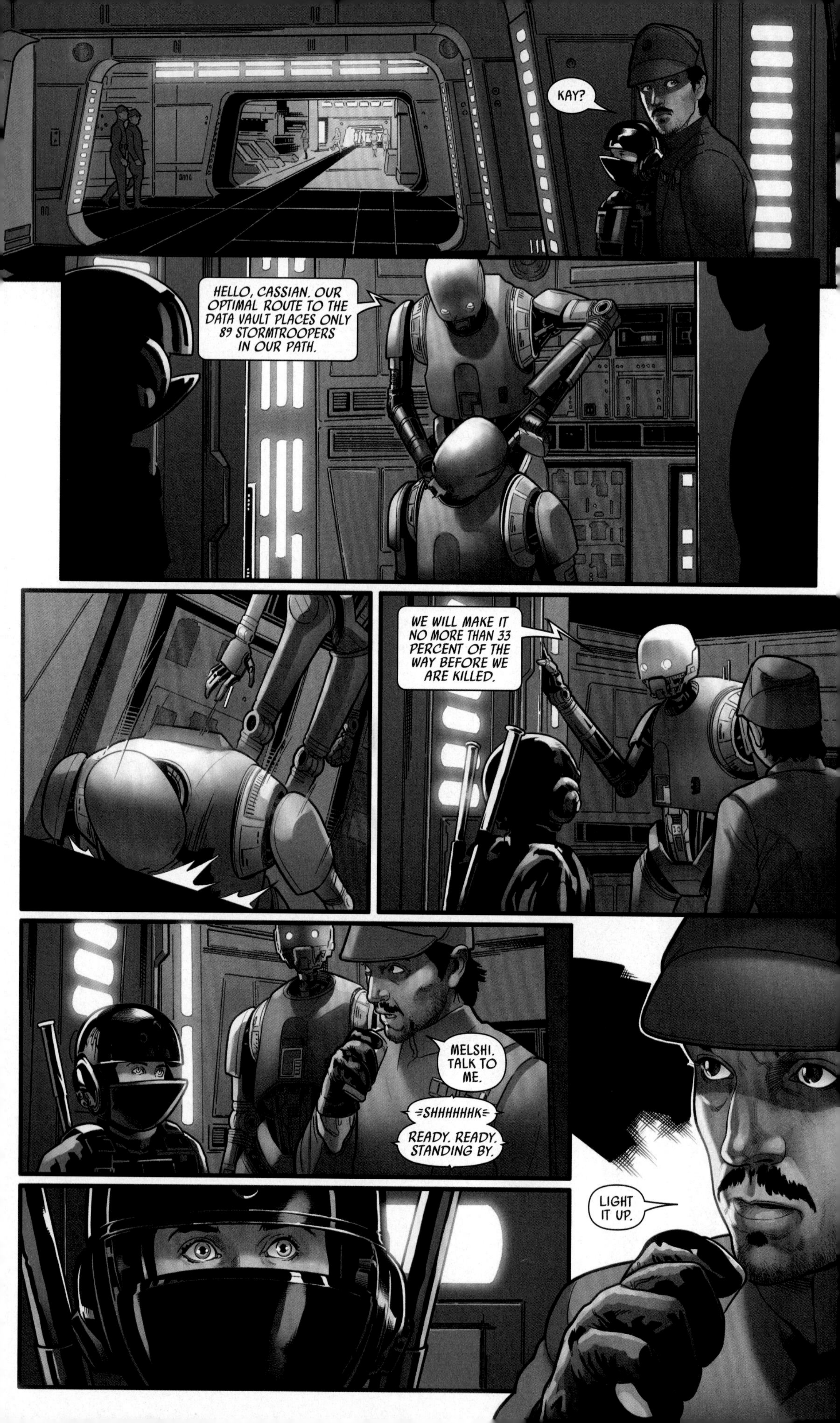
KAY?
HELLO, CASSIAN. OUR OPTIMAL ROUTE TO THE DATA VAULT PLACES ONLY 89 STORMTROOPERS IN OUR PATH.
WE WILL MAKE IT NO MORE THAN 33 PERCENT OF THE WAY BEFORE WE ARE KILLED.
MELSHI, TALK TO ME.
SHHHHHHK
READY. READY. STANDING BY.
LIGHT IT UP.

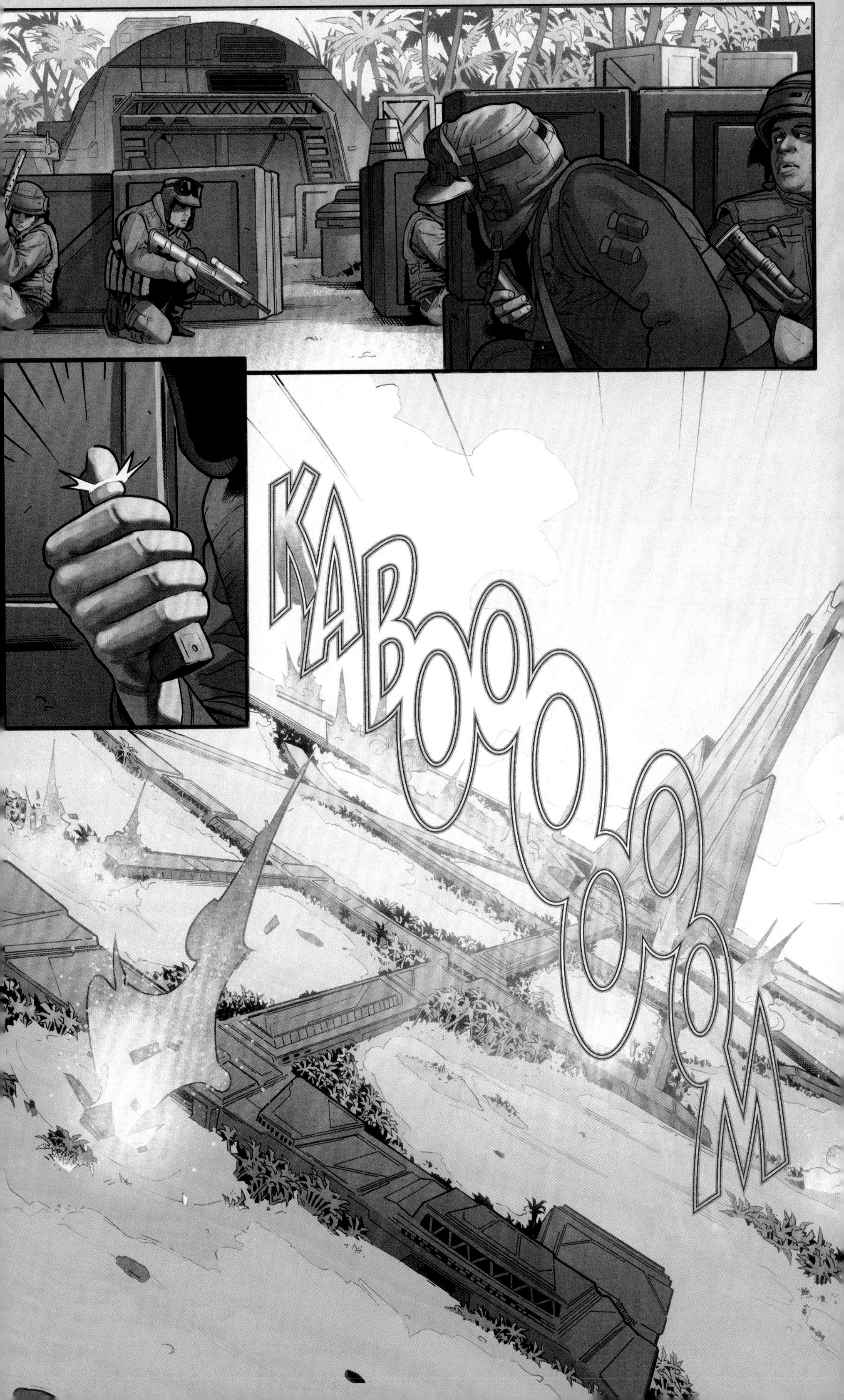
KABOOOOOOOOM

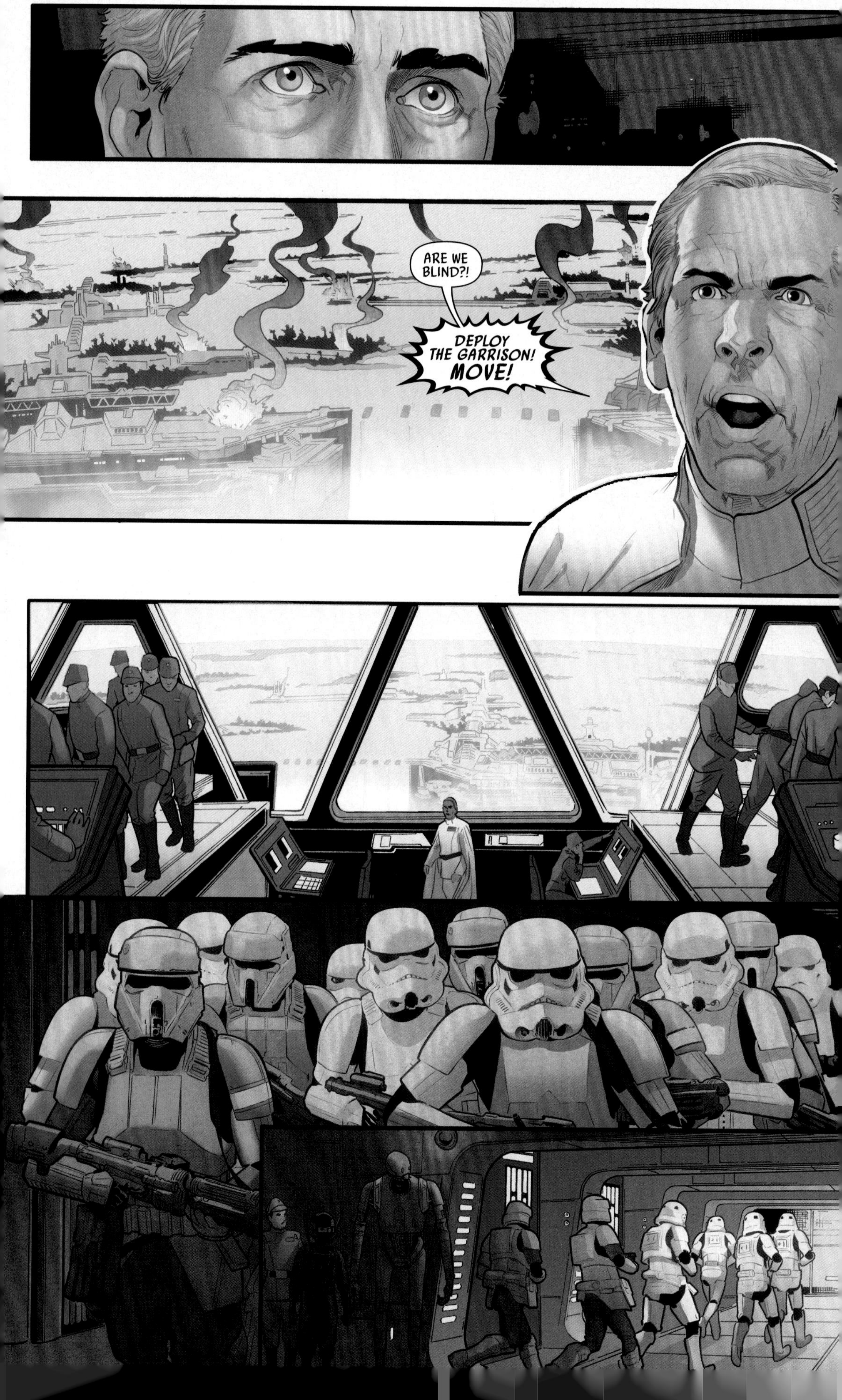
ARE WE BLIND?!
DEPLOY THE GARRISON! MOVE!

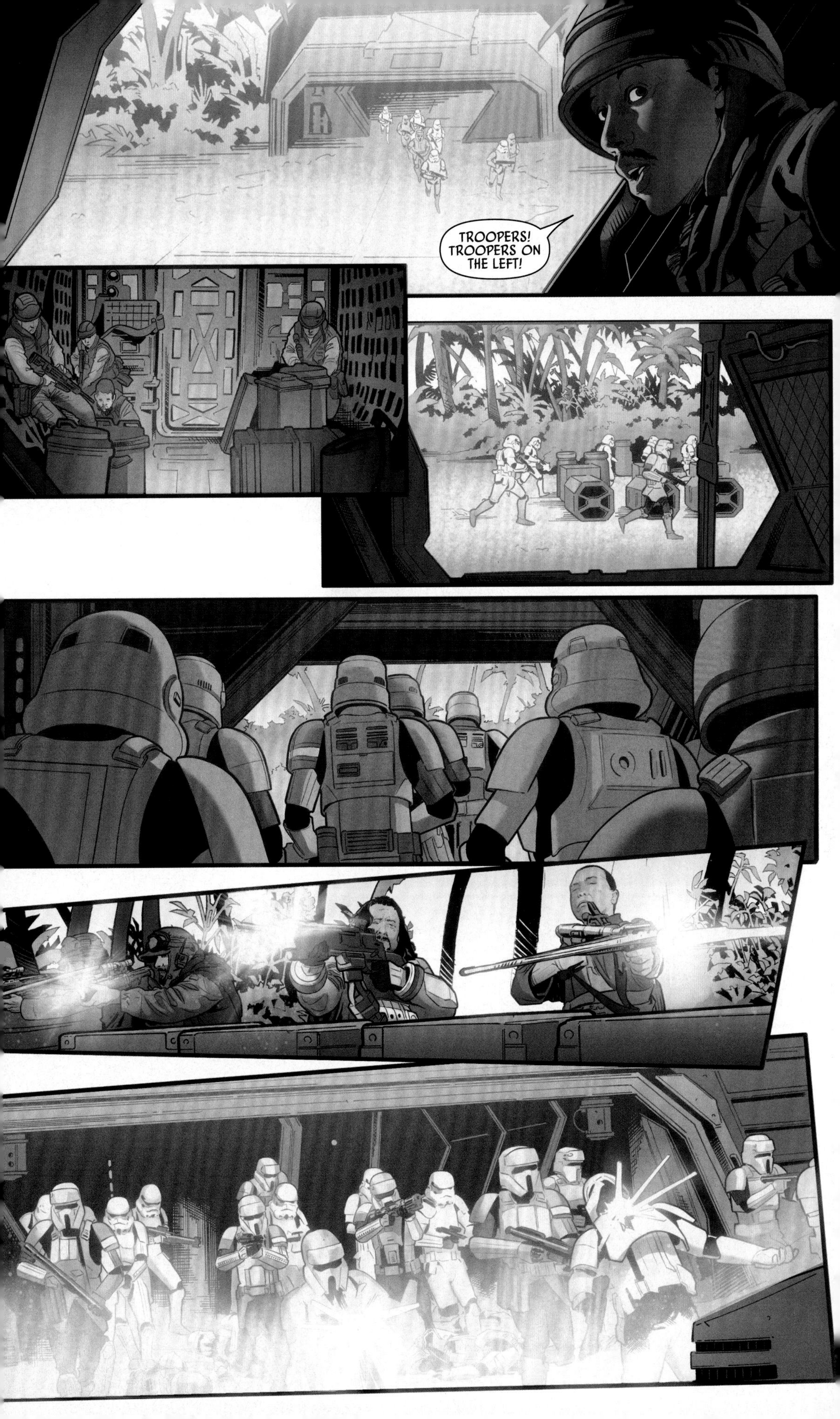
TROOPERS! TROOPERS ON THE LEFT!

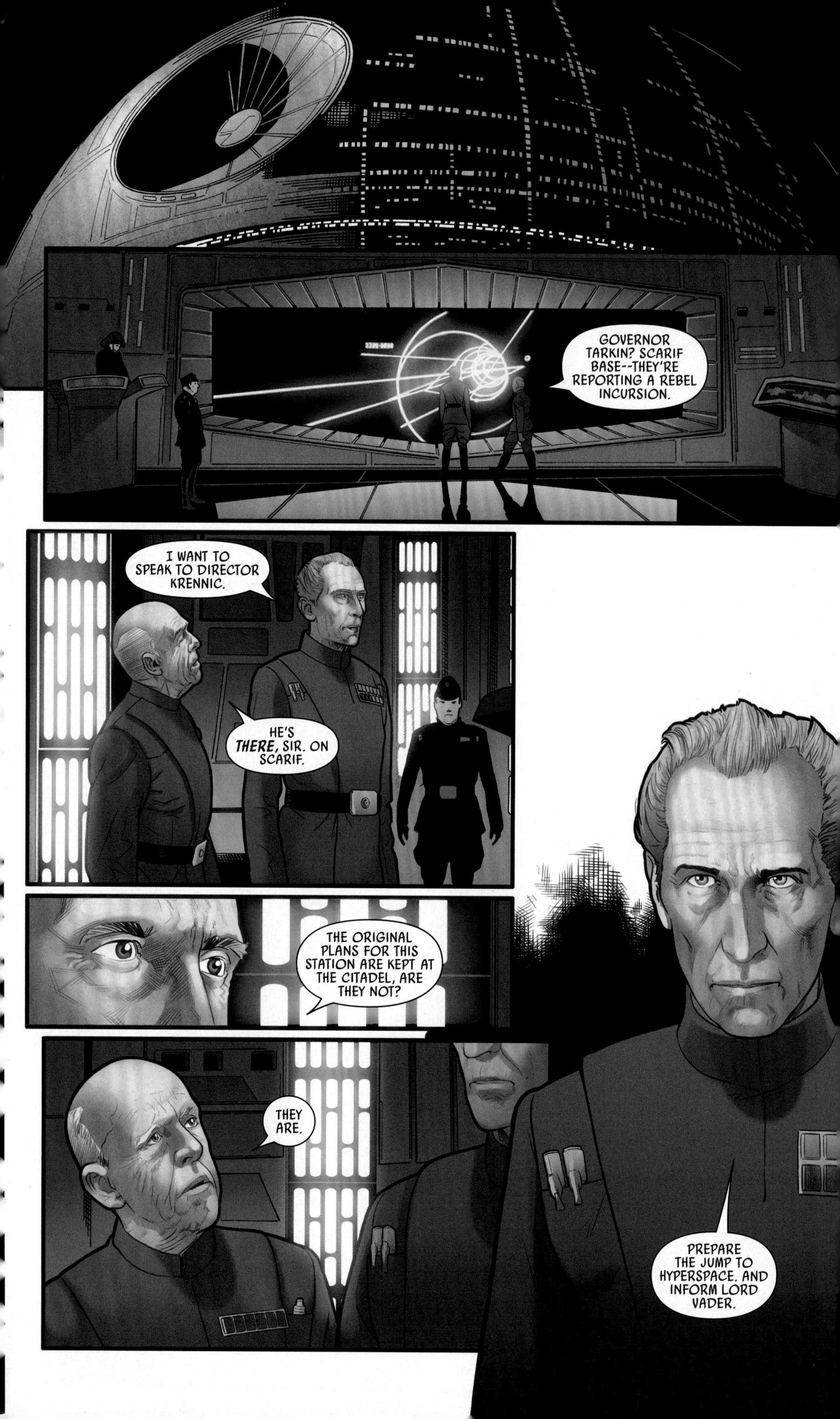
GOVERNOR TARKIN? SCARIF BASE--THEY'RE REPORTING A REBEL INCURSION.
I WANT TO SPEAK TO DIRECTOR KRENNIC.
HE'S THERE, SIR. ON SCARIF.
THE ORIGINAL PLANS FOR THIS STATION ARE KEPT AT THE CITADEL, ARE THEY NOT?
THEY ARE.
PREPARE THE JUMP TO HYPERSPACE. AND INFORM LORD VADER.

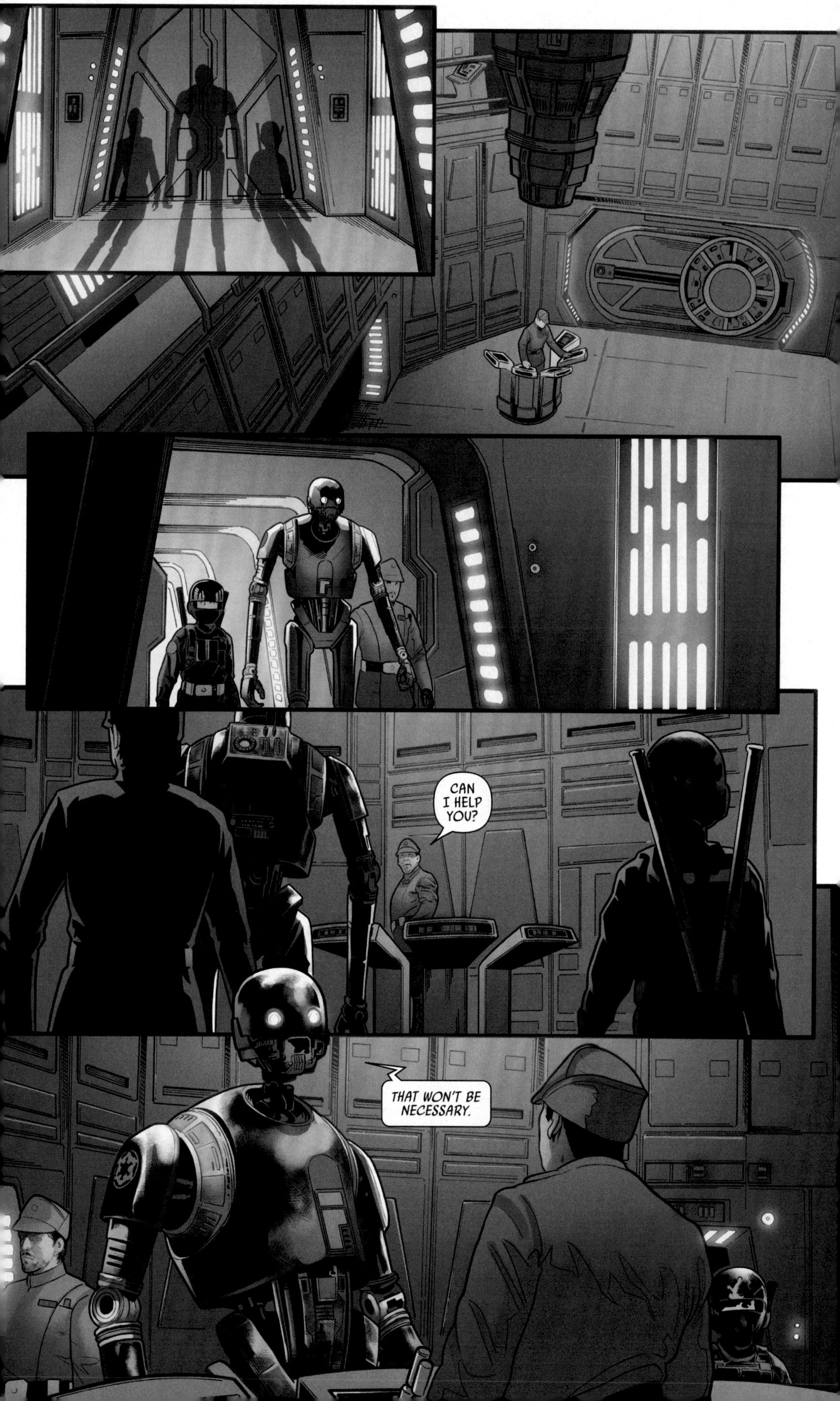
CAN I HELP YOU?
THAT WON'T BE NECESSARY.

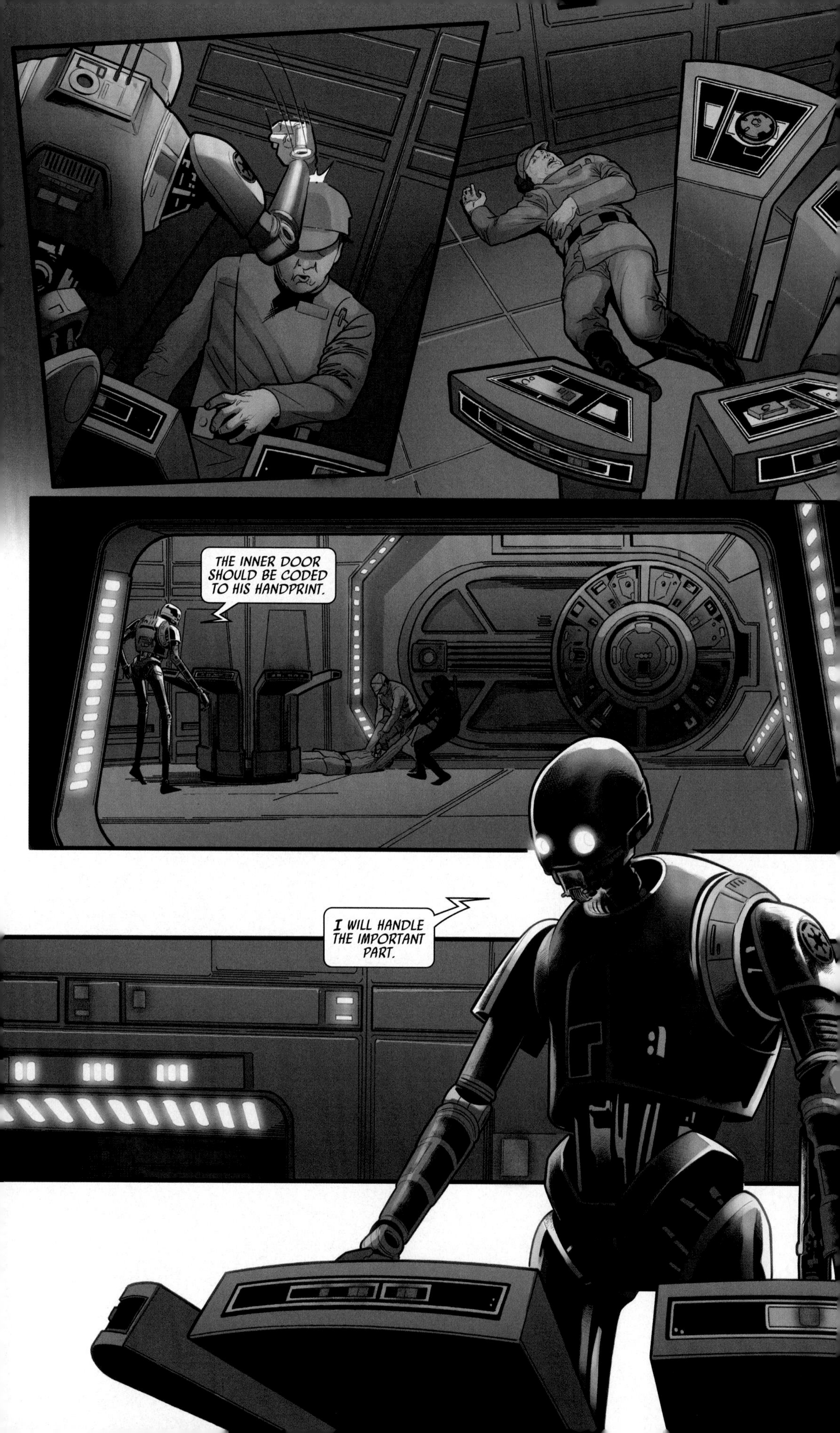
THE INNER DOOR SHOULD BE CODED TO HIS HANDPRINT.
I WILL HANDLE THE IMPORTANT PART.

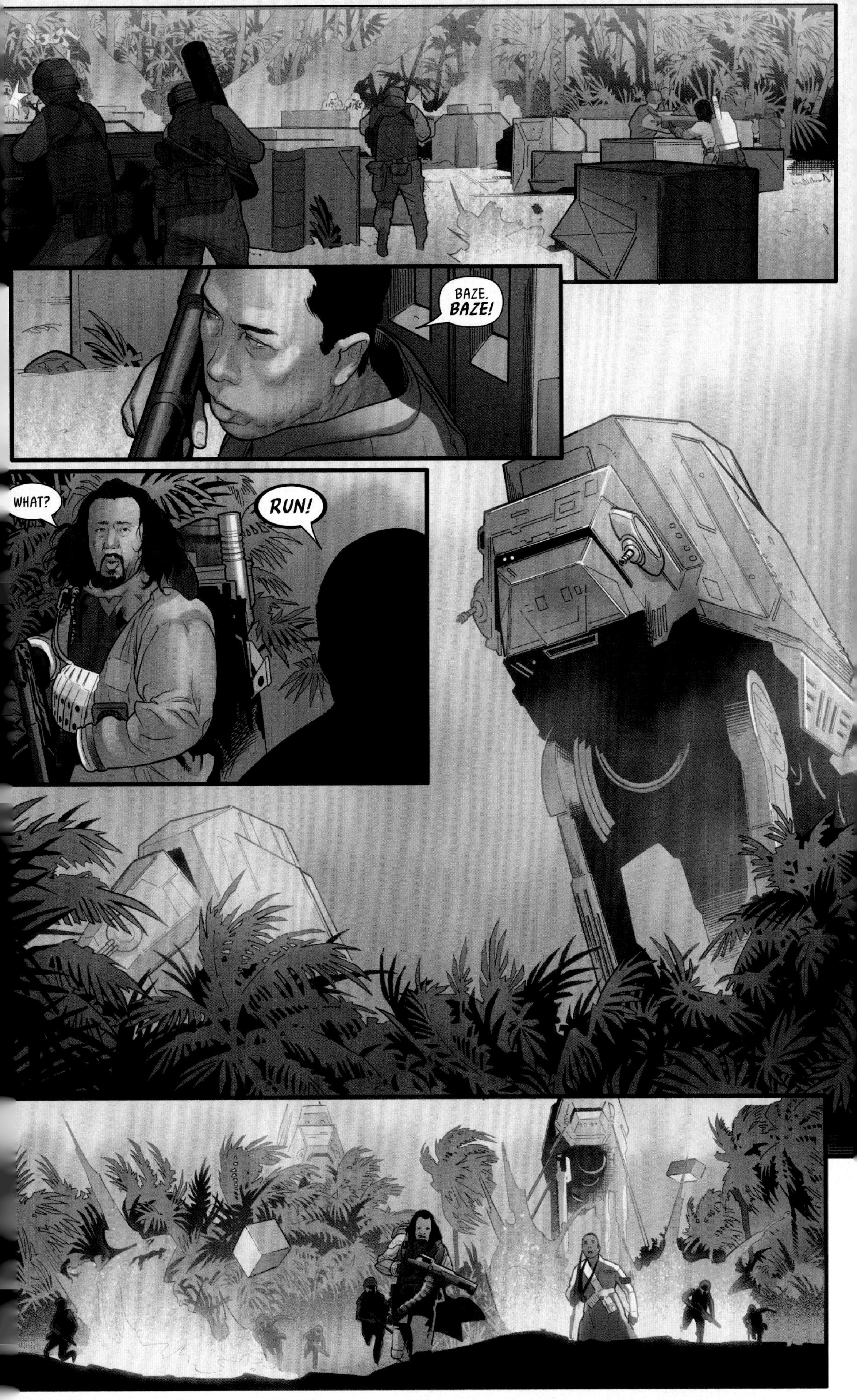

BAZE.
BAZE!
WHAT?
RUN!

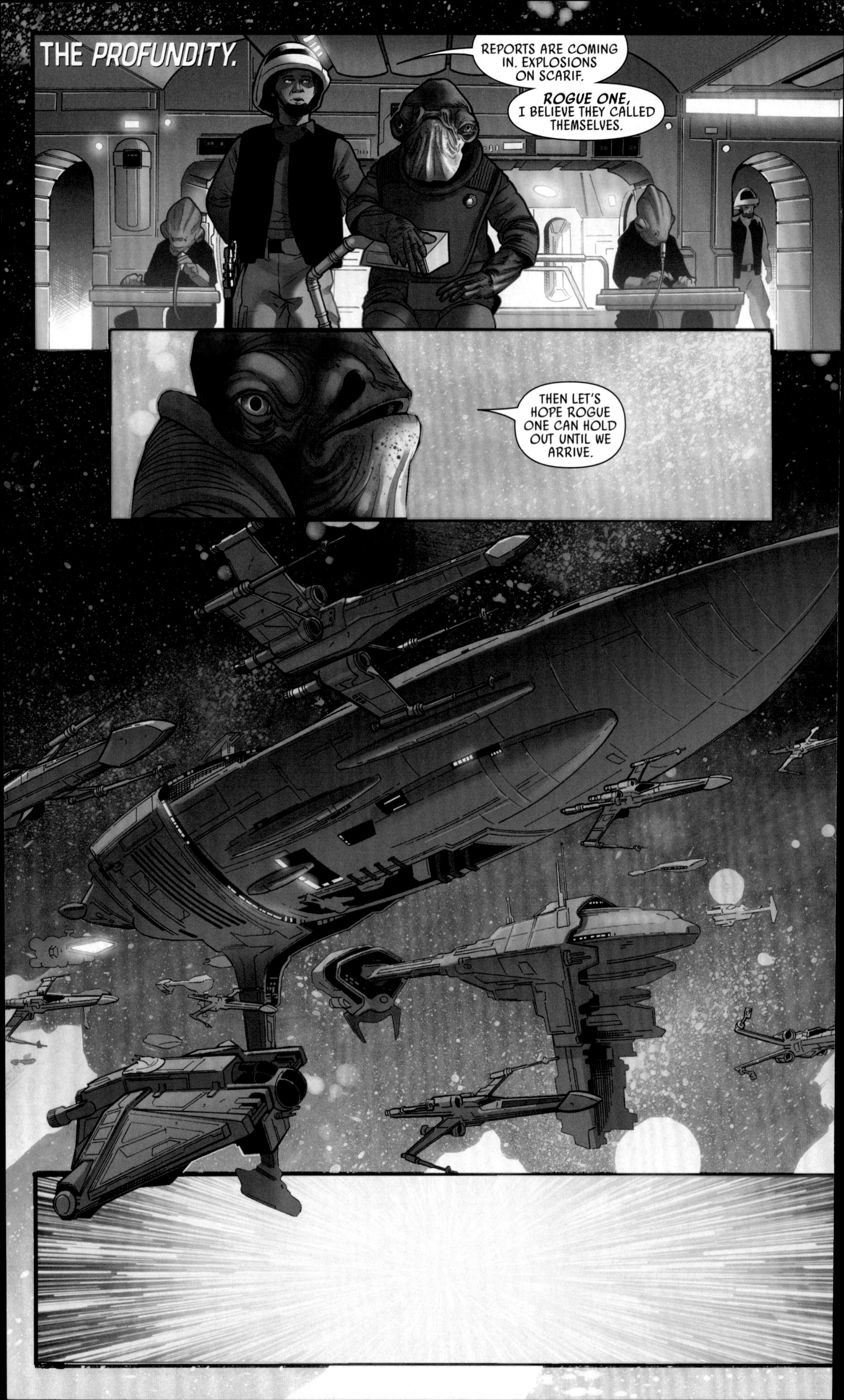
THE PROFUNDITY.
REPORTS ARE COMING IN. EXPLOSIONS ON SCARIF.
ROGUE ONE, I BELIEVE THEY CALLED THEMSELVES.
THEN LET'S HOPE ROGUE ONE CAN HOLD OUT UNTIL WE ARRIVE.

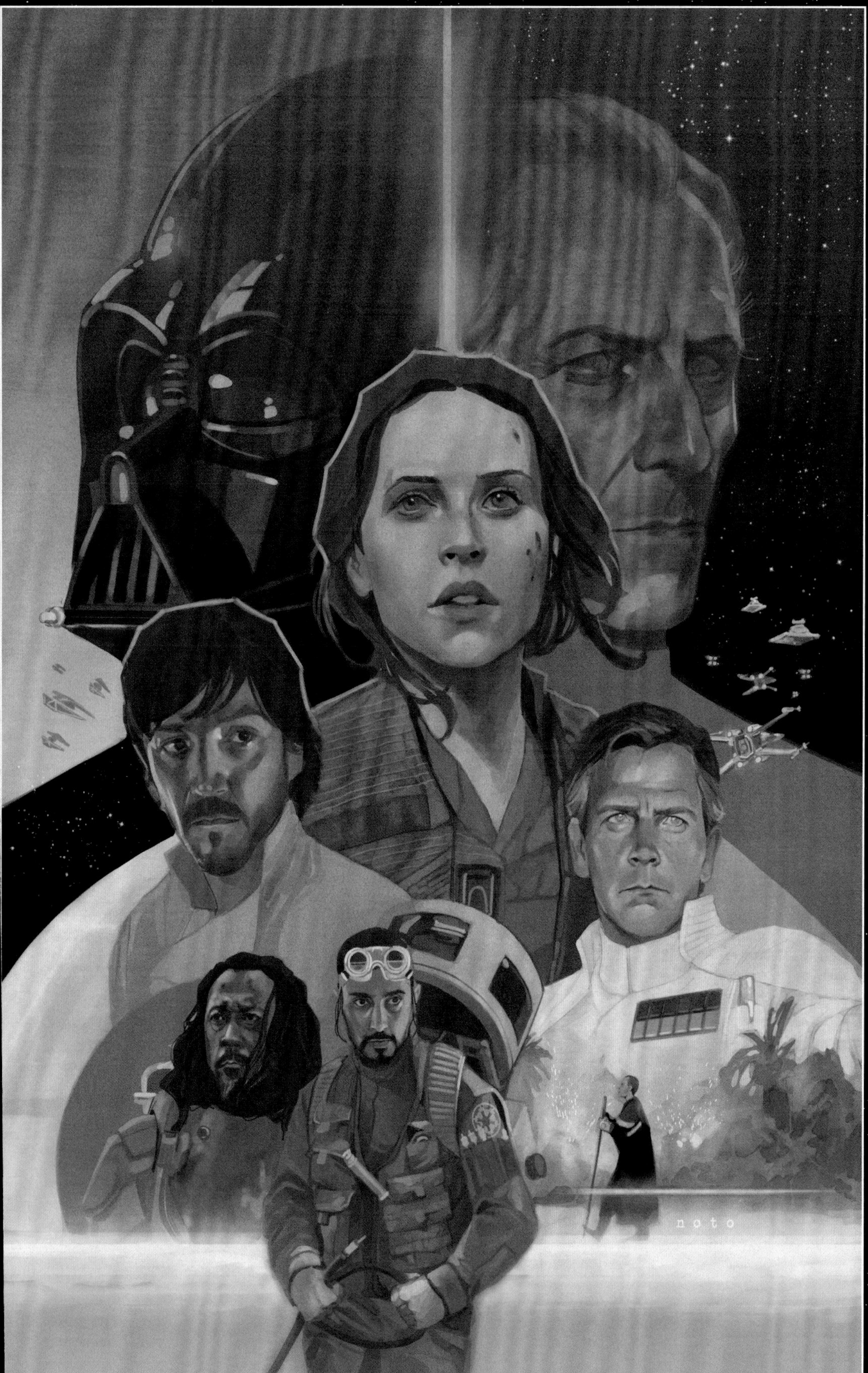
noto

ROGUE ONE #6

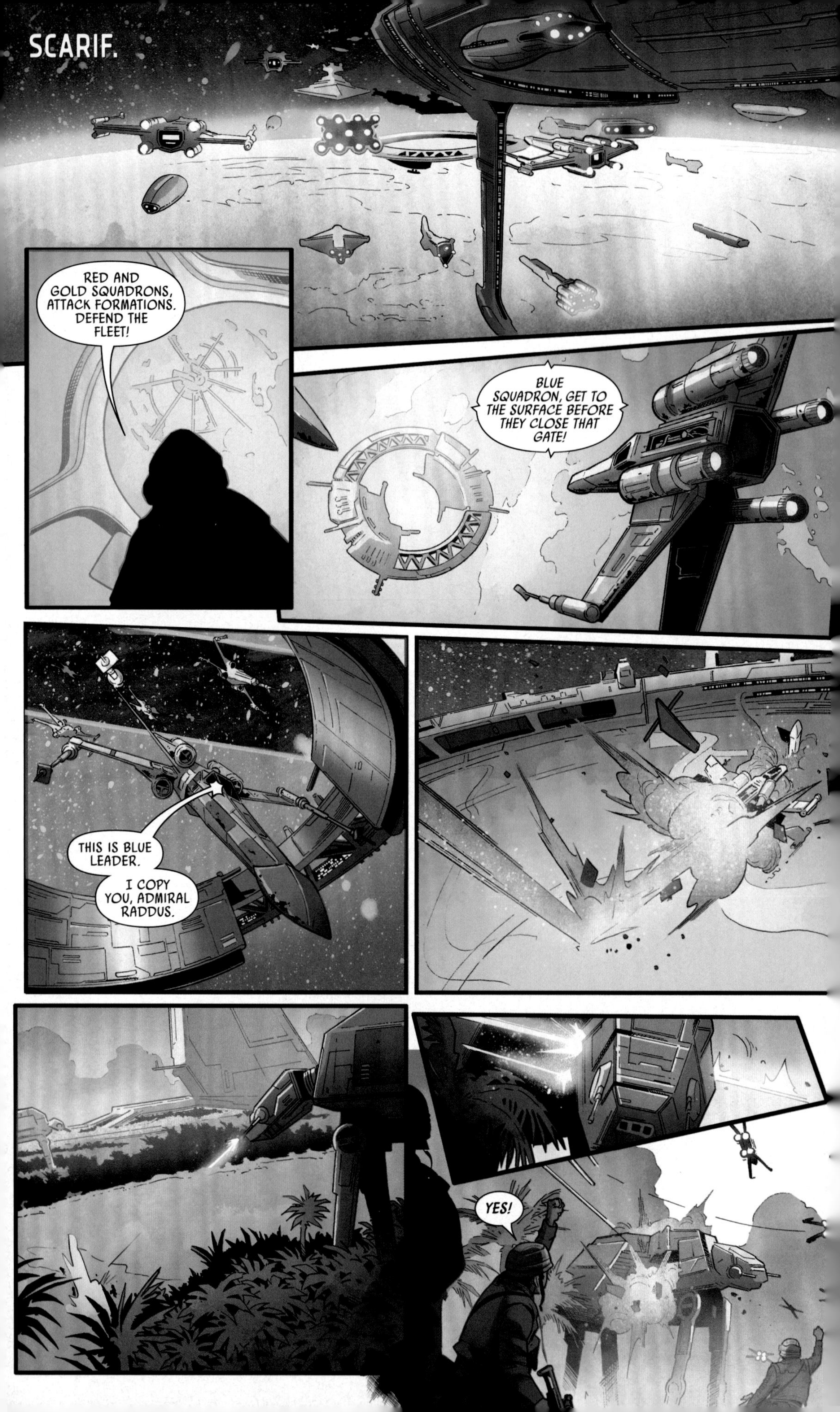
SCARIF.
RED AND GOLD SQUADRONS, ATTACK FORMATIONS. DEFEND THE FLEET!
BLUE SQUADRON, GET TO THE SURFACE BEFORE THEY CLOSE THAT GATE!
THIS IS BLUE LEADER.
I COPY YOU, ADMIRAL RADDUS.
YES!

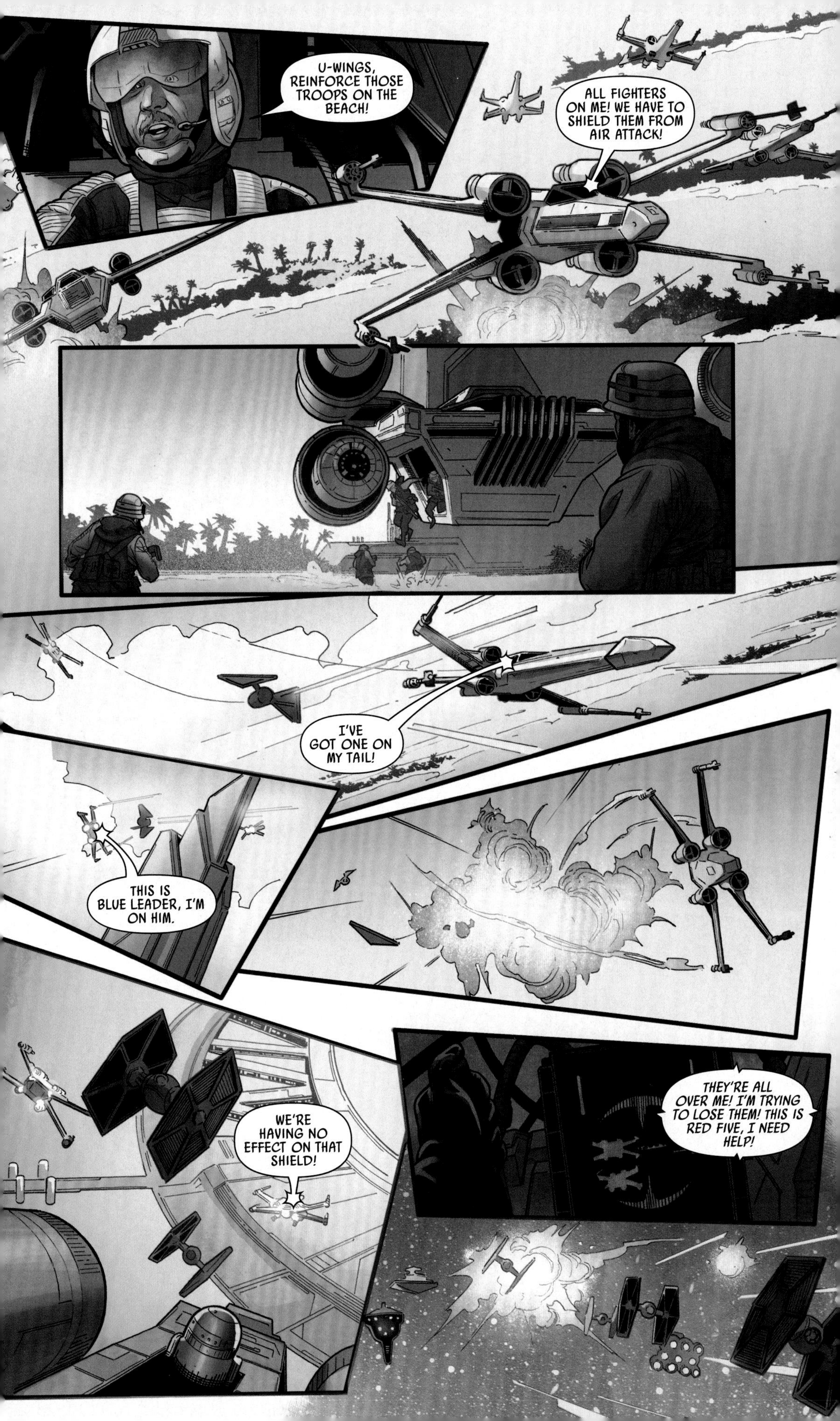
U-WINGS, REINFORCE THOSE TROOPS ON THE BEACH!
ALL FIGHTERS ON ME! WE HAVE TO SHIELD THEM FROM AIR ATTACK!
I'VE GOT ONE ON MY TAIL!
THIS IS BLUE LEADER, I'M ON HIM.
WE'RE HAVING NO EFFECT ON THAT SHIELD!
THEY'RE ALL OVER ME! I'M TRYING TO LOSE THEM! THIS IS RED FIVE, I NEED HELP!

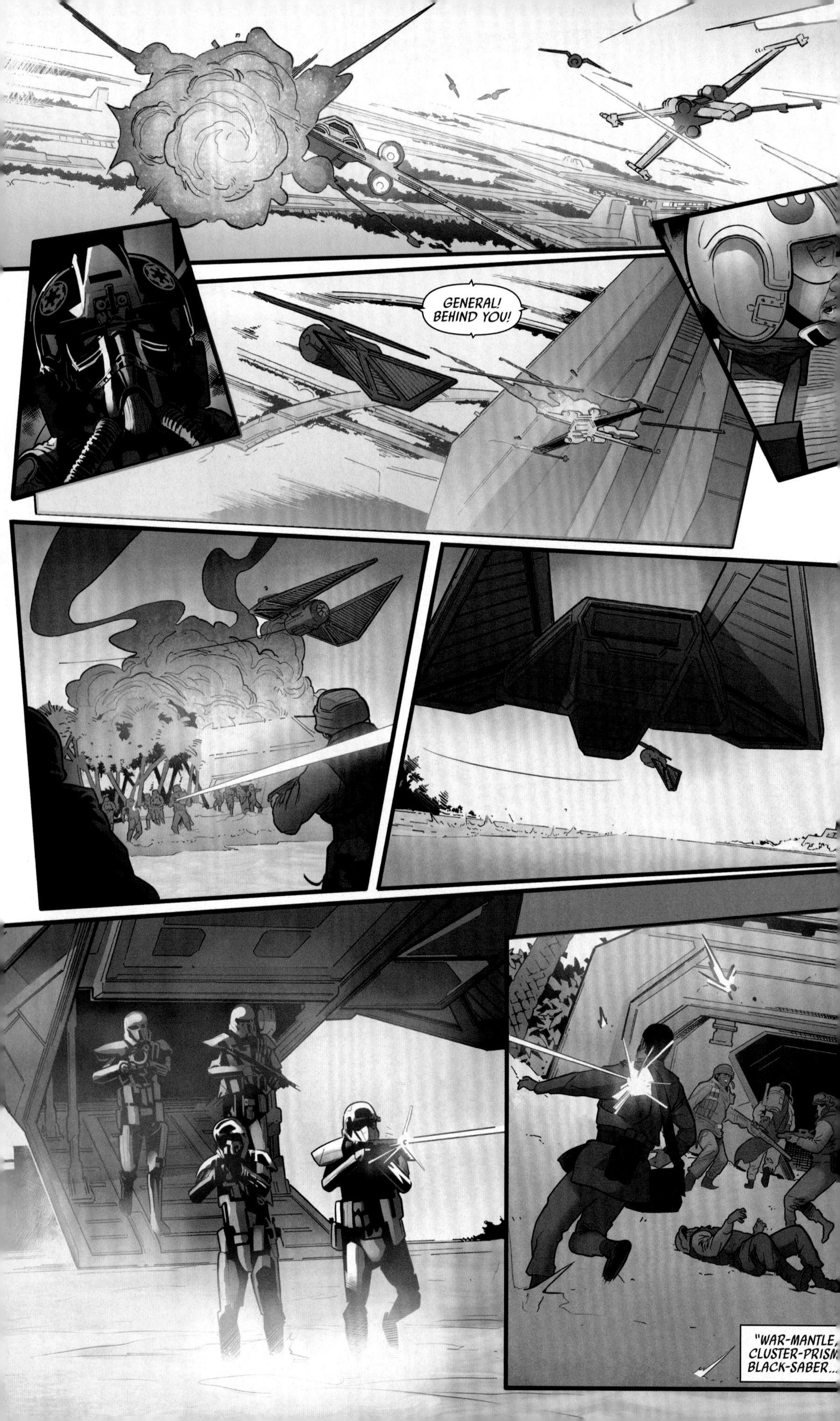
GENERAL! BEHIND YOU!
"WAR-MANTLE, CLUSTER-PRISM, BLACK-SABER...

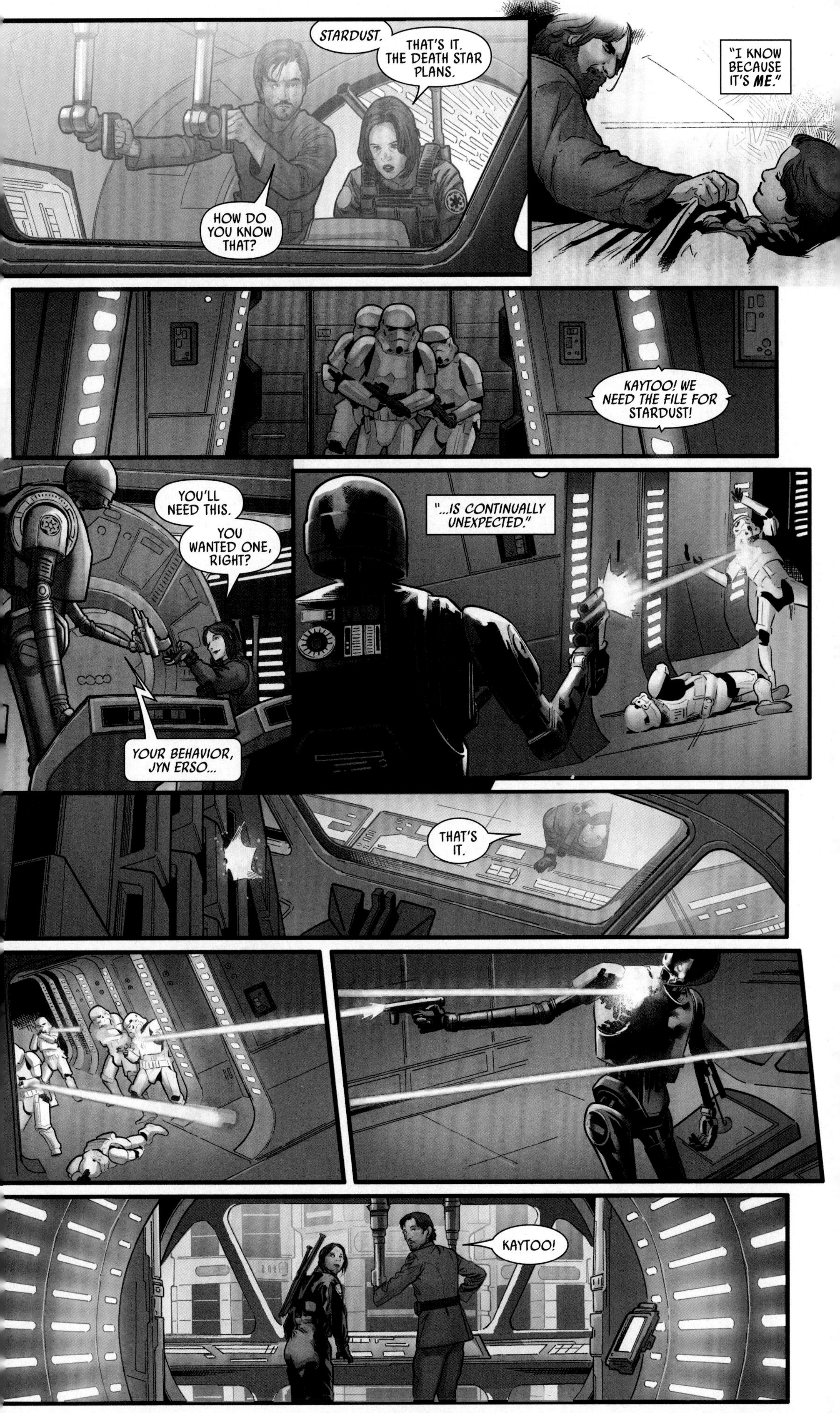
STARDUST.
THAT'S IT. THE DEATH STAR PLANS.
HOW DO YOU KNOW THAT?
"I KNOW BECAUSE IT'S *ME.*"
KAYTOO! WE NEED THE FILE FOR STARDUST!
YOU'LL NEED THIS.
YOU WANTED ONE, RIGHT?
YOUR BEHAVIOR, JYN ERSO...
"...IS CONTINUALLY UNEXPECTED."
THAT'S IT.
KAYTOO!

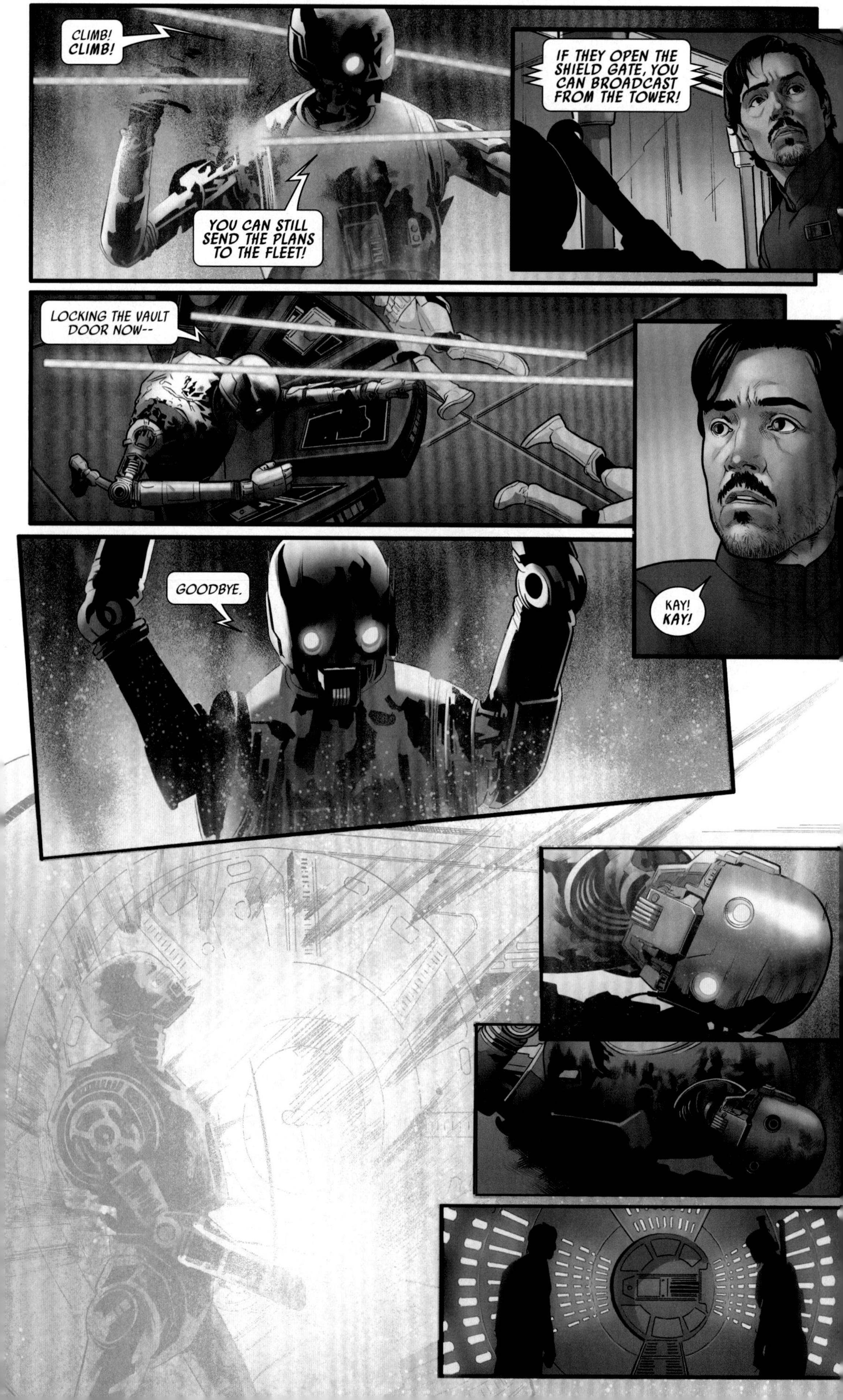
CLIMB! CLIMB!
IF THEY OPEN THE SHIELD GATE, YOU CAN BROADCAST FROM THE TOWER!
YOU CAN STILL SEND THE PLANS TO THE FLEET!
LOCKING THE VAULT DOOR NOW--
GOODBYE.
KAY! KAY!

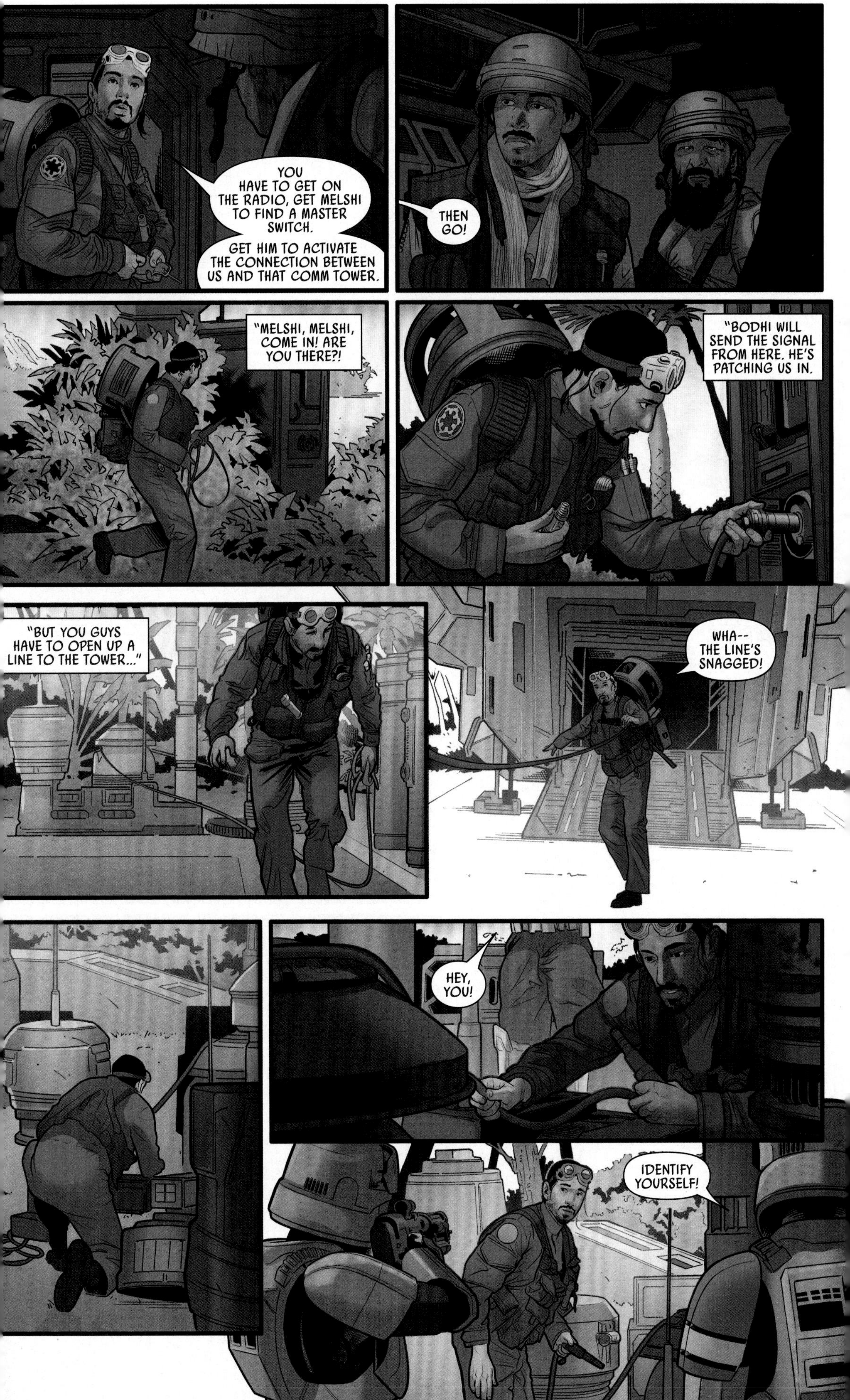
YOU HAVE TO GET ON THE RADIO, GET MELSHI TO FIND A MASTER SWITCH.
GET HIM TO ACTIVATE THE CONNECTION BETWEEN US AND THAT COMM TOWER.
THEN GO!
"MELSHI, MELSHI, COME IN! ARE YOU THERE?!
"BODHI WILL SEND THE SIGNAL FROM HERE. HE'S PATCHING US IN.
"BUT YOU GUYS HAVE TO OPEN UP A LINE TO THE TOWER..."
WHA-- THE LINE'S SNAGGED!
HEY, YOU!
IDENTIFY YOURSELF!

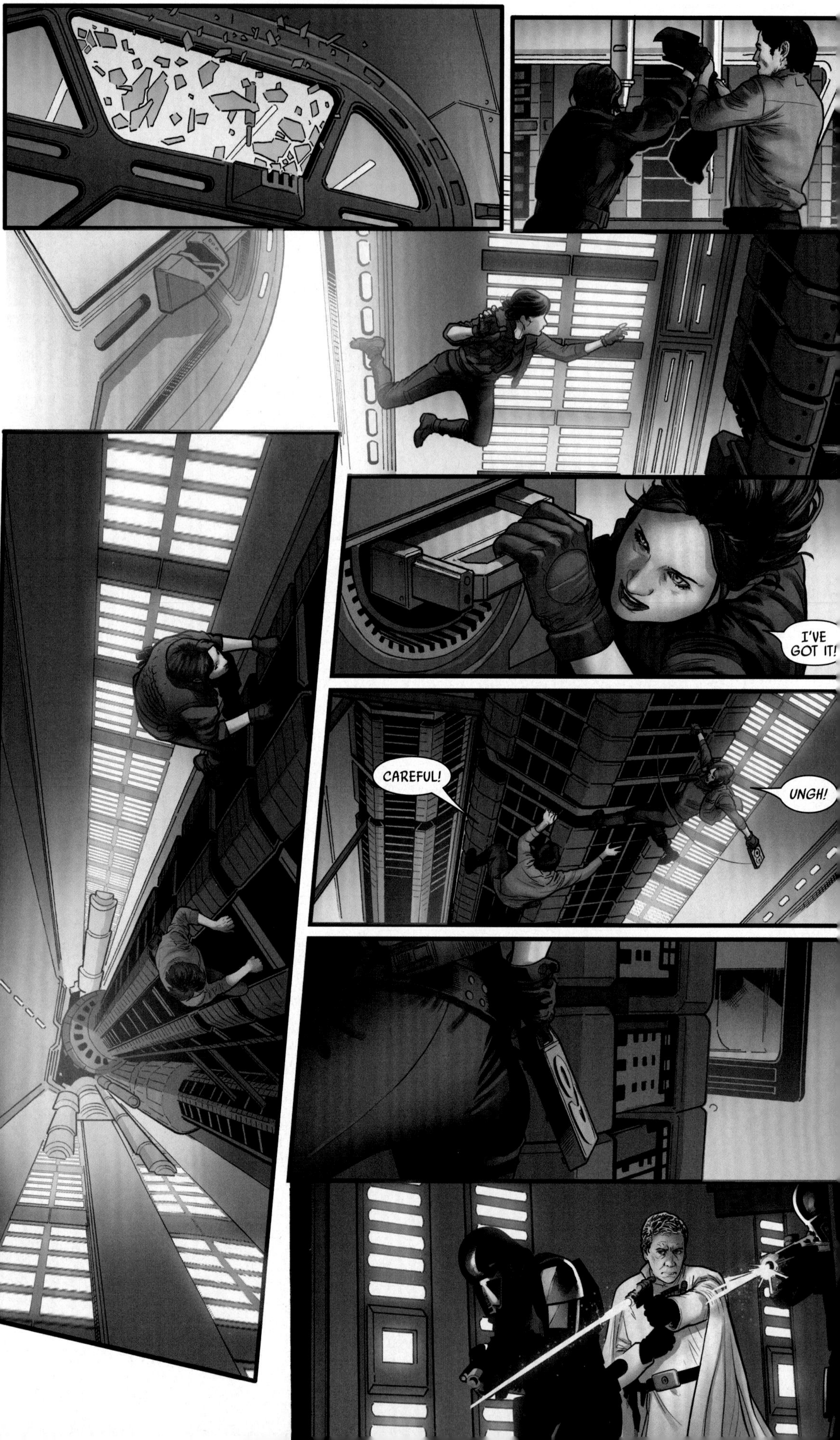
I'VE GOT IT!
CAREFUL!
UNGH!

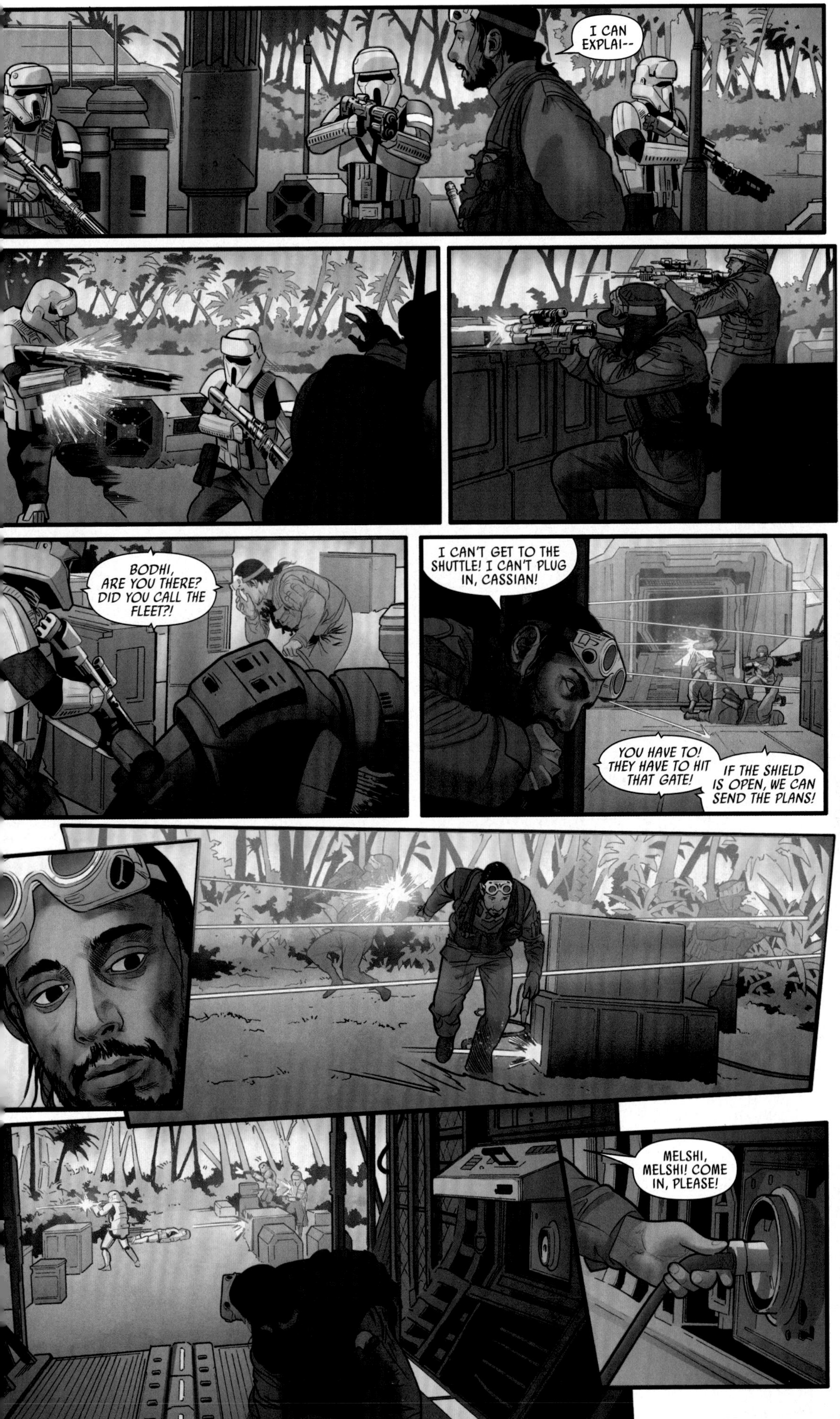
I CAN EXPLAI--
BODHI, ARE YOU THERE? DID YOU CALL THE FLEET?!
I CAN'T GET TO THE SHUTTLE! I CAN'T PLUG IN, CASSIAN!
YOU HAVE TO! THEY HAVE TO HIT THAT GATE!
IF THE SHIELD IS OPEN, WE CAN SEND THE PLANS!
MELSHI, MELSHI! COME IN, PLEASE!

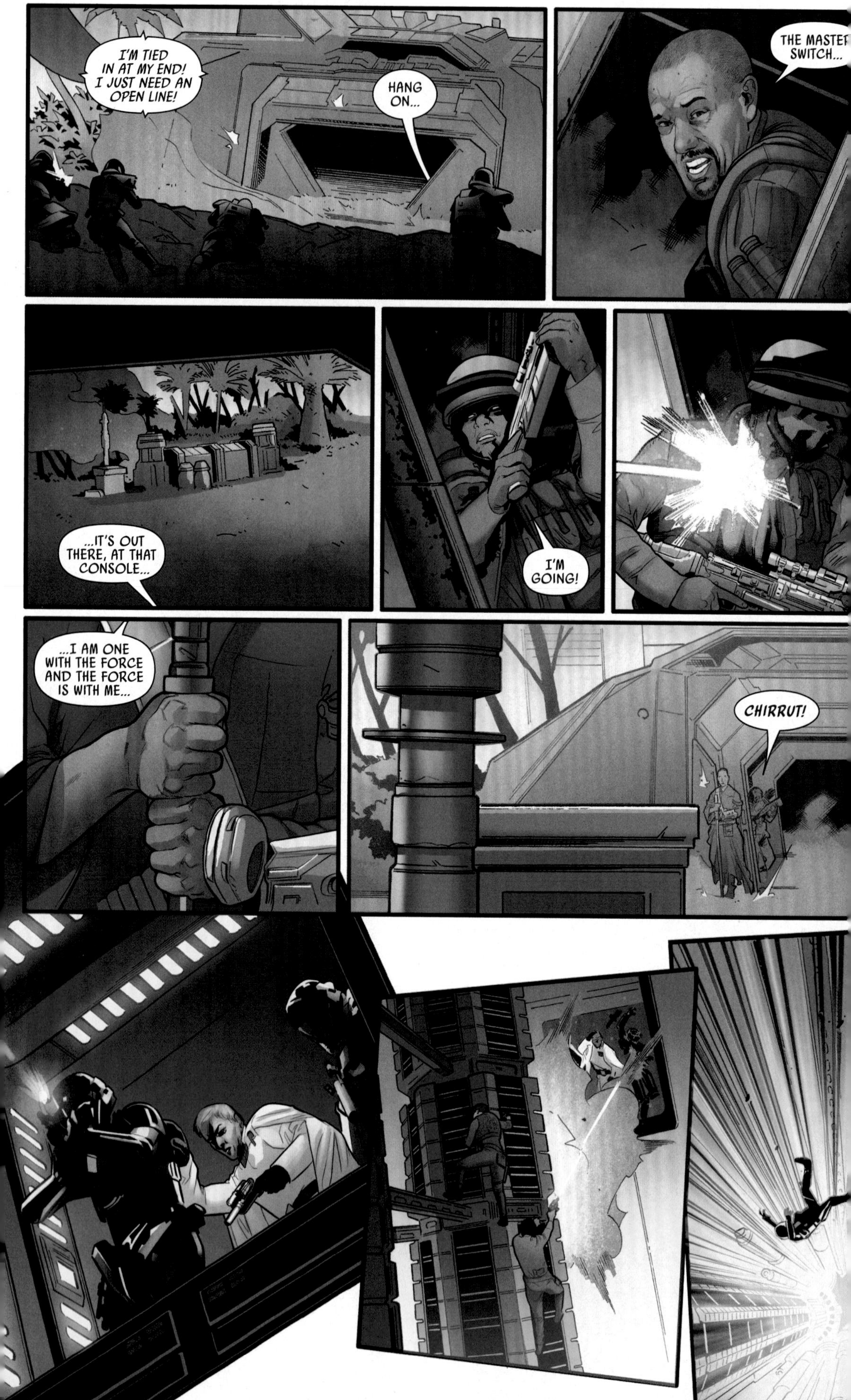

I'M TIED IN AT MY END! I JUST NEED AN OPEN LINE!
HANG ON...
THE MASTER SWITCH...
...IT'S OUT THERE, AT THAT CONSOLE...
I'M GOING!
...I AM ONE WITH THE FORCE AND THE FORCE IS WITH ME...
CHIRRUT!

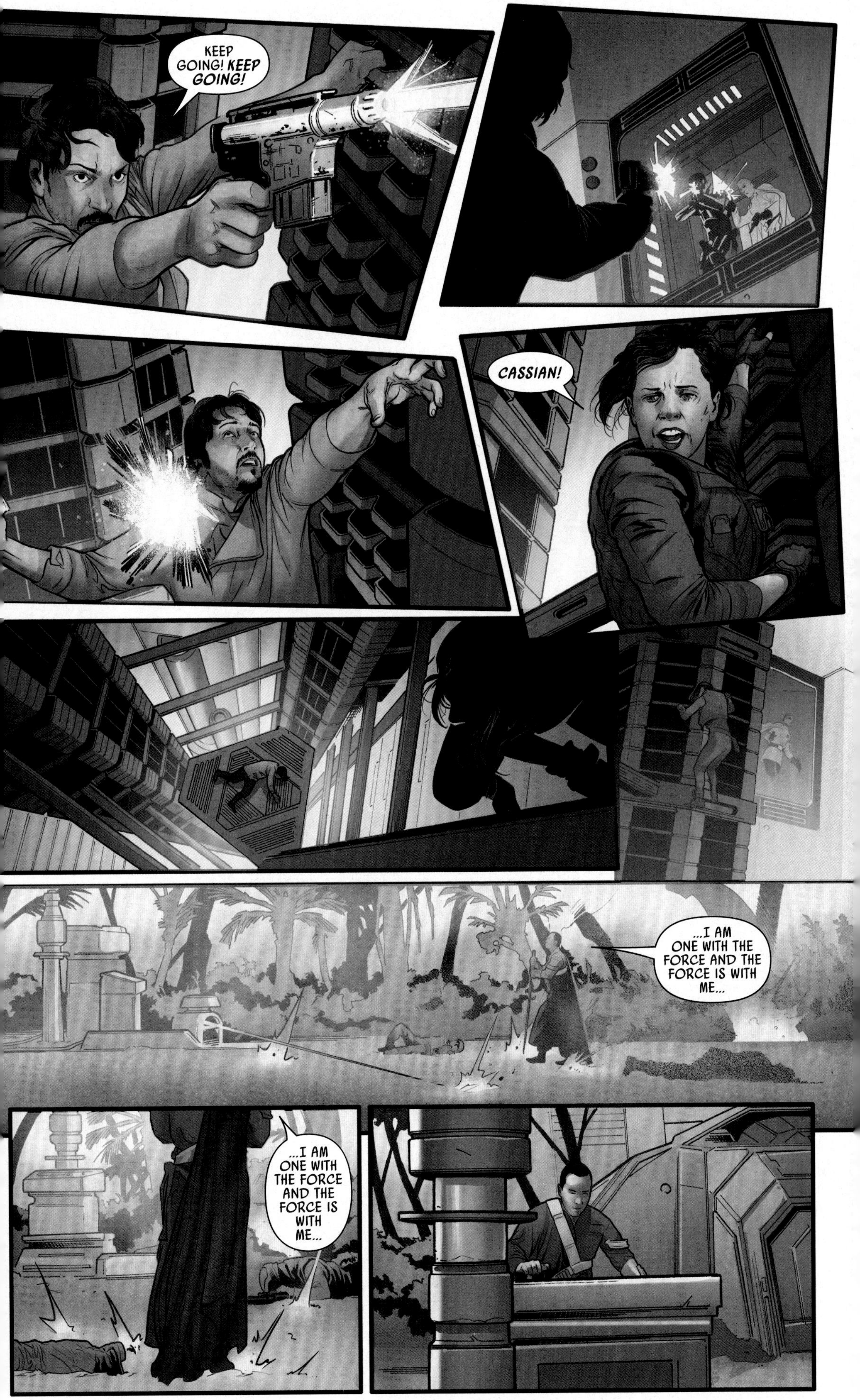
KEEP GOING! KEEP GOING!
CASSIAN!
...I AM ONE WITH THE FORCE AND THE FORCE IS WITH ME...
...I AM ONE WITH THE FORCE AND THE FORCE IS WITH ME...

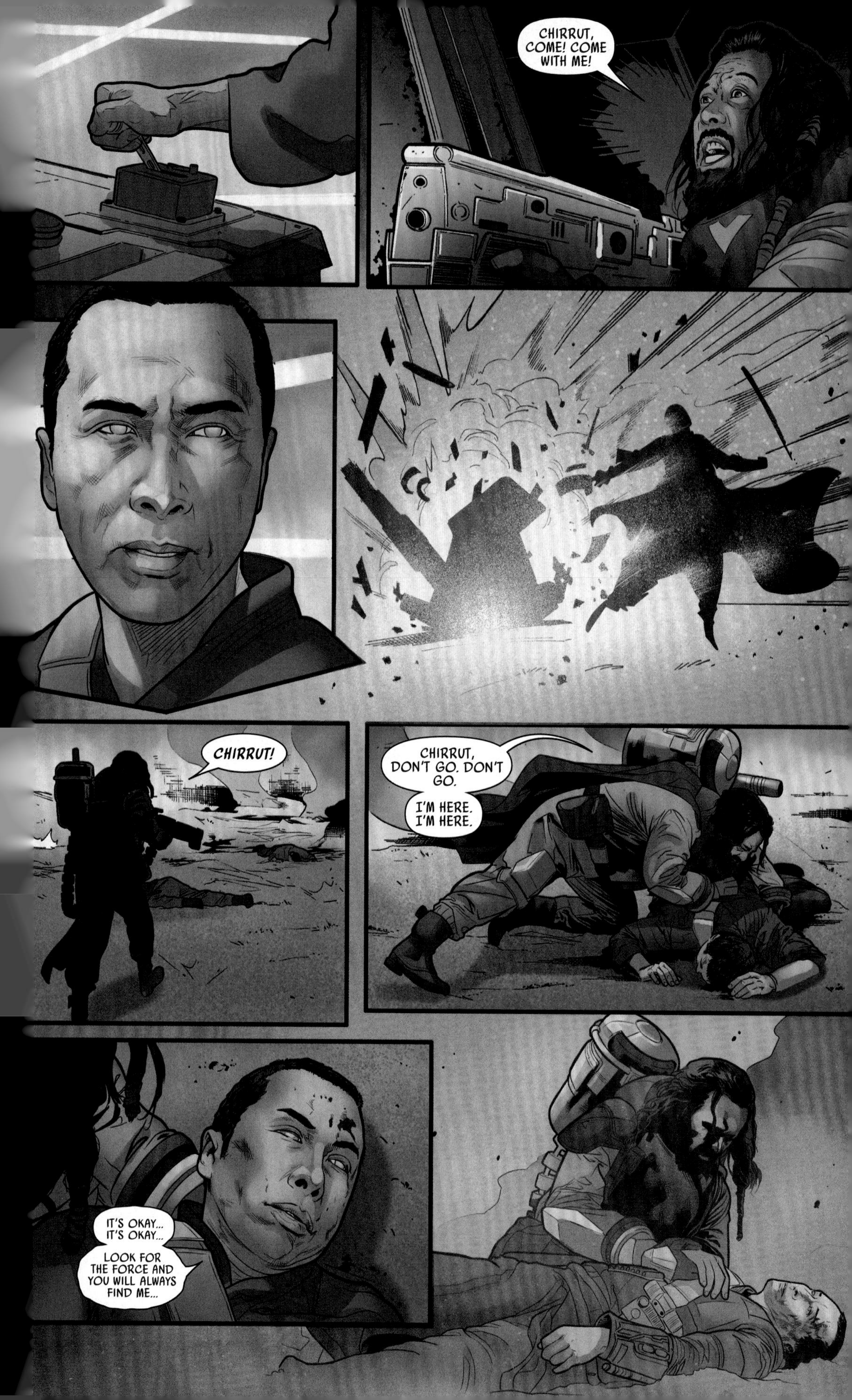
CHIRRUT, COME! COME WITH ME!
CHIRRUT!
CHIRRUT, DON'T GO. DON'T GO.
I'M HERE. I'M HERE.
IT'S OKAY... IT'S OKAY...
LOOK FOR THE FORCE AND YOU WILL ALWAYS FIND ME...

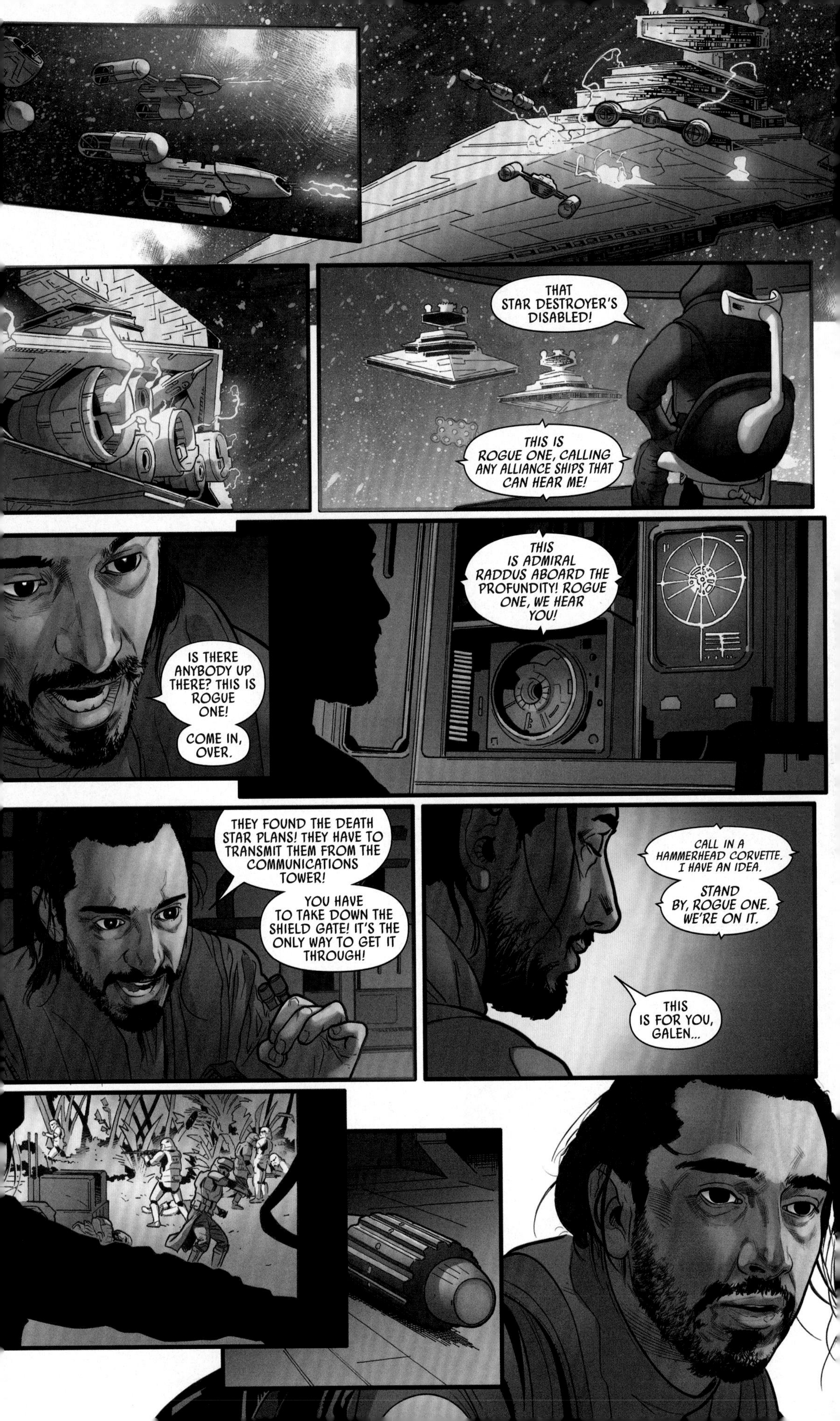
THAT STAR DESTROYER'S DISABLED!
THIS IS ROGUE ONE, CALLING ANY ALLIANCE SHIPS THAT CAN HEAR ME!
IS THERE ANYBODY UP THERE? THIS IS ROGUE ONE!
COME IN, OVER.
THIS IS ADMIRAL RADDUS ABOARD THE PROFUNDITY! ROGUE ONE, WE HEAR YOU!
THEY FOUND THE DEATH STAR PLANS! THEY HAVE TO TRANSMIT THEM FROM THE COMMUNICATIONS TOWER!
YOU HAVE TO TAKE DOWN THE SHIELD GATE! IT'S THE ONLY WAY TO GET IT THROUGH!
CALL IN A HAMMERHEAD CORVETTE. I HAVE AN IDEA.
STAND BY, ROGUE ONE. WE'RE ON IT.
THIS IS FOR YOU, GALEN...

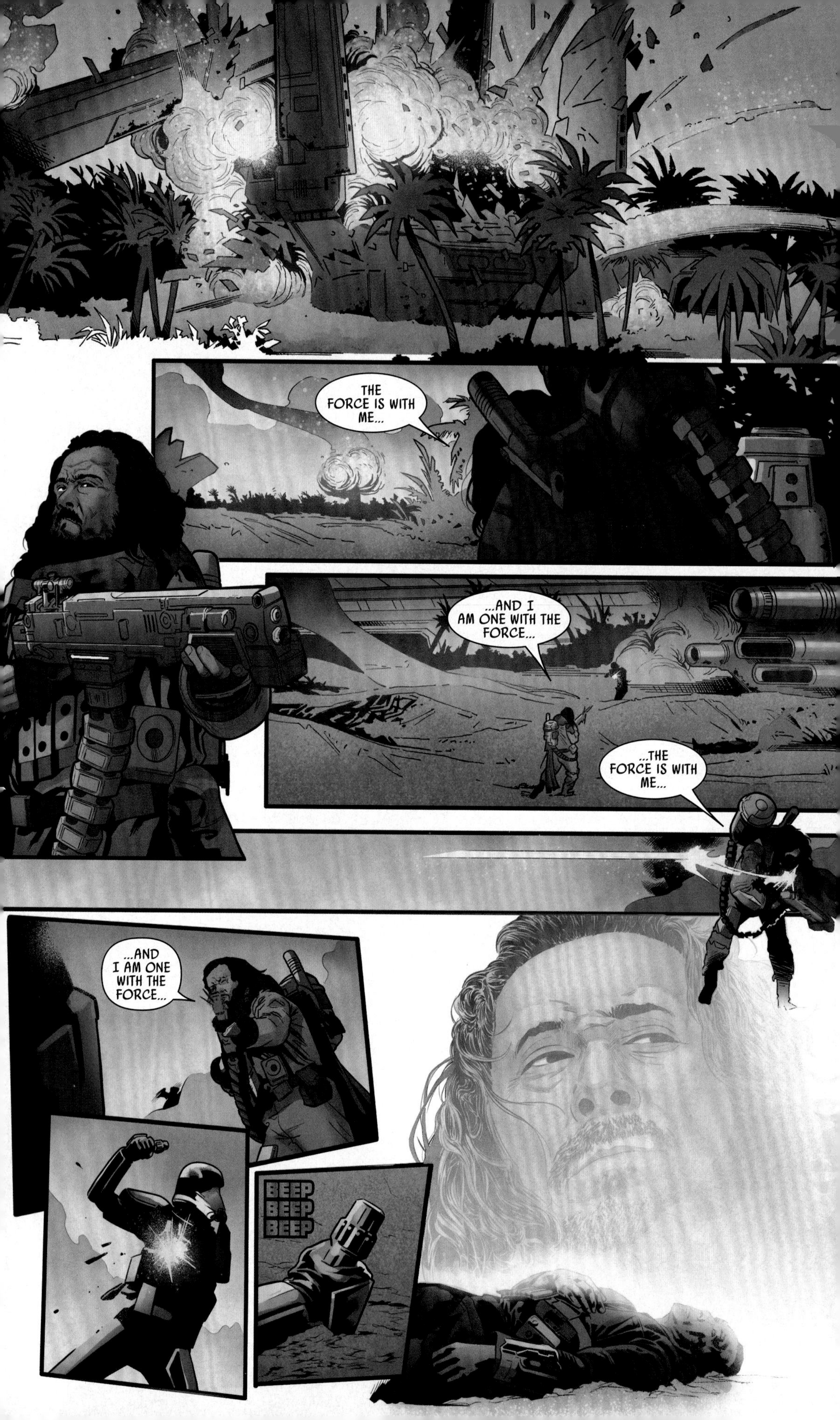
THE FORCE IS WITH ME...
...AND I AM ONE WITH THE FORCE...
...THE FORCE IS WITH ME...
...AND I AM ONE WITH THE FORCE...
BEEP BEEP BEEP

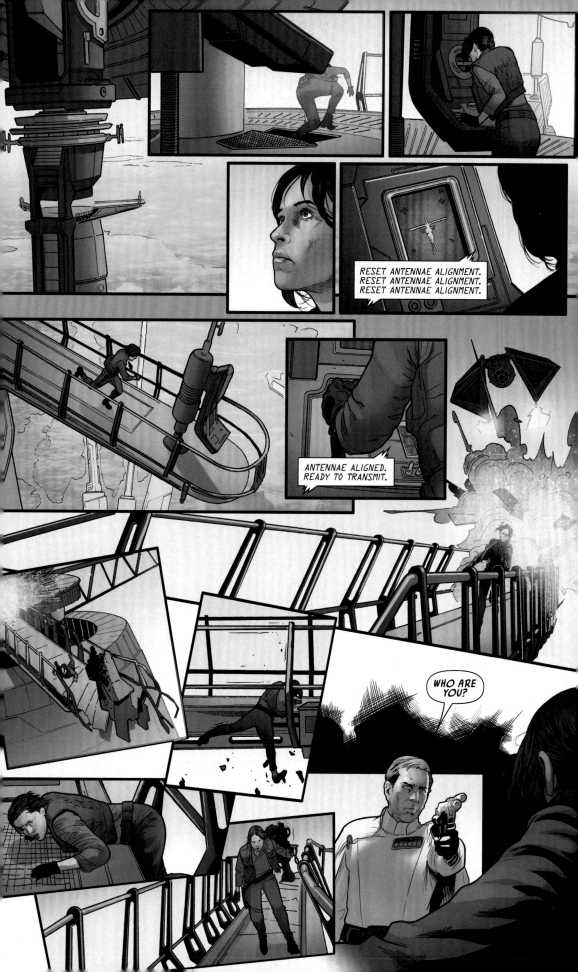

RESET ANTENNAE ALIGNMENT.
RESET ANTENNAE ALIGNMENT.
RESET ANTENNAE ALIGNMENT.

ANTENNAE ALIGNED.
READY TO TRANSMIT.

WHO ARE YOU?

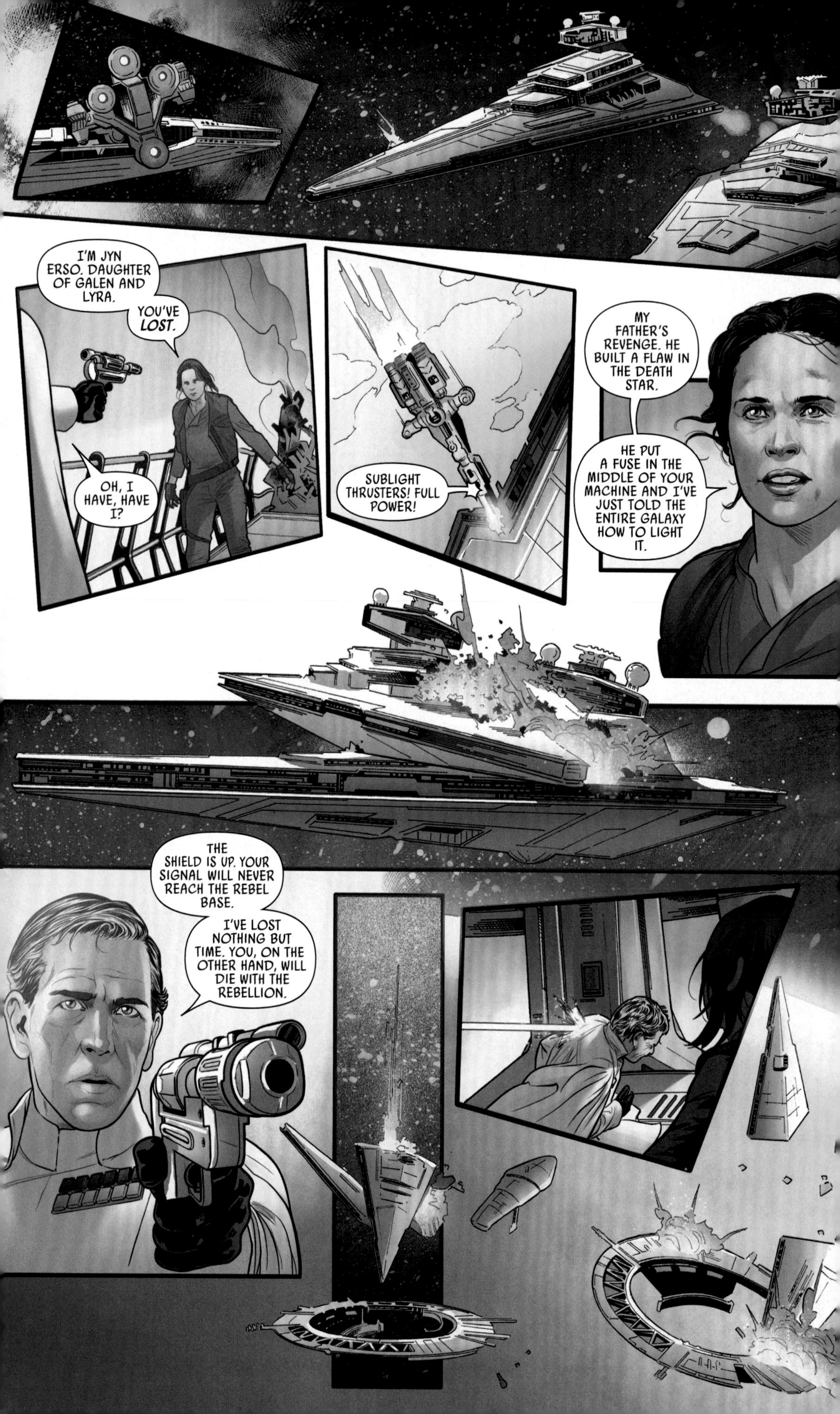
I'M JYN ERSO. DAUGHTER OF GALEN AND LYRA.
YOU'VE *LOST*.
OH, I HAVE, HAVE I?
SUBLIGHT THRUSTERS! FULL POWER!
MY FATHER'S REVENGE. HE BUILT A FLAW IN THE DEATH STAR.
HE PUT A FUSE IN THE MIDDLE OF YOUR MACHINE AND I'VE JUST TOLD THE ENTIRE GALAXY HOW TO LIGHT IT.
THE SHIELD IS UP. YOUR SIGNAL WILL NEVER REACH THE REBEL BASE.
I'VE LOST NOTHING BUT TIME. YOU, ON THE OTHER HAND, WILL DIE WITH THE REBELLION.

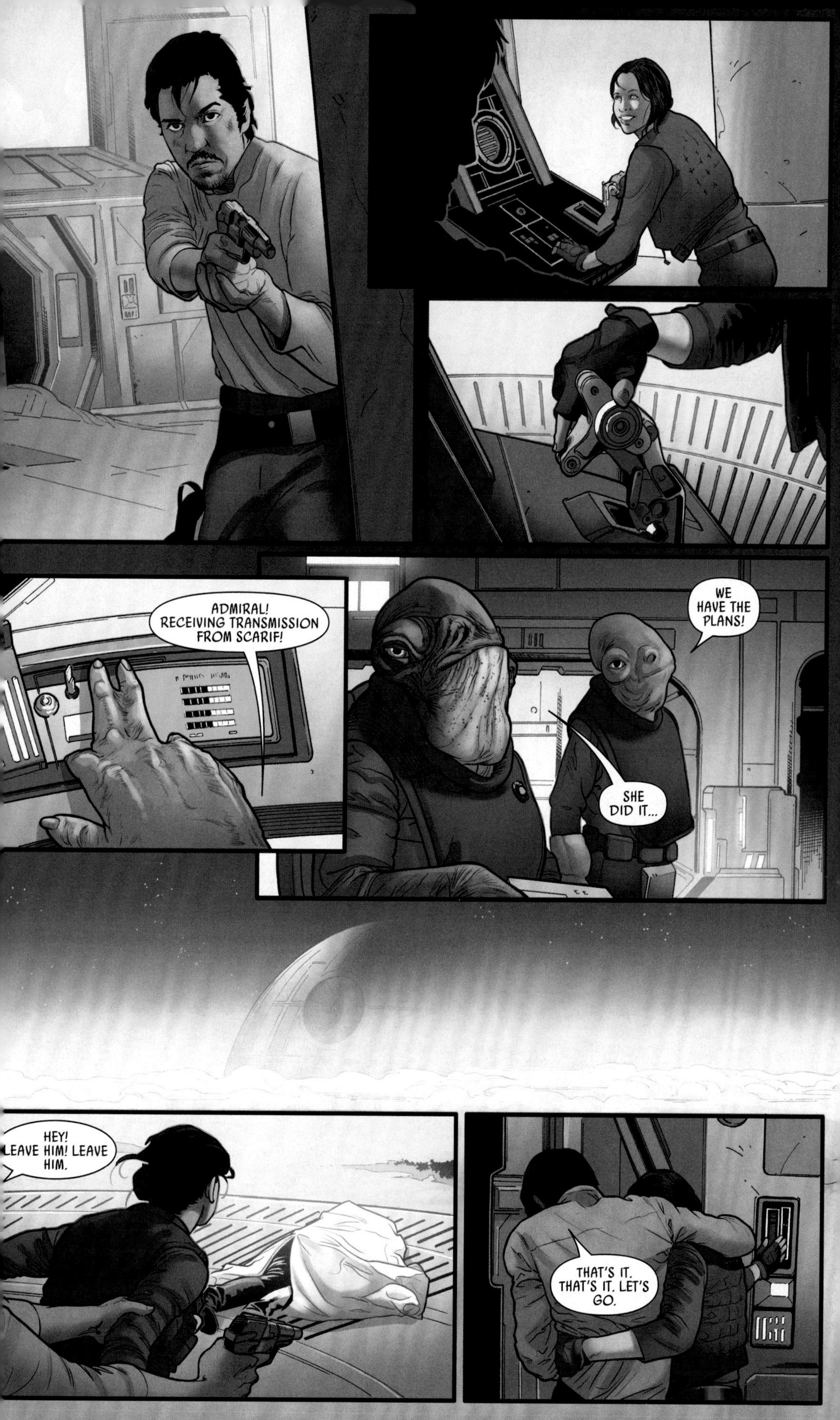
ADMIRAL! RECEIVING TRANSMISSION FROM SCARIF!
WE HAVE THE PLANS!
SHE DID IT...
HEY! LEAVE HIM! LEAVE HIM.
THAT'S IT. THAT'S IT. LET'S GO.

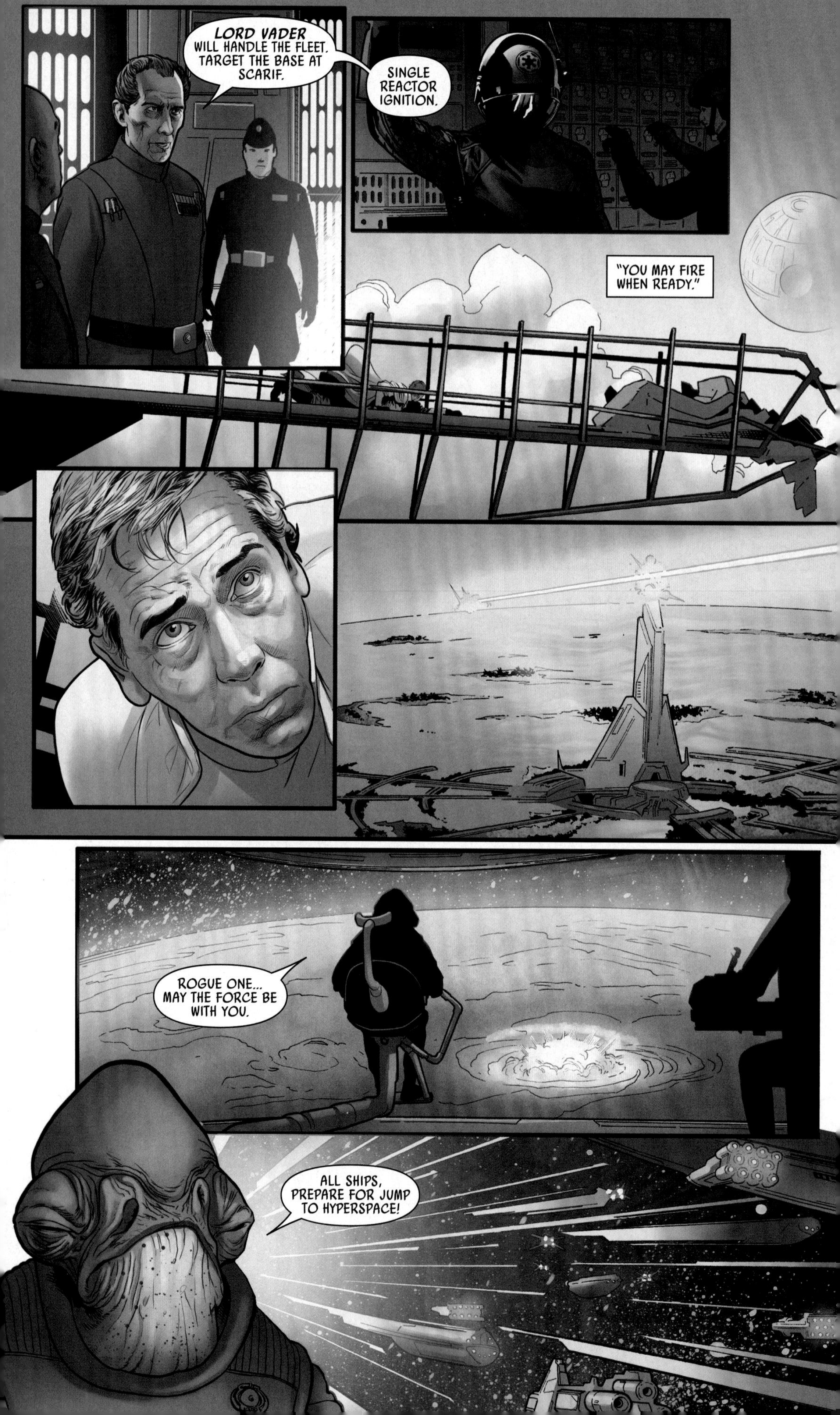
LORD VADER WILL HANDLE THE FLEET. TARGET THE BASE AT SCARIF.
SINGLE REACTOR IGNITION.
"YOU MAY FIRE WHEN READY."
ROGUE ONE... MAY THE FORCE BE WITH YOU.
ALL SHIPS, PREPARE FOR JUMP TO HYPERSPACE!

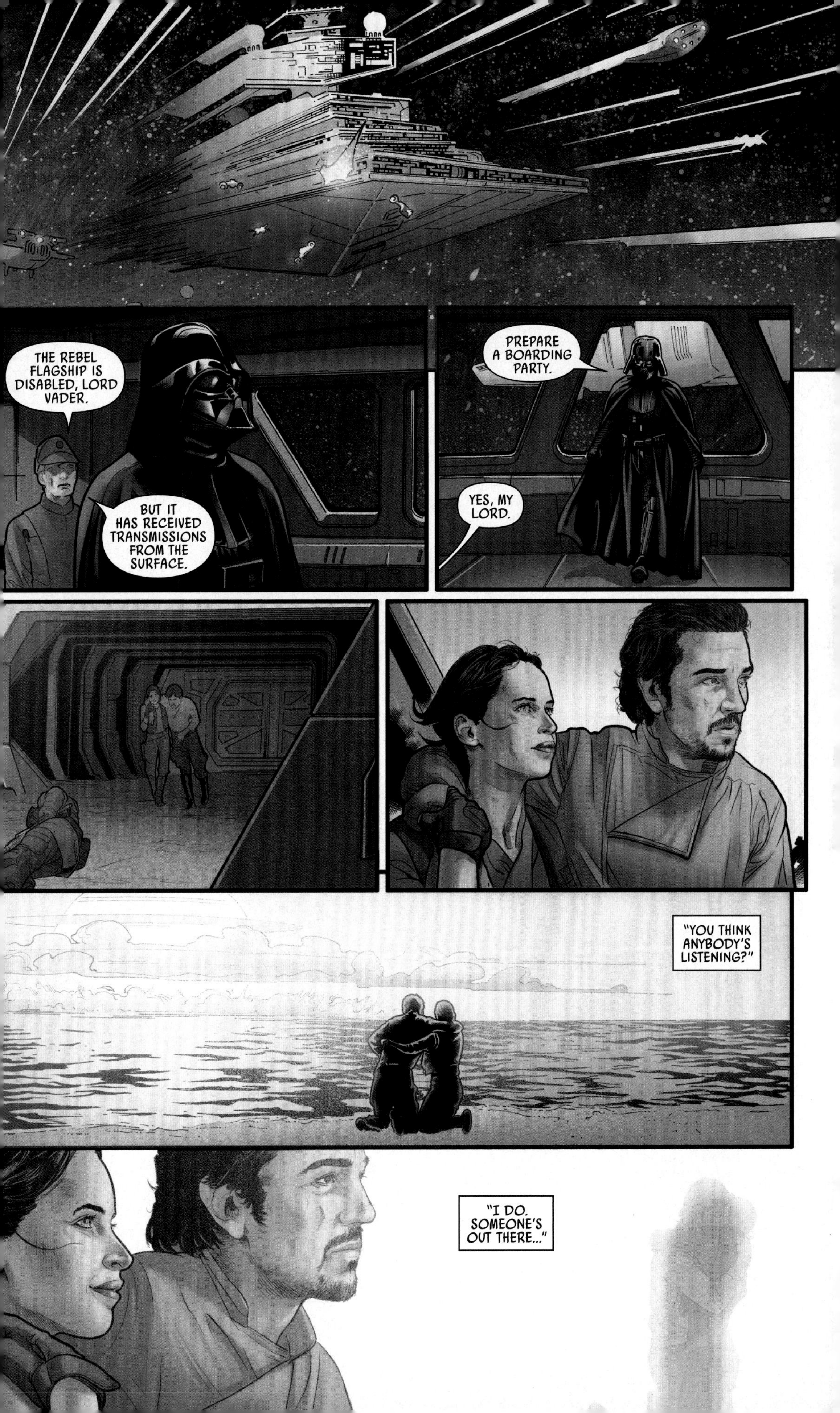
THE REBEL FLAGSHIP IS DISABLED, LORD VADER.
BUT IT HAS RECEIVED TRANSMISSIONS FROM THE SURFACE.
PREPARE A BOARDING PARTY.
YES, MY LORD.
"YOU THINK ANYBODY'S LISTENING?"
"I DO. SOMEONE'S OUT THERE..."

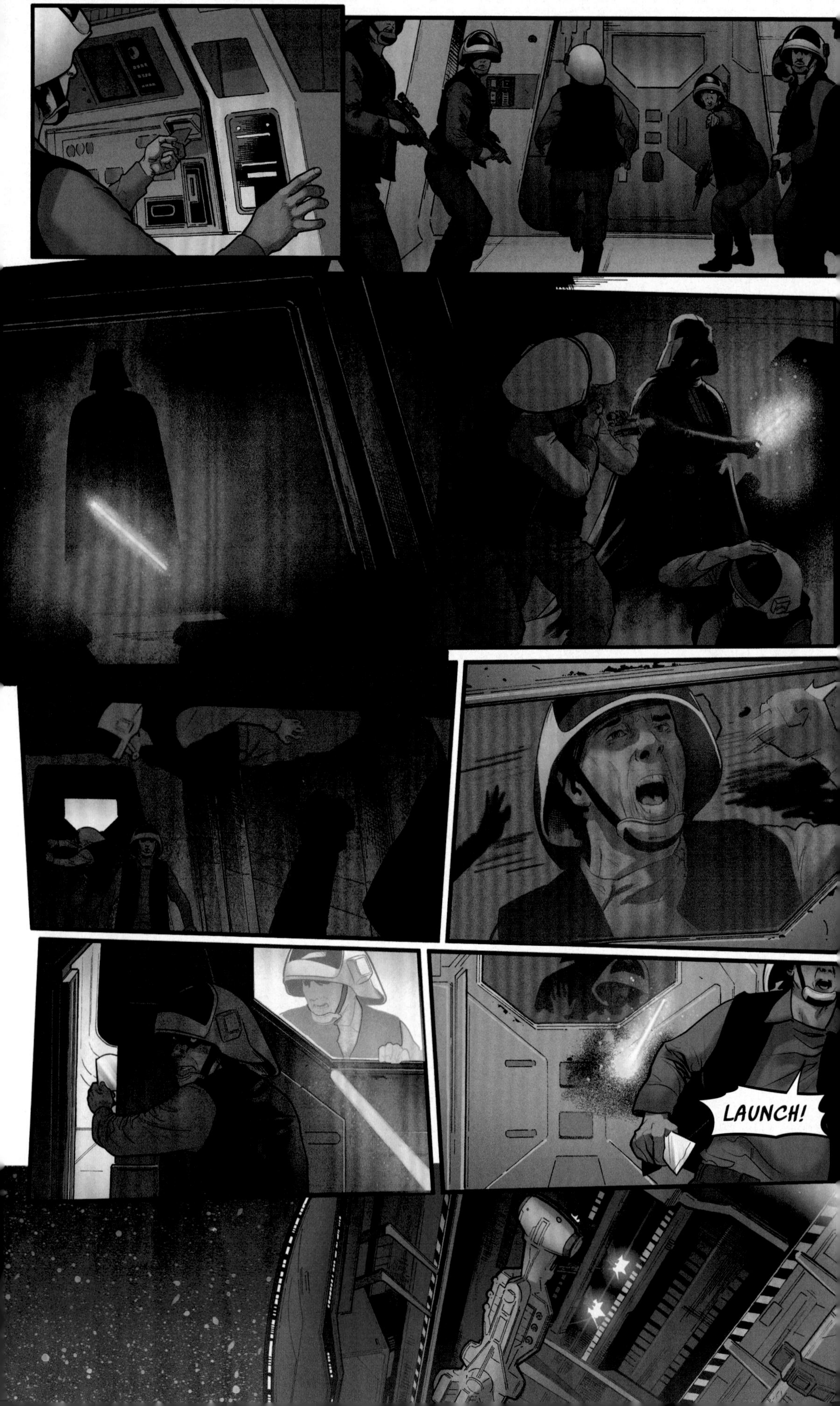
LAUNCH!

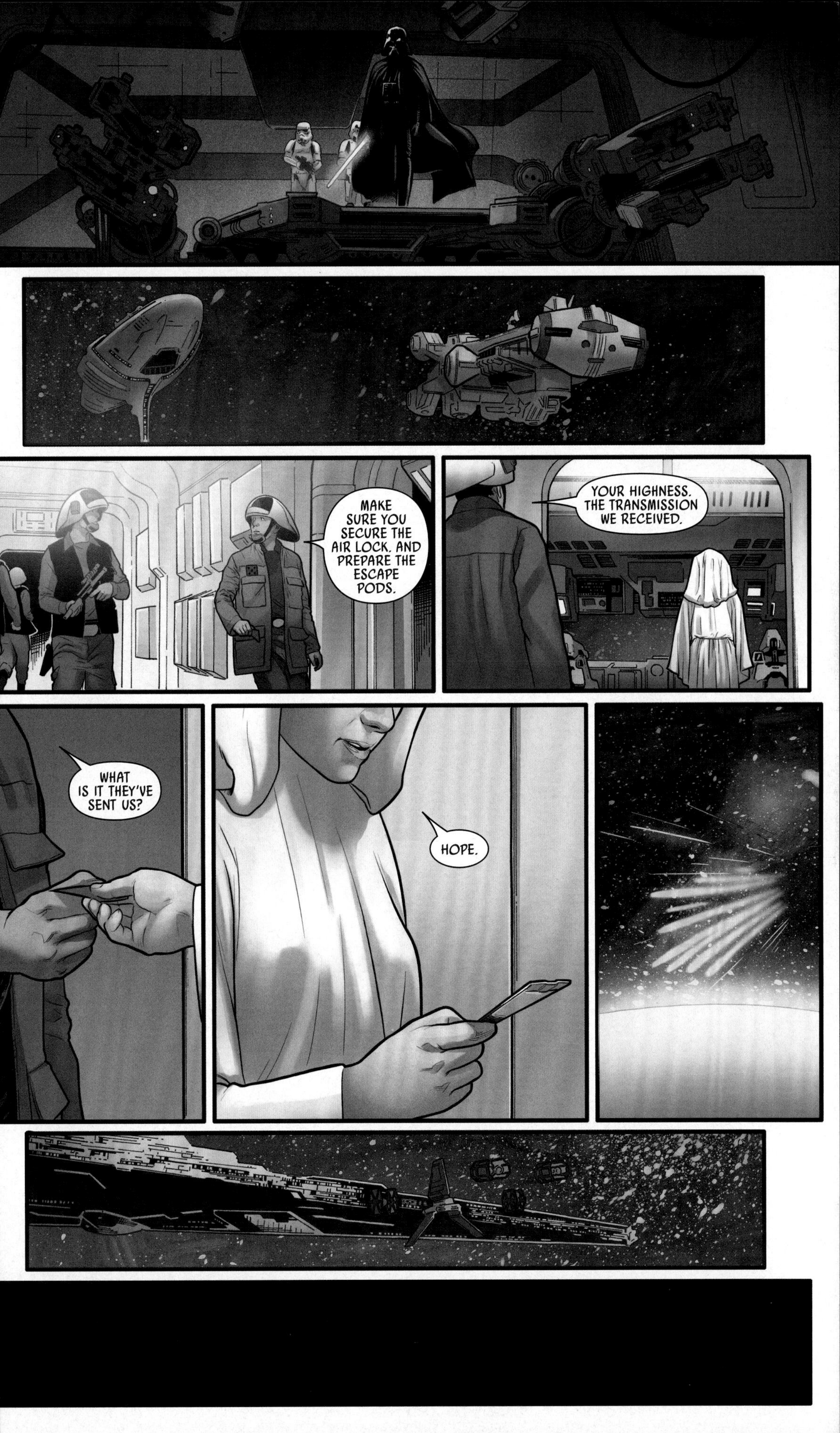
MAKE SURE YOU SECURE THE AIR LOCK. AND PREPARE THE ESCAPE PODS.
YOUR HIGHNESS. THE TRANSMISSION WE RECEIVED.
WHAT IS IT THEY'VE SENT US?
HOPE.

A NEW HOPE

It is a period of civil war.
Rebel spaceships, striking
from a hidden base, have won
their first victory against the
evil Galactic Empire.

During the battle, Rebel spies
managed to steal secret plans
to the Empire's ultimate
weapon, the DEATH STAR, an
armored space station with
enough power to destroy an
entire planet.

Pursued by the Empire's
sinister agents, Princess Leia
races home aboard her
starship, custodian of the
stolen plans that can save he
people and restore freedom t
the galaxy....

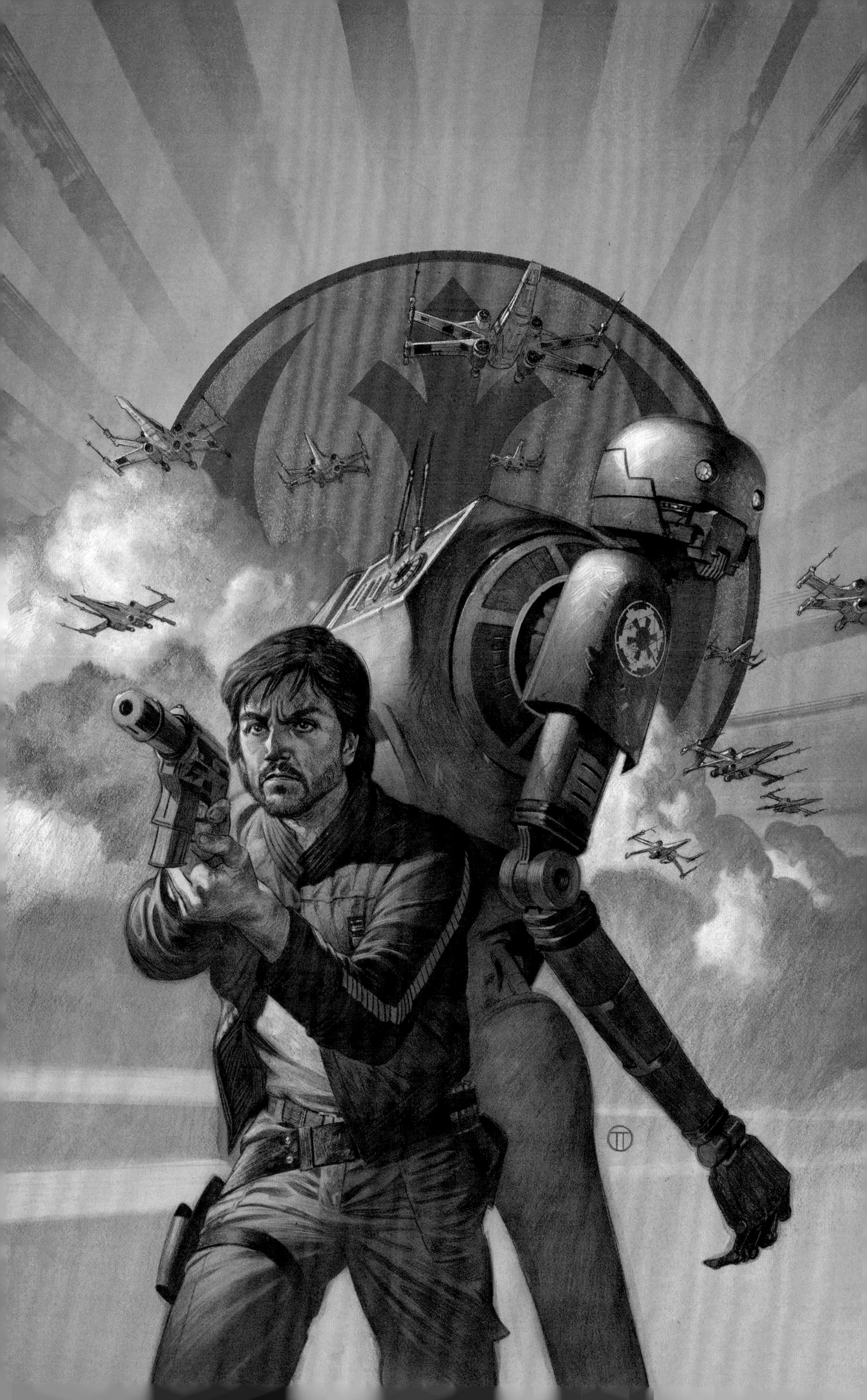

REBEL'S REPORT

OPERATIVES:

Rebel intelligence officer Cassian Andor rebel spies Kertas and Rismor.

CAPTAIN CASSIAN ANDOR

KERTAS & RISMOR

MISSION:

Extract Imperial security protocols.

NOTES:

Attempt to evade detection.

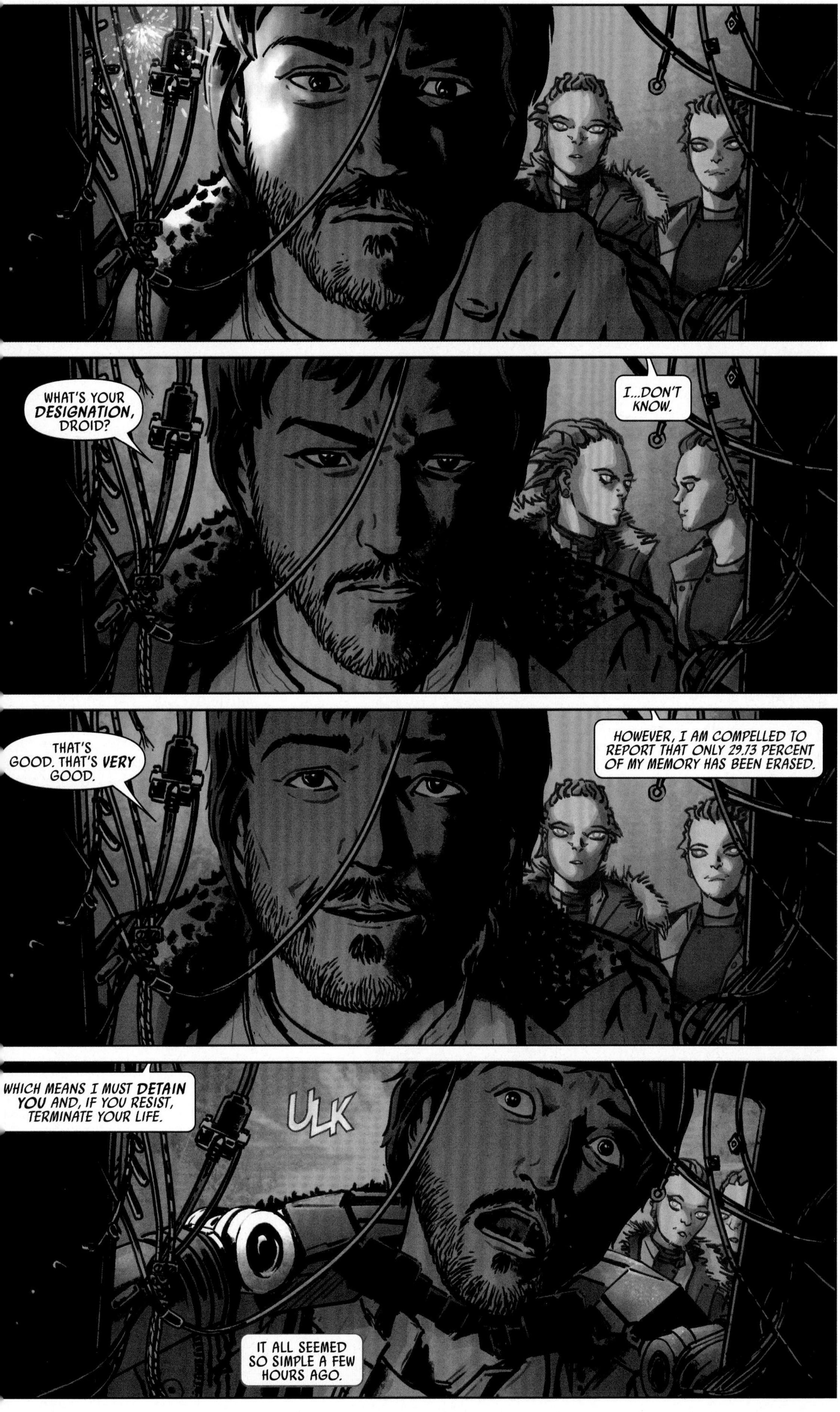
WHAT'S YOUR DESIGNATION, DROID?
I...DON'T KNOW.
THAT'S GOOD. THAT'S VERY GOOD.
HOWEVER, I AM COMPELLED TO REPORT THAT ONLY 29.73 PERCENT OF MY MEMORY HAS BEEN ERASED.
WHICH MEANS I MUST DETAIN YOU AND, IF YOU RESIST, TERMINATE YOUR LIFE.
ULK
IT ALL SEEMED SO SIMPLE A FEW HOURS AGO.

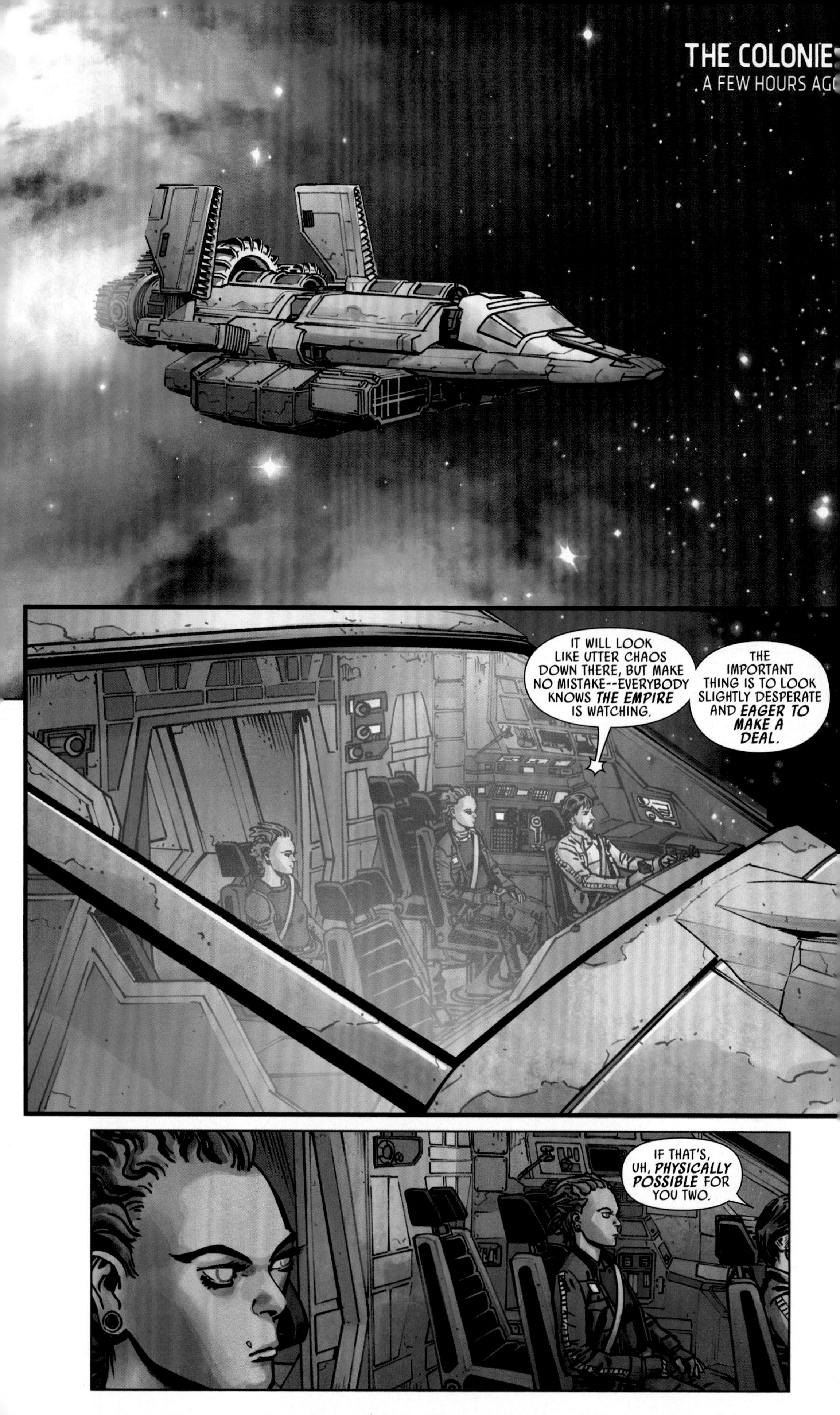
THE COLONIE
. A FEW HOURS AGO
IT WILL LOOK LIKE UTTER CHAOS DOWN THERE, BUT MAKE NO MISTAKE--EVERYBODY KNOWS THE EMPIRE IS WATCHING.
THE IMPORTANT THING IS TO LOOK SLIGHTLY DESPERATE AND EAGER TO MAKE A DEAL.
IF THAT'S, UH, PHYSICALLY POSSIBLE FOR YOU TWO.

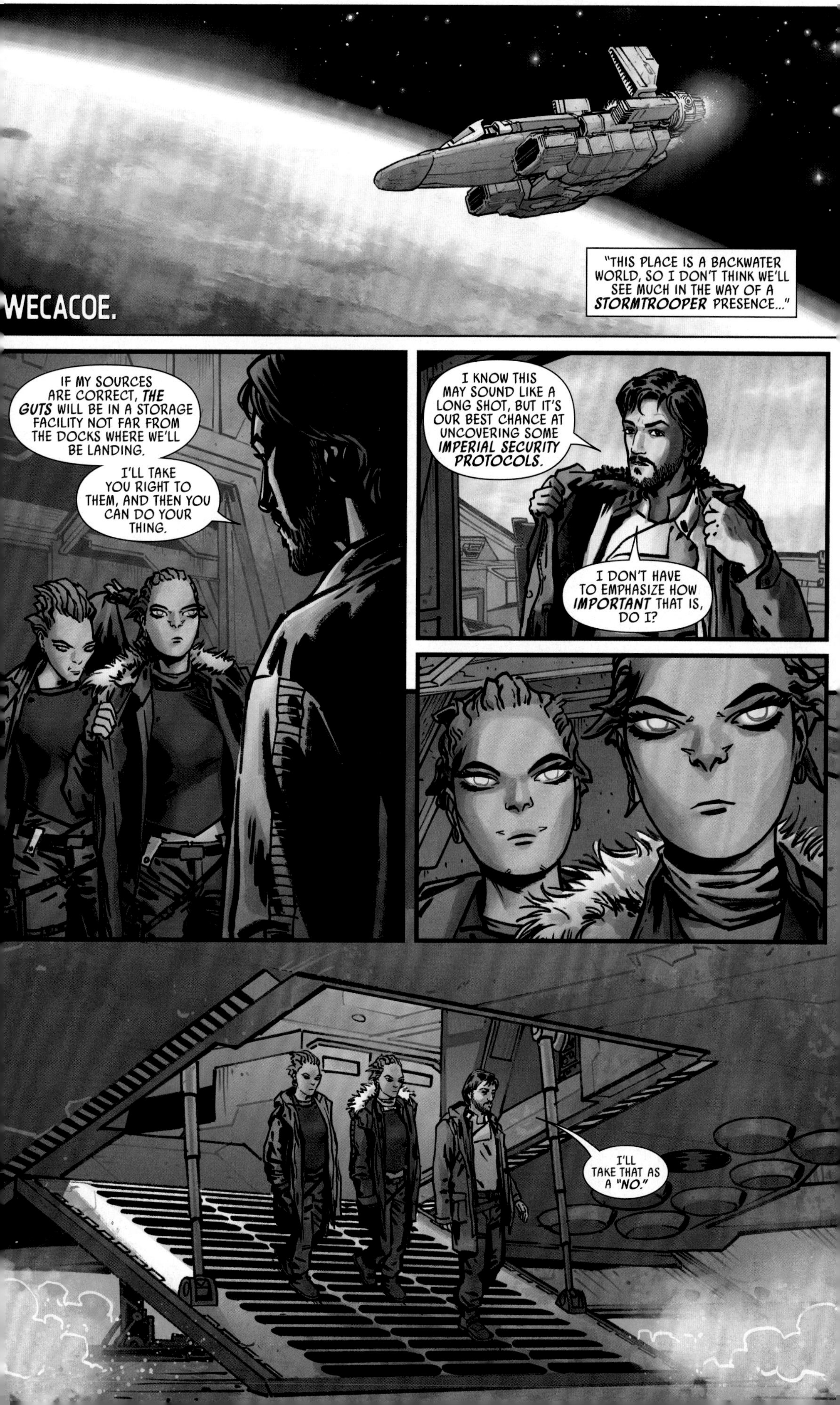
WECACOE.
"THIS PLACE IS A BACKWATER WORLD, SO I DON'T THINK WE'LL SEE MUCH IN THE WAY OF A STORMTROOPER PRESENCE..."
IF MY SOURCES ARE CORRECT, THE GUTS WILL BE IN A STORAGE FACILITY NOT FAR FROM THE DOCKS WHERE WE'LL BE LANDING.
I'LL TAKE YOU RIGHT TO THEM, AND THEN YOU CAN DO YOUR THING.
I KNOW THIS MAY SOUND LIKE A LONG SHOT, BUT IT'S OUR BEST CHANCE AT UNCOVERING SOME IMPERIAL SECURITY PROTOCOLS.
I DON'T HAVE TO EMPHASIZE HOW IMPORTANT THAT IS, DO I?
I'LL TAKE THAT AS A "NO."

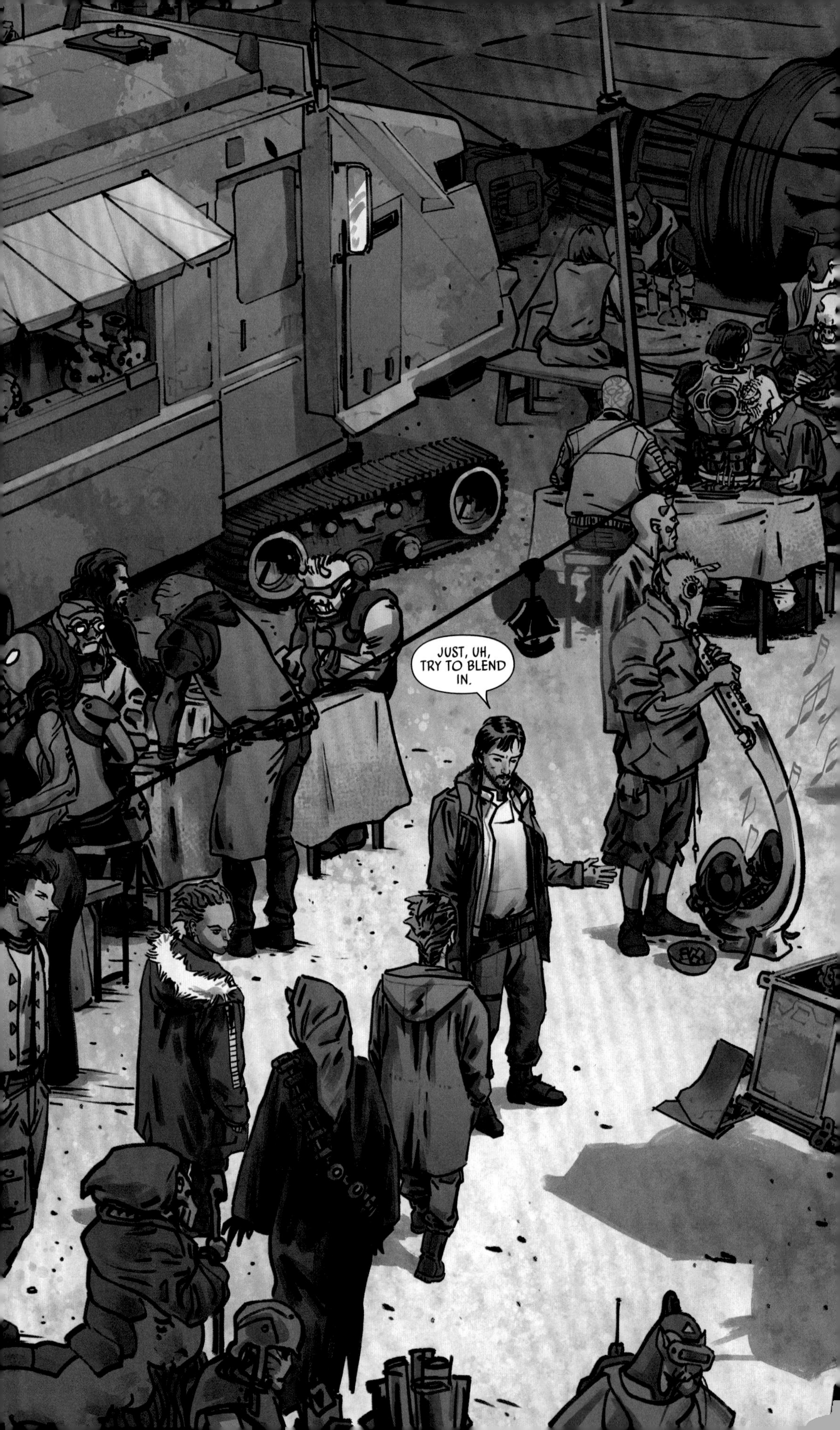

JUST, UH, TRY TO BLEND IN.

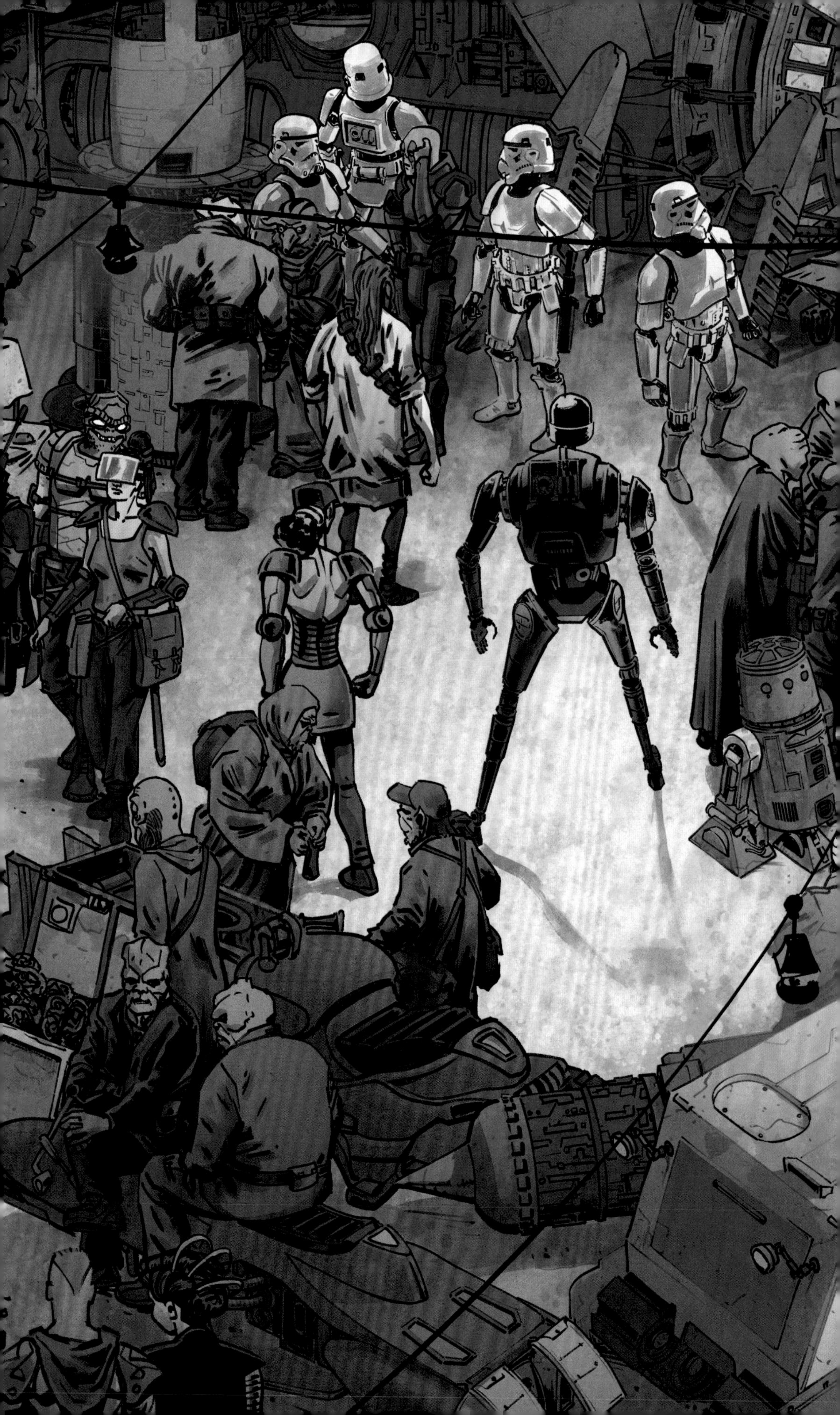

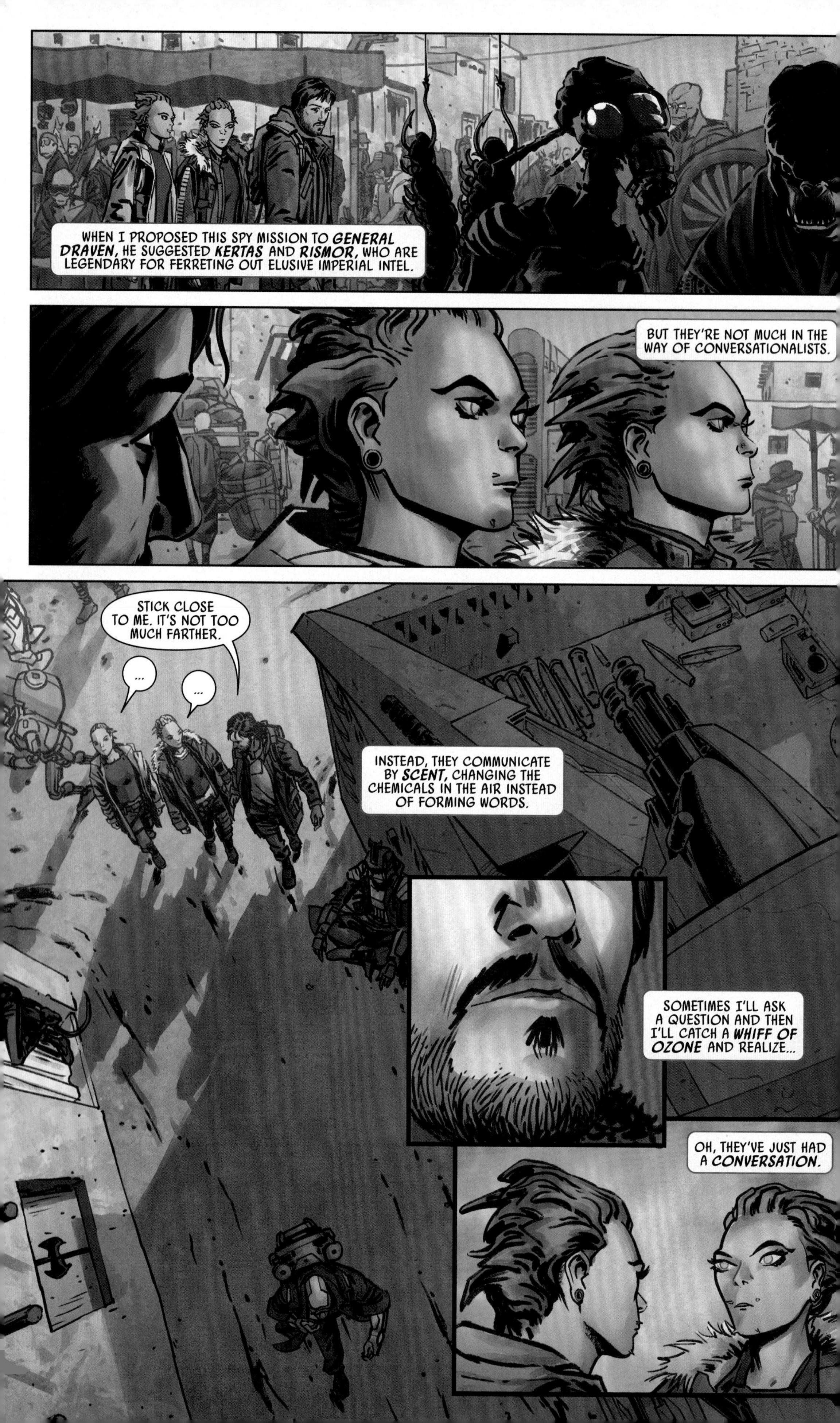
WHEN I PROPOSED THIS SPY MISSION TO GENERAL DRAVEN, HE SUGGESTED KERTAS AND RISMOR, WHO ARE LEGENDARY FOR FERRETING OUT ELUSIVE IMPERIAL INTEL.
BUT THEY'RE NOT MUCH IN THE WAY OF CONVERSATIONALISTS.
STICK CLOSE TO ME. IT'S NOT TOO MUCH FARTHER.
...
...
INSTEAD, THEY COMMUNICATE BY SCENT, CHANGING THE CHEMICALS IN THE AIR INSTEAD OF FORMING WORDS.
SOMETIMES I'LL ASK A QUESTION AND THEN I'LL CATCH A WHIFF OF OZONE AND REALIZE...
OH, THEY'VE JUST HAD A CONVERSATION.

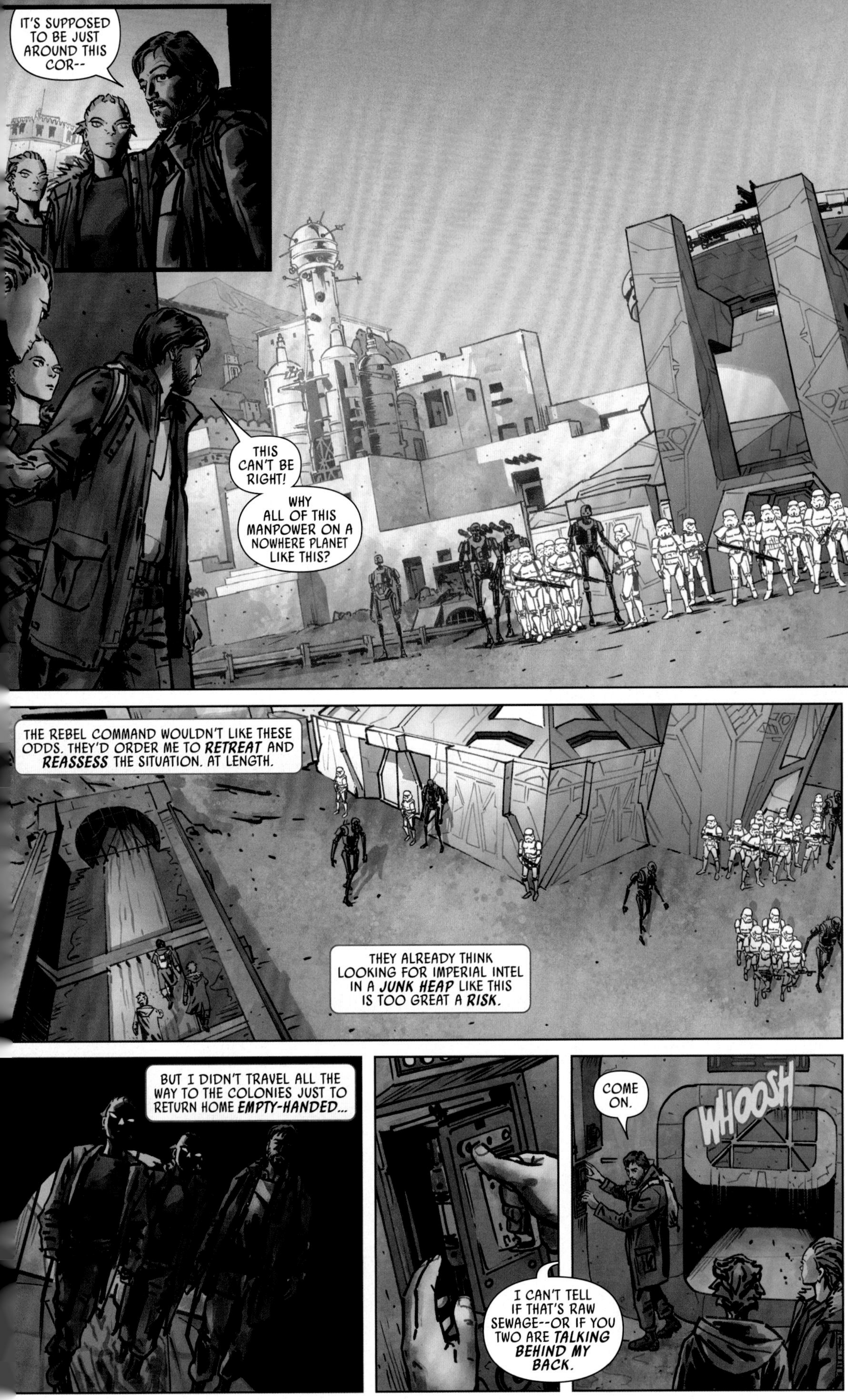

IT'S SUPPOSED TO BE JUST AROUND THIS COR--
THIS CAN'T BE RIGHT!
WHY ALL OF THIS MANPOWER ON A NOWHERE PLANET LIKE THIS?
THE REBEL COMMAND WOULDN'T LIKE THESE ODDS. THEY'D ORDER ME TO RETREAT AND REASSESS THE SITUATION. AT LENGTH.
THEY ALREADY THINK LOOKING FOR IMPERIAL INTEL IN A JUNK HEAP LIKE THIS IS TOO GREAT A RISK.
BUT I DIDN'T TRAVEL ALL THE WAY TO THE COLONIES JUST TO RETURN HOME EMPTY-HANDED...
I CAN'T TELL IF THAT'S RAW SEWAGE--OR IF YOU TWO ARE TALKING BEHIND MY BACK.
COME ON.
WHOOSH

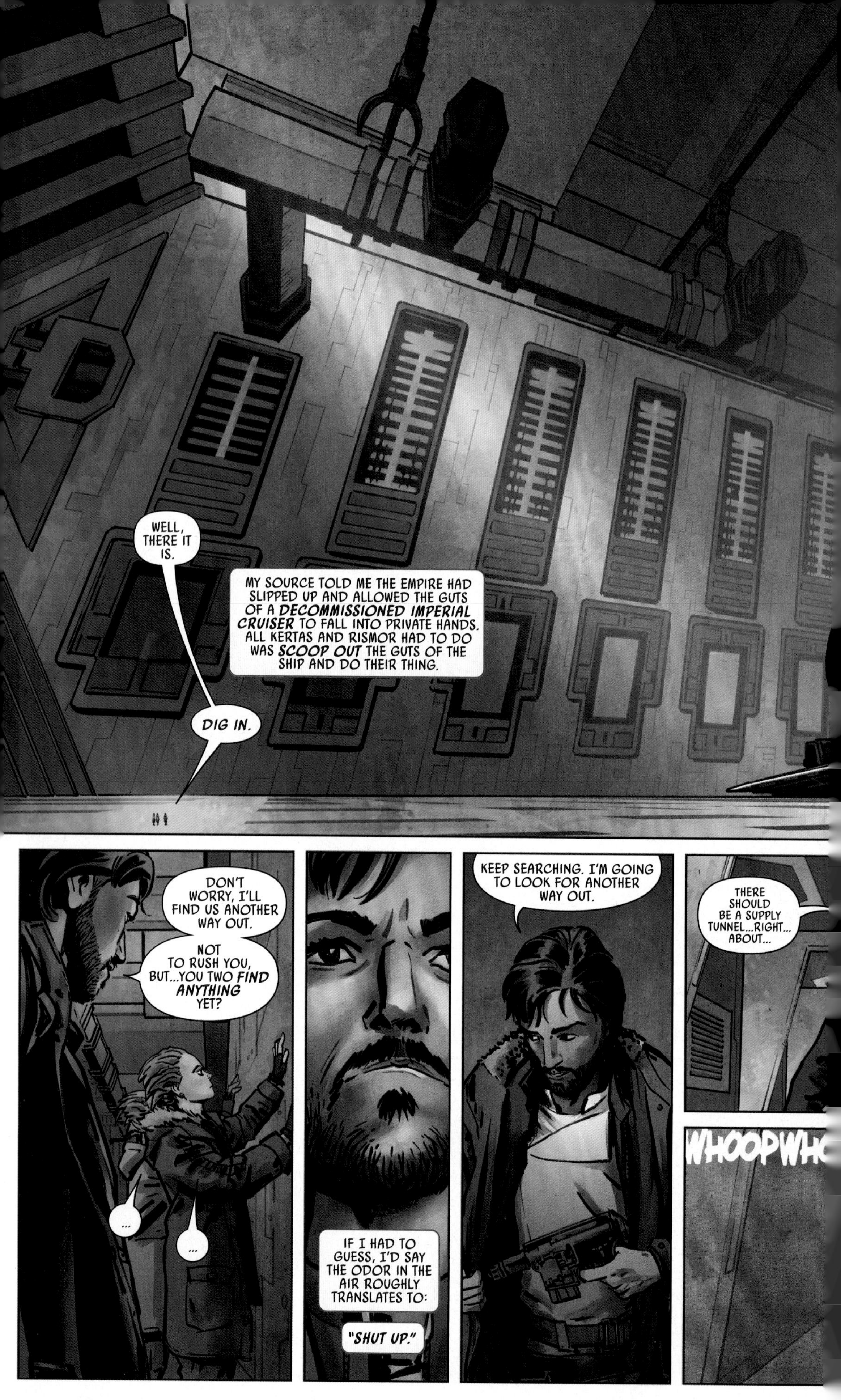
WELL, THERE IT IS.
MY SOURCE TOLD ME THE EMPIRE HAD SLIPPED UP AND ALLOWED THE GUTS OF A DECOMMISSIONED IMPERIAL CRUISER TO FALL INTO PRIVATE HANDS. ALL KERTAS AND RISMOR HAD TO DO WAS SCOOP OUT THE GUTS OF THE SHIP AND DO THEIR THING.
DIG IN.
DON'T WORRY, I'LL FIND US ANOTHER WAY OUT.
NOT TO RUSH YOU, BUT...YOU TWO FIND ANYTHING YET?
...
...
IF I HAD TO GUESS, I'D SAY THE ODOR IN THE AIR ROUGHLY TRANSLATES TO:
"SHUT UP."
KEEP SEARCHING. I'M GOING TO LOOK FOR ANOTHER WAY OUT.
THERE SHOULD BE A SUPPLY TUNNEL...RIGHT... ABOUT...
WHOOPWHO

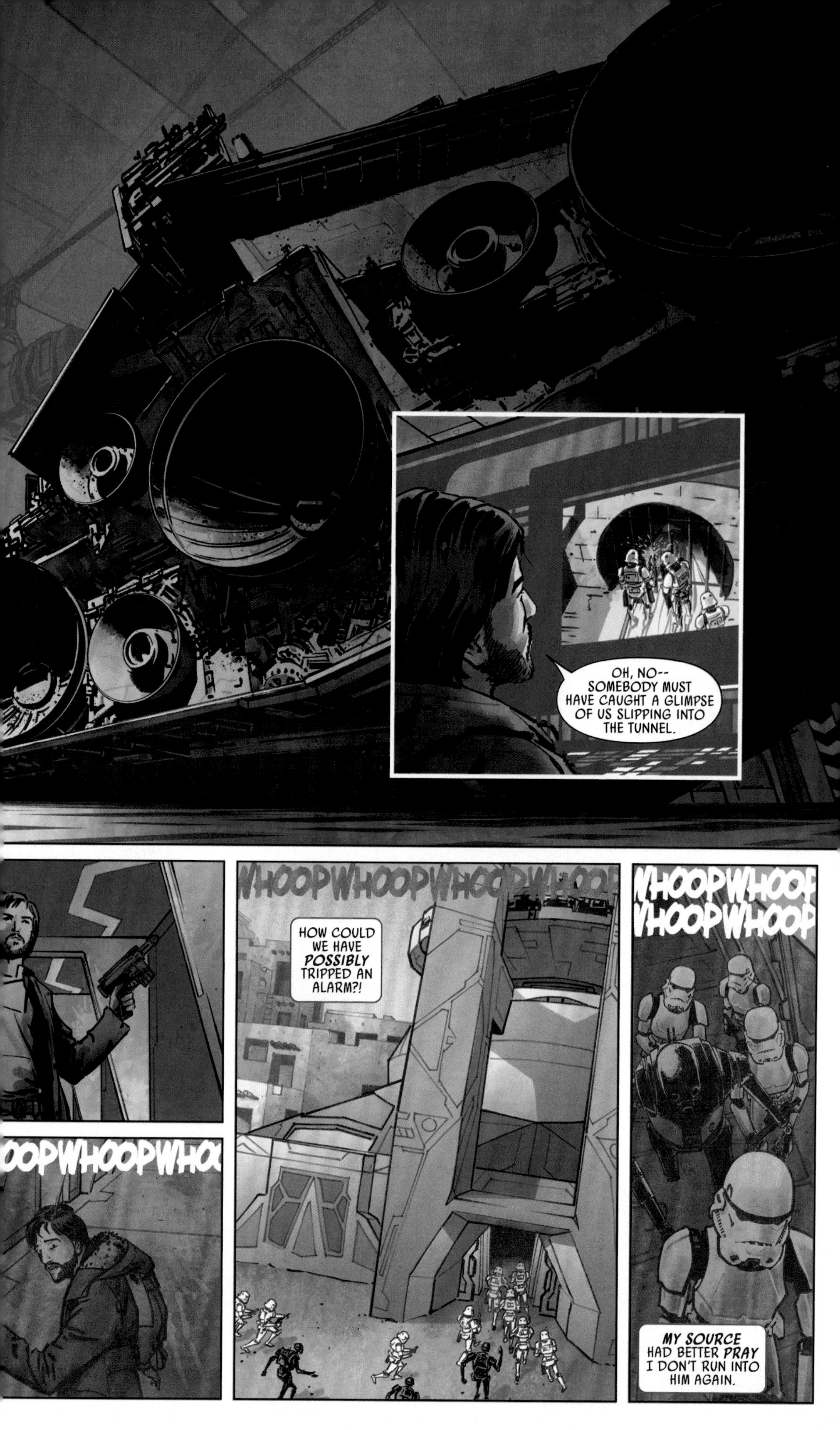
OH, NO--
SOMEBODY MUST
HAVE CAUGHT A GLIMPSE
OF US SLIPPING INTO
THE TUNNEL.
WHOOPWHOOPWHOOPWHOO
OOPWHOOPWHOO
HOW COULD
WE HAVE
POSSIBLY
TRIPPED AN
ALARM?!
WHOOPWHOOP
WHOOPWHOOP
MY SOURCE
HAD BETTER PRAY
I DON'T RUN INTO
HIM AGAIN.

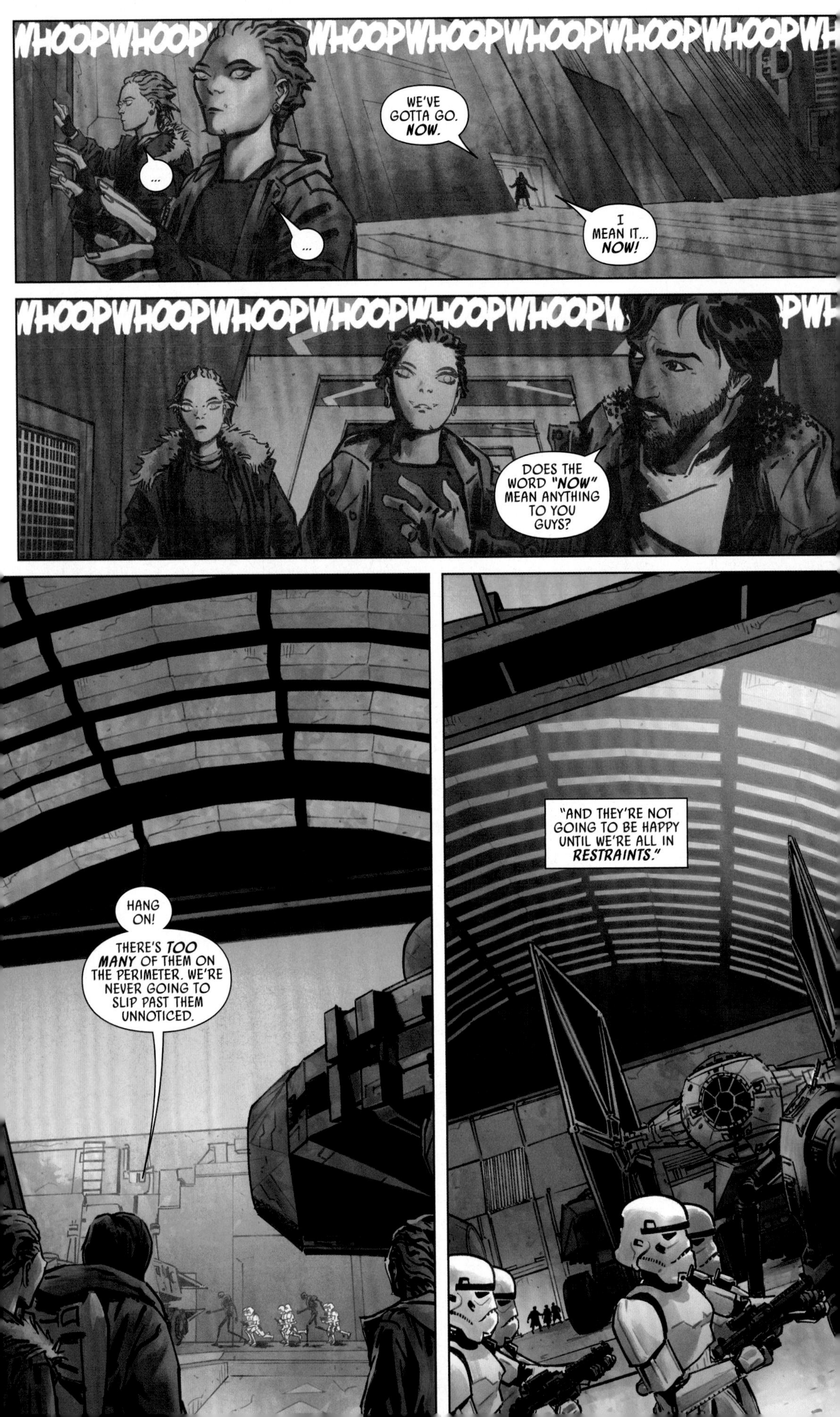
WHOOPWHOOPWHOOPWHOOPWHOOPWHOOPWHOOPWH
...
...
WE'VE GOTTA GO. NOW.
I MEAN IT... NOW!
WHOOPWHOOPWHOOPWHOOPWHOOPWHOOPWH
DOES THE WORD "NOW" MEAN ANYTHING TO YOU GUYS?
HANG ON!
THERE'S TOO MANY OF THEM ON THE PERIMETER. WE'RE NEVER GOING TO SLIP PAST THEM UNNOTICED.
"AND THEY'RE NOT GOING TO BE HAPPY UNTIL WE'RE ALL IN RESTRAINTS."

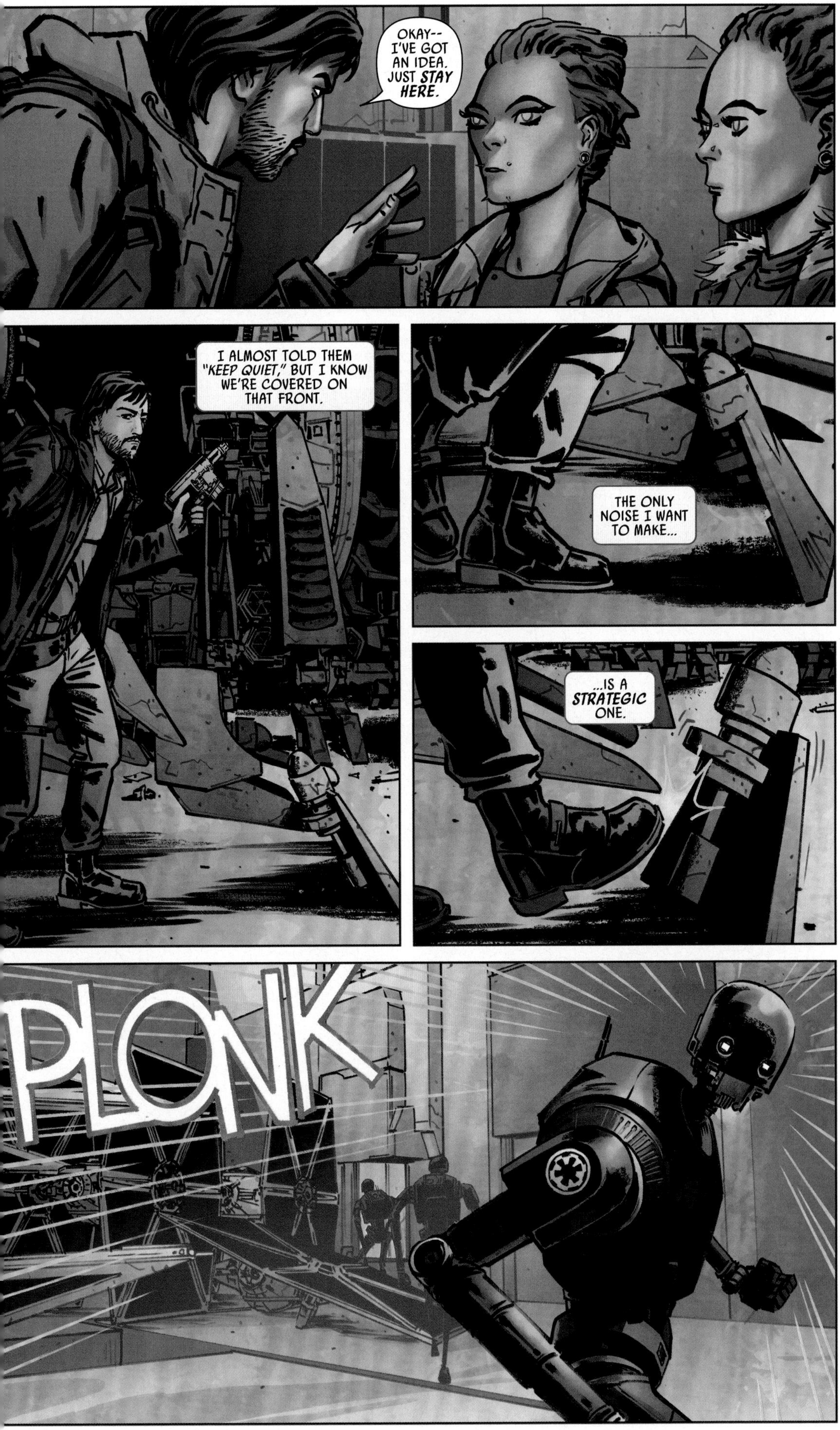
OKAY-- I'VE GOT AN IDEA. JUST STAY HERE.
I ALMOST TOLD THEM "KEEP QUIET," BUT I KNOW WE'RE COVERED ON THAT FRONT.
THE ONLY NOISE I WANT TO MAKE...
...IS A STRATEGIC ONE.
PLONK

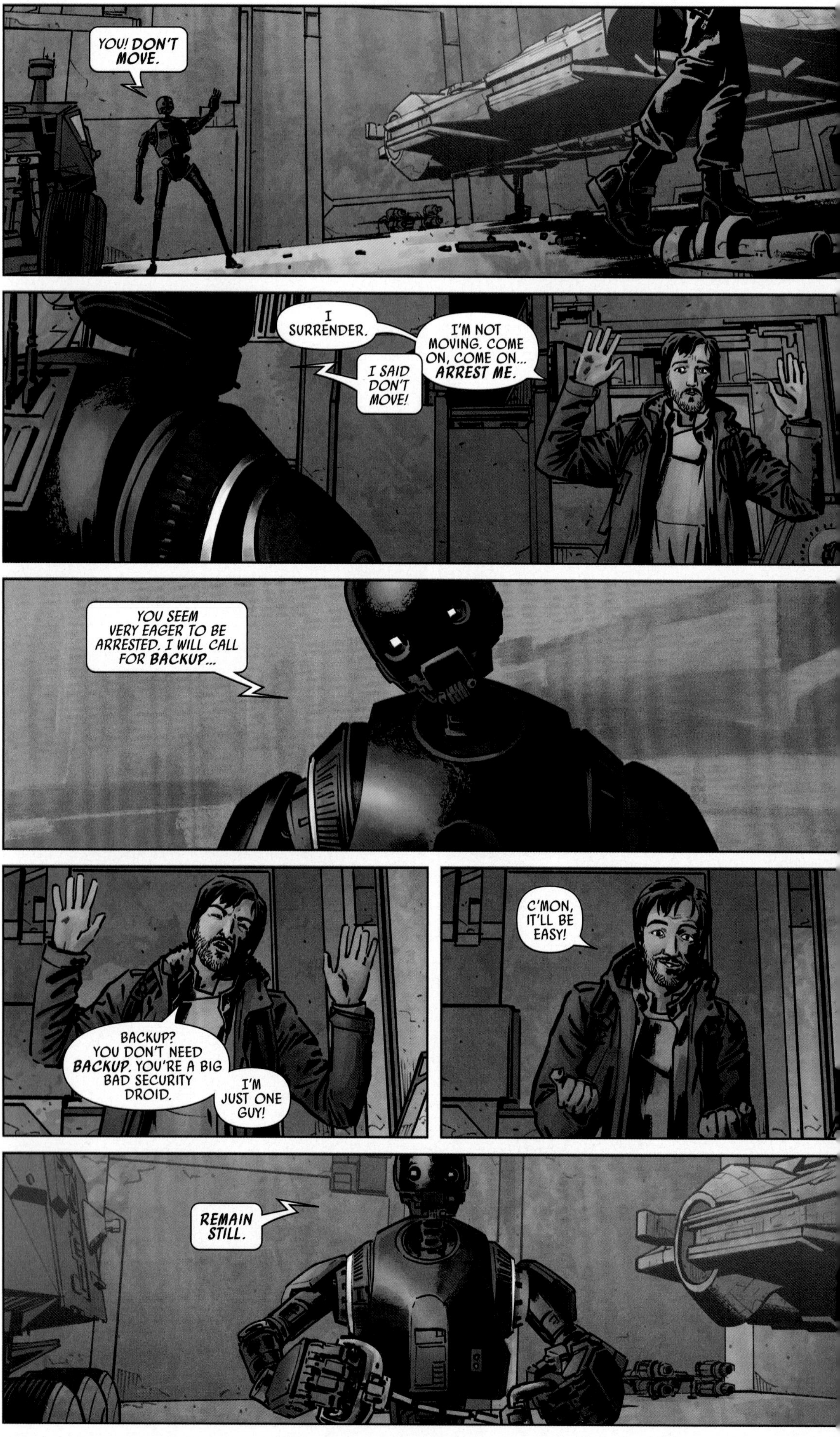
YOU! DON'T MOVE.
I SURRENDER.
I'M NOT MOVING. COME ON, COME ON... ARREST ME.
I SAID DON'T MOVE!
YOU SEEM VERY EAGER TO BE ARRESTED. I WILL CALL FOR BACKUP...
BACKUP? YOU DON'T NEED BACKUP. YOU'RE A BIG BAD SECURITY DROID.
I'M JUST ONE GUY!
C'MON, IT'LL BE EASY!
REMAIN STILL.

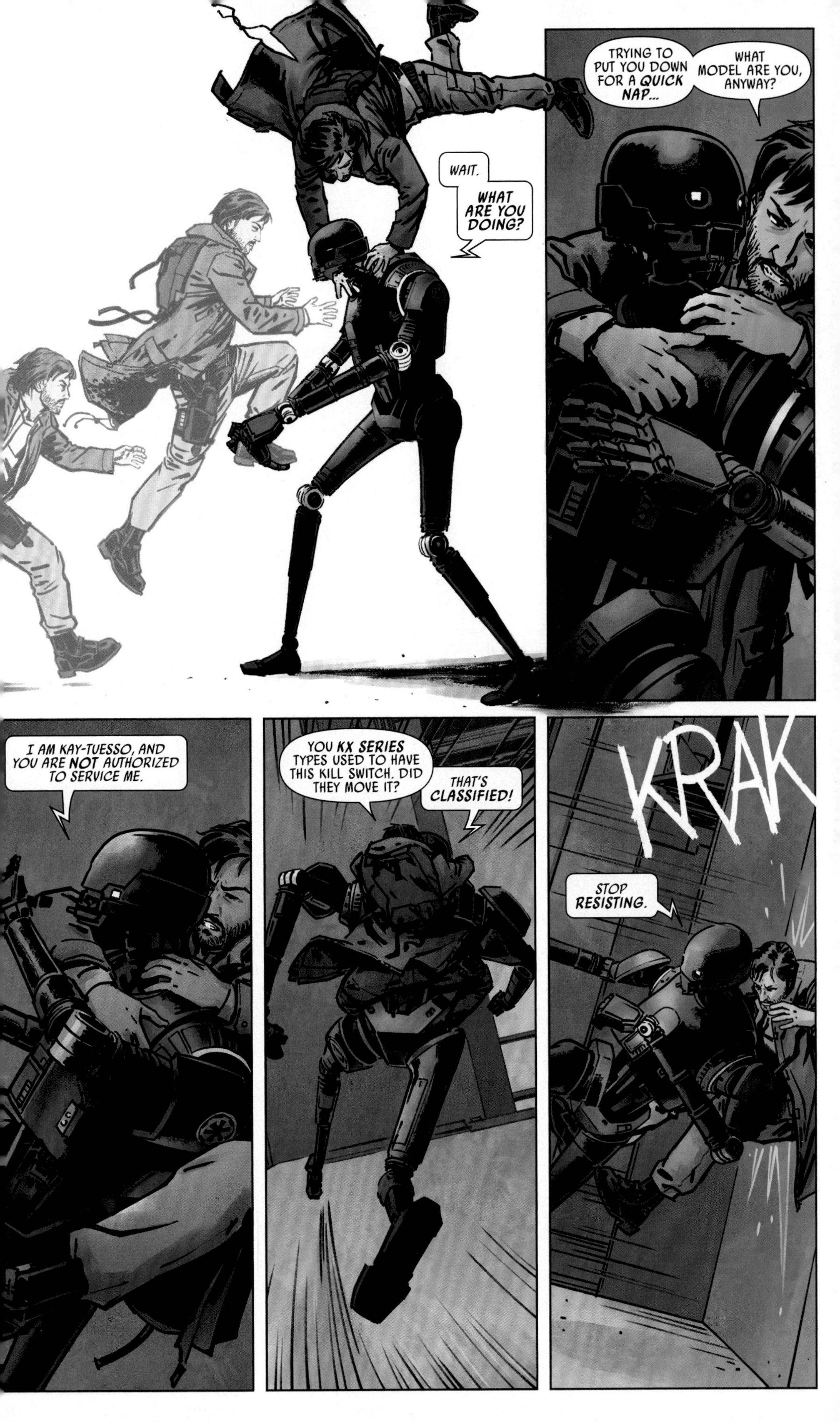
WAIT.
WHAT ARE YOU DOING?
TRYING TO PUT YOU DOWN FOR A QUICK NAP...
WHAT MODEL ARE YOU, ANYWAY?
I AM KAY-TUESSO, AND YOU ARE NOT AUTHORIZED TO SERVICE ME.
YOU KX SERIES TYPES USED TO HAVE THIS KILL SWITCH. DID THEY MOVE IT?
THAT'S CLASSIFIED!
KRAK
STOP RESISTING.

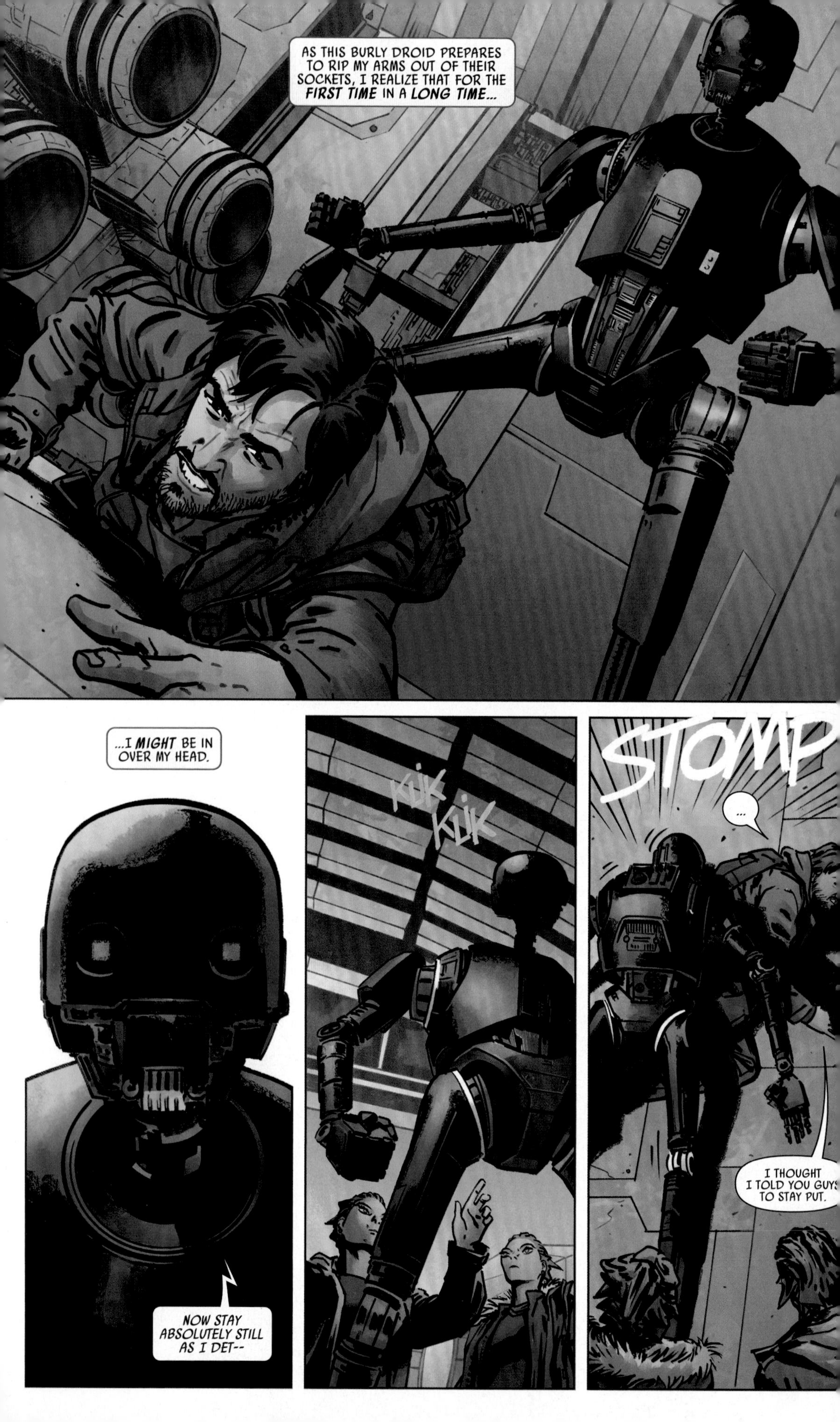
AS THIS BURLY DROID PREPARES TO RIP MY ARMS OUT OF THEIR SOCKETS, I REALIZE THAT FOR THE FIRST TIME IN A LONG TIME...
...I MIGHT BE IN OVER MY HEAD.
NOW STAY ABSOLUTELY STILL AS I DET--
KLIK KLIK
STOMP
...
I THOUGHT I TOLD YOU GUYS TO STAY PUT.

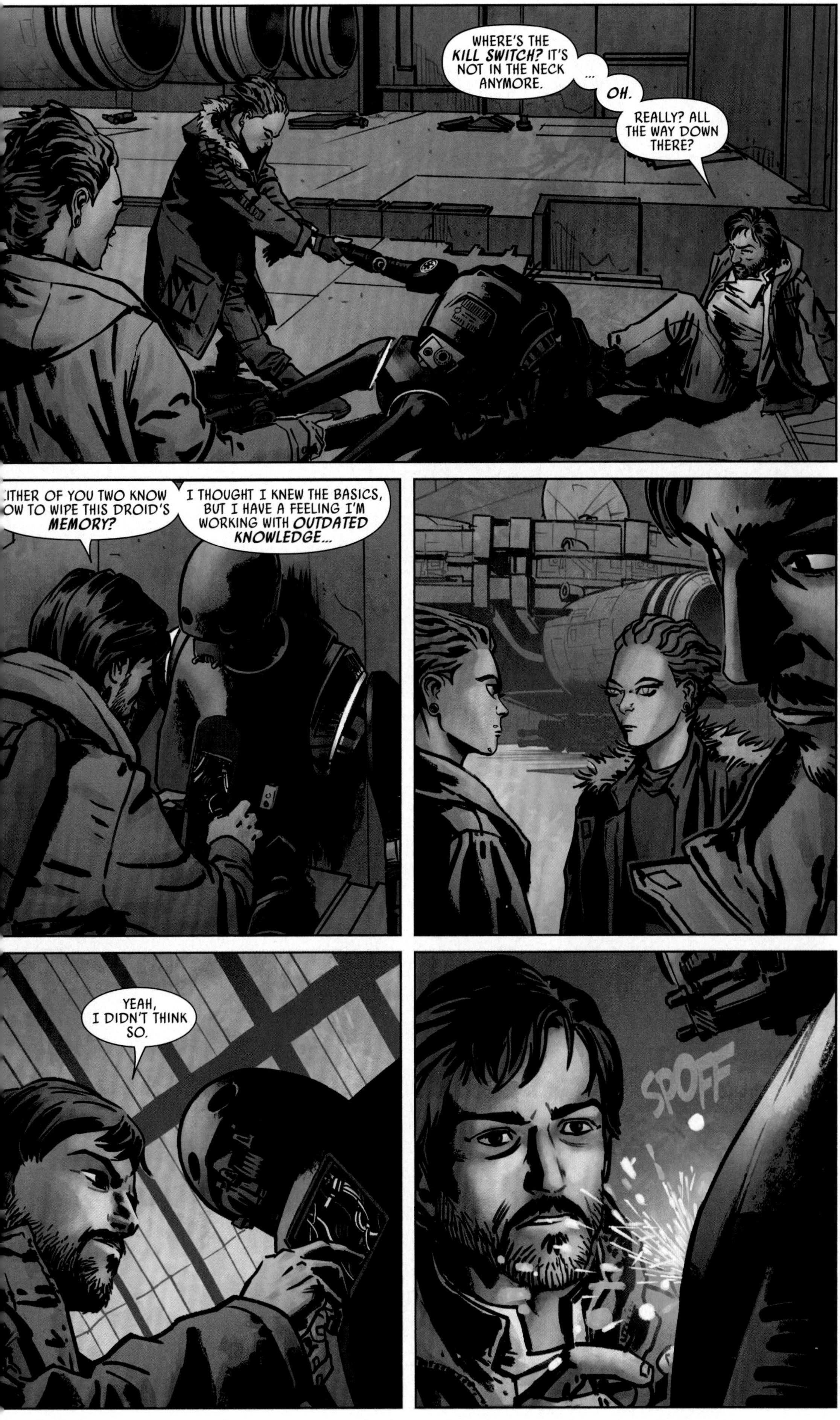
WHERE'S THE KILL SWITCH? IT'S NOT IN THE NECK ANYMORE.
...
OH.
REALLY? ALL THE WAY DOWN THERE?
ITHER OF YOU TWO KNOW OW TO WIPE THIS DROID'S MEMORY?
I THOUGHT I KNEW THE BASICS, BUT I HAVE A FEELING I'M WORKING WITH OUTDATED KNOWLEDGE...
YEAH, I DIDN'T THINK SO.
SPOFF

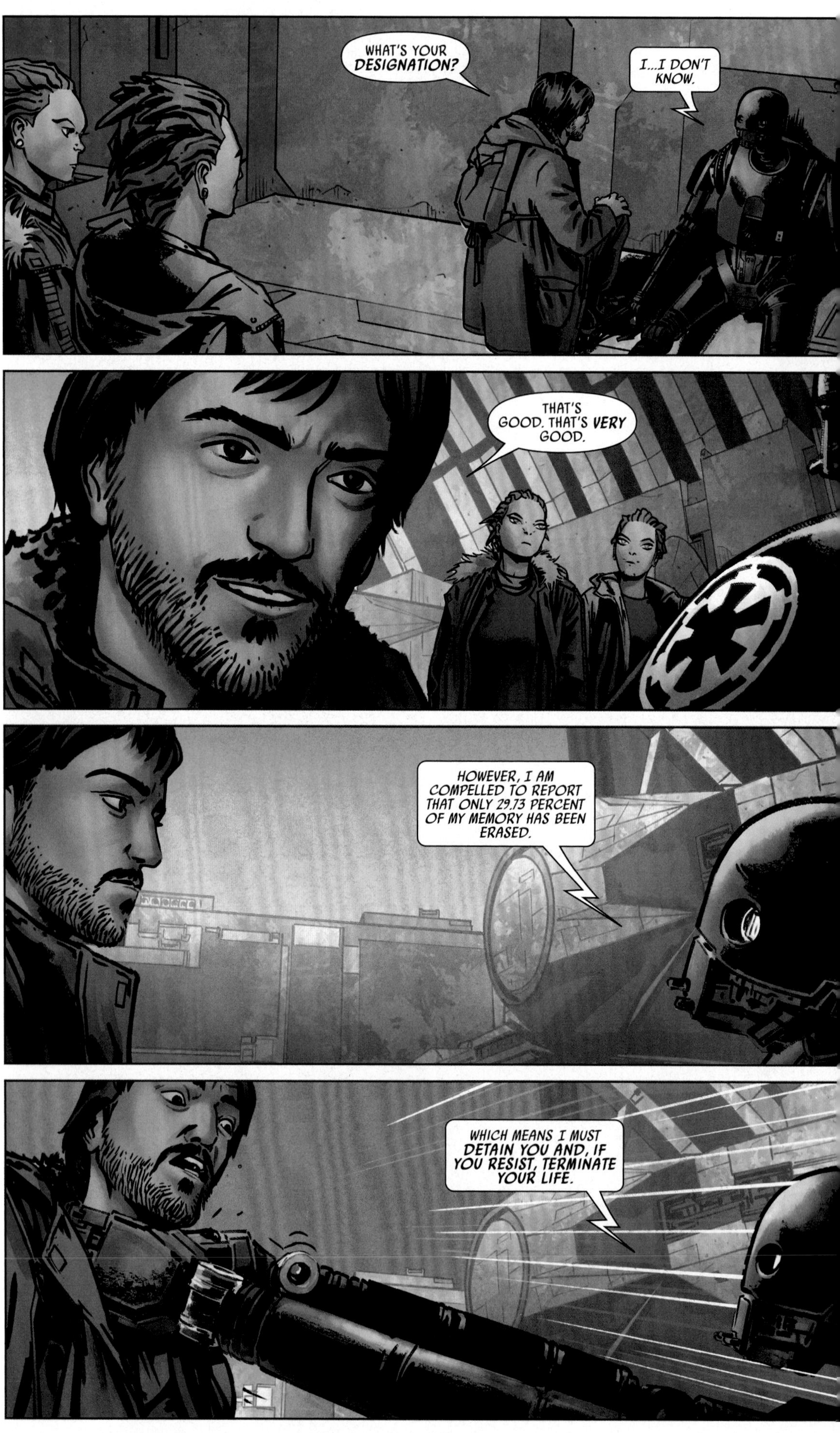
WHAT'S YOUR DESIGNATION?
I...I DON'T KNOW.
THAT'S GOOD. THAT'S VERY GOOD.
HOWEVER, I AM COMPELLED TO REPORT THAT ONLY 29.73 PERCENT OF MY MEMORY HAS BEEN ERASED.
WHICH MEANS I MUST DETAIN YOU AND, IF YOU RESIST, TERMINATE YOUR LIFE.

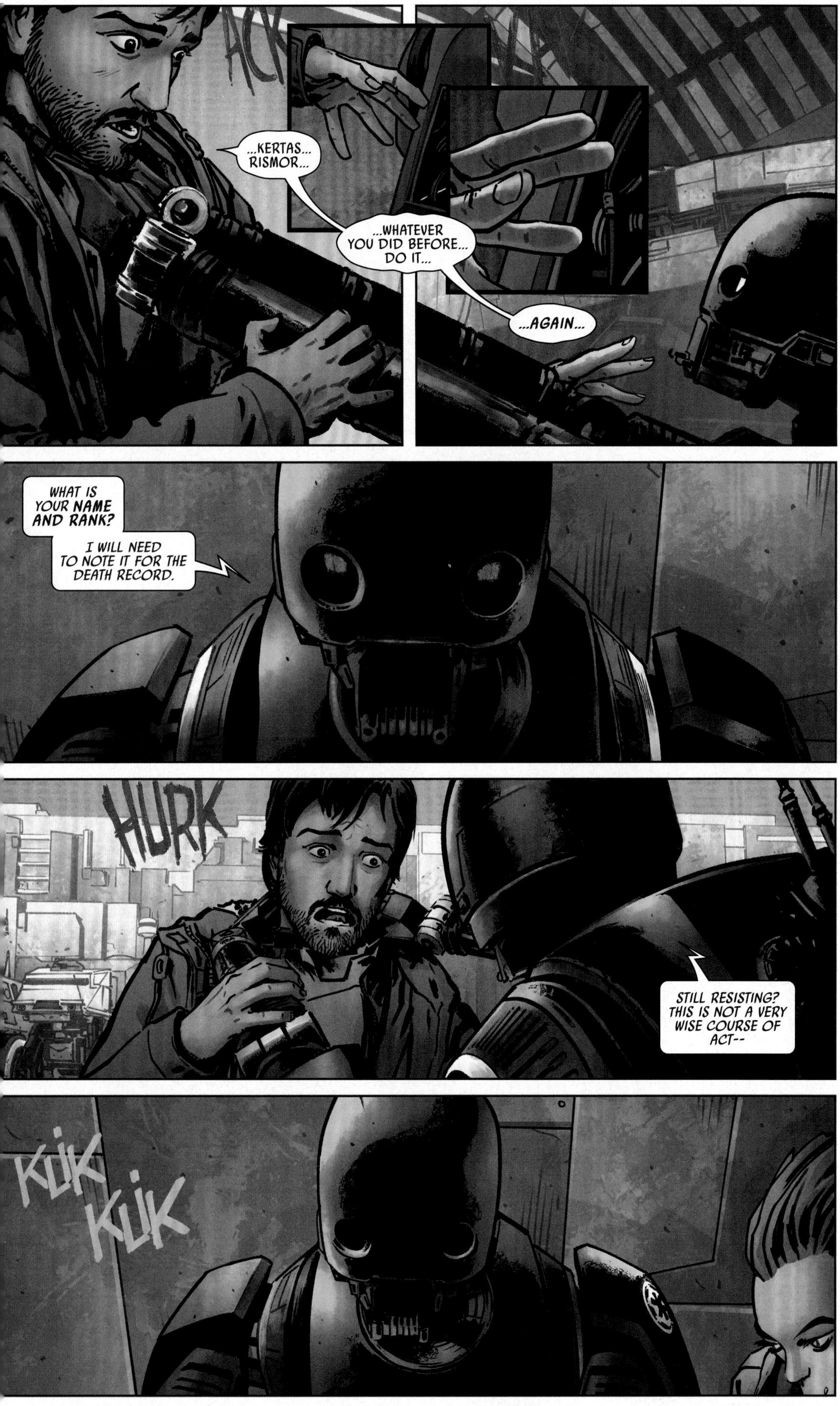
ACK
...KERTAS... RISMOR...
...WHATEVER YOU DID BEFORE... DO IT...
...AGAIN...
WHAT IS YOUR NAME AND RANK?
I WILL NEED TO NOTE IT FOR THE DEATH RECORD.
HURK
STILL RESISTING? THIS IS NOT A VERY WISE COURSE OF ACT--
KLIK KLIK

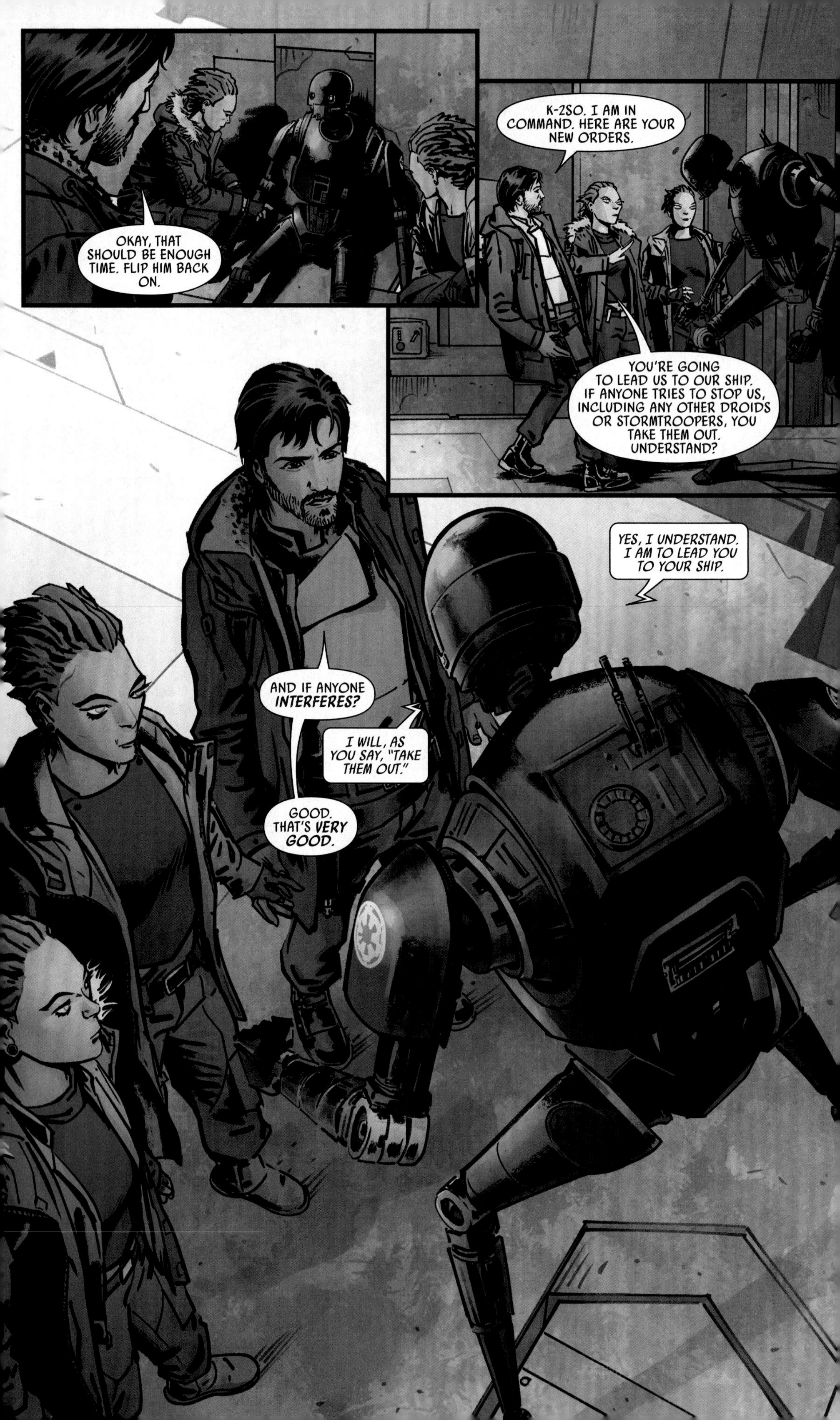
OKAY, THAT SHOULD BE ENOUGH TIME. FLIP HIM BACK ON.
K-2SO. I AM IN COMMAND. HERE ARE YOUR NEW ORDERS.
YOU'RE GOING TO LEAD US TO OUR SHIP. IF ANYONE TRIES TO STOP US, INCLUDING ANY OTHER DROIDS OR STORMTROOPERS, YOU TAKE THEM OUT. UNDERSTAND?
YES, I UNDERSTAND. I AM TO LEAD YOU TO YOUR SHIP.
AND IF ANYONE INTERFERES?
I WILL, AS YOU SAY, "TAKE THEM OUT."
GOOD. THAT'S VERY GOOD.

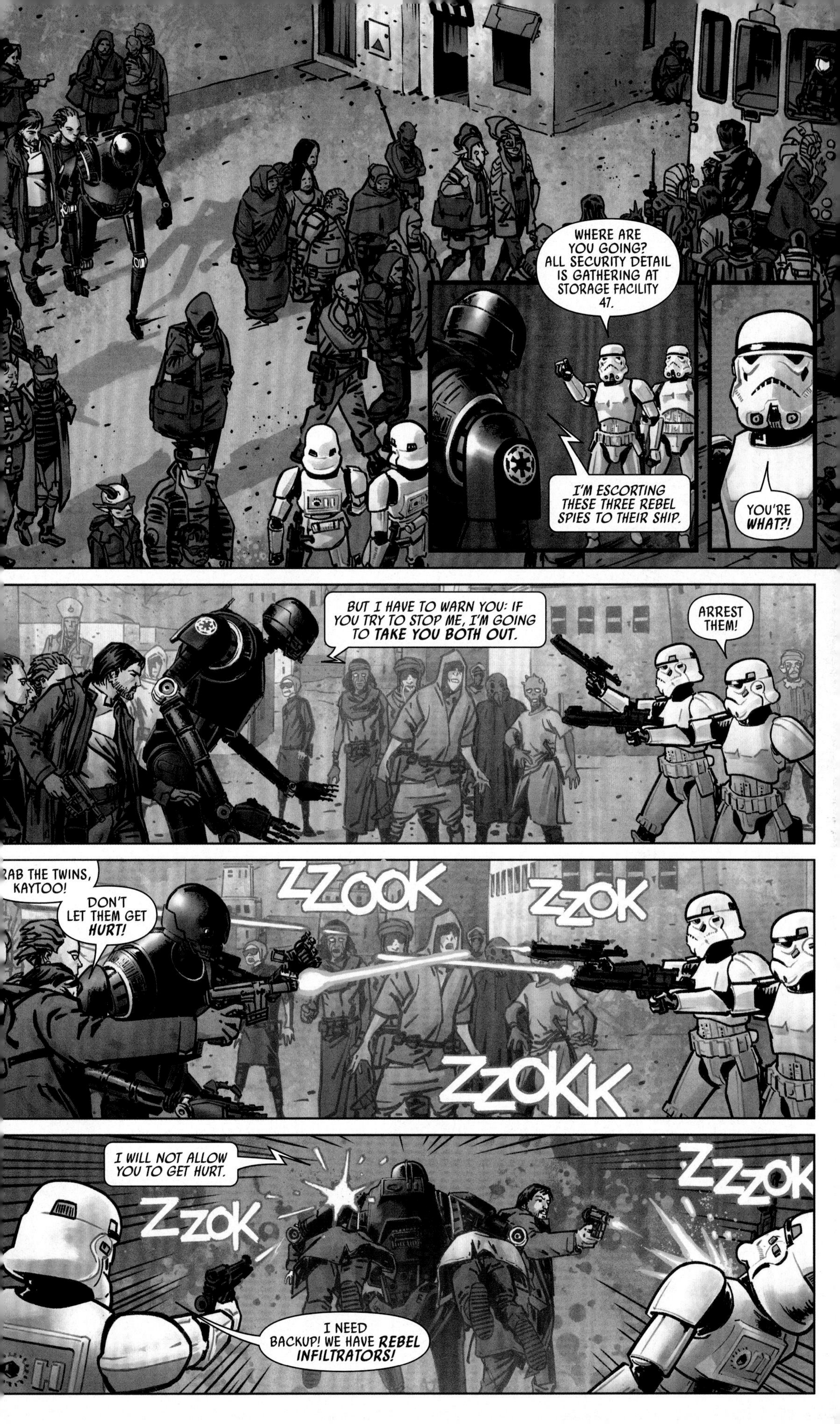
WHERE ARE YOU GOING? ALL SECURITY DETAIL IS GATHERING AT STORAGE FACILITY 47.
I'M ESCORTING THESE THREE REBEL SPIES TO THEIR SHIP.
YOU'RE WHAT?!
BUT I HAVE TO WARN YOU: IF YOU TRY TO STOP ME, I'M GOING TO TAKE YOU BOTH OUT.
ARREST THEM!
RAB THE TWINS, KAYTOO!
DON'T LET THEM GET HURT!
ZZOOK
ZZOK
ZZOKK
I WILL NOT ALLOW YOU TO GET HURT.
ZZOK
ZZZOK
I NEED BACKUP! WE HAVE REBEL INFILTRATORS!

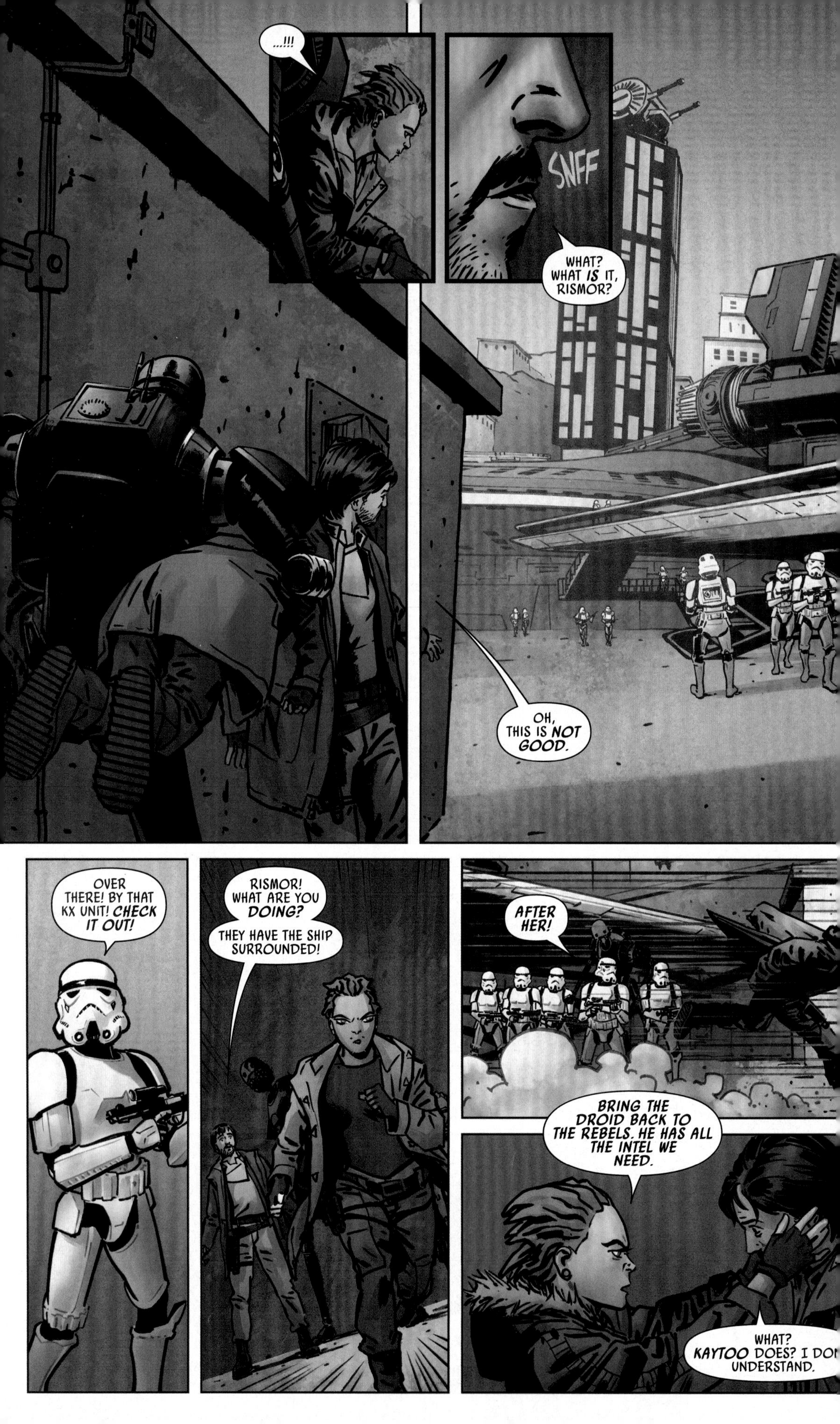

...!!!
SNFF
WHAT? WHAT *IS* IT, RISMOR?
OH, THIS IS *NOT* *GOOD.*
OVER THERE! BY THAT KX UNIT! *CHECK IT OUT!*
RISMOR! WHAT ARE YOU *DOING?*
THEY HAVE THE SHIP SURROUNDED!
AFTER HER!
BRING THE DROID BACK TO THE REBELS. HE HAS ALL THE INTEL WE NEED.
WHAT? *KAYTOO* DOES? I DON'T UNDERSTAND.

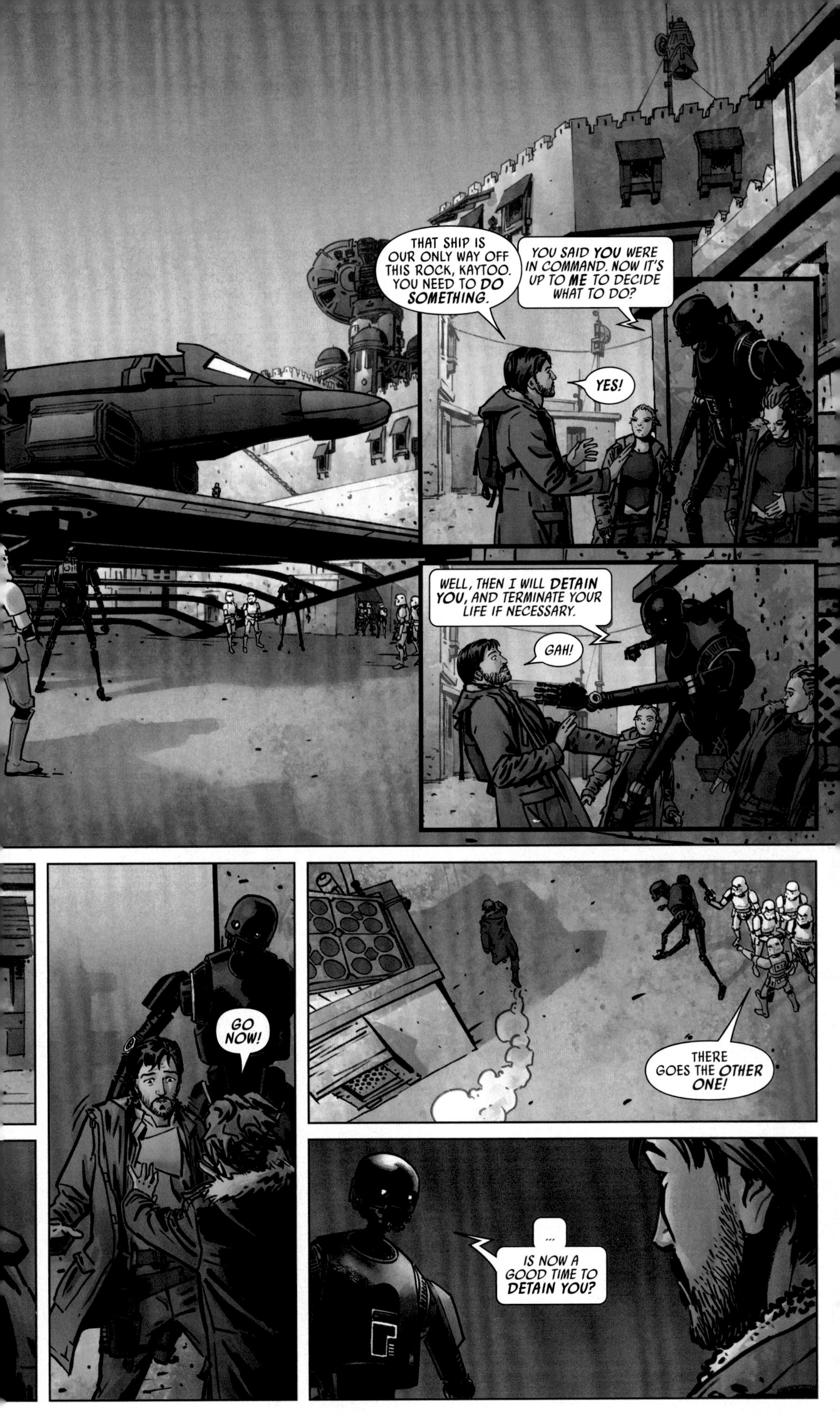
THAT SHIP IS OUR ONLY WAY OFF THIS ROCK, KAYTOO. YOU NEED TO DO SOMETHING.
YOU SAID YOU WERE IN COMMAND. NOW IT'S UP TO ME TO DECIDE WHAT TO DO?
YES!
WELL, THEN I WILL DETAIN YOU, AND TERMINATE YOUR LIFE IF NECESSARY.
GAH!
GO NOW!
THERE GOES THE OTHER ONE!
...
IS NOW A GOOD TIME TO DETAIN YOU?

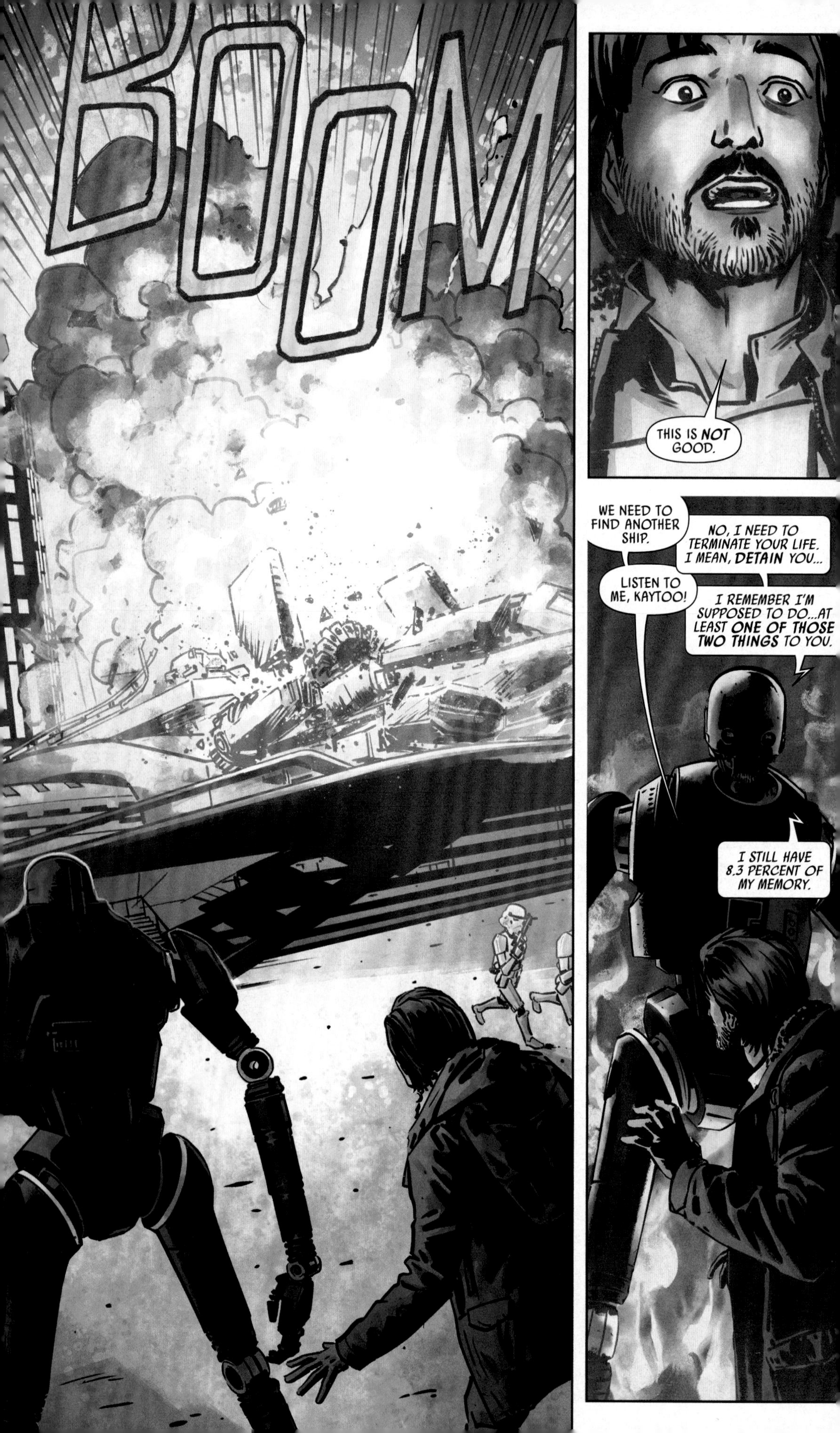
BOOM
THIS IS NOT GOOD.
WE NEED TO FIND ANOTHER SHIP.
NO, I NEED TO TERMINATE YOUR LIFE. I MEAN, DETAIN YOU...
LISTEN TO ME, KAYTOO!
I REMEMBER I'M SUPPOSED TO DO...AT LEAST ONE OF THOSE TWO THINGS TO YOU.
I STILL HAVE 8.3 PERCENT OF MY MEMORY.

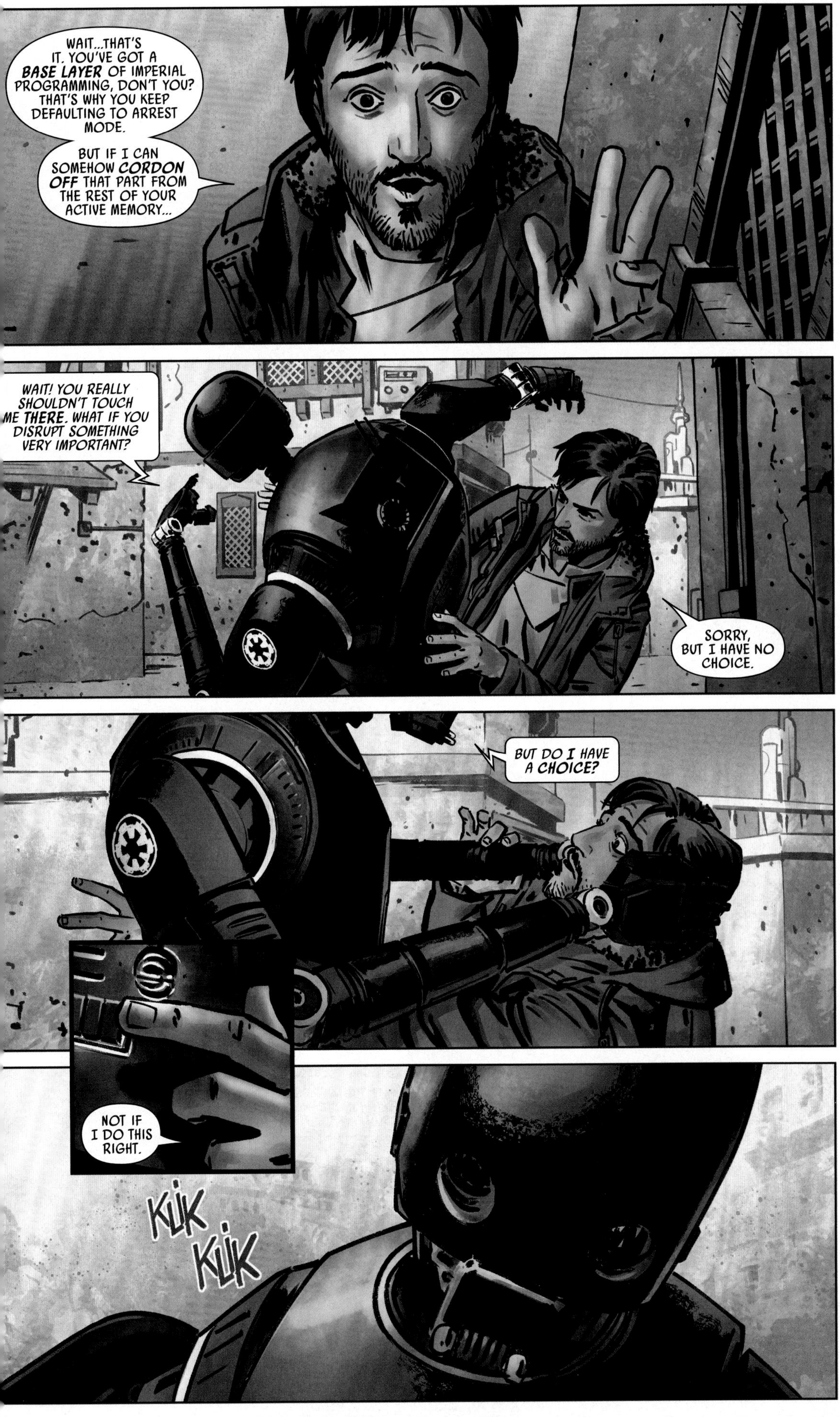
WAIT...THAT'S IT. YOU'VE GOT A BASE LAYER OF IMPERIAL PROGRAMMING, DON'T YOU? THAT'S WHY YOU KEEP DEFAULTING TO ARREST MODE.
BUT IF I CAN SOMEHOW CORDON OFF THAT PART FROM THE REST OF YOUR ACTIVE MEMORY...
WAIT! YOU REALLY SHOULDN'T TOUCH ME THERE. WHAT IF YOU DISRUPT SOMETHING VERY IMPORTANT?
SORRY, BUT I HAVE NO CHOICE.
BUT DO I HAVE A CHOICE?
NOT IF I DO THIS RIGHT.
KLIK KLIK

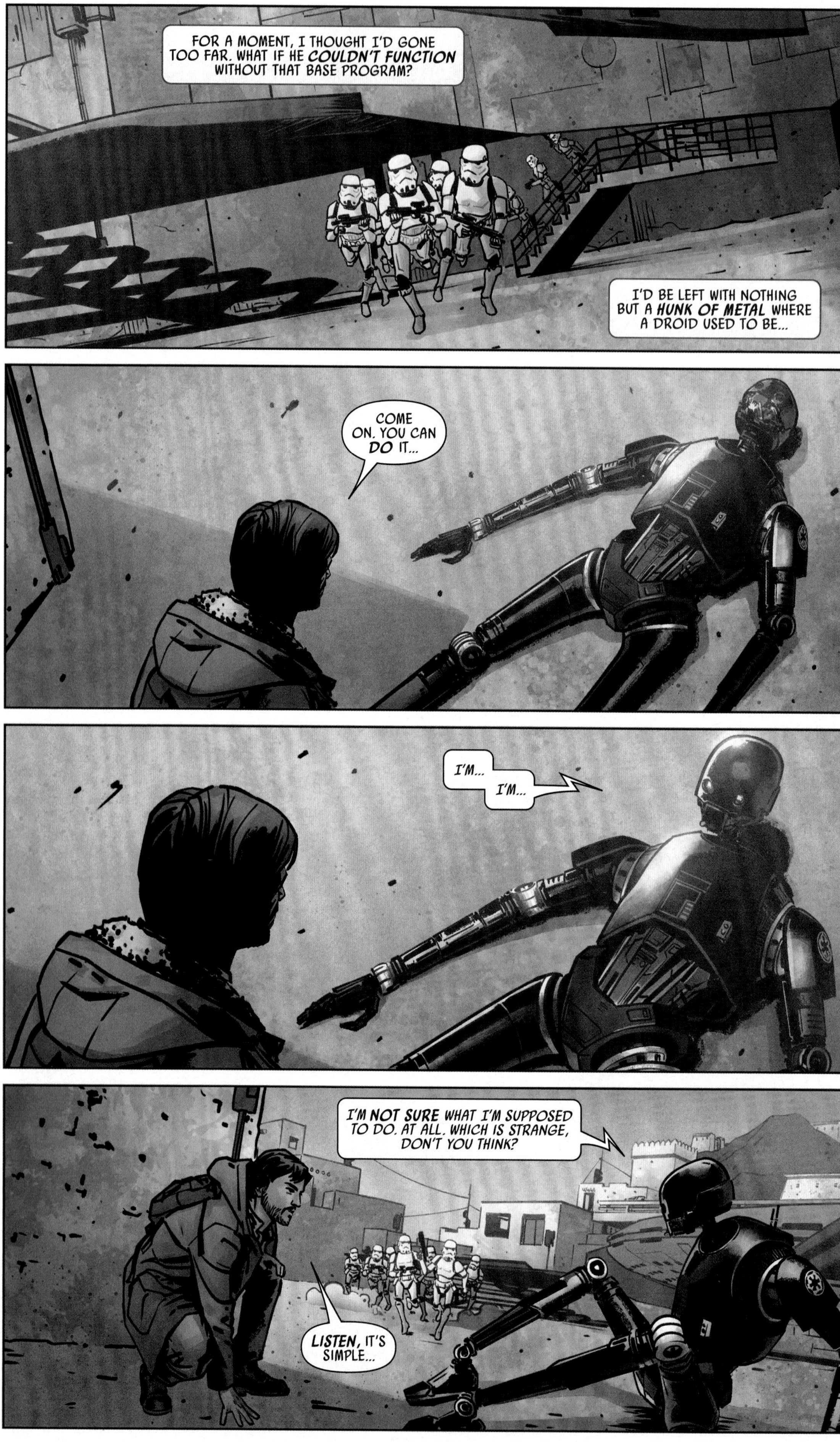
FOR A MOMENT, I THOUGHT I'D GONE TOO FAR. WHAT IF HE COULDN'T FUNCTION WITHOUT THAT BASE PROGRAM?
I'D BE LEFT WITH NOTHING BUT A HUNK OF METAL WHERE A DROID USED TO BE...
COME ON. YOU CAN DO IT...
I'M...
I'M...
I'M NOT SURE WHAT I'M SUPPOSED TO DO. AT ALL. WHICH IS STRANGE, DON'T YOU THINK?
LISTEN, IT'S SIMPLE...

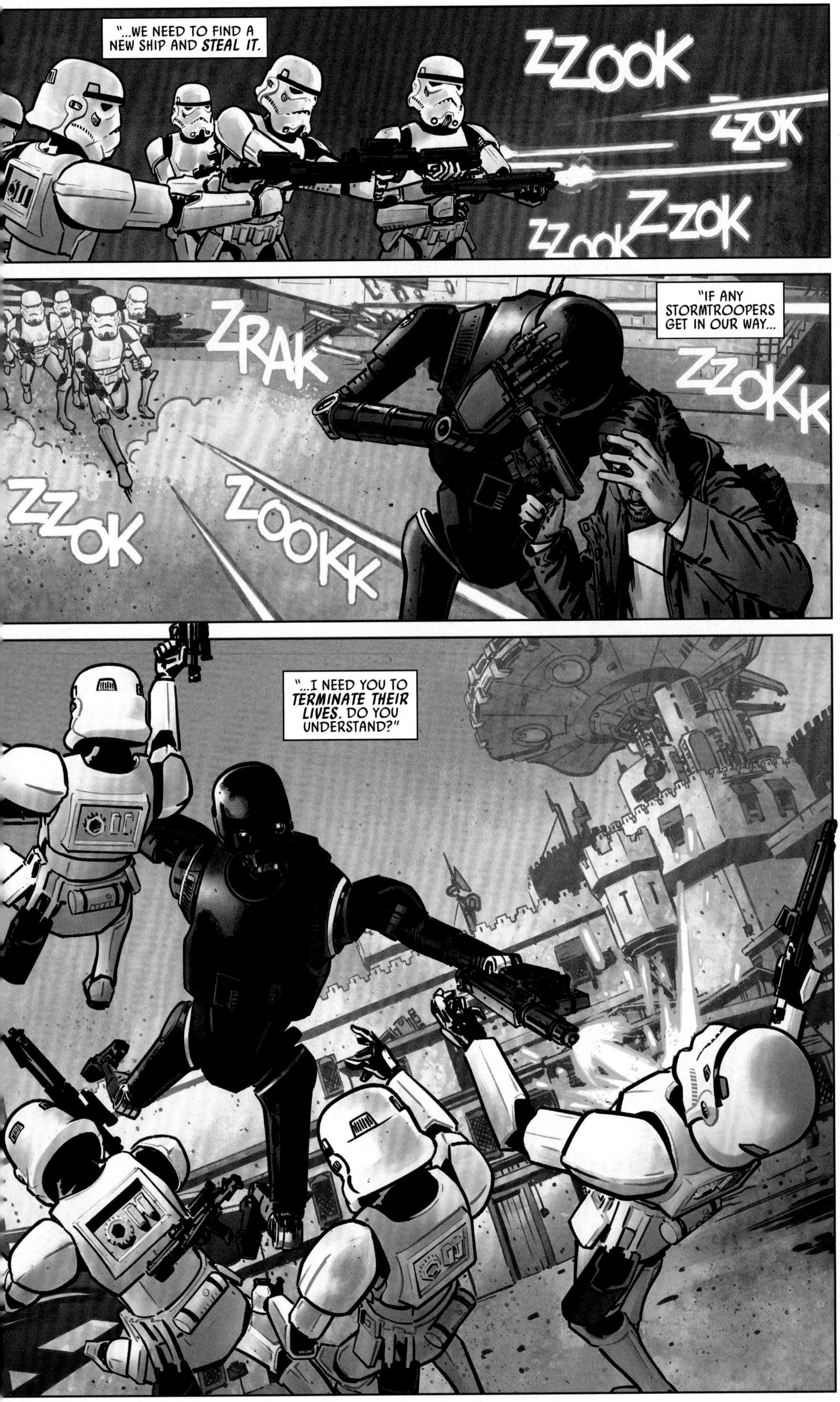
"...WE NEED TO FIND A NEW SHIP AND STEAL IT.
ZZOOK
ZZOK
ZZOOK
ZZOK
"IF ANY STORMTROOPERS GET IN OUR WAY...
ZRAK
ZZOKK
ZZOK
ZOOKK
"...I NEED YOU TO TERMINATE THEIR LIVES. DO YOU UNDERSTAND?"

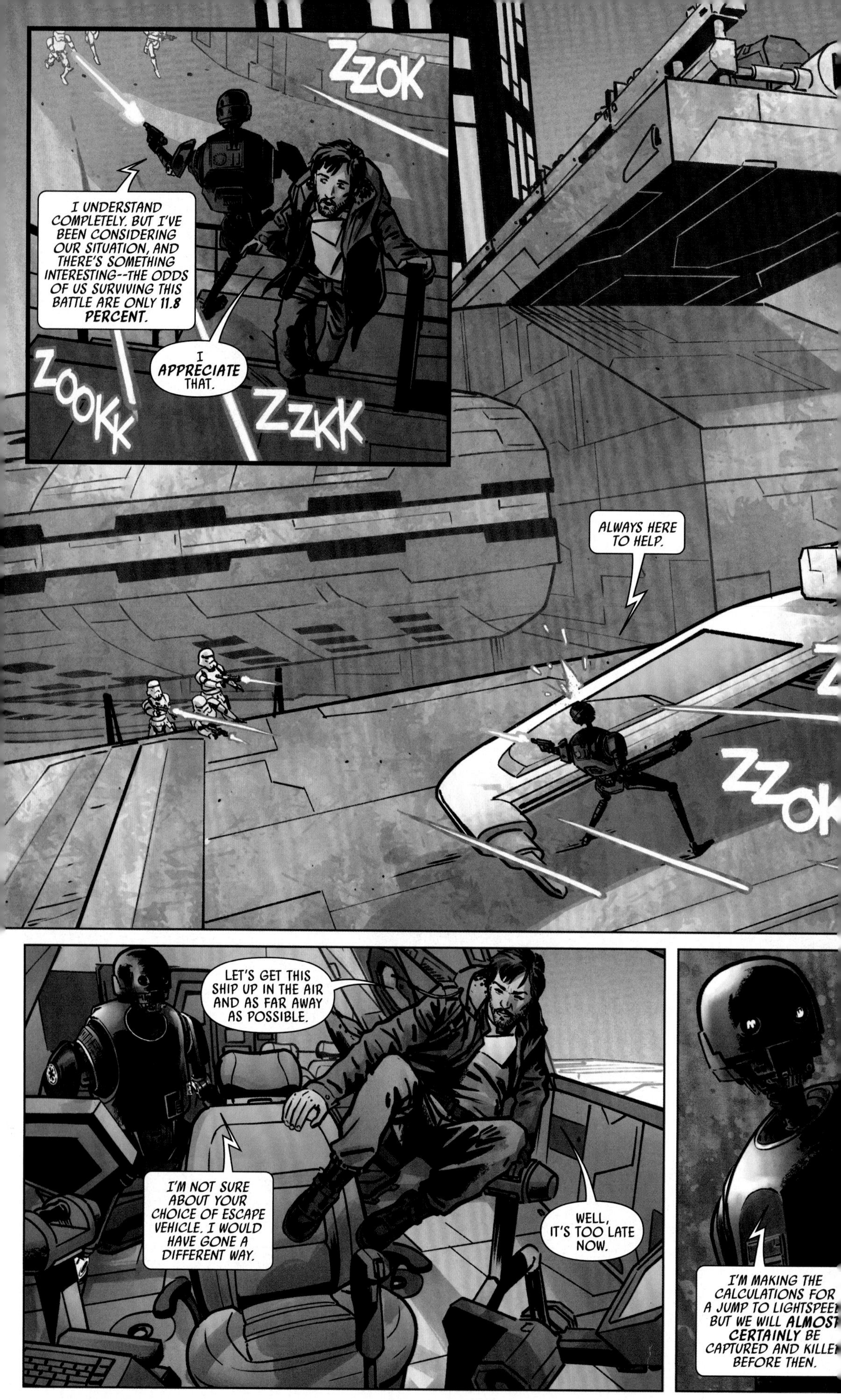
ZZOK
I UNDERSTAND COMPLETELY. BUT I'VE BEEN CONSIDERING OUR SITUATION, AND THERE'S SOMETHING INTERESTING--THE ODDS OF US SURVIVING THIS BATTLE ARE ONLY 11.8 PERCENT.
I APPRECIATE THAT.
ZOOKK
ZZKK
ALWAYS HERE TO HELP.
ZZOK
LET'S GET THIS SHIP UP IN THE AIR AND AS FAR AWAY AS POSSIBLE.
I'M NOT SURE ABOUT YOUR CHOICE OF ESCAPE VEHICLE. I WOULD HAVE GONE A DIFFERENT WAY.
WELL, IT'S TOO LATE NOW.
I'M MAKING THE CALCULATIONS FOR A JUMP TO LIGHTSPEE BUT WE WILL ALMOST CERTAINLY BE CAPTURED AND KILLE BEFORE THEN.

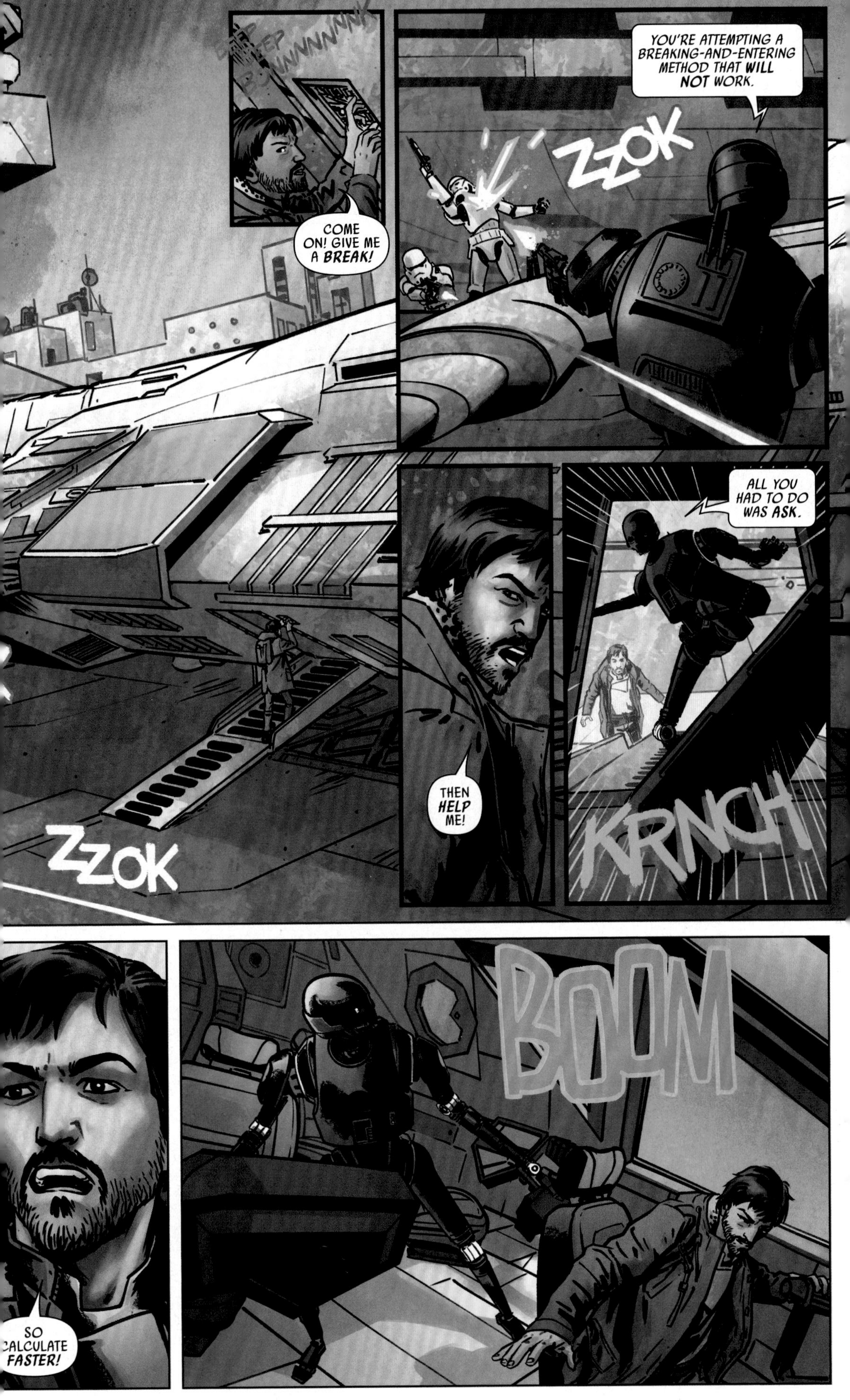
COME ON! GIVE ME A *BREAK!*
YOU'RE ATTEMPTING A BREAKING-AND-ENTERING METHOD THAT **WILL NOT** WORK.
ZZOK
ZZOK
THEN *HELP* ME!
ALL YOU HAD TO DO WAS **ASK.**
KRNCH
SO CALCULATE *FASTER!*
BOOM

KZZOKK
ZZOK
ZZOKK
KZZOK
ZK!

VVVRRRRMMMMM

GO! NOW! NOW!

RUSHING THESE CALCULATIONS COULD LEAD TO A VERY QUICK DEMISE.

DESPITE THE ODDS, WE HAVE ESCAPED.

THANKS FOR THAT VOTE OF CONFIDENCE.

YOU'RE WELCOME.

I NEVER LEARNED YOUR NAME. FOR MY DATA FILES, OF COURSE.

I AM.

CAPTAIN CASSIAN ANDOR. AND YOU'RE STILL KAY-TUESSO?

WHICH MEANS YOU STILL HAVE THAT IMPERIAL PROGRAMMING SOMEWHERE INSIDE OF YOU.

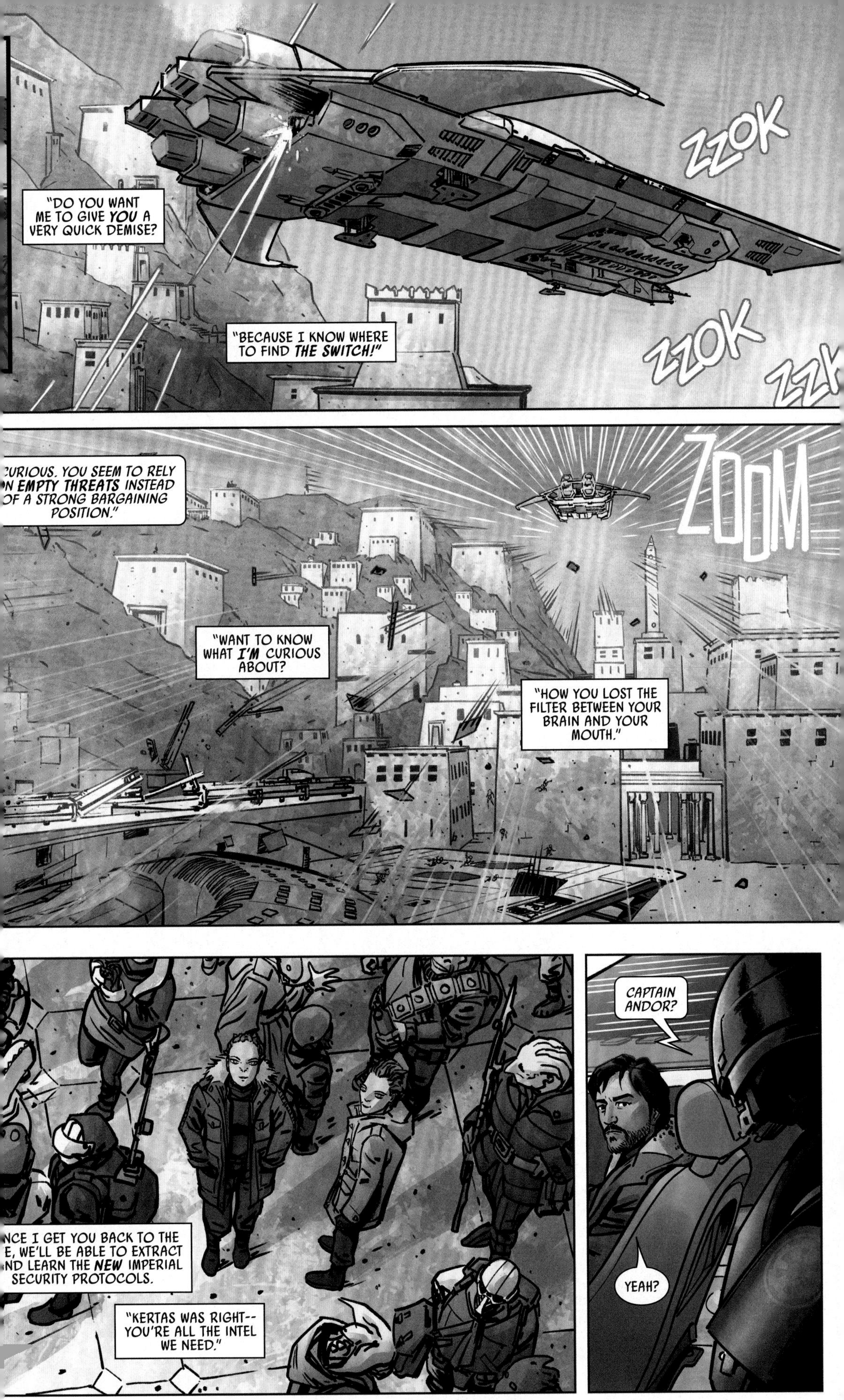

ZZOK
"DO YOU WANT ME TO GIVE YOU A VERY QUICK DEMISE?
"BECAUSE I KNOW WHERE TO FIND THE SWITCH!"
ZZOK
CURIOUS. YOU SEEM TO RELY ON EMPTY THREATS INSTEAD OF A STRONG BARGAINING POSITION."
ZOOM
"WANT TO KNOW WHAT I'M CURIOUS ABOUT?
"HOW YOU LOST THE FILTER BETWEEN YOUR BRAIN AND YOUR MOUTH."
NCE I GET YOU BACK TO THE E, WE'LL BE ABLE TO EXTRACT ND LEARN THE NEW IMPERIAL SECURITY PROTOCOLS.
"KERTAS WAS RIGHT-- YOU'RE ALL THE INTEL WE NEED."
CAPTAIN ANDOR?
YEAH?

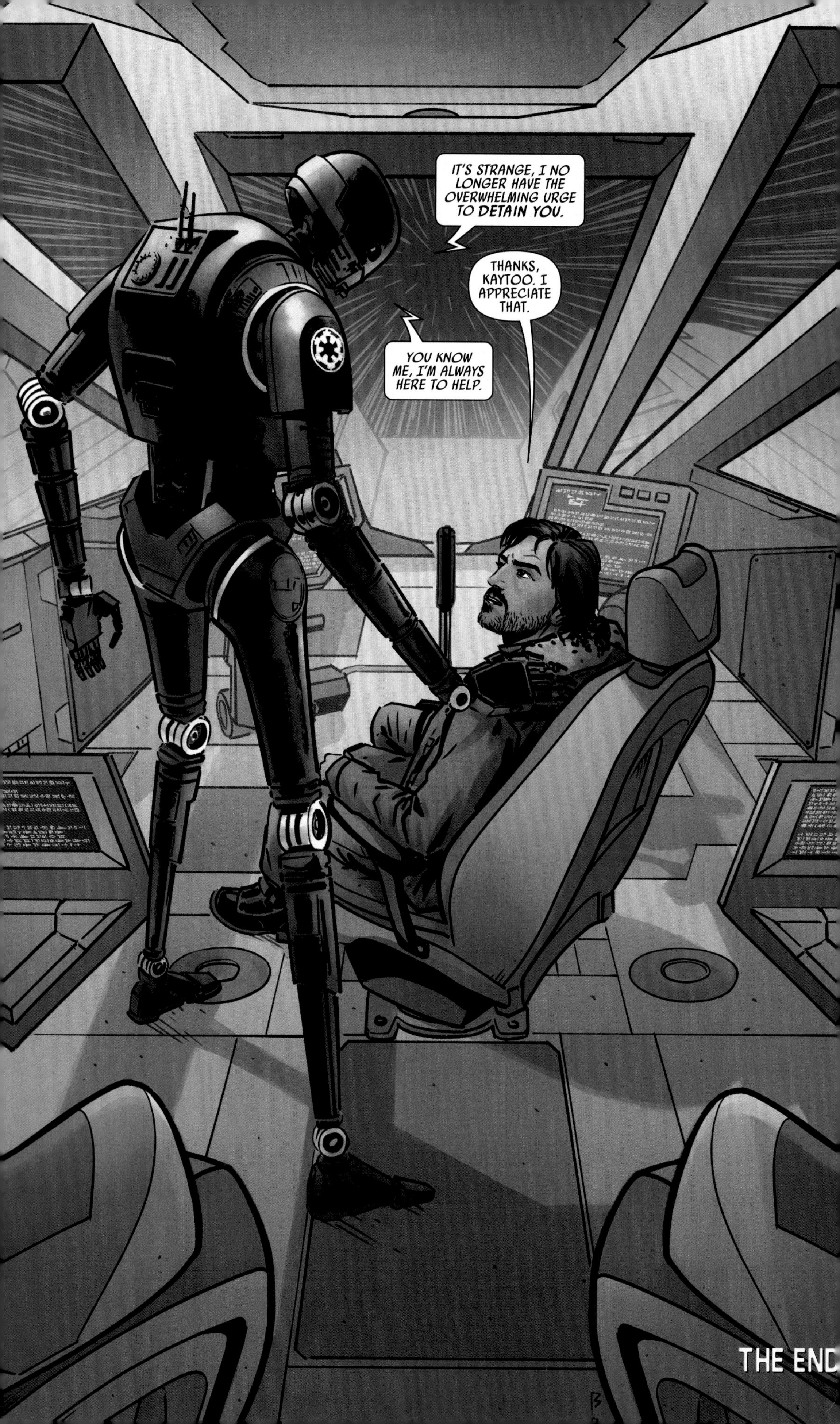
IT'S STRANGE, I NO LONGER HAVE THE OVERWHELMING URGE TO DETAIN YOU.
YOU KNOW ME, I'M ALWAYS HERE TO HELP.
THANKS, KAYTOO. I APPRECIATE THAT.
THE END

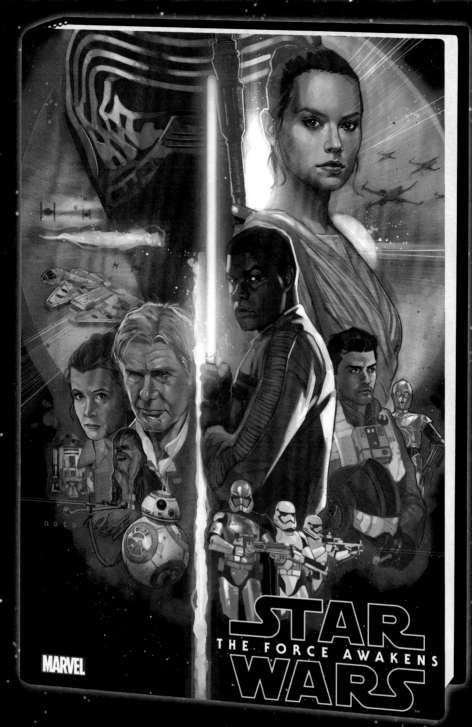

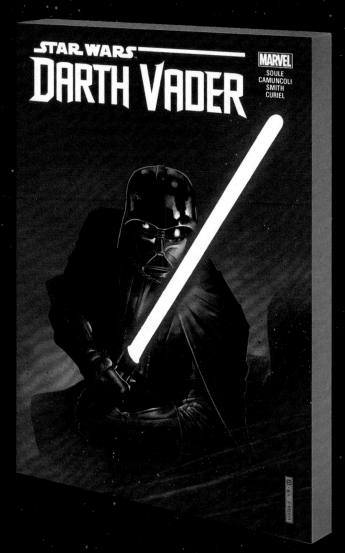

THE DARK LORD OF THE SITH'S FIRST DEADLY MISSION

STAR WARS: DARTH VADER: DARK LORD OF THE SITH
VOL. 1: IMPERIAL MACHINE TPB
978-1302907440

ON SALE NOVEMBER 2017
WHEREVER BOOKS ARE SOLD

TO FIND A COMIC SHOP NEAR YOU, VISIT COMICSHOPLOCATOR.COM